The Italian Cooking Course

The Italian Cooking Course

Katie Caldesi
Photography by Lisa Linder

Kyle Books

This edition published in 2012 by
Kyle Books
An imprint of Kyle Cathie Limited
www.kylecathie.com
Distributed by National Book
Network
4501 Forbes Blvd., Suite 200,
Lanham, MD 20706
Phone: (301) 459 3366
Fax: (301) 429 5746

First published in the US in 2010
under the title *Cook Italy*

ISBN 978-1-906868-96-3

Text © 2009 by Katie Caldesi
Design © 2009 by Kyle Cathie
Limited
Photography © 2009 by Lisa
Linder

Editors Kyle Cathie,
Katharina Hahn
Editorial assistance Vicki
Murrell, Laura Wheatley
Copy-editors Stephanie Evans,
Sheila Keating, Susannah
Marriott, Susie Johns
Design Rashna Mody Clark
Photography Lisa Linder
Creative Direction Lisa Linder
Proofreading Vicki Murrell
Indexer Alex Corrin
Production Gemma John

Katie Caldesi is hereby
identified as the author
of this work in accordance with
Section 77 of the Copyright,
Designs and Patents Act 1988.

Color reproduction by
Scanhouse
Printed and bound in China by
Toppan Leefung Printing Ltd.

ACKNOWLEDGMENTS

My parents have always been obsessed by food and I thank them so much for passing on their obsession. When my family travelled, it was for the food and the views. We had picnics in woods and on mountainsides, my mother always bringing wonderful things for us to eat and my father delighting in them. As children we learnt to savour a tomato and onion salad in France or to enjoy blackberries with thick cream in Gruyère, in Switzerland. My father would always order something weird from the menu in a restaurant, 'You have to try new things,' he would say as we waded through some revolting sausage made of the finest breed of pig's entrails.

My father told me many years ago that he would not be happy with my career until I had my own restaurant. He recognised my passion for food. Luckily, when I met Giancarlo 12 years ago I met a kindred spirit, and he encouraged me to work in the kitchen and develop my passion. I painted murals for Giancarlo—that is how we met; while I painted, he cooked for me. It wasn't long before I hung up my paint brushes, put on my chef's whites, and cooked with him.

I love the theatre of the kitchen. I like the machismo, the testosterone-fuelled atmosphere, the commanding chefs who come alive during a busy service. I get a kick out of the fury and pace and even the bawdy sense of humour. I would like to say a huge thank you to our chefs Stefano Borella, Monserrato Marini and Gregorio Piazza who have shared their knowledge, time and recipes with me. They have encouraged and helped me so much, and this book would never have existed without them. I know I have tested their patience on occasion, but fortunately their sense of humour never failed.

Thank you to Stefano's father Gino Borella, who was Head Chef of San Lorenzo in Knightsbridge for more than 30 years. He has taught me two hugely important principles of cooking; patience in cooking times and courage in seasoning. His pot roasts have changed the way I cook.

I have also been lucky enough to work with Franco Taruschio, who with his wife Anne ran The Walnut Tree in Wales and wrote many cookbooks. From Franco I have learnt to use different cuts of meat and long, slow cooking techniques.

Thanks to six Italian mothers—Rina Rancati, Teresa Cotone, Ninfa Bono, Sabia Tortella, Nicoletta Salvato and Anna Pino—who came over to work with us, I now understand why home cooking tastes so good; it is made with *amore* they told me.

Thanks to Kyle Cathie for coming up with the idea and asking me to do it, Lisa Linder for her amazing and inspiring photographs, Rashna Mody Clark for her superb design, Katharina Hahn and Danielle Di Michiel from Kyle Cathie, editors Susannah Marriott and Sheila Keating, Stephanie Evans. Also to Sheila Abelman, my literary agent, for her constant encouragement and faith, and Mary Dowey for her fascinating chapter on wine.

The research team and the experts
Daniela White, India Amos, Francesca Da Ros, Jo Hynes, Liz Bentham-Clark, Philip Beresford, Richard Bertinet, Brian Macleod, Paolo Arrigo, Mauro Vignali, Carole Borella, Annabel Ward, Patricia Michelson and Fabio Antoniazzi.

The chefs and cooks
Antonietta Mirizio and Vito Brescia from La Vecchia Taverna in Monopoli, Puglia; Rita Guastamacchia from Masseria Serra dell'Isola, near Mola di Bari, Puglia; Dino at La Colonna restaurant in Milan; Giusy from Il Giardinetto di Via Tortona in Milan; Cristiano Rossi; Maria Barbuti from Parma; Livia and Nello from Tuscany; Giovanna Simonelli from Casa Villara near La Spezia, Liguria, for her cooking lessons; Paola Cavazzini and Maurizio Rossi from La Greppia restaurant in Parma; Ediglio from Osteria di Maesta near Parma; Maria Pasqualini and Giuseppe Navarro from Naples; Giuseppina the chef and the owners of La Mola, Santa Maria di Castellabate, Cilento.

The exacting recipe testing team
Carolina Català-Fortuny, Fabrizio Tarpei, Carrie Darby and Ian Bethwaite, Shella Rushton, the mothers from Gayhurst School.

The locations
The Frescobaldi family for their generous loan of two castles for our shoot in Tuscany and the loan of their wonderful staff—Carina, Fabio, Antonella and Monica. Chiara Agnello for use of her family's beautiful agriturismo, Fattorie le Mose, Agrigento, Sicily. Anna Pino and Gianfranco Poddighe for the use of their wonderful family home in Sardinia.

Suppliers
La Fromagerie (www.lafromagerie.co.uk), La Credenza (020 7070 5070), Lina Store (020 7437 6482), Fratelli Camisa (www. camisa.co.uk), The Ginger Pig (www.thegingerpig.co.uk), Savoria (www.savoria.co.uk), Machiavelli Food (www.machiavellifood.co.uk), Partridges (www.partridges.co.uk), Shipton Mill Flour (www.shipton-mill.com), Valvona & Crolla (www.valvonacrolla.co.uk), Callebaut chocolate (www.callebaut.com). www.flexmorefarm.co.uk (for buffalo products)

VALLE
D'AOSTA

LOMBARDIA

TRENTINO
ALTO
ADIGE

FRIULI
VENEZIA
GIULIA

PIEMONTE

VENETO

LIGURIA

EMILIA ROMAGNA

Balsamic Vinegar

TOSCANA

MARCHE

UMBRIA

Olive Oil

LAZIO

ABRUZZO

SARDEGNA

MOLISE

CAMPANIA

BASILICATA

PUGLIA

CALABRIA

SICILIA

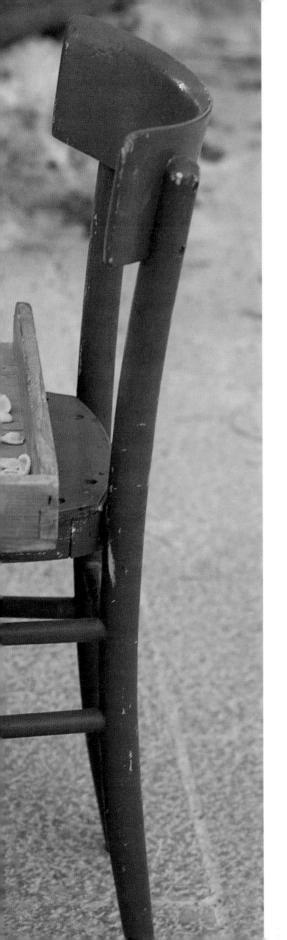

*To my children Giorgio and Flavia.
With my love, I pass on the work
of an older generation of cooks
to a new one.*

CONTENTS

Foreword

BY GIANCARLO CALDESI

Katie may have been born in an English seaside town, but with this book she has become an honorary Italian. Her dedication to authenticity has, if I am honest, far, far exceeded my expectations, as has her understanding not only of the food, but of its place in what we call *costume e cultura*—the local culture, which differs from village to village in every region of Italy.

Like a London taxi driver who does The Knowledge in order to understand how to get from street to street, Katie has taken on a marathon Knowledge of Italy, learning how to navigate from region to region via recipes and ingredients. It has taken dedication, stamina, stubbornness and a great deal of determined travelling around Italy over the last few years for Katie to achieve what she wanted, and on the way she has come to truly understand and love Italy in its totality. It is no mean feat; no mean feat at all.

We have journeyed together, and I have learnt a great deal too. Like all Italians, I am fiercely loyal to my region—in my case, Tuscany. Italians always think that the way we do things in our locality, which is the way our mothers and our grandmothers did things before us, is the best. For centuries, in different parts of the world, people have produced foods that suit the local climate and conditions and combined them in the best ways possible—and the recipes that have been handed down determine who you are and what you are. I really believe that. But the truth is that most Italians know very little about the food and culture of the regions outside their own. So it has been very interesting for me to travel with Katie and discover different ideas.

I must stress that this is Katie's project through and through, and she has done things her own way, cooking with people in their own homes, collecting recipes that have never before been written down, and then trying them over and over again back in London. The only way to truly understand about ingredients and recipes is to keep preparing and cooking them yourself, and we are lucky in that we have two restaurants and a cooking school whose staff come from all over Italy and have been happy to share their knowledge and help Katie in whatever way they can.

From the person I first met who was a good cook and loved food, Katie has become a truly confident, accomplished, imaginative cook, who can explain Italian cooking in a way that non-Italians understand. But more importantly, she has learned to treat ingredients as an Italian would and not to twist or change the recipes to suit English taste. That is why this book is so very true to Italy.

Katie, you have done a great job for my country, and if you are able to convey even 10 percent of the delight you have in the Italian way of life and of eating, then this will be a magical book.

Introduction

Ask my family and friends and they will tell you that I have become obsessed with Italian food—but then it would be impossible not to fall in love with a food culture that is so resonant with history, so absorbing and so totally fascinating. Of course, there is not really any such thing as "Italian food," because from north to south, city to country, region to region, everyone has a different view of what should go into a dish. People talk endlessly about food in Italy. You can follow a couple down the road and hear them discussing the relative merits of mozzarella or *fior di latte*; you can go to the hairdresser and overhear arguments about who makes the best *ribollita* soup. I am not exaggerating. Once I could understand Italian, I was astounded to discover how preoccupied everyone was with food. As someone who loves to cook and eat, I felt immediately at home.

So, although my aim in writing this book is to give a comprehensive course in Italian cuisine, based on my experience of running an Italian cooking school in London, a summer school in Tuscany and two Italian restaurants with my Tuscan husband, Giancarlo—in reality there can never be an all encompassing "complete history" of Italian food, because it is just too diverse. And that is what is so wonderful about it.

Campanilisti is the Italian word for staunch supporters of their home town, its customs, football team—and local *salami*! It literally means "people who live near the bell tower"—rather like our Eastenders, who must be born within the sound of the Bow Bells to be real Cockneys. Italians never refer to themselves as Italian, but instead as Sardo, Sicilian, or Tuscan. Simply calling them Italian just won't do, and if they meet someone from the same region it has to be stated from which province within that region they are from. Being English, I often feel slightly embarrassed about how openly

This is a book for people who come home from holiday in Italy, or just from a great meal at an Italian restaurant, wishing they knew how to make that seafood pasta or focaccia that they enjoyed so much.

disparaging Italians are about the people, food, and cooking of other regions, but it is an accepted part of the banter that all Italians love.

I know from teaching at our cooking school that there is a huge hunger to learn more about such regionality, about Italian ingredients, Italy's culinary history, and above all how to successfully prepare classic, traditional Italian recipes as well as some with a more modern twist. So, as well as highlighting the ingredients typically found in an Italian kitchen, I have devised a series of masterclasses which show you the way we teach certain dishes.

Although I have a background in food history—as part of my degree in art and theater design, I wrote a dissertation on medieval food and banquets—my reasons for writing this book are not to explore what Pliny thought, or what the Etruscans cooked—fascinating as they are, being often pictured as a rotund race who knew how to party! This is a book for people who come home from a holiday in Italy, or just from a great meal at an Italian restaurant, wishing they knew how to make that seafood pasta or the focaccia that they enjoyed so much.

I want to take you on my journey of discovery over the last 12 years, which I have spent surrounded by Italians, both here and abroad. I want to show you the recipes and skills, and share the ideas and tips that have changed my style of cooking from English to Italian. I want to take you inside the homes I've visited and show you the families I've met, their food and how they eat. The recipe introductions and Lisa's beautiful and accurate photography set the dishes in context. I have been privileged to travel with my Italian colleagues from the cooking school and restaurants, and to stay with their families, and I have been overwhelmed by everyone's generosity, hospitality, and knowledge. I have cooked into the wee hours of the morning

I have been privileged to travel with my Italian colleagues from the cooking school and restaurants, and to stay with their families, and I have been overwhelmed by their generosity, hospitality, and knowledge.

with many of these people, and they never seem to tire of showing me their traditions, knowing that if I write them down they will be preserved. I hope I have done them justice—I have only changed the recipes subtly, where essential, to suit our ingredients. I am sure every Italian family could show me something I haven't seen before, and that there are hundreds more recipes out there, but I had to stop somewhere!

The book follows the courses of a typical Italian meal, starting with wine and bread and ending with cheese and preserves. I have selected what I consider to be the essential recipes, as well as giving some lesser known wonders that I simply couldn't leave out. I wanted to show the diversity of Italy's regional dishes—from the light and summery fish dishes of Sardinia to the comfort food of the Dolomites in the north. The common perception of Italian eating is of families enjoying lunch and dinner al fresco in the sunshine, but don't forget that Italy is 75 percent alpine.

Aside from regional differences, I have discovered that seasonality and seasoning are the essence of Italian flavor, and that to cook well one has first to select good ingredients and second be brave with food. I have understood how to be patient with stews and pot-roasts, leaving them long enough for the meat to melt in the mouth, just as I have learnt to cook something briefly, as for Steak Robespierre (see page 119) or *Saltimbocca* (see page 307), and how to tell when a steak or chicken breast is just right, rather than being paranoid about food poisoning and overcooking meat to resemble leather. I have been taught to be bold with seasoning and herbs to accentuate the natural flavors of fish or meat rather than mask them.

Way beyond my love of Italian food, Italy and its lifestyle touches me deeply; perhaps it is a love affair all the more romantic for the fact that I don't live there. I love the way Italians don't wait to eat—if they go to someone's house, they would rather eat their pasta while it is hot than wait patiently until the host sits down. And the host wouldn't expect anything different. "*Mangia, mangia*," or "Eat, eat," will be the cry.

I am charmed also by the way that gathering the family around the table to eat and talk is all important, despite the television blaring in the corner during dinner—inevitably showing a bicycle race interspersed with a scantily clad woman on a chat show.

And I've often been infuriated by the men of the house, who don't seem to do dirty plates, set the table, or help much around the house. They work long hours, provide food and money, and hunt occasionally, and the roles at home are clearly divided. It's pointless asking them to help; they simply won't know where the cutlery drawer is!

Not spending all my time in Italy, I can dip in and out of its beauty without suffering the hardships of daily life. I don't see the unemployment, I don't have to deal with the often ridiculous bureaucracy, I cannot hear the provincial small-mindedness that I know exists. Instead, I dream that Giancarlo and I will live there one day, and I feel homesick for a land that is not my own.

A Way of Eating

It is impossible to generalize about family eating in Italy, but Italians tend to follow the traditions learned from previous generations. Every Italian family has its own recipe for *ragù*, for example, handed down from grandmother to grandchild and so on. It appears to me that the Italians are as passionate about retaining original recipes as we are about changing them, and will happily share them with you when you eat something you enjoy.

Many families live close to one another, so a meal can be shared on a weekly, if not a daily, basis. Except in some of Italy's busy cities, lunch is still often eaten at home or lingered over with friends at an *osteria*.

Meeting and eating with family and friends, together with regular trips to bars for essential caffeine boosts, forms the backbone of the day, which usually begins with *colazione*. Italians have no love for breakfast as we know it. It is really a matter of a cappuccino and croissant or a great big doughnut stuffed with custard at the bar on the way to work. Sweet foods are preferred to savory—offer a bacon sandwich and it is anathema; I've tried!

Spuntino is a light snack at any time of day, such as a *panino* or cake, while *l'ora di pranzo* is "the time to lunch," usually at 1pm. Giancarlo's father always ate at that time exactly, as though his life depended on it—such was the respect given to his digestion.

In the afternoon there is often a snack, normally sweet, and usually given to school children, which is known as *merenda*. Then, come evening, there may be an *aperitivo* in a bar, where free nibbles of food are given with drinks, followed by *cena*—dinner—at home or in an *osteria*, *trattoria,* or *ristorante*.

Rich and Poor—The Sources of Italian Cooking

Much of Italy's cooking comes from two distinct sources: *cucina povera*, or the cooking of the poor, and *cucina nobile*, the rich man's diet. Since the days of the Romans and even further back to the Etruscans, cooking for the different classes has been divided. The Romans, for example, considered brown bread only to be suitable for the poor, whereas bread for the wealthy was made from white flour—indeed, this was so celebrated that it was worn as face powder by rich women wishing to make themselves appear paler.

As necessity is the mother of invention, many wonderful dishes have arisen from the tradition of *cucina povera*, making the most of leftovers, using what little is available at any time of the year, and preserving. Yesterday's bread, for example, has hundreds of uses, forming the basis of the Tuscan soup *Ribollita* (see page 130), and *Gnocchi gnudi*, the spinach dumplings of the north (see page 203).

Cucina nobile has also left its mark, harking back to the feasts enjoyed by the wealthy, when chefs showed off for their patrons by using spices and exotic fruits brought to Italy by visiting traders, and employing culinary skills learnt from the Arabs. Think of sorbets, made originally with snow and fruit juice and sweetened with honey (see Passion Fruit Sorbet, page 438), John Dory Stew with Potatoes and Saffron (see page 244), or Saddle of Venison (see page 357) and you have a flavor of *cucina nobile*.

Italians still follow the traditions learned from previous generations. Every Italian family has their own recipe for ragù, for example, handed down from grandmother to grandchild and so on.

Italians generally still buy seasonal produce, because they know this is the way to get the best flavor from food. They will pick over fruit and vegetables in the markets with great attention.

Feste e Sagre—Festivals and Food Fairs

Italy's strong religious past has resulted in many festival foods which are only made at certain times of year, and many of these traditions are still alive today. The shop windows in Siena at Christmas heave with *panforte*, while the Sicilians hang marzipan fruits from their trees. Ligurians picnic on Easter Monday with their traditional Easter tart—*Torta Pasqualina* (see page 75).

Carnevale has pre-Christian origins and was celebrated by the ancient Romans. This is the time just before Lent when fatty foods such as *Frittelle* (see page 461) are eaten with relish. The English equivalent is Pancake Day, which some of us still celebrate with races. All over Italy, towns hold processions of children and adults in costume, but none more so than Venice and Viareggio, where the party atmosphere can last for days.

Sagre are food festivals that celebrate the ripening or harvest of a particular food from a particular place. The origins of the *sagre* are sometimes religious, sometimes pagan or sometimes a mix of the two. I suppose they are the equivalent of us wassailing apple trees in Britain. Families and friends, old and young unite at this time to socialize, eat, and celebrate. It could be the start of hunting for wild boar or the peak of the porcini mushroom season. Typical of this kind of event is a chestnut festival I attended in a sports pavilion in Tuscany, with long tables and stalls selling whole chestnuts, chestnut flour, chestnut liqueur and so on, and serving a delicious menu of chestnut pasta, polenta, and porcini.

At a *festa*, a festival celebrating a saint's day or a national holiday, food is sometimes made to raise money for a local cause. There are also political celebrations, such as the annual *Festa dell'Unità* held in most towns all over Italy. This celebration of the left-wing party with concerts, debates, and stalls is peculiarly Italian. Food, naturally, is one of the key elements, and often people enjoy both local and ethnic dishes, such as Indian and Chinese. Frequently, there is a strong link with ethical trade organizations, so people can not only eat "green" food but also buy it.

Local and Seasonal Food

To cook Italian means using mainly local ingredients and following traditions learnt from previous generations that define the characteristics of the region. Italy has been living a food renaissance recently, led by movements such us the Slow Food organization, which began as a reaction to a McDonald's opening by the famous Spanish Steps in Rome. The Slow Food movement has created the Ark of Taste, with the sole purpose of saving artisan foods and promoting ingredients from specific areas, such as Lardo di Colonnata or the balsamic vinegar of Modena. DOP (*Denominazione d'Origine Protetta*) or Protected Designation of Origin certification has also been vital in preventing the otherwise inevitable degradation of regional products. Because of this legislation, no chile can be added to Parmigiano-Reggiano, for instance, and you won't find a cumin seed spicing up a leg of Parma Ham. Local food isn't just for tourists; it is eaten by everyone, though it might be packaged differently for visitors to the region. On a trip to Bergamo I found the windows of the delis crammed with *plin* (a type of pasta) and *gnocchi all'ortica* (nettle gnocchi)—the pasta was sold loose by weight for the locals, whereas it was done up in pretty packages tied with raffia for the tourists.

Many Italians grow their own vegetables wherever they can, and if they don't have their own garden will have an *orto*, or allotment, yielding fresh produce. Most people also raise basil, rosemary and thyme plants. Italians in general are still forced to live with the seasons, since you won't find imported food at the weekly or daily markets. So they set great store by drying and preserving foods to eat during the rest of the year. You cannot get a fresh chile for love nor money outside late summer, for example, so many people grow them in pots on their balconies, then dry them on the window sills when they are ripe.

Supermarkets are less faithful to local suppliers and seasonal produce. Avocados, for instance, are not indigenous to Italy but are now available in supermarkets and have become more widely used in cooking (see Scallops Wrapped in Pancetta with Avocado Sauce, page 275). Even so, Italians generally still buy seasonal produce, because they know this is the way to get the best flavor from food. They will pick over fruit and vegetables in the markets with great attention—and not only in the markets, but in supermarkets, too, using the disposable plastic gloves that are compulsory if you want to touch the food. I once spent ages picking out peppers in a market in Puglia to help a local woman who was teaching me how to make a dish, only to find later that when my back was turned she had put them all back and selected smaller, tighter ones, muttering in dialect about English women not knowing their peppers from their elbows.

In different parts of Italy, farmers are raising animal breeds that had at one time almost disappeared. There is also an association—*Associazione Nazionale Formaggi Sotto il Cielo*—which is trying to encourage people to use meat and dairy products made from cattle that are allowed to roam free *sotto il cielo*, "under the sky," rather than being confined to barns.

Food and Health

Italians are much more concerned with their digestion than the British—and don't hold back on the subject at the dinner table. They believe that some foods are best eaten at certain times of day. For example, melon is eaten before a meal, not after, while an espresso will help you to digest your food if taken almost immediately after a meal. To an Italian it is simply unthinkable to drink cappuccino after eleven in the morning and they are genuinely horrified when they see a tourist drinking one in the afternoon or, even worse, after eating pizza for dinner. The reason, they say, is that milk is quite tough to digest after the first part of the day.

Italians generally eat something if they drink alcohol, to avoid becoming drunk and because they believe that ingesting alcohol on its own is harmful to health, which is why during the famous *aperitivo* when Negroni or Spritz might be drunk, light snacks will usually be brought to the table.

Italians in general are still forced to live with the seasons, since you won't find imported food at the weekly or daily markets. So they set great store by drying and preserving foods to eat during the rest of the year.

Fashion in Food

Most of Italy's cuisine is firmly rooted in the past; however, change is happening here, just as it is all over the world. In larger modern towns, such as Milan, more "contemporary" food is celebrated and welcomed. Sushi bars abound and almost any type of food is available, although Italian food still predominates.

As in the rest of the world, "fusion cuisine" is becoming more and more popular in Italy. Smart restaurants use a variety of ingredients, including cinnamon, star anise, cumin, and ginger. Arguably, these ingredients were available in Italy centuries ago, during the time of the great spice trade, but they are only now being rediscovered. Fusion is evident not only in the ingredients used, but in the method of cooking, too. Thanks to Asian (especially Japanese) influences, raw food is becoming popular, and if it is not served raw, then fish and meat is frequently served very rare.

Today, despite the Italian reverence for long meals, traditional and much-loved slow-cooked *ragù* sauces, known as *stracotti* (meat cooked in wine or broth for hours), are becoming harder to find on many restaurant menus in the cities because of the pressure and trend for faster food.

The popular *gelaterie* are trend-following hotspots, and always have the latest flavors and mixtures. Even savory ice creams have made a comeback in Italy, possibly influenced by our famous experimental British chefs. I say comeback because the Roman scholar Pliny refers to a friend choosing to go out with some dancing girls rather than come around to his place for a savory salad sprinkled with snow. My favorite savory ice creams sampled in Italy are Parmesan Cream and Truffle.

Yes, times are changing, but to listen to the young Italians who work in Caffè Caldesi and our restaurant Caldesi in Campagna in Bray, you would think, actually, they are not really changing that much. How many English twenty-somethings could argue as forcibly and knowledgeably about the relative merits of different Cheddars as these young people do about Parmigiano Reggiano or Grana Padano? Or recall with such fondness canning tomatoes with their great grandmothers, or pine for a particular pasta their nonna makes? I am privileged to work with young people from regions as diverse as Abruzzo and Sardinia who like nothing better than to contradict each other about the correct way to make a dish.

One day in the restaurant at Caffè Caldesi I noticed that the fries we were serving with a particular dish were slightly undercooked, so I told the chef that they were a bit sad, and not up to standard. He told me apologetically that he was sad, so the chips were sad. The next day they were beautiful: perfectly cooked inside and crispy outside. "Today," he said, "I made them with love." This is something I hear all the time from my Italian friends—"You have to make it with love"—and it always makes me smile because it is so genuine, and so lovely to hear. My husband Giancarlo says the same thing, "If you don't make it with love, it won't happen." So, no, I don't think Italian food is changing that much.

"You have to make it with love"—this is something I hear all the time from my Italian friends, and it always makes me smile because it is so genuine, and so lovely to hear. My husband Giancarlo says the same thing, "If you don't make it with love, it won't happen."

The Wines of Italy

There has never been a better time to put an Italian bottle on your table. Just when wine enthusiasts have grown weary of overplayed international grape varieties, such as Chardonnay, Cabernet Sauvignon, and Merlot, Italy is able to open the door to a new world of distinctive flavors. Carpeted with vines from top to knobbly toe since the time of the ancient Greeks, Italy has managed to maintain a vast array of unique wine styles. Suddenly the world is ready to lap them up.

The diversity of wines produced in Italy is remarkable. All the wine regions —which cover the country like a mottled patchwork stocking—have clung to their own traditions, and usually have a proud adherence to local grape varieties. This means that today Italy makes wine from about two hundred different grapes, ranging from the familiar Pinot Grigio and Sangiovese to the tantalizingly obscure Tintilia, Timorasso, Casavecchia, and Pignol.

Approaches to winemaking are varied too—fiercely traditional in some places and determinedly modern in others. Put all the variables together and you have a head-spinning choice of wine, from the simple and rustic (the liquid equivalent of a homemade pizza, say) to the suave and sophisticated. Steady improvements in quality over the past decade are another plus. None of this means that it is compulsory to serve Italian wine with Italian food, of course—but what a pity not to!

Italy's finest classic wines—all well known—are mainly red. They include the Piedmont legends Barolo and Barbaresco, based on the tar-and-rose-petal-scented grape Nebbiolo, and the super-concentrated Amarone, made in the Veneto from partially dried grapes. Then there are the best Chianti Riservas and Tuscany's other Sangiovese stars, Brunello di Montalcino and Vino Nobile de Montepulciano. Like most premium wines, these shine with simple food that allows the wine to be the focus of attention—serve them with roast beef, filet mignon, venison, or wild boar. Except for Amarone, which is so sweetly luscious that it often tastes best at the end of a meal, served with a chunk of Parmesan or all by itself.

The style of many top reds like these has changed in recent years. They have become fruitier, richer, and smoother in texture—less austere. More controversially, some are strongly stamped with the cedar and mocha notes of new French oak barrels, the favorite fashion accessory of swish wineries the world over. In Tuscany, however, the pendulum is swinging back towards tradition. The SuperTuscans—internationally acclaimed wines like Tignanello, Sassicaia, and Ornellaia, incorporating Cabernet Sauvignon and Merlot—are these days somewhat overshadowed by pure expressions of Sangiovese.

All well and good... but darned expensive. What about the more affordable end of the spectrum? The picture couldn't be more positive. Interesting, well-priced wines of all descriptions are arriving on our shelves from every part of Italy. Some regions which until recently suffered from a poor image have raised their game and begun to prove how impressive their wines can be: Valpolicella and Soave are prime examples. Others have emerged from semi-obscurity to refocus attention on their exciting heirloom grape varieties: Collio close to Slovenia, for instance, with its racy Ribolla Gialla; Campania with a mineral-edged Greco di Tufo, floral Fiano, and pineappley Falanghina; Sicily with chocolatey Nero d'Avola; and Puglia with chunky Negroamaro, to name but a tiny handful.

Although central Italy is producing a wider assortment of unusual wines than before, especially in the Marche and Abruzzo, the cool north and sunbaked south are the real pacesetters. The north-west is as significant as the north-east for revitalized whites: Piedmont's Arneis and improved (but not necessarily expensive) Gavi are counterpoints to Lombardy's Lugana and the Veneto's Bianco di Custoza. Surprisingly, the south, home of robust reds, is also proving adept at delicious whites, particularly in Campania. Fashion has played a role in Italy's wine renaissance. Even non-drinkers know about the rollicking success of Prosecco and Pinot Grigio (some good, but much of it as flavorless and forgettable as industrial mozzarella).

The focus on previously little-known grapes and regions, combined with a wealth of familiar styles, creates a range of possibilities so broad that it may seem baffling. Charged with finding the right wine for a particular dish, how are frazzled cooks to find shortcuts through the maze? The first tip is to zone in on the region from which a dish originated (if it has regional roots—and many do). You know, for example, that risotto belongs to northern Italy, so, depending on the ingredients, team it with a light white or red wine from the north. White Bianco di Custoza or Soave Classico would be just right for a Risotto with Seafood (see page 213) or a Spring Risotto of green vegetables (see page 217), while red Dolcetto or Valpolicella Classico would harmonize perfectly with a Borlotti Bean and Sausage Risotto (see page 212). Similarly, pasta dishes with punchy flavors like anchovies, chile, and capers hail from the south and suit a robust red from Italy's foot or heel (like Puglia's Salice Salentino), or from Sicily or Sardinia. The natural flavor affinity between local foods and local grapes is difficult to beat.

Don't panic, though, if you are unable to pin down a dish by its region. Look at it this way: you now have the perfect excuse to come up with some intriguing combinations of your own, and this is where the true fun of food-

The focus on previously little-known grapes and regions, combined with a wealth of familiar styles, creates a range of possibilities so broad that it may seem baffling.

and-wine-matching lies. For best results follow two basic rules. First, match the weight of the wine with the weight of the dish. Light, delicate food requires light, delicate wine, while rich flavors on the plate need to be balanced with weighty concentration in the glass. This may sound insultingly obvious, but it is often lost sight of, especially at dinner parties when there may be an urge to serve blockbuster wines, no matter what is on the menu.

Once this balancing act has determined roughly the style of wine you are aiming for, think about specific flavors. A beef stew made with tomatoes will taste good with a tangy young Barbera, for example—picking up on the fresh acidity of the tomatoes. A beef casserole with mushrooms will have other requirements. An older wine—a Chianti, perhaps, with its earthy edge —should have developed faint mushroom or truffle notes which will gloriously amplify the flavors of the dish. Let's look at a few more possibilities suggested by recipes in the book. I'd choose a light, zesty white for *Spaghetti al limone* (see page 196); there's enough richness in the cream already. Lobster Spaghetti (see page 264) or Lobster Mezzelune (see page 265) on the other hand call for a partner with substance—a decent Gavi or a generously flavorsome Greco di Tufo. Calf's Liver with Onions (see page 314) would be delicious with a subtle northern Pinot Nero, while Tuscan Rabbit with Olives (see page 356) would be well matched by a rustic middleweight, such as Montepulciano d'Abruzzo.

Remember, the main ingredient in a dish won't necessarily point towards the perfect wine by itself; consider its accompanying elements, too. Even salad dressings may hold clues—lemon suggesting lighter, tangier wines than balsamic, which marries with richer flavors. But it's a mistake to get too precious about food and wine partnerships. If you feel befuddled, just bear in mind that virtually all Italian wines taste better with food; that fact should carry you comfortably across a confusing morass of minor subtleties.

To desserts, finally. Everybody knows Tuscany's powerful amber Vin Santo (it's best with *panforte* or little *cantucci* biscuits—it can overwhelm tiramisu). But do try some of Italy's other dessert wines, such as Marsala (good with toffee flavors) or Recioto. The white Recioto di Soave is yummy with baked peaches and is generally cake and caramel-friendly, while Recioto della Valpolicella, the sweet red cousin of Amarone, is good with blue cheese or dark chocolate. If all these concentrated sweets sound a bit too overpowering, a good-quality Moscato d'Asti may be the answer—brilliantly low in alcohol and wonderfully palate-cleansing, especially with tongue-clinging desserts like meringues, zabaglione, soufflés, or ice cream.

Having chosen your wine carefully, it's worth taking the trouble to serve it with panache. The Italians, after all, are masters of style—not just pioneers of today's tall, elegantly tapered wine bottles and design-led labels, but schooled to serve even modest wine with such a flourish that it often tastes way better than it should. Follow their lead. Choose generous, tulip-shaped glasses: this shape helps to trap the aromas that are so central to the enjoyment of wine. This gives your guests a head start as they breathe in those quintessentially Italian smells—lemons and almonds, perhaps, in the whites, and the heady scent of damp earth and cherries in the reds.

Everybody knows Tuscany's powerful amber Vin Santo (best with panforte or little cantucci biscuits— it can overwhelm tiramisu). But do try some of Italy's other dessert wines such as Marsala (good with toffee flavors) or Recioto.

Be adventurous. Try wine styles you have never tasted before as often as you can. You may not strike gold every time, but you'll unearth some thrilling finds, every one distinct and different from the rest.

Don't serve white wines too cold (only sparkling and sweet wines should be chilled; everything else benefits from a few more degrees), or reds too warm (above 17°C they may taste syrupy and flat). And don't fill glasses higher than the widest point of the tulip, leaving plenty of space to swirl and release the precious aromas that intensify a wine's taste. (Swirling is not pretentious, by the way. The popularity of wine-appreciation classes has made it commonplace, thank goodness.) Well-filled wine glasses may appear generous, but most wine enthusiasts consider them crass.

After all those do's and don'ts, I've saved the most crucial advice for last. Be adventurous. Try styles you have never tasted before as often as you can. You may not strike gold every time, but you'll unearth some thrilling finds, every one different from the rest. With all its complications—scores of regions, hundreds of grapes, thousands of estates—Italy makes that as easy as pie.

by Mary Dowey

Pane

CHAPTER 1: BREAD, PIZZA, AND SAVORY TARTS

Pane

INTRODUCTION

Many years ago, an Italian friend came to stay and she helped set the table for dinner. By each place setting she laid slices of the only bread I had in the house (embarrassingly, a very ordinary white loaf). Since we were having pasta, I thought this quite bizarre, but now I know the Italian psyche better, it's obvious that she tried to find the best bread, however unappetizing it might be! No Italian would dream of serving a meal without it.

read is eaten throughout the day, every day in Italy, dipped into coffee in the morning, used to scoop up food or mop juices from the plate at lunch or dinner (the Italians call a piece of bread used for this purpose *scarpetta*), and dipped into soup, served with salad, or eaten as a snack. In Tuscany, bread is used for tasting the first olive oil of the season, simply rubbed with garlic and drizzled with the olive oil. It's called *Fettunta*.

Italians especially love *bruschetta* (bread toasted on a grill), usually rubbed with olive oil and topped with chopped tomatoes and basil, or *crostone* (large toasts) and *crostini* (small toasts) topped with a variety of ingredients, such as dressed beans, chicken livers or vegetables. These are eaten on their own at family gatherings and parties, or served as antipasti (see pages 76–119). The words bruschetta and crostini often seem interchangeable, and Italians are usually vague about the difference, but in general, bruschetta refers to simple, grilled bread—the bread itself is the hero, often only with good oil drizzled over—whereas crostini is toasted bread that acts as the carrier for all kinds of combinations of ingredients.

There is still a great deal of religious symbolism surrounding bread and pastries. At one time it was considered sacrilegious to turn a loaf upside down because it symbolises Christ's body, and I have seen Italians kiss dough or bread before throwing it away as a sign of respect. Various specialities and specific shapes of bread are often only made at the time of religious festivals. To celebrate Easter, for example, bread is formed into a ring in Naples and baked with whole eggs still in their shells—this symbolizes fertility and spring, and probably has pre-Christian origins. In Liguria at Easter, *torta pasqualina* was originally made with 33 layers of pastry, each one symbolizing a year of Jesus's life, and the famous Easter *colomba* cake is made in the shape of a dove.

In this spirit of celebration, I love to give home-baked Italian bread as presents. At the risk of sounding like a 1950s housewife who has nothing

better to do than bake, when I go to someone's house for dinner it makes me happy to take a freshly baked loaf wrapped in parchment paper and tied with rustic string, perhaps decorated with a sprig of rosemary. The recipient may be secretly less than grateful and wish I had brought flowers or chocolates, but thanks to the polite manners of my friends I will never know! A selection of grissini also makes a lovely gift since breadsticks keep well. When we were taking photos of grissini in Sardinia, Anna, whose house we had borrowed, showed me how she folded a piece of parchment paper in half and cut out a semi-circle shape. She then folded it again and made several snips with a pair of scissors around the edge to make little decorative holes (see the photo on page 70). It was so simple but effective that I have copied her many times since when putting bread or cakes on a plate.

It was the Greeks who taught the Romans how to bake bread with natural leavens and wheat flour in around 170BC. Before that they ate *puls*, a sort of grain mush. It became cool for Romans to have a Greek baker in their local bakery or to keep a Greek slave baker at home, and by 147BC, these bakers were considered important in Roman society. The Greeks baked around 50 kinds of bread using fine-milled flour and large ovens.

In her fascinating book *The Italian Baker*, Carol Field talks of bakers in 25BC leavening bread with pieces of dough left over from the previous day and using beer yeast introduced by the Gauls and Germans. At the same time, they were also using a *biga*, or starter dough, made from fermenting wheat flour and grape must. They also made enriched doughs containing egg, oil, honey, and cheese in various forms.

According to Field, in later Roman times less wheat was grown as fields were given over for cattle, and with the expansion of the Roman Empire, wheat was brought in from abroad. When the Roman Empire fell apart, Rome was no longer able to import wheat from Egypt and Africa, so bread virtually disappeared. It was the Byzantines who brought it back by growing wheat at the edges of the Tiber River. Fortunately, breadmaking skills had been preserved in the monasteries and by AD800, under Charlemagne's control, bread had become more important again and mills re-established. The legacy of the Romans persisted into the 1950s, however, with bread being eaten according to class: *pane nero*, or wholewheat bread, was still typically for the poor, while the rich ate bread made with fine white flour.

After the fall of the Roman Empire, the Italian regions became better established and more local styles of bread developed. By the Middle Ages, bakers were concentrating on elaborate speciality breads, using ingredients specific to their locality. The Black Death had a devastating effect in the 14th century, bringing famine to Italy, and the high cost of wheat at this time made bread scarce.

By the Renaissance, however, things had improved again, and bread was baked with sophistication by Italian bakers until the Viennese, across the

There is something distinctly appetizing and comforting about the smell of freshly made bread. So much so that supermarkets pipe the scent to the front of the shop to lure us in. Baking bread at home is not so hard; if you're a beginner, try the Quick White Bread (see page 45) or Rosemary Focaccia (see page 62).

In small communities baking bread brought people together to share a work and oven space. In this shared space, tips, knowledge, and recipes passed through the generations. The religious symbolism of bread also passed on as loaves were blessed or made into particular shapes to celebrate church festivals.

border, began to rival the Italian bakers with the beautiful pastries and breads in their coffee houses, and Napoleon introduced French white bread to Italy. Puff, flaky, and other pastries were developed at this time and became commonplace over the following years. There is great debate about who taught whom. In her *Gastronomy of Italy*, Anna Del Conte says that the Tuscans claim to have taught the French how to make choux pastry; apparently, one of Caterina de Medici's cooks, Pantanelli, took the recipe with him when he accompanied her to France. Certainly profiteroles and the similar *bignè* are still popular all over Italy today—but who knows who really made such things first?

Loaves were traditionally marked with an identifying symbol in Italy before being baked. This sign, called a *marchio*, was particularly important before the 1950s and 60s, when bread began to be made on an industrial scale. Before this time, ovens were often shared, or you would take your bread to the local bakery to be baked for a set fee. Obviously each family's loaves had to be recognizable after baking, hence the mark. This was still the case when Giancarlo was young; he remembers families taking it in turns to fire up their ovens so local people could come and bake their bread. Every 10 days it would be his family's turn and they would get up at 4am to stoke the fire and start baking. He says it was his favorite day of the week as it caused a big commotion and the smell was so wonderful.

An Italian artisan baker I work with in London still makes marks on his loaves and can recognize those of other bakers. Frequently, a cross is made in the dough before it goes into the oven. This helps the loaf to expand easily, but the intent is also to bless it, so that the bread is good.

In Italy, as in the UK and America, artisan bakeries producing traditionally made bread have been making a comeback in the face of more industrialized breadmaking. Stalls at markets sell bread made by small producers, or you can buy loaves from the back of an *ape*, (one of those annoying little scooters converted into a small van). As well as traditional and regional specialities (see panel page 30), you will find a whole range of breads these days, including organic, wholewheat, spelt, and seeded loaves. Fashionable flours include manitoba, a Canadian flour that is high in gluten and therefore strong and good for bread, and kamut, a type of low-gluten wheat sold in America and Europe and made by a company of the same name. The original kamut grains are supposedly descended from a few grains found in a stone box in a tomb near Dashur in Egypt in the 1940s. This is unlikely, however; there is no evidence that the ancient Egyptians grew any wheat other than spelt, and the maximum life-span of wheat (unless frozen) is 200 years. It is more likely that kamut is a strain that, over the centuries, adapted itself to grow away from its source in Egypt. Rice and soy flour are also becoming popular in Italy, with the increase in numbers of people with a wheat intolerance, and pasta and bread made with these flours are available from health food shops.

Traditional styles of bread

Shapes of bread differ from region to region and there are far too many to mention, however the most popular are as follows:

Panino—common roll used to make filled snacks or light lunches.

Rosetta—crusty white roll

Michetta—crispy light roll from Milan.

Pagnotta—large loaf, popular all over Italy, made to last the week. Typical are the sourdough durum wheat breads made in Altamura in Puglia which are full of holes and can weigh up to 4 lb, or those made in the Dolomites that at one time were made to last for up to a year and had to be cut with a special knife. These big loaves are hard to bake at home, requiring a stone base to allow them to bake from underneath.

Filone—long loaf, like a fat baguette.

Ciabatta—the slipper loaf that is now so popular outside Italy.

Pane senza lievito—across Italy you will find unleavened bread such as piadina from Romagna, testo bread from Umbria, pane carasau from Sardinia, and pita from Calabria, which is served filled and re-heated or as an accompaniment to salumi and cheese.

Pane integrale—wholewheat bread

Pane carré—a sliced white loaf used for *mozzarella in carozza* or *tramezzine*, the crustless sandwiches found in bars and cafés.

Never waste bread

Traditionally, bread is never thrown away in Italy. In various regions it is seen as bad luck to discard bread, however stale. Old bread, known as *pane raffermo* (bread that has become firm or hard) is used in recipes all over Italy. Indeed, I could write an entire book with the title *1001 Ways to Use Up Stale Bread*.

Stale bread can be used to pad out soups such as *Ribollita* (see page 130) or *Acquacotta* (see page 130), or soaked in vinegar and squeezed out to reconstitute for adding to the Tuscan salad *Panzanella* (see page 402). In the Veneto, sliced dry bread is imbibed with flavored stock and served as a soup.

Breadcrumbs, too, are a staple of the kitchen. Semi-stale crumbs are mixed with meat for stuffing or for use in the soup known as *passatelli*. Very dry crumbs are used to coat veal in the Milanese fashion. Often they will *impanare* a piece of meat, which means dipping it in flour, egg, and then bread-crumbs before frying.

Soft breadcrumbs
Italians call the soft white breadcrumbs from inside a loaf *mollica*. They use these in meatballs and meatloaf. Slightly stale bread from a white loaf is often soaked in milk and then used. However this only works when you have a properly made country loaf with a crumb that is quite solid and full of holes. Most commercial white bread simply turns to putty when soaked and doesn't bounce back to life like an Italian country loaf. So I prefer to whizz soft bread into breadcrumbs using a food processor and then add a couple of spoonfuls of milk to the recipe if it feels a little dry. If you are doing this with a recipe that includes herbs or garlic, whizz them at the same time and the flavor will be wonderful. If you don't have a food processor, use a grater instead.

Medium-soft breadcrumbs
If you are making something with a crust, such as Oven-baked Salmon with Pistachio and Honey Crust (see page 239), use medium-dry breadcrumbs or fresh breadcrumbs, and don't sieve them: the crunch is better if the breadcrumbs are not too fine.

Dry breadcrumbs
You can make hard breadcrumbs from very stale bread. Italian mammas could give you a thousand recipes for ways to use these, but here, you'll find them in Veal Milanese (see page 306), Summer Sunday Chicken (see page 332) and Peperonata (see page 106). When coating veal, first sieve the breadcrumbs so that you are left only with the smallest crumbs.

Freezing breadcrumbs
Breadcrumbs can be frozen, so stick a small bag or two in the freezer. But don't freeze massive quantities; you won't be able to use them up quickly enough.

If you only have fresh bread and you need dry breadcrumbs, tear the bread into chunks and bake them in the oven for 10–20 minutes to harden up. Let them cool and then whizz into fine breadcrumbs.

the dough will continue to rise and the top of the bread will be forced away from the bottom. This "oven spring" also happens if the dough hasn't risen enough before going into the oven.

Water

A dough recipe is generally comprised of 60–65 percent water to flour. The Neapolitans swear that the dough for their famous pizza is better than anywhere else because of the region's water. I am sure that water can make a difference—a heavily chlorinated water, for example, could affect the growth of natural yeast—but I find my tap water is fine. And whether your water is hard or soft makes little difference to the finished bread. If you are concerned, though, simply use bottled water, especially for making starters. When I refer to tepid water, it should be the same temperature as your hand—72–75°F. You can test the temperature by looking away as you put your finger in a cup of water. If it is tepid, you should be unable to tell when your finger is in or out of the water, since there will be no sensation of hot or cold.

Salt

There is usually 2.5 percent salt to flour in a dough recipe to inhibit the yeast from working too quickly and give depth of flavor. Mix salt into the flour before the yeast—direct contact soon kills the yeast. In Tuscany bread is made without salt, but I find it pretty unpalatable.

Sugar or honey

If used at all in a dough, these comprise 0.5–1 percent of the ingredients, to "push" the fermentation. If using honey, add it to the water; mix sugar into the flour. Sugar gives a better color and crust.

Covering the dough

Dough should be covered when left to rise or proof. Give it a light coating of oil first—put the dough in a lightly oiled bowl, then turn until all its surfaces are covered. This will stop it from developing a crust. Then cover with plastic wrap or a linen kitchen towel (in hot weather, wet it first). Dough can also be left in a floured, linen-lined bowl.

Rising

It is possible to shape a loaf immediately after kneading and achieve a perfectly good close-crumbed bread. If you require more spring and airiness, let the dough rise before shaping and then let it prove (rise a second time) before

Katie's baking notes

Temperature

Bakeries are warm places, so try to mimic them in your kitchen. Close the doors, turn up the oven, and get cozy with your dough. Although yeast will work slowly even in the refrigerator overnight, a kitchen temperature of 68–73°F gives an unhurried rise; to speed up fermentation, try a temperature of 75–100°F. Some ovens have settings for rising dough, but a warm, draft-free place is ideal. You will find the perfect place in your home, such as an airing cupboard or a shelf over the tumble dryer—I taught one lady who found that her humid indoor pool room was perfect!

Bread needs to be baked at a very high temperature. Most of the recipes here call for around 425–500°F. This heat allows the dough to expand until it reaches 140°F, when the yeast is killed. If the oven is not hot enough, baking. When the dough has doubled in size and remains depressed if you touch it lightly with a finger, it is ready for baking, or for shaping before the next rising.

Steam

For a good crust, steam is required at the beginning of baking. Bakers use steam-injection ovens. To simulate this at home, spray the oven (being careful to avoid the light and the loaf) 10–15 times with water from a refillable spray bottle. Some people put a pan of hot water in the bottom of the oven to create steam.

When is the bread done?

I have always found tapping the base of bread to see if it sounds hollow quite difficult. Although it may not help first-time bakers, I feel it is better to trust your instinct and feel the weight of the loaf. Bread loses 20 percent of its weight during baking, so if it feels heavy, it is probably underbaked and should be left in longer. After you have baked a particular bread a few times, you will get the feel of this. Don't be afraid to adjust the oven temperature; all ovens are different and often have a hot spot. Allow loaves to cool on a wire rack before cutting.

Storing bread

Wrap completely cooled focaccia tightly in plastic wrap. It will be slightly hard but still good next day. Focaccia is good toasted when past its best—use it for crostini.

Equipment

Digital scales

Weighing using digital scales is a quick and exact way to measure ingredients. I wouldn't be without mine, especially when using very small amounts of yeast or salt. However, don't worry too much about weighing when you are used to a recipe; most Italians don't even have scales in the house—all is done *all'occhio* (measuring by eye).

Tablespoons and teaspoons

Having an accurate tablespoon and teaspoon measure on hand helps when measuring oil and salt, although salt can also be measured on a digital scale.

Measuring cup

This is necessary if you don't use a digital scale.

Mixing bowls

Ours are very cheap plastic bowls bought from Italian markets for a euro each. The thin plastic adapts quickly to the temperature around it, easing the rising process.

Mixer

I like to use a heavy-duty mixer with a dough hook for kneading if I am short of time, if the dough is very wet, or I want to get on with something else while the dough churns and turns all by itself. However, since I hardly ever knead any dough for longer than 10 minutes and enjoy the exercise, I usually do it by hand—the other plus is that hand-kneading means fewer things to wash.

Dough scraper

This essential utensil is used for mixing the dough, transferring it to the bowl, cutting shapes, and cleaning the work surface afterwards. Our chefs used to make their own scrapers from discarded plastic containers. However, you can easily buy metal or plastic dough scrapers through cookware shops today; once you get used to using one, you will wonder how you survived without it.

Linen cloths

Ideal to place beneath the rising dough, since floured linen does not stick. In very dry conditions, wet cloths are good for introducing humidity into the dough.

Sharp knife or razor blade

Use these to slash dough before it goes into the oven.

Pala or peel

This thin wooden board is great for transferring the bread from work surface to oven. If you don't have one, a thin baking sheet without a lip is ideal.

Refillable water spray

Use for misting the oven to ensure a good crust.

Baking stones

Buy from a cookware shop to transfer heat to the bottom of a loaf and help a home oven simulate a baker's oven. A large unglazed stone or tile from a DIY shop works fine, too. We use a terracotta tile to make pizzas in our oven at home.

farina

FLOUR OF ITALY

Grades of flour

The difference between "0" and "00" flours is in the level of refining and therefore the percentage of grain left after milling. Flour used to be categorised into "00," "0," "1" and "2" grades, "00" being the finest and whitest and working down to the almost wholewheat grade "2" flour. Today, however, the most readily available flours using this categorization are "0" or "00" grades. Both are suitable for bread-making.

"0" flour: Many people suggest that "0" flour has a higher level of gluten, as in bread flour, but it is not as straight-forward as "0" flour being strong and "00" soft. Italians are divided as to which one is better for making bread, and both parties are, of course, sure they are right. I prefer to use "0" flour, as the "00" grade seems to make the bread slightly cakey in texture, but in tests I have done with focaccia it is hard to see any real difference.

"00" flour: Because it is milled more than "0" flour, this is the most refined grade with the lowest level of bran. Some people say that some of the protein is lost during the milling process, resulting in a lower gluten flour. "00" is popular for making pasta in northern Italy when egg is used.

For patisserie, the most commonly used among the *grano tenero* (soft wheat) flours is "00" grade, which can be a mixture of different types of wheat: 30 percent Canadian manitoba, 30 percent Austrian, 20 percent French, and 20 percent Italian wheat.

Organic and local flour Where possible, I prefer to buy organic flour to be certain that it is as pure as can be, and does not contain traces of pesticides or too many additives. Locally produced flour is great because it prevents unnecessary transportation, although unfortunately the European climate is unable to produce flour as strong as the Canadian flours. Italian flour has always been weak (apart from the hard durum wheat variety used for dried pasta) which is one reason that a *biga* was traditionally used to help the flour. This also accounts for the popularity of manitoba flour, which is more reliable than Italian flour. Due to the high cost of importing flour in Italy, they are usually sold a mix of local and Canadian flours, which marries the weak and the strong as well as the local and the imported.

TYPES OF FLOUR
Bread flour

Because of the proteins in the grain used to make strong flour, it yields higher quantities of gluten. The extra gluten makes bread-making more successful. Although most countries measure their flour in terms of gluten levels, Italy does not, which means you cannot directly compare Italian flour with flour from other parts of the world.

***Semola* and semolina**

Creamy colored *semola* is milled durum wheat. Its name means "semi-milled" indicating that it is coarser than regular "00" and "0" white flour. *Semola rimacinata* is more finely ground and this is used to make pasta or bread by hand in the south of Italy.

Semola acts like little ball bearings on a *pala* (the thin board for shunting pizza or loaves into the oven). Rather than sticking, the dough glides from the pala onto the hot baking sheet in the oven.

As *semola* is often difficult to find, a good substitute is the finest semolina, made from soft wheat that has not been completely ground to flour. The recipe for Semolina Bread (see page 50) makes a particularly tasty loaf that lasts well, and here semolina is combined with strong flour.

All-purpose flour
This "soft" flour is not available in Italy, but because it is finely milled, it is similar to "00" flour. Plain flour contains less gluten than "0" or "00" flours, making it suitable for cakes and pastry which do not need a high gluten quantity. Do not use it for making bread.

Self-rising flour
Simply flour with baking powder added, this is unheard of in Italy. Instead, Italians use "00" flour and add little blue packets of *pane degli angeli,* baking powder that may contain vanilla flavoring. Since there are also E numbers in these packets, I prefer to use all-purpose or "00" flour and add my own baking powder. If I need vanilla, I use the seeds from a pod or vanilla extract.

Wholewheat flour
This is becoming more popular in Italy among artisan bakeries and those adopting healthy or high-fiber diets. All bread and pasta was once wholewheat. However, over time the rich opted for white flours, and there is still a snobbery about only eating white-flour products. Cetina, who made bread with me in Sicily, said rather disparagingly, "Only people on diets use wholewheat bread so they only eat small amounts, hence all the *sfilatini*—long, small loaves—in the shops."

Farina di grano Saraceno—buckwheat flour
This is not suitable for bread, although it could be added for flavor. It is used for making *pizzoccheri* pasta.

Farina di grano Turco—corn flour
Corn, or maize, came to Italy from America, but it was assumed at the time that it came from Turkey hence the name "Turkish grain." Finely ground corn flour is used to thicken sauces such as *crema pasticcera* (see page 424). When corn is semi-ground, it is used to make polenta (see page 222). Polenta is sometimes used in bread-making to form a crusty coating on bread or breadsticks.

Farina di segale—rye flour
Common in Central Europe, where it is used to make the traditional brown bread—and vodka—rye is common in northern Italy, especially in Valle D'Aosta and Trentino Alto Adige, where the traditional food has been influenced by Austria and Switzerland. Often breads made with rye flour are flavored with caraway seeds. As rye gluten is very weak, it needs to be mixed with bread flour for bread-making.

Farina di farro—spelt or emmer wheat
Spelt and emmer wheat are types of farro, which is the most ancient cereal used by humankind. It has a high level of fiber and it works really well for baking. Some people say that the Romans won their empire on farro, because their soldiers could fight and travel for longer on the slow-releasing carbohydrate gained from mush made from the grains. The gluten contained in farro is more easily digested than in wheat, making it good for people with a wheat intolerance. The hard exterior to the grain gives it protection against insects and therefore the crop does not require pesticides. The flavor is good too. It may be psychological, but I am sure I feel better when I have baked a farro loaf.

lievito

YEAST

Yeast is a single-celled fungus that eats carbohydrate as it multiplies. As it does so, it produces carbon dioxide gas in the form of little bubbles, which are perfect for making bread. A few cells of yeast are all you need, but the amount of yeast required to make dough rise varies hugely in accordance with the result you are seeking. I would use as little as 1 teaspoon yeast to 5 cups flour in some recipes to produce a very slow fermentation that gives an acidic flavor to the finished loaf. But I have also listed recipes here with 7 tablespoons yeast to 5 cups flour, for example a Pugliese-style focaccia (see page 59). In this recipe, the bubbles rise quickly to the surface and the bread is light, airy, and quick to make. As a general rule, the less yeast you use, the longer the fermentation and therefore the better the flavor.

Natural yeast
Natural airborne yeasts are all around us and can be harvested simply by leaving food out for them. This is what must have first happened a few thousand years ago when someone accidentally left the dough out and it started to ferment from the natural yeast in the air. When it was baked, or mixed first with fresh dough, this leavened bread would have tasted really rather nice! Since then, people have been making their own starter doughs (often called a mother), from natural yeast found in the air or from fermenting substances like fruit, including grapes (or grape must), apples, and oranges. This was how all bread was leavened before beer yeast was marketed in fresh or dried form. If you want to make your own starter in this way, follow the instructions for making your own *madre* (mother) on page 39.

Fresh yeast
Though you can achieve equally good results with fresh or dried commercial yeast, I prefer to use fresh yeast. It feels more natural and is generally preferred in Italy, where you can buy it in shops and supermarkets. Here, it is a little harder to find, but you can usually buy it from health food stores, organic shops or the bakeries in some supermarkets. Fresh yeast keeps in the fridge for up to three weeks if it is covered, and you can rub it straight into the flour when you start making your bread. However I prefer to melt it in tepid water first to prevent any lumps of yeast from appearing in my dough.

If you buy a large block of fresh yeast, cut it into small portions, wrap them in plastic wrap and store in the freezer for up to three months. You should defrost them before use... that said, on occasion I have had to use frozen yeast and as soon as it hits the tepid water it quickly melts.

Dried yeast
The advantage of dried yeast is that you can keep it in a cupboard and bring it out as necessary rather than worrying about using up the fresh yeast stored in the fridge within its three-week shelf life. Just make sure you observe the use-by date as even dried yeast eventually perishes. Use half the quantity of dried yeast to fresh.

Old-fashioned dried yeasts had to be brought back to life with warm water and a touch of sugar, but today's fast-acting or easy-blend yeasts can simply be mixed in with the flour.

Everlasting starter
(madre)

Starter dough
(biga)

Pane
MASTERCLASS

Writing a chapter about Italian bread is like negotiating a maze: it is full of traps, contradictory information, and differing opinions. Bread is made differently all over Italy, and those differences are not simply regional: bread-making varies from town to town, street to street, and home to home. What I want to convey here, then, is the spirit of Italian bread and the ease of making classics such as focaccia and pizza, which are still made in most households today. As you grow in experience, I hope you'll be encouraged to try making breads using a *madre*, such as the Rustic White Bread (see page 42), or with a *biga*, such as the Spelt Bread (see page 54) or Rye Bread (see page 54). First, though, a little explanation about how the rising is achieved.

Starters

Using a fermentation starter helps to develop flavor and create a more open texture and chewy crust. This is the flavor that hits you when you break into a wonderful artisan loaf and release the slightly beery, acidic smell inside. The longer the starter is given to ferment, the more pronounced these qualities. There are three types of starter: the everlasting starter (or *madre*) made from natural yeast, the starter dough (or *biga*) made from beer yeast a day or two before the dough is made, and used in its entirety, and the mother dough which is literally a piece of dough kept back from the previous day's baking and added to the next batch. All these starters, to a greater or lesser degree, give the bread qualities that cannot be found in a loaf made without a starter. Of the three, the *madre* produces the highest acidity, the most flavor and a good crust.

Traditional Italian wheat flour is weak in gluten and so using a starter of any kind helps to form a good, well-risen loaf. Today, imported Canadian flours are far stronger than they were in the past, making a starter less necessary to ensure bread made with this type of flour rises, but a starter is still good for flavor. Some of the Italians I have worked with tell me that now beer yeast and good flour are readily available, they no longer use a starter as their mothers did 20 or 30 years ago. Some Italian bakers use a *poolish*, the starter used by French bakers. This is more liquid than a *biga*, usually containing the same amount of water to flour, and its name derives from the Polish bakers whose techniques were taken to France. However, it is not nearly as popular as the firmer, more traditional *biga*.

Everlasting starter (*madre*)

This is sometimes referred to in English as a mother or sourdough starter and in Italian as *lievito di madre*, *madriga*, or *pasta acida*. Before beer yeast was readily available, each household would make its own starter from airborne yeasts or those found in fermenting fruits such as grapes. It's easy enough to create your own yeast culture from flour, water and honey over about a week. This can then be kept in the fridge, fed regularly with flour and water, and used to give bread a wonderful flavor, crust, and texture. Such starters are everlasting: some bakeries in America claim to have had their starter for over one hundred years. It can be made out of white or wholewheat flour. I have used both successfully, but if you want a pure white bread you cannot use a wholewheat starter; bear in mind, though, that a wholewheat starter works more quickly. It is better to choose the type of flour according to the bread you are most likely to make—if you are a lover of wholewheat, stick to a wholewheat starter.

Pane

1¾ cups organic bread flour or organic strong
   wholewheat bread flour, or a mixture of the two
⅔ cup tepid water
1 teaspoon organic mild honey, such as acacia

Mix all the ingredients together well and leave in a plastic container in a warm place with the lid slightly ajar. In a day or two the contents will start to ferment and bubble, and a strong smell of alcohol will develop. I was convinced this was wrong the first time I made this *madre* and threw it away! Perservere; the flavor will moderate over time and with regular feeding, and the resulting flavor of your bread will be delicious. After two days, discard 3½ oz of the fermented mixture and feed it with another 1¾ cups of the same type of flour and ⅔ cup water. Mix them in well, including any crust that has developed. This can be done by processing in a food processor. Repeat every now and again to ensure that the *madre* has a smooth consistency. Leave the mixture again, lid on this time, in a warm place for another 48 hours and then discard another 3½ oz and feed as before. Leave for one more day, then the *madre* is ready to use according to the instructons in the recipe.

From now on keep the *madre* in the fridge with the lid on. All you need to remember is to use (or discard) 12 oz a week and then to feed it with flour and water as before. Don't worry too much about the timing, though; at the low temperature of your fridge, the *madre* will forgive you if you leave it for up to ten days without nourishment. If you have too much because of lack of use and subsequent feedings, throw away a little more of the *madre* each time to compensate. If I want to use the *madre* the day after feeding it, I leave it out of the fridge to speed up the fermentation. Similarly, if I know I won't be using it for another few days, I immediately put it back in the fridge to slow down the fermentation.

If I do not have an everlasting starter in my fridge, I make a *biga* (see right) a couple of days before or even the night before I want to make bread. This type of starter dough can also be frozen. Just remember that it needs to defrost for 3 hours at room temperature to return to its bubbly and active old self. I find I can make most Italian bread successfully in this way.

A *biga* usually consists of half the amount of water to flour and a very small percentage of beer yeast (*lievito di birra*). As with other starters, there are several ways of preparing a *biga*, and each recipe can differ according to the type of bread being made. I have worked out a simple method here that can be added to a variety of recipes. Either mix it with the water first or knead into the rest of the ingredients when they form a dough—whichever you find easier. For best results when using a *biga*, be patient, and give the dough a few hours to rise to let the flavor really emerge. As a general rule, the slower the fermentation, the better the flavor of the bread.

Starter dough (*biga*)

2¼ cups "0" flour, all-purpose
   flour or bread flour
⅔ cup tepid water
1 teaspoon yeast

Put the flour in a bowl, mix the water and the yeast together and then pour them into the bowl. Mix together well, cover the bowl with plastic wrap and leave overnight. If the room is cold, leave the bowl out; if you have the central heating on, put it in the fridge. It will ferment and bubble overnight. Next day, take the *biga* out of the fridge and allow it to come to room temperature. Now mix with the other ingredients as instructed in the recipe you are using.

Mother dough

The third form of starter is a piece of dough kept back from the previous day's baking. If I am in the throes of breadmaking, I keep back 7 oz of dough from the current batch and allow it to ferment, covered, in the fridge for a day or two. I add this to the new batch and put a 7 oz piece from the fresh dough in a covered container in the fridge. Many Italian bakers do this; it's amazing to smell this fermenting dough and see what it does to your bread. Another advantage to this method is that this piece of dough can be frozen and simply defrosted before use.

Pane

MASTERCLASS
CIABATTA

7 oz *biga* or *madre* (½ quantity of recipe
  on page 39)

5 cups bread flour
2 teaspoons fine salt
½ oz fresh yeast
14 oz tepid water
5 tablespoons olive oil

Put the flour and salt in a bowl. Dissolve the yeast in
the water and add 3 tablespoons of the oil. Pour into
the bowl and mix roughly, then add the *biga* or *madre*.
This is a wet dough, so use a mixer, mix by hand with
a plastic dough scraper until amalgamated, or follow
the method for Crispy Pugliese Focaccia on page 59.

Pour the dough into an oiled bowl and drizzle 1
tablespoon of the remaining oil over the surface of the
bread. Use the scraper to scrape down the sides of
the bowl, tucking the dough in as you go until all the
dough is covered in oil. Try to get the oil beneath the
dough so it does not stick to the bowl. This helps the
dough to rise and pour easily when you are ready to
shape it. Leave to rise until doubled in size, about
1½ hours (or 1 hour in a warm kitchen). The dough
doesn't need to be covered because the surface is
coated with oil. For slower fermentation and extra
acidity of flavor, leave to rise in the fridge overnight.
Bring the dough to room temperature before the
next stage.

Preheat the oven to 425°F and put in two baking
sheets upside down. Heavily flour the work surface
and two *palas* or flat baking trays. Pour the ciabatta
mixture onto the work surface, using the dough
scraper to cut it free. Form it into a rough rectangle
using the scraper. Scatter flour over the top and cut
into 4 lengths. Pick up each length of dough from
either end with your hands and transfer to the *palas*
or baking trays, pulling it out to lengthen it. The less
you fiddle with the loaves now the better to keep the
air bubbles inside. Sprinkle a little flour over and leave
to rise for 1½ hours, or until doubled in size.

Slide the loaves from the *palas* or trays onto the hot
inverted baking sheets and spray the oven with water.
Bake for 20–25 minutes, until golden and the bottoms
sound hollow when tapped. Or bake for 15 minutes,
cool, freeze, and bake for 15–20 minutes from frozen.

Ciabatta, which literally translates as "slipper
bread," is originally from Como. This recipe
is based on one I learnt from Thane Prince,
who really gave me the confidence to make
ciabatta. She claimed it was one of the
easiest breads to make. I didn't believe her
until I tried her method—she explained that
ciabatta doesn't need kneading, which is just
as well as the dough has to be very wet.
Thane uses a mother for her ciabatta, which
gives the necessary acidity of flavor to the
loaf. I have adapted her recipe to use my *biga*
or *madre* starter (see page 39). The *biga*
recipe makes 14 oz, so either use half for
something else, freeze it, or only make half
the *biga* recipe to start your ciabatta.

BREAD, PIZZA, AND SAVORY TARTS **41**

Rustic White Bread with Madre

This big rustic white loaf, often referred to as the *pagnotta*, or "loaf," is found in various guises across Italy. It takes a while to prepare since the dough is left to rise, and is reshaped and molded four times over 24 hours. Start it in the evening and leave the dough to rise overnight. The dough relies solely on the natural ferment in the *madre*. It should be full of holes, have a wonderful acidity and a chewy, crispy crust. After making this loaf you will appreciate the difference between artisan loaves and industrially made white bread.

Makes 1 large loaf

12 oz *madre* (see recipe page 39)

5 cups bread flour
3 teaspoons salt
2 teaspoons honey
1¼ oz tepid water

Mix the flour and the salt in a bowl. Add the honey to the water and blend with a small whisk or your hands. Pour into the flour and add the *madre*. Using your hands or a plastic dough scraper, bring the ingredients together until you have a loose ball of dough. Transfer to a lightly floured work surface and knead for 10 minutes, until smooth. Try to use additional flour sparingly. Put the dough in a floured bowl and cover with a kitchen towel. Let it rise for 1 hour.

Re-knead the dough and form it into a ball; leave to rest for another hour. Repeat this process once more. Put the dough in a basket lined with a loose-weave linen kitchen towel sprinkled with flour. Cover with a cloth and leave in a cool place or the fridge to rise for 14–15 hours. It is ready when doubled in size and it springs back slowly to the touch.

In the last hour, preheat the oven to 475°F. Put in a baking sheet upside down. When the dough is ready, gently turn it out onto a *pala* or baking tray sprinkled with semolina. Spray the oven with water. Slash the top of the dough with a cross and slide it onto the hot inverted tray. Spray the oven with water and quickly close the door to trap the steam inside. Bake for 10 minutes, then turn the oven down to 425°F and bake for 25–30 minutes. If it begins to burn after 25 minutes and is not cooked through, turn the oven down to 350°F. The loaf is ready when light to the touch and hollow-sounding if tapped on the bottom.

Cetina

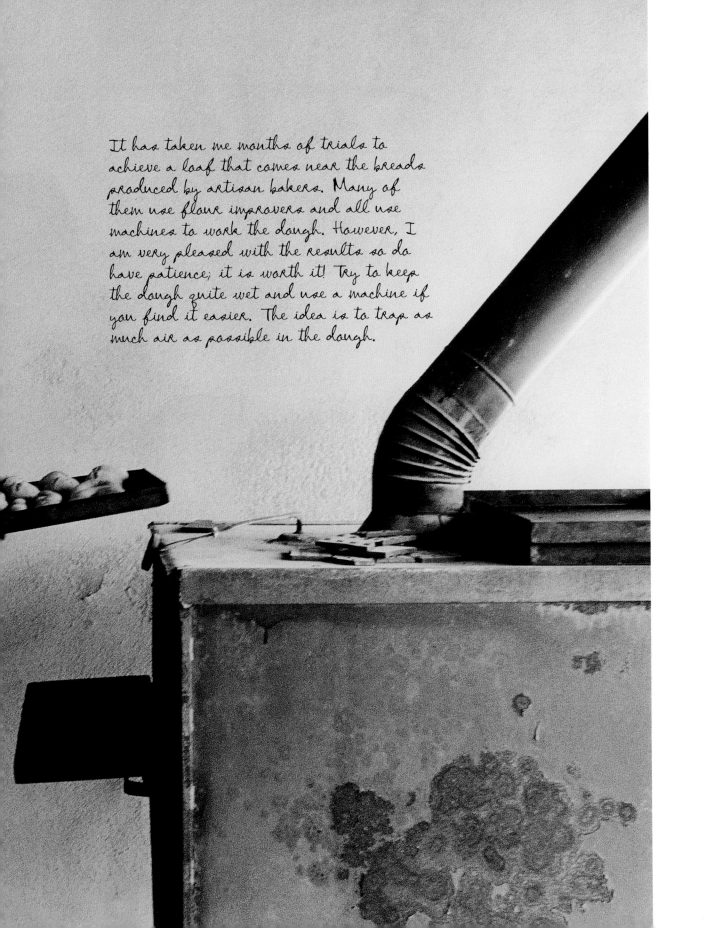

It has taken me months of trials to achieve a loaf that comes near the breads produced by artisan bakers. Many of them use flour improvers and all use machines to work the dough. However, I am very pleased with the results so do have patience; it is worth it! Try to keep the dough quite wet and use a machine if you find it easier. The idea is to trap as much air as possible in the dough.

Pane semplice
Quick White Bread

This is a quick white dough without a *biga* or *madre*. It can be used as a basic dough for the Spinach and Ricotta Rolls, the Roasted Vegetable Rolls (see page 46) and the Walnut and Olive Breads (see page 48). One of our chefs, Gregorio, used to make a large batch of this dough and leave it in the fridge overnight to rise. He would then turn it into seeded rolls, focaccia, pizza for the staff lunch, and *grissini*. By leaving it to rise slowly, he ensured the dough developed its flavor through slow fermentation rather than adding a starter. The simplicity of this recipe is that it has one rising after being kneaded and shaped. This gives a close-grained loaf. If you have time and prefer a more open grain, leave to rise in a bowl for an hour or two or overnight like Gregorio, then shape and allow to prove again.

Makes 2 large loaves; 10 Spinach and Ricotta, Roasted Vegetable, or Sesame Seed Rolls; or 2 Walnut and Olive Breads

2 teaspoons salt
5 cups bread flour
½ oz fresh yeast, ¼ oz dried yeast
1½ cups tepid water

Mix the salt into the flour on a board or into a bowl and make a well in the center. Blend the yeast into the water with a small whisk or your hands, then pour it into the well in the mound of flour. Bring the dough together with your fingers or a dough scraper and collect it into a ball.

Try to use additional flour sparingly; a good dough should be as wet as possible without being impossible to handle. Establish a pattern of pushing the dough out into a long oval, then fold it back towards you, trapping air inside. Next give a quarter turn and push it out again. Keep thinking: stretch it, fold it, turn it; stretch it, fold it, turn it. In the photographs, Cetina worked so fast that it was hard to see the different movements, but slow steady strokes work just as well until you pick up speed. The dough is ready when it is springs back to the touch, feels elastic and stops sticking to the board. If the amount you are making is big, split the dough into 2 to make it easier to knead.

Preheat the oven to 425°F. Shape the dough as required and place it on a flat piece of wood or baking sheet dusted with flour or semolina. This helps it slide into the oven when risen. Leave in a warm place to rise until doubled in size, 45–60 minutes. When ready, the dough should slowly bounce back to the touch. Make a cross in the top of the dough, then put in the oven on an oiled baking sheet. Bake the loaves for 25–30 minutes, the rolls for about 20 minutes.

Gregorio

Rotolini agli spinaci e ricotta
Spinach and Ricotta Rolls

Makes 10 spiral rolls

1 quantity of Quick White Bread dough (see page 45)

½ cup cooked spinach, thoroughly squeezed dry
8 oz ricotta
¼ cup Parmesan, finely grated
grated nutmeg, to taste
salt and freshly ground black pepper

Follow the instructions for the Quick White Bread until the dough is shaped. Preheat the oven to 400°F and oil a large baking sheet.

Make the stuffing by combining the ingredients in a bowl, seasoning to taste. Roll the dough into a rectangle ½ inch thick. Spread the spinach mixture over the dough and roll it up into a log shape. Cut crosswise into ten even pieces. Transfer the rolls to the baking sheet, making sure they have enough space around them to increase in size. Set aside in a warm place, covered with a kitchen towel, until doubled in size, about 45 minutes. Bake for 20–25 minutes, or until golden and cooked through.

Rotolini alle verdure arrosto
Roasted Vegetable Rolls

Makes 10 spiral rolls

1 quantity of Quick White Bread dough (see page 45)

1 medium eggplant
1 medium red bell pepper
1 medium zucchini
2 tablespoons olive oil
salt
3 sprigs of thyme
2 garlic cloves, unpeeled and lightly crushed

Preheat the oven to 400°F. Slice the eggplant and zucchini into circles about ½ inch thick, then in half again and lay them in a roasting pan.

Cut the pepper lengthwise into 1-inch thick slices—you should get around 8 slices from each pepper. Add the peppers to the eggplant and brush all the vegetables with the oil. Season with salt to taste, and tuck the thyme sprigs beneath the peppers. Tuck the garlic cloves between the vegetables and bake for 20 minutes.

Remove the vegetables from the oven when they are cooked through and lightly browned at the edges. Leave to cool, then substitute for the spinach and ricotta stuffing in the recipe above. The vegetables can also be pan-fried (see photo).

Pane bianco
White Bread with Biga

This is a good crusty loaf and quicker to make than the Rustic White Bread on page 42. It is speeded up by the addition of beer yeast and can be made with either a *biga* or a *madre*. This recipe has two risings, giving a lighter loaf. It could be made with just one like the Quick White Bread (see page 45), resulting in a denser loaf but still with a good crumb, but the *biga* gives a much better flavor and crust. For bigger holes in the dough and a more even, lighter result, let the dough rise three times before baking.

*Makes 1 big white loaf or
2 smaller loaves*

7 oz *biga* (½ quantity of recipe on page 39)

4½ cups bread flour
1¼ cups tepid water
1 oz fresh yeast
2 teaspoons salt
1 tablespoon sesame seeds

Follow the instructions for preparing the Quick White Bread until you have a loose ball of dough. Add the *biga* and knead on a lightly floured work surface for 10 minutes, until smooth. Try to use additional flour sparingly. For a lighter loaf, leave the dough to rise in an oiled bowl, covered in a little oil and then with plastic wrap or a kitchen towel. This should take about 1 hour.

Preheat the oven to 425°F. Shape the loaf or loaves and leave on a large oiled baking tray to rise for 30–40 minutes, until light and puffy-looking and doubled in size. When ready, put the sheet in the oven, spraying around the loaf with water. Quickly close the door, trapping the steam inside. Bake the bread for 15 minutes and then lower the temperature to 350°F and bake for a further 10–15 minutes, or until cooked through.

Pane con noci e olive nere
Walnut and Olive Breads

Bread with olives is made in various forms in Italy. In Milan I bought short sticks flavored with olives and others with walnuts but there is no reason not to mix the two. Or to swap the olives for raisins; we served a raisin and walnut bread with cheese at our restaurant in Bray.

Makes 2 loaves or 6 Sesame Seed Rolls

1 quantity of Quick White Bread dough (see page 45)

5 oz olives, coarsely chopped and dried on paper towels
½ cup walnuts

Follow the instructions for preparing the Quick White Bread, leave the dough to double in size and then put it on a floured work surface, spreading it out into an oval about 1¾ inch thick. Lay over the olives and/or walnuts. Fold the dough over from either side into the center. Now pull the dough from the top and bottom edges into the center and push down on the seam, creating a backbone. Give the dough a quarter turn and repeat the folding 15–20 times, until the olives and nuts are all incorporated. (Some will fall out; pop them back in the center and keep folding and turning until amalgamated.)

Form the shape into two rounds and slash a cross in the top. Leave on a large oiled baking sheet until doubled in size, 1–1½ hours. Meanwhile, preheat the oven to 425°F. Bake for 20–25 minutes, or until golden brown and cooked through.

Variation: Sesame Seed Rolls
Split the risen dough into six portions. Fold the sides of each piece in, then pull the top and bottom edges into the center and push down on the seam to create a backbone. Give the dough a quarter turn and repeat the folding five times. Roll each piece gently to give a longer shape, seam side down. Brush with a little egg white and pat on some sesame seeds. Slash the tops and leave to rise until doubled in size. Bake as above.

Making the Wholewheat Bread

Pane di semola
Semolina Bread

This bread is made mainly in the south of Italy, where *semola* flour is frequently used. This flour produces a pale straw-colored loaf with a slightly crunchy texture. It lasts well. I was shown how to make this bread in Sicily, but also requested the help of my friend Ursula Ferrigno, who was the first person to get me making bread since my school days. Her books and her enthusiasm are a great inspiration. Apart from my *biga*, this recipe is based on Ursula's semolina bread rolls from *The New Family Bread Book*.

Makes 4 loaves or 16 small rolls or Mafalda

7 oz *biga* (see recipe page 39), you can freeze any leftover *biga*

3¾ cups bread flour
2¾ cups semolina, plus extra for sprinkling over the loaves
2¼ teaspoons salt
1 teaspoon coarsely ground black pepper
½ oz fresh yeast
1¾ cups tepid water

Mix the flour, semolina, salt, and pepper together in a large mixing bowl. Put the yeast into the tepid water and mix with a small whisk or your fingers. Make a well in the flour and pour in the yeasted water and the *biga*. Mix together using a dough scraper, turn out the dough and knead for about 10 minutes, or until smooth.

Put the dough into a lightly oiled bowl and leave for 1½–2 hours, or until doubled in size. Shape the loaves or rolls and put them onto an oiled baking tray. Make a cross with a very sharp knife in the top of each one and leave to prove again until doubled in size. Preheat the oven to 425°F. Sprinkle a little semolina over the top of the bread. Bake the loaves for 30–35 minutes, the rolls for around 15 minutes, or until they feel light and sound hollow when tapped.

Variation: *Mafalda*
Roll out a long sausage of dough, then fold it in on itself, concertina fashion, following the masterclass on page 52. Finsh by securing one end over the top before baking.

Pane nero alla Siciliana o integrale
Wholewheat Bread with a Biga

The "wholewheat" flour we usually buy is actually a mix of wholewheat and bread flour. Bread made purely with wholewheat flour would be very heavy, so you may need to experiment with some less common brands by adding a little white flour to balance them. Originally, all bread was wholewheat, but as the Romans starting milling flour and separating the husk from the white part—the endosperm—white bread became a more popular choice for the rich.

A baker named Cetina (in the photo above) showed me this recipe in Sicily. Cetina uses a *biga* to improve the dough. She made it into a loaf of *pane nero*, as they call it, as well as into braids, rolls, *chicori*—horseshoe shapes— and twists, or *torchiglioni*.

Makes 1 loaf or 6 round rolls, plaits or chicori

7 oz *biga* or *madre*, either wholewheat or white (½ quantity of recipe on page 39)

5 cups strong wholewheat (bread) flour
2 teaspoons sugar or honey
2 teaspoons salt
½ oz yeast
1½ cups tepid water
2 tablespoons olive oil

Combine the flour, the sugar, if using, and the salt in a large bowl. Mix the yeast with the tepid water, the *biga*, the honey if using, and the oil using a plastic dough scraper or your hands. Make a well in the flour and pour in the yeasted water and *biga* mixture. Knead for 10 minutes, then place in a lightly oiled bowl, cover with a little more oil and then plastic wrap or a kitchen towel, and leave until doubled in size, about 45–60 minutes.

Preheat the oven to 425°F. Turn the dough onto a lightly floured surface and cut into even-sized pieces, depending on whether you are making a large loaf or six rolls. Shape into the required shapes following the masterclass on page 52 and leave to rise until doubled in size once more. Bake the loaf for 30–40 minutes, the rolls for about 15 minutes.

Pane
MASTERCLASS
ROLL-SHAPING

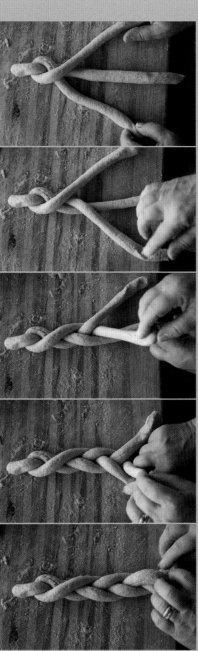

Mafalda concertina rolls

To make *mafalda* rolls, roll out a long sausage of dough and bend it back and forth in a concertina pattern. Fold the last length along the middle of the folds to secure them in place. Sprinkle with some sesame seeds. If you find they are not sticking, lightly brush a little water over the surface before putting the seeds on.

Braid masterclass

Make one long sausage of dough around 12 inches in length. Make another around 24 inches in length. Secure the longer length at its halfway point around the top of the shorter length. Now use the three lengths to make a braid of dough. Secure at the bottom with a little water, if necessary, to hold the braid in place.

Twists

Roll one long sausage-shaped length of dough. Fold it in half and then hold it in the air and give a twist. The ends will spin and twist around one another. Secure at the bottom with a little water, if necessary.

Pane di farro
Spelt Bread

This is enjoyed by the health
conscious in Italy, who try to eat
grains with a lower gluten content.
The loaf is dense, but I like it, and
sometimes I add sunflower and/or
pumpkin seeds. Spread it with a
good homemade jam, and I am
in heaven! You can reduce the
density of this loaf by replacing
half the spelt flour with bread flour.
An extra 5 minutes' kneading also
helps to give more air and lightness
to the dough.

Makes 2 loaves

7 oz *biga* (½ quantity of recipe
  on page 39)

5 cups spelt flour
½ oz yeast
1 tablespoon salt
1½ cups tepid water
2 tablespoons olive oil
1 teaspoon honey

Preheat the oven to 425°F. Combine all the
ingredients, knead for 15 minutes, and
leave to rise for 1 hour, or until doubled in
size, in a lightly oiled bowl covered with
plastic wrap.

Knock down the dough and shape into two
loaves, either long or round. Sprinkle with a
little flour and then slash the top
lengthwise. Leave to rise again for about
1 hour, or until doubled in size. Place on a
floured baking sheet and bake for 35–40
minutes.

Tip: If the bread starts to color too much on the
outside, lower the oven temperature to 350°F.

Pane di segale
Rye Bread

This recipe is from the Valle
d'Aosta in the north of Italy,
where the Austrian influence on
baking is obvious from the use
of caraway seeds. It is known as
pane nero or black bread in the
north, whereas in the south *pane
nero* refers to wholewheat bread.
Try this with cheese or Speck, the
smoked ham of the same region.

Makes 2 loaves

7 oz *biga* (½ quantity of recipe
  on page 39)

2¼ cups rye flour
2¼ cups bread flour
½ oz yeast
1 tablespoon salt
1½ cups tepid water
2 tablespoons olive oil
1 teaspoon honey
1 tablespoon caraway seeds

Preheat the oven to 425°F. Combine all the
ingredients, knead for 10 minutes, and
leave to rise for 1 hour, or until doubled in
size, in a lightly oiled bowl covered with
plastic wrap.

Knock down the dough and shape into
two loaves, either long or round. Sprinkle
with a little flour and then slash the top
lengthwise. Leave to rise again for about
1 hour, or until doubled in size. Place on
a floured baking sheet and bake for
30 minutes.

Pane con sarde
Sicilian Panini with Anchovies, Mozzarella, Tomatoes, and Basil

These beautiful, freshly made panini are filled with the glorious colors and flavors of Sicily. My Sicilian friends use their local fresh sheeps' cheese called *primo sale* because its mild flavor complements the salty anchovies—but mozzarella works just as well. Although *pane con sarde* means bread with sardines, this recipe has salted anchovies because my friends prefer their sharper taste. Sicilians from the east of the island use *pane nero*, a dark loaf similar to crusty wholewheat or rye bread. A white loaf with sesame seeds works really well, too, provided the loaf is well cooked; be sure not to undercook the bread, which results in soggy sandwiches. When in doubt, use a loaf of sourdough bread instead.

Serves 4

4 anchovy fillets in salt or oil, or 2 tinned sardines
1 loaf of crusty white bread with sesame seeds or 1 wholewheat loaf
a good pinch of salt and pepper
2 tablespoons olive oil
2 ripe tomatoes, ends discarded, thinly sliced
10 green olives, pitted and torn coarsely
1 x 4 oz ball of fresh mozzarella
a small handful of basil leaves, washed and coarsely chopped

Prepare the fish by removing any obvious bones and rinsing them if they are salted. Pat dry. Cut the loaf in half horizontally separating the crusty top from the base. Scatter a little salt over each cut side. Use a sharp knife to make diagonal slashes over the soft part of the loaf, taking care not to cut all the way through. Now make more slashes along the opposite diagonal. Pour over half the olive oil and lay over little pieces of anchovy or sardine. Replace the bread "lids" and press down to squeeze the oil into the bread. Open them again and lay over the tomatoes and the olives. Sprinkle over more salt and pepper to taste and drizzle with the remaining olive oil. Top with pieces of the cheese and the basil leaves. Press down the lids, cut, and serve.

Crescia di formaggio
Easter Cheese Bread

Resembling a savory panettone, *crescia* takes various forms around Le Marche, Umbria, and even Tuscany. It can be cooked in a terracotta flowerpot or made as flat discs and eaten topped with prosciutto. *Crescia* always contains cheese, either Parmesan, pecorino, or both. It is particularly popular at Easter, when the shops around Lesi in Le Marche are full of them—and the aroma of melting cheese. This version comes from Franco Taruschio, former owner of The Walnut Tree Inn in Abergavenny, Wales, whose family are Marchegiani. He forms the dough into braids and cooks them in brioche molds or 2½ x 2½ inch dariole molds, but if you don't have these, try using similar-sized terracotta flowerpots lined with parchment paper. Otherwise, bake as four larger loaves in charlotte pans. This bread freezes well.

Makes 16 in dariole molds, flowerpots or brioche molds, or 4 loaves in charlotte pans

5–5½ cups bread flour or "00" flour
1¼ cups freshly grated pecorino
1 cup freshly grated Parmesan
1½ teaspoons salt
½ teaspoon black pepper
⅓ cup olive oil
⅓ cup warm water
2½ oz fresh yeast
5 eggs, beaten
butter, for greasing
5 oz young pecorino, cubed

Put 5 cups of the flour, the grated cheeses, and salt and pepper into a large bowl. Add the oil and water to the yeast and mix until blended, then add to the flour, followed by the beaten eggs. Form the mixture into a dough, if necessary adding a little more flour (this depends on the size of the eggs). Turn out onto a lightly floured surface and knead by hand for 10 minutes. Leave the dough in an oiled bowl, covered with a cloth, in a warm place to rise until doubled in size, up to 1 hour. Meanwhile butter the molds or pans generously or line the flowerpots with parchment paper.

Preheat the oven to 325°F. Cut the dough into four. Fold one quarter of the cubed pecorino into each lump, allowing it to poke out slightly. If making loaves, follow the loaf-shaping masterclass on page 48 and put the loaves in the charlotte pans seam side-down. If using dariole molds or flowerpots, divide each portion into fourths again and make 16 small rolls using the same method. Put the balls in the molds or pans. Cover with a kitchen towel and leave to rise until doubled in size. Bake for 35–40 minutes, the rolls for 20 minutes. Unmold and cool on a rack.

Piadina
Flatbread

This is a soft flatbread from Romagna in the north of Italy. It is usually made with all-purpose flour, lard (or olive oil), salt, and water. The dough was traditionally cooked on a terracotta dish (called a *teggia* in the local dialect), although today flat pans or electric griddles are commonly used. You can use a non-stick, heavy-bottomed frying pan, although the heat on my stovetop is so fierce that I have frequently burnt pans in the process, so I now use the oven to make *piadine*, which are very popular with my family for a quick lunch. *Piadine* are usually eaten as soon as they are cooked, although the dough can be prepared in advance. They are often sold at specialist kiosks, or *piadinerie*. The choice of fillings is endless, but they are frequently served with a wonderfully named soft white, cheese called *squacquerone*, and with Swiss chard or spinach. Alternative fillings include *stracchino*, Taleggio or mozzarella, Parma ham, and arugula.

Makes 6

5 cups all-purpose flour or "00" flour
1½ teaspoons salt
5 oz lard, at room temperature
⅔ cup water
½ teaspoon baking soda

Preheat the oven to its highest setting—somewhere between 525°F and 550°F is ideal. Put two oven trays upside down in the oven if you can (so that you can quickly slide the *piadine* onto them), or use two baking sheets.

Sift the flour and the salt together in a mixing bowl, add the butter and the water to the dough. Mix together with your hands until you have a soft, pliable dough that you will be able to roll out. Be prepared to add a little more flour or water if necessary. Leave to rest for 30 minutes in the fridge.

Turn out the rested dough onto a floured work surface and divide it into six balls. Roll them out into circles no more than ½ inch thick. Put them onto another upturned, floured baking sheet and then slide into the hot oven for 2–4 minutes, or until cooked through and lightly browned. If you are using a frying pan, allow 2–3 minutes on each side.

When done, spread your chosen filling over half the surface and fold the other half over the top. If they puff up, slide a knife around the edge and fill without folding. Serve at once.

Schiacciata all'uva
Sweet Focaccia with Grapes

In the Tuscan town of Consuma, the local speciality is a shallow focaccia named *schiacciata*, meaning "squashed," which can be filled with various ingredients: sweet grapes and sugar, porcini mushrooms, prosciutto cotto and cheese, and many more besides. About three different bakeries in the town make schiacciata every day and people travel from miles around to eat them. This is my favorite type, made with a sweet dough. For savory versions, use the Foccacia dough on page 62.

Serves 10

5 cups bread flour
a pinch of salt
⅔ cup sugar
4 tablespoons butter, softened
¾ oz yeast
⅔ cup tepid water
1 egg, plus 1 egg beaten for the glaze
1 tablespoons olive oil
9 oz plum or dark fruit jam
1 lb seedless red grapes
2 tablespoons water

Mix the flour, salt and ¼ cup of the sugar in a large bowl, and rub in the butter. Blend the yeast into the tepid water with your fingers until no lumps remain. Add the yeasted liquid and 1 egg to the flour and mix using a plastic dough scraper or your hand. When incorporated, bring the ingredients into a ball with your hand. Use it to pick up bits from the sides, leaving the bowl clean.

Turn the dough onto a lightly floured work surface and knead it by pulling, stretching, and folding for around 10 minutes. The dough should be soft, but if really sticky add a little more flour. When the dough is worked enough it should bounce back to the touch and feel elastic; if not, keep kneading.

Fold the edges of the dough underneath to make a smooth, rounded ball. The top side is the surface of the focaccia. Grease the bowl with the olive oil to prevent the dough from sticking. Put the smooth top of the dough head-first into the oiled bowl and turn to coat the top and sides with oil. Cover with plastic wrap or place a kitchen towel over the bowl and leave in a warm, draft-free spot for about 1 hour, or until doubled in size.

Preheat the oven to 425°F. Put the dough on a lightly floured surface. Roll it out to about ½ inch thick. Spread the jam over half of the rectangle, fold the dough over and push it down with your fingertips, starting in the center and working outwards. Push the grapes into the top, then brush twice with the beaten egg. Sprinkle with 2 tablespoons of the remaining sugar and bake for 25–30 minutes, until golden and cooked through. Meanwhile make a sugar syrup by boiling the remaining sugar and water together for 5 minutes. Remove from the oven and brush the syrup over the top.

Focaccia sud Barese
Crispy Pugliese Focaccia

This is a completely different way of making bread, with a very wet dough. I learnt to make this in Puglia from a couple of women who lived near Bari. They taught me to make my hand into the shape of a duck's foot, as if I had a webbed hand. "Flap, flap, flap," they told me until sweat formed on my brow; I was only allowed to stop flapping when bubbles appeared on the surface of the dough.

Serves 10

1 medium potato (about 5 oz), peeled and roughly chopped
5 cups bread flour or "00" flour
1 level teaspoon salt
2 cups tepid water (use the potato cooking water)
1½ oz fresh yeast
½ teaspoon sugar
3 tablespoons olive oil, plus extra for greasing

FOR THE TOPPING
olives, oregano, cherry tomatoes, etc.

This is usually made in a large, thin circular pan about 11 inches across and 2 inches deep, but I have also made it successfully in a thin, rectangular roasting pan. First cut a circle of parchment paper to line the bottom.

Put a small saucepan of water on to boil and put the potato in to cook. Meanwhile, mix the flour and the salt together in a large mixing bowl. Once the potato is tender, drain but reserve the cooking water. Pour the water into

Crispy on the surface and with the consistency of a biscuit inside, this is a wonderful, light bread. The traditional topping is oregano and halved cherry tomatoes, but olives are good, too.

a measuring cup and top it up to 2 cups, keeping the temperature of the water tepid.

Mix the yeast and sugar into this water with your fingers until it is completely blended and no lumps remain. Put the warm potato through a ricer, or mash with a fork, and add to the flour mixture. Add the tepid water and, making your hand into the shape of a webbed foot, hit the dough and pull it up one side of the bowl. The higher you pull the dough, the more air will be incorporated and the quicker this form of kneading will be. Use the other hand to hold the bowl steady against your stomach. If necessary, add a little more tepid water from the tap to obtain a dough with the consistency of wet porridge.

Repeat this motion, picking up speed as you go. It becomes tiring,

but you will see the air getting trapped in the dough. Stop to rest every few minutes and watch the dough. Once you see bubbles rise to the surface and pop, it is ready.

Pour half the oil into the lined pan and rotate to ensure it is coated generously all over. Pour the focaccia dough into the pan and pat the rest of the oil over the surface of the dough with your fingers so that it is covered in oil. This prevents a crust from forming while it rises. Leave to rise in a warm, draft-free spot for about 1½ hours, or until the surface is covered in bubbles.

Meanwhile preheat the oven to 400°F. Once the dough is risen, add your chosen topping. Place the pan in the oven and bake for around 50–60 minutes, or until the bread is crispy and golden brown.

Focaccia di Recco
Ligurian Focaccia

This bread is from the town of Recco on the Ligurian coast. It contains no yeast, but the oil and water make the dough very elastic and strong. This means it can be rolled out very finely and stretched over huge pans, topped with cheese and then covered with a second fine layer of pastry. It is baked very quickly in an extremely hot oven and served right away. Every restaurant in Recco offers this bread as an appetizer; it is so delicious that it's hard to leave room for anything else. *Crescenza* or *stracchino* cheese is a soft, creamy cow's milk variety, but Taleggio tastes good, too.

Serves 8

2¼ cups bread flour or "00" flour
1 level teaspoon salt, plus a good pinch for
 scattering over the focaccia
4 tablespoons olive oil
½ cup tepid water
12 oz *crescenza* or *stracchino*

Mix the flour and the salt together in a large mixing bowl. Pour in 1½ tablespoons of the olive oil and the tepid water, then work the ingredients into a smooth dough using your hands. Turn out onto a lightly floured work surface and knead for 10 minutes. Leave to rest in the bowl, covered, for at least 40 minutes.

Meanwhile select your thinnest metal baking sheet or roasting pan, around 14 x 18 inches. It must have a 1–1½ inch lip. Line the bottom only with parchment paper and grease well with ½ tablespoon of the olive oil. Mix the remaining 1½ tablespoons of oil with 1½ tablespoons of cold water and set aside. Preheat the oven to maximum, usually 475°F.

Turn out the dough and cut it in half. Roll out both pieces on a well-floured surface until each one is 1mm thick and the shape of the prepared pan. (You should be able to blow the side of the rolled-out dough and see it lift from the surface.) Roll up one piece of dough, lay it in the pan and unroll it to lie flat, up to and onto the lipped edges. Cut it off around the edge of the pan.

Tear the cheese into small pieces and dot them over the surface of the dough. Now place the second piece of dough over the top and secure the edges by pressing them onto the dough beneath. Make small tears in the surface to allow the steam out and then drizzle over the oil and water mixture. Sprinkle with salt and bake in the oven for 7–8 minutes, or until golden brown on top. Remove from the oven, cut into large rectangles, and serve right away.

Carta da musica
Rosemary and Sea Salt Bread

This parchment-like Sardinian "music paper" bread earned its name because it is very thin and creamy in color. This method, though not strictly traditional, makes it easy to prepare. The bread is especially delicious served with drinks.

Makes 3 slabs (oven trays)

2¼ cups *semola*, fine *semolina*,
 "00" or pasta flour
½ cup tepid water
2 tablespoons olive oil, plus extra
¼ oz fresh yeast or half a ¼ oz
 envelope active dry yeast
fine sea salt
2 sprigs of rosemary

Make the dough by combining all ingredients except the salt and rosemary in a food processor or blend by hand. Turn out the dough onto a floured work surface and knead for 5–10 minutes or until it is even in color and springy. Coat the surface of the dough in oil and leave in a bowl covered in plastic wrap to rise for an hour in a warm place.

Preheat the oven to 425°F. Remove from the fridge and divide into thirds. Roll out each piece as thinly as possible on a well-floured surface. It should be as thin as paper. Grease three baking sheets with olive oil and transfer the rolled dough to the sheet. Sprinkle with some salt and drizzle with olive oil. Bake for 7–10 minutes or until golden brown and crispy.

Remove from the oven and sprinkle with over the rosemary and drizzle with oil. Serve at once.

Focaccia al rosmarino
Rosemary Focaccia

was taught how to make focaccia by a Tuscan baker. He told me to tuck the flavorings into bed and pull the duvet over them! He explained that if you leave sprigs of rosemary sticking up they burn and do not offer any flavor to the bread, so push them in and partially cover them with dough.

Tip: Focaccia doesn't keep well, but if you want to eat it next day, allow it to cool then wrap in plastic wrap to stop it drying out. To use up any leftover focaccia, split it in half, cut into large pieces and toast. Top with Cheese Paste (see page 471), Squashed Oven-dried Tomatoes (see page 372) or Sun-dried Tomato, Caper and Olive Paste (see page 487).

Serves 10

5 cups bread flour
2 level teaspoons salt
¾ oz fresh yeast or dried equivalent (usually half the amount of fresh; follow packet instructions)
1¼ cups tepid water
2 tablespoons extra virgin olive oil
all-purpose flour, for dusting
coarse or rock salt, for sprinkling prior to baking
1 large sprig of rosemary

OTHER TOPPING IDEAS
thyme, olives, red onion slices

Mix the flour and the salt together in a large mixing bowl. Blend the yeast into the water with your fingers until no lumps remain. Add the yeasted liquid to the flour and mix well using a plastic dough scraper or your hand. When the liquid is incorporated, bring all the ingredients together into a ball of dough with your hand. Use the dough to pick up the bits from the sides of the bowl so that you leave the bowl clean.

Turn out the dough onto a lightly floured surface and knead it by pulling, stretching and folding for around 10 minutes. The dough should be soft, but if really sticky add a little more flour. When the dough is worked enough it should bounce back to the touch and feel elastic; if not, keep kneading.

Fold the edges of the dough underneath so that you have a smooth rounded ball. The top side will be the surface of the focaccia. Grease the bowl with a little of the remaining oil to prevent the dough from sticking to it. Put the smooth, top side of the dough head-first into the oiled bowl and turn to coat the top and sides with oil. (This will prevent a crust from forming and stop it sticking.) Cover with plastic wrap or place a tea-towel over the bowl and leave it in a warm, draft-free spot for about an hour, or until it has doubled in volume.

Preheat the oven to 425°F. Next slide the dough onto an oiled baking sheet or roasting pan. Gently ease it out from underneath, trying to keep a good rounded edge. Then use your fingertips to make indentations in the dough, flattening it into an oval about 1½ inches thick. Add your choice of toppings and drizzle over the oil, but no salt yet. Break sprigs of rosemary or thyme off the main stem and tuck into the dough; press olives and onion rings into the dough to stop them from burning.

Return the dough to rise in its warm place until it is about half as high again, 30–40 minutes. When it has risen, use your fingertips gently to press more indentations into the dough and sprinkle with the rock salt. Bake for 15–20 minutes, until golden brown. If the bottom is not cooked, turn the focaccia over and bake for 5 minutes longer. Let cool in a basket or on a wire rack so that it cannot sweat underneath.

PIZZA

Romans baked a flat bread known as *picea*; centuries later it was still popular, but had changed from a plain bread to something similar to the pizza we know today.

Ferdinand II, the Bourbon monarch, loved the pizzas of famous *pizzaiolo* Don Domenico Testa so much that he made him a *monzu* (from the French word *monsieur*), which in 18th-century Naples was an honor normally reserved for the great French chefs who cooked for the rich. Ferdinand even had pizza ovens built in his garden so that he and his guests could enjoy this Neapolitan delight.

In the book *Usi e costumi di Napoli e contorni*, published in 1858, Emanuele Rocco wrote that pizza, as it was called by then, could be finished with an assortment of toppings, such as basil, fish, cheese, and oil. If you were to fold this over it would be known as *pizza calzone*.

In 1861, Umberto I, from the House of Savoy, came to the throne of Naples and visited the city. His wife Margherita was presented with a pizza by the chef Raffaele Esposito which was topped with ingredients in the colors of the unified Italy—red tomatoes, white mozzarella, and green basil—hence the Pizza Margherita.

Pizza, like everything else, differs across the country. In Naples, the crust is thicker than elsewhere in Italy. This helps keep the filling inside the parameters of the circle of dough. They are also more generous with their toppings in Naples. In Rome, the pizzas have thinner bases or are often made as tray pizzas.

KATIE'S TIPS

I normally use bread flour for making pizza, but this does make the dough so elastic that when you roll it into shape it can spring back. I gleaned a tip from Hugh Fearnley-Whittingstall to help avoid this: mix bread and all-purpose flours (or "0" and "00" flours) together.

Many pizzaioli make pizza balls the night before and leave them in the fridge overnight to rise slowly. This gives a better flavor to the dough and reduces work next day.

Pizza are usually baked at 750°F, but in a domestic oven just turn it up as high as you can. Don't forget that you are trying to imitate the wood-burning pizza ovens of Italian restaurants! Put a baking sheet or a pizza stone into the oven first to get really hot, which will help to get the bottom crisp. If you turn the baking sheets upside down so that there is no lip, you can slide the pizzas easily in and out of the oven.

To make pizza bianca just drizzle hot pizza bread with your best olive oil, a little chopped garlic, and some sea salt. For other pizzas it is important that there is not too much topping, or the base will be soggy. But too little topping and your pizza will be dry...

In Naples, pizza is often made with *fior di latte* mozzarella made with cow's milk. This is because the very fresh mozzarella, traditionally made with buffalo milk, is very watery and would make the pizza soggy. I still like using buffalo mozzarella, but I let it drain first in a sieve.

Pizza Parmigiana
Ninfa and Teresa's Parmesan Pizza

These two women said that this type of pizza with *sarde* (which were actually anchovies, not sardines) was from Naples and it was served always with Parmesan or *Grana Padano* and never with mozzarella, because mozzarella and fish don't go together. Those of you who know Italian mammas will understand that it's best not to argue, particularly as an English woman. I didn't dare tell them that only a few months previously I had eaten pizza in Naples smothered with anchovies and mozzarella. Whatever its origins, this pizza is delicious and a favorite with our children, one who likes the anchovies and the other who pushes them off. Ninfa and Teresa use *semola* flour for their base as they like it crunchy. I like it too for a change, but our semolina is not quite the same as *semola*, so it is best to use half semolina and half bread flour.

Makes 4 pizzas

FOR THE PIZZA BASE
5 cups *semola* flour, or
  2½ cups bread flour and
  2½ cups fine semolina
½ oz fresh yeast
2 teaspoons salt
2 tablespoons olive oil
1¼ cups tepid water

FOR THE TOPPING
a few anchovies (optional)
1 quantity of Tomato Sauce
  (see recipe page 66)
1 garlic clove, chopped
1 tablespoon olive oil (optional)
1 cup Parmesan, finely grated

Make the pizza dough following the masterclass on page 66 and roll out the dough into four circles. Push some little pieces of anchovy, if using, into the dough and then cover with a generous amount of the tomato sauce. (The semola base can take more liquid than a normal base). If you are using the garlic and olive oil, drizzle this over the top of the pizzas, scatter the Parmesan on top and bake as directed in the masterclass.

This is the very basic pizza— tomato, cheese, and basil. Its former name was Marinara, topped with tomato, garlic, and sometimes anchovies, because it was eaten by Neapolitan fishermen who couldn't take cheese on their trips. We make pizza at home on weekends; I leave the dough to rise while we go shopping or walking and once we get back everyone helps out—turning the oven up high, flattening out the pizzas, and putting on their favorite toppings. We always leave enough dough to make one Camicia da Notte (see page 448) with Nutella and banana to finish.

Makes 4 pizzas

FOR THE PIZZA DOUGH
½ oz fresh yeast or 1 (¼ oz)
   envelope active dry yeast
1⅓ cups tepid water
5 cups bread flour or "0" flour
   (or half bread flour, half
   all-purpose or "00")
2 teaspoons salt

FOR THE TOMATO SAUCE
(*makes enough for 4–6 pizzas*)
14 oz Italian canned plum
   tomatoes
1 heaping teaspoon dried
   oregano
1 teaspoon salt
2 tablespoons olive oil
semolina, to help the pizza
   glide from *pala* to oven tray
2 x 4 oz balls of mozzarella,
   drained and sliced
a handful of fresh basil leaves,
   to garnish

Add the yeast into the tepid water, then mix together all the ingredients for the dough. Knead for 8–10 minutes, until the dough is smooth and elastic. Shape it into a ball, put in an oiled bowl and cover with plastic wrap or a kitchen towel. Leave in a warm, draft-free spot to rise until doubled in size. If you have time, make the dough the night before you need it and leave it to rise very slowly in the fridge. This ensures a good acidity and flavor to the dough.

After the dough has risen, split it into four even-sized balls and leave to rise until doubled in size again. Meanwhile, make the tomato sauce: put the tomatoes in a bowl and squash them into pieces with your hands (or use a hand blender for a really smooth sauce). Add the oregano, the salt, and the oil, and stir well. Use right away or store in the fridge for a couple of days.

Put a couple of baking sheets, spaced apart, upside down in the oven. This gives a flat surface to cook the pizza on and since upside-down trays have no lip, you can slide the pizza into the oven easily. Have a thin wooden chopping board or *pala* (a thin piece of wood or metal used for transferring the pizza to the oven) and the semolina nearby.

Preheat the oven to its hottest setting—475–550°F would be perfect. Roll out the dough on a floured work surface using a rolling pin. Scatter some semolina onto the *pala* in readiness for the pizza. When the dough is rolled out to the required thickness, pull it onto the *pala* and spread over a tablespoon of tomato sauce. Top with a quarter of the mozzarella or other toppings (see below). Now slide the pizza into the oven and quickly pull the *pala* away so that the pizza glides onto the hot, upturned oven tray. Leave to cook for 7–10 minutes. The base should be golden underneath and the cheese bubbling. Garnish with the basil leaves and serve.

Other additions
The many variations and whims of fashion make the list of additional pizza toppings endless, so I asked two Neapolitan friends for their favorites. Maria likes her pizza topped with anchovies and Giuseppe prefers a smoked cheese like *provola* or *scamorza* and ham. His other favorite is *calzone*, the folded over version (like the Camicia da Notte, see page 448), filled with ricotta, *provola*, and little pieces of fried *lardo* and served with tomato sauce on top. My favorite topping is salami with marinated artichokes in oil and sun-dried tomatoes.

Pizza frutti di mare
Seafood Pizza

This has to be one of my favorite pizzas. I ate it about 20 years ago in Viareggio on the coast of Tuscany where there is a daily fish market, and it still stays in my mind. When telling my children about my travels, I said the fish on the pizza was so fresh, the squid got up and ran away. I hope they don't believe me, but it really was one of the best pizzas I have ever eaten.

Make the pizza dough following the masterclass on page 66, roll out the dough balls to a thickness of about ½ inch and place them on one or two oiled baking sheets. Spread a little of the tomato sauce over each one and top with a quarter of the seafood. Mix the oil, parsley, chile, if using, garlic, and salt and pepper to taste in a small cup. Drizzle over the seafood and bake for a few minutes in the oven until cooked through and bubbling hot.

Serves 4

1 quantity of pizza dough
  (see recipe page 66)
1 quantity of Tomato
  Sauce (see recipe page 66)

12 jumbo shrimp
12 oz fresh mussels, cleaned
12 oz fresh clams, scrubbed
4 small squid, cut in
  ½ inch rings
4 tablespoons olive oil
1 tablespoon finely chopped
  flat-leaf parsley
½ chile pepper, sliced (optional)
2 garlic cloves, finely chopped
salt and freshly ground
  black pepper

Pissadella
Tomato, Anchovy and Olive Pizza

Also known as *sardinaira*, this pizza is baked in a tray and served in rectangles and resembles the Provençal *pissaladière*, which is no surpise as Liguria touches Provence. *Pissadella* has a topping of sweet onions, tomatoes, and anchovies and is served without cheese.

Make the dough following the masterclass on page 66 and prepare the tomato sauce. While the dough is rising and the sauce cooking, sauté the red onions and the garlic in the oil over medium-low heat. Stir frequently, adding 2 tablespoons of water if they start to dry out. Cook for 20 minutes, or until the onion is soft and cooked through. Add the honey 5 minutes before the end of cooking. When the tomato sauce is ready, add the onions and set aside.

Preheat the oven to 350°F and oil a baking sheet. When the dough is doubled in size, roll out a rectangle to the size of the baking sheet. If the dough is difficult to stretch and retracts, let it rest for 5 minutes and try again. Lay it on the tray and gently push it up to the edges. Pour over the sauce, spreading it evenly, then make a lattice with the anchovies. Put an olive in each diamond, sprinkle with the capers and season to taste. Bake for 20–30 minutes until the base is golden and cooked underneath.

Serves 8–10

1 quantity of pizza dough
  (see recipe page 66)
1 quantity of Franca's
  Tomato Passata (see page
  166) or Tomato Sauce
  (see page 66)

2 red onions, halved
  and thinly sliced
  into rings, then cut
  in half
3 fat garlic cloves,
  thinly sliced
4 tablespoons extra virgin
  olive oil
1 teaspoon honey
1 large sprig of basil
  (about 5 leaves)
25–30 anchovy fillets in
  oil, drained, or salted
  anchovies, rinsed
  and dried
4 oz small black olives,
  such as *Taggiasca*
1 tablespoon capers,
  rinsed and drained
salt and freshly ground
  black pepper

Pane

MASTERCLASS
GRISSINI
TORINIESI

These long, thin breadsticks, known as *grissini torinesi*, hail from Turin, where they have been made since the 14th century and are still made in large quantities today. They are eaten with drinks or served with soup instead of bread. This recipe is for cheese breadsticks, which for me are the most interesting, but you can omit the cheese or use focaccia or pizza dough instead. These *grissini* make a good gift, wrapped in parchment paper and tied with rustic string. For a party, make a variety and stand them in a vase as a dramatic centerpiece. My children help me to make these breadsticks and I let them use their imagination as to what flavorings to add.

Makes 80

2½ cups "00" flour
½ oz fresh yeast or 1 (¼ oz) envelope dry active yeast
⅔ cup tepid milk
4 oz Parmesan
8 tablespoons soft butter
1 teaspoon salt

Preheat the oven to 325°F. Mix the yeast with the tepid milk. Blend the remaining ingredients together in a bowl. Pour in the yeasted milk, and use your fingers to incorporate everything evenly and bring to a dough. Turn onto a lightly floured board and roll out to a thickness of ⅕ inch. Cut into lengths about 16 inches long and ½ inch wide. Place on a greased baking sheet and cook for 25–30 minutes, or until a rich golden brown. Leave to cool, then store in a tall airtight jar, such as a spaghetti jar. *Grissini* will keep for about a month. Use as they are or wrap in a thin slice of ham.

Variations

Sesame seed—spread a layer of sesame seeds on a plate and roll each stick in them before cooking.
Rosemary—spread a layer of finely chopped rosemary leaves on a plate and roll each stick in them before cooking.
Thin grissini—you can also put the dough through a pasta machine: roll it through the widest setting a couple of times, then put it through a tagliatelle cutter. Lay the stips on a floured baking sheet and bake for 10–12 minutes, until golden brown.
Cheese and black olive twists—use the recipe for pizza dough on page 66 and roll out the dough into a rectangle to the thickness of ⅕ inch. Scatter some chopped pitted olives and finely grated Parmesan over one half of the rectangle, fold the other halves over, and cut into lengths ½ inch wide. Roll and twist the lengths, lay them on an oiled tray and bake immediately for around 10 minutes or until golden brown at 400°F.

(This idea is courtesy of Richard Bertinet, a fantastic French baker who also makes great Italian and English bread!)

Calzone di cipolle
Scallion and Leek Pie

Apparently the origins of this pie lie in the Spanish *calzon*, since the Bourbons ruled southern Italy as well as Spain for centuries. It is often served as part of antipasti in Puglia or eaten as a hot snack from bakeries. I was shown how to make it by a lady named Rita who lives in a beautiful *masseria* (a traditional farmhouse) near Bari. Her incredibly thin pastry is made with wine, which gives off a wonderful aroma as it is heated. The Pugliesi use the local *sponsale*, a type of onion that is more bulbous than a scallion and has a milder flavor. You can sometimes find them sold as "continental onions." I have used a mixture of scallions or continental onions and leeks, which prove to be equally delicious. The best olives—if you can find them—are *Taggiasca*; otherwise buy small whole black olives and remove the pits.

Serves 8

FOR THE PASTA FROLLA RUSTICA (WHITE WINE PASTRY)
butter, for greasing
2¼ cups "00" flour or all-purpose flour
3 tablespoons olive oil
⅓ cup dry white wine
½ teaspoon salt

FOR THE FILLING
8 oz continental or scallions (bulbs and half the green parts), thinly sliced
1 lb leeks, thinly sliced
3 tablespoons olive oil
a good pinch of salt and freshly ground black pepper
3 tablespoons water
¼ cup golden raisins
½ cup black olives, pitted and coarsely chopped
¼ cup Parmesan, finely grated

Preheat the oven to 350°F. Grease a 10-inch tart pan with a removeable bottom with butter, dust with flour then tap out the excess.

Make the pastry by mixing the ingredients in a bowl with a large spoon or plastic dough scraper. Use your hands to bring the mixture into a ball. Collect the bits from around the bowl with the dough, then turn it onto a lightly floured work surface. Knead until well amalgamated and evenly colored. Wrap in plastic wrap and chill in the fridge for at least 20 minutes or overnight.

For the filling, cook the onions and leeks in a large frying pan with the oil, salt and pepper. After a couple of minutes, add the water and continue to cook over medium heat for 10–15 minutes. When the excess water has evaporated, add the raisins and olives. Stir well to combine and remove from the heat. Stir in the Parmesan, adjust the seasoning as necessary, and set aside.

Thinly roll out one-third of the pastry into a circle on a well-floured surface. Keep rolling until it is just 1mm thick (you should be able to blow underneath and see it lift off the surface). Place the pan upside down on the pastry and draw around it with the tip of a knife. This is the pie lid. Roll out the remaining pastry to 1mm thick and line the pan, allowing a 1½ inch overhang. Trim with scissors. Pour in the leek filling and cover with the pastry lid. Roll and twist the overhanging pastry inwards over the lid to seal. Finish by making two holes in the center with a sharp knife to allow steam to escape. Bake in the preheated oven for 35–45 minutes, until the top is golden. Leave to cool on a wire rack. Remove the sides of the pan, drizzle a little extra olive oil over the top, and serve at room temperature.

Panelle
Sicilian Chickpea Fritters

I never thought I would see a french-fry sandwich for sale on a hot sunny day in a Sicilian market! The "chips" were actually triangular fritters made with chickpea (gram) flour wedged into a soft bread roll, but the carbohydrate intake was the same! I prefer the fritters without the bread as antipasti or a snack. They are sometimes flavored with parsley or fennel seeds. I have also eaten these fritters made into chunky chip shapes in Liguria as a delicious accompaniment to Pot-roasted Loin of Pork with Prune, Apple, and Rosemary Stuffing (see page 320).

Serves 6–8

3 level teaspoons salt, plus extra for serving
1 teaspoon black pepper, finely crushed
2 teaspoons finely chopped flat-leaf parsley (optional) or 2 teaspoons fennel seeds, lightly crushed
6 cups cold water
5 cups chickpea (gram) flour
oil, for deep frying

There are two ways of cutting *panelle,* so decide on your method before embarking on this first stage and have the equipment ready. You will either pour the thickened mixture onto a clean work surface to be rolled out, or you can pour the mixture into a mold with sides about 2 inches deep (a small lasagne pan is perfect).

Begin by thoroughly mixing the salt, pepper, and parsley or fennel seeds with the flour. Pour the water into a large saucepan and add the flour to the water little by little, stirring with a whisk. Put over the heat and stir with a wooden spoon for 15–20 minutes, until it thickens.

Now either pour the thickened mixture onto the clean surface, cover with parchment or wax paper and roll out to a thickness of ½ inch, or pour it into your chosen mold. Leave to cool until set, for around 30–40 minutes.

Cut the cooled mixture (it will be stiff) into triangles measuring 2 x 2 x 3 inches for traditional *panelle* or into chunky french-fry shapes.

Heat the oil in a large saucepan or a deep-fat fryer to 350°F, or hot enough to brown a small piece of bread instantly. Fry the fritters for about 5 minutes, or until golden brown on all sides. Drain on paper towels and sprinkle with a little salt to taste before serving.

Torta salata di verdure
Oretta's Chicken and Vegetable Pie

This pie was shown to me by our friend Simone, whose mother makes it in Padua. You can vary the contents to use up leftover meat and vegetables such as broccoli or potatoes.

Serves 8

¼ cup olive oil
1 red bell pepper, cut into ¾ inch dice
1 zucchini, cut into ¾ inch dice
1 small eggplant, cut into ¾ inch dice
2 sprigs of thyme
1 garlic clove, lightly crushed
1 chicken breast, cut into bite-size chunks
salt and freshly ground black pepper
2 eggs
⅓ cup heavy cream
½ cup Parmesan, finely grated
2 sheets puff pastry, ready rolled
flour for dredging

Preheat the oven to 350°F and grease a 9½ inch fluted tart pan with a removeable bottom.

Heat ⅓ cup of the oil in a large frying pan and cook the vegetables, thyme, and garlic until browned and cooked through. Remove the vegetables from the pan with a slotted spoon and set aside in a colander to drain. Discard the garlic and thyme. Season the chicken with salt and pepper and toss in the flour to coat, tapping off the excess. Add the rest of the oil to the pan and fry the chicken until golden brown on all sides and cooked through. Set aside in a colander to drain.

Combine one of the eggs in a mixing bowl with the cream and Parmesan. Season with salt and pepper to taste.

Line the bottom of the pan with one sheet of the puff pastry and arrange the vegetables and chicken on top. Drizzle with the cream and egg mixture and cover with the second sheet of pastry. Trim the edges and make a cross in the center to allow steam to escape. Beat the remaining egg and brush over the pie. Bake for 30 minutes, until golden brown.

Tortine di zucchini e peperoni rossi in crosta di Parmigiano
Zucchini and Red Pepper Tarts with a Parmesan Crust

I tasted a tart similar to this at Marchesi, a beautiful *pasticceria* in Milan, and was so struck by its delicate taste and texture that I asked what was in it. The difference, the owner explained, between French quiche and Italian *tortina* is that the Italians use ricotta and Parmesan cheese. The filling varies according to the season, and may include plain cheese, Speck, mushrooms (see page 395 for Giancarlo's *Funghi Trifolati*, which is delicious as a filling), peas, and asparagus. For my version, I have added cheese and a pinch of chili powder to the pastry for extra bite.

Preheat the oven to 350°F and and grease the fluted tart pan(s). To make the filling, cut the zucchini into ⅕ inch slices, trim and dice the pepper, and put them on a baking sheet with the garlic, thyme, and salt and pepper to season. Drizzle with the olive oil. Toss well together and bake for 20–25 minutes, or until lightly browned. Set aside to cool.

For the pastry, sift the flour into a mixing bowl. Add the lard or butter, the grated cheese, the chili powder (if using), and the salt, and rub together with your fingers until the mixture resembles fine breadcrumbs. Add the water and bring the crumbs into a ball (this can be done in a food processor). Knead on a lightly floured work surface until you have a smooth dough. Wrap in plastic wrap and chill in the fridge for 20 minutes.

Meanwhile, in a bowl, whisk together the eggs, cream, milk, most of the Parmesan, and salt and pepper to taste. Spoon in the ricotta and mix gently (I like the texture of ricotta to show, so I don't overblend it). Set aside.

Remove the pastry from the fridge and roll it out to ⅛ inch thick. Line the tart pan(s) with the pastry, pressing lightly into the fluted sides. Prick the bottom with a fork, cover the surface with parchment paper and fill with baking beans or rice. Bake blind for 10 minutes then take out of the oven, remove the rice and paper, and allow to cool.

When the vegetables are at room temperature, put them on the pastry case(s) and pour in the cream and egg mixture. Bake in the oven for 30–40 minutes, or until the pastry is golden brown and has shrunk away slightly from the edges of the pan(s). Leave to cool slightly before serving with a Pecorino Cheese Sauce (see page 473) or with a simple dressed salad. This tart will reheat successfully.

Makes 6 individual (4 inch) quiches or 1 large (10½ inch) quiche

FOR THE PASTRY
1¾ cups all-purpose flour or "00" flour
6 tablespoons lard or butter, or half and half, cubed
½ cup Parmesan, finely grated
a good pinch of chili powder (optional)
a good pinch of salt
4 tablespoons cold water

FOR THE FILLING
2 large zucchini (about 1 lb in total)
1 large red bell pepper
2 garlic cloves, smashed
4 sprigs of thyme
salt and freshly ground black pepper
½ tablespoon olive oil
3 medium eggs
⅔ cup heavy cream
3 tablespoons milk
½ cup Parmesan, finely grated, (some reserved for the topping)
⅓ cup ricotta (sheep or cow's milk)

Torta Pasqualina
Easter Tart

This Ligurian tart is made at Easter and eaten on picnics on Easter Monday. The tart usually contains the soft cheese *prescinsoeua,* but this is hard to find so I suggest crème fraîche. Swiss chard is used traditionally but spinach is easier to find. If you are making the pastry, roll it by hand or use a pasta machine.

Serves 8–10

FOR THE PASTRY

3½ cups all-purpose flour or "00" flour
¾ cup water
2 tablespoons olive oil
a good pinch of salt

or 16 sheets filo pastry, plus extra olive oil
  for brushing

FOR THE FILLING

3 tablespoons olive oil
1 white onion, finely chopped
1 lb cooked spinach (weight after being cooked
  and squeezed dry)
salt and freshly ground black pepper
1 cup crème fraîche
1 egg
1 cup Parmesan, finely grated
1 tablespoon finely chopped fresh parsley,
6 eggs (1 reserved for the glaze)

Preheat the oven to 350°F. Grease and line a 10 inch tart pan, preferably with a removeable bottom. Make the pastry by mixing the ingredients by hand in a bowl or in a food processor. Knead briefly on a floured work surface, then divide the pastry into six equal balls. Let them rest in the fridge while you make the filling.

For the filling, heat the oil and cook the onion for 5 minutes or until softened, then add the spinach to heat through, and season with salt and pepper. Remove from the heat and pour into a mixing bowl to cool. Add the crème fraîche, the egg, Parmesan, and parsley, and mix well.

Roll each ball of pastry into a circle 1mm thick and large enough to fit the pan. Cover the bottom of the pan with three layers of pastry. Fill the tart with the stuffing and make five shallow holes for the eggs. Break the eggs into the holes. Cover with the remaining layers of pastry. Seal the edges with oil. Bake for 35–40 minutes. Serve right away or refrigerate overnight, covered, until needed.

Torta fritta
Hot Fried Dough Squares

On the winding roads around the hills of Parma there are signs outside restaurants promoting *torta fritta*, delicious fried puffs of dough. These are great with drinks before dinner. I encourage guests to tear the top off the little pockets and fill them with sliced Parma ham, *lardo di colonnata,* or soft *stracchino* cheese so that it melts in the heat. There are many versions of *torta fritta*, or *gnocchi fritti*, around Italy as I have come to discover; in Liguria we ate *sgabei*, which are traditionally eaten with *stracchino*, a soft cheese, and salumi. In Naples the dough is wrapped around broccoli florets or cheese to form balls before being fried. They are sold from *friggitori*, shops devoted to fried food.

Serves 6

1 medium potato (about 5 oz), boiled in its skin
½ oz fresh yeast or 1 (¼ oz) envelope
  active dry yeast
5 cups "00" or all-purpose flour
2 teaspoons salt
1 tablespoon extra virgin olive oil
approximately 1¼ cups tepid milk
oil or lard, for frying

Peel and mash the potatoes while still hot or, better still, pass through a *passatutto* or a food mill.

Crumble the fresh yeast (or mix, if dried) into the flour, and transfer to a food processor or bowl with the salt and potato. Combine the ingredients with the oil and then add enough tepid milk to form a smooth and soft dough. Leave the dough to rest in a bowl for about 1 hour or until doubled in size. Roll it out on a floured surface to a thickness of ⅕ inch. Cut the dough with a knife or a wavy pasta cutter into rectangles measuring roughly 3 x 4 inches.

Heat enough oil or lard to fill a pan to a depth of about 2 inches. To test the heat, drop a little piece of bread into the oil to see if it quickly becomes brown. When the oil is hot enough, carefully drop in a few *torte* to fry. You will need to work in batches. Turn when you see the edges of the underside becoming brown; they should only take about 1 minute on each side. Drain on paper towels and serve at once with Parma ham, salame, or *lardo*.

tipasti

CHAPTER 2: ANTIPASTI

Antipasti

When I first went to stay with Giancarlo's family in Italy, I made the error that I suspect many English people have made before me, of mistaking the antipasti for the whole meal. We arrived on a warm evening at his cousin's house to find the most beautiful array of food: mozzarella, prosciutto, stuffed vegetables, breads, olives…. How lovely, I thought; all this wonderful food that you can just pick up with your hands. His cousins remarked constantly on my healthy appetite and offered me more. They were delighted that I tried everything, and the more they encouraged, the more I ate. Then they said, "Now we will bring the pasta!"

ow naive of me not to know—and of course Giancarlo hadn't helped me at all; it never occurred to him to warn me. The whole meal lasted for hours. After the pasta came the meat course, the vegetables, and then the dessert. His family was so impressed at my capacity to enjoy food that I couldn't let them down, and it was all so delicious that I ate everything put in front of me. But it was a sharp learning curve. Now I know that almost always in Italy, whether you are joining friends at home or eating out at a restaurant, you begin a meal with antipasti, however humble or elaborate.

Antipasto, in fact means "before the meal" not, as people often think, "before the pasta." The custom dates back to Roman times, when many different appetizers would be served to begin a banquet. The most popular were seasoned eggs and egg-based dishes, mushrooms and truffles, vegetables, salads, assorted shellfish, cheese with herbs, olives, sausages, and even more filling dishes—like complicated *fricassées* and casseroles—which today really would be considered complete meals.

Caffè Caldesi is inspired by a place I ate at in Tuscany—I even had the same carpenter make the bar, which we brought all the way from Italy to London! But it was the antipasti in this café that I loved most, served on wooden platters. It has become fashionable now in London restaurants to serve antipasti this way, but we have been doing it for years: it is such a wonderful way to share food.

Every region in Italy has its favorite antipasti, which vary according to the geography—coastal or mountainous—and local produce. Almost always, though, there will be *salumi*—which is not a mis-spelling of salami, as I have often been admonished—but the generic term for cured meats. A plate of *affettati misti* might be offered (*affettati* refers to mixed sliced cured meat, as opposed to *salumi*, the name for mixed meats, which may or may not be sliced). There are also some classic antipasti cooked all over Italy, predominantly vegetable dishes, such as *sottaceto* (pickled vegetables), *sott'olio* (artichokes, mushrooms, or eggplants marinated in oil and herbs), pickled onions, grilled peppers, and sun-dried tomatoes. To go with these there will always be bread or bruschetta (see pages 40–75).

It is probably wise to learn from my experience with Giancarlo's family when planning an antipasto and to keep in mind the other dishes you are going to make to follow it, so that your antipasti stimulate the appetite rather than satisfying it.

salumi

COLD CUTS

People often ask me if *salumi* is a misprint—should it be *salami*? I was even challenged by a waiter once, who insisted on correcting me when I asked about *salumi*, replying, "Does madam mean salami?"

Salumi, not *salami* (the name given to cured sausage), is the generic term for cured meats, which have been well known since Greek and Roman times, especially those made with pork. In Rome, there is still an ancient market road called *Via Panisperna*, meaning "bread and ham." In the Middle Ages, during the barbarian invasions, the produce of the pig was one of the most important sources of income for a village, often used in place of money. Making *salumi* was a way of preserving meat before the invention of the fridge, and of using up all parts of the animal, including the blood. During the 19th century, the first *salumerie* (charcuterie delicatessen) appeared, and Italian *salumi* started to be appreciated abroad.

There are two main types of *salumi*: either cured pieces of meat, such as prosciutto and bresaola; or *insaccati*, which means chopped meat stuffed into a casing, as for *salame*. *Salumi* may be made with pork, beef, or game cured with salt and sometimes spices. In the Valle d'Aosta, Tuscany and Sardinia, donkey and horse meat are also used. It is the pig, however, that is king. Alongside the more commercial varieties of pig, there are four main traditional breeds of swine, known as *autoctono*, which means "from a particular area": the *Cinta Senese* from Tuscany, which are black with a white belt, the *Mora Romagnola* from the Apennine side of Emilia-Romagna, the *Nero dei Nebrodi* from Sicily, which resemble a wild boar, and the *Razza Casertana* from the Cilento area of Campania.

As always, every Italian region boasts typical local cured meats of extraordinary taste, whose method of production is often related to the climate. When you buy *salumi* unsliced, look for a label specifying the origins—the DOP (Protected Designation of Origin) symbol is a guarantee both of quality and traditional methods of production.

Salumi are good eaten alone—in Italy that means with bread—or with preserved vegetables. Ham and melon are like a married couple, while potato purée and spinach pair up with Italy's famous cotechino sausages, made from pork, fat and spices.

A guide to salumi

Salami

Every region has a variation on the basic salami recipe: chopped meat and hard fat, seasoned and sometimes spiced, then forced into a casing and hung to cure. They vary in coarseness: finer grain salami are known as *grana*. Traditionally, better cuts of meat—shoulder, rump, thigh—are reserved for salami, the rest being for sausages. Our Sardinian friend Gianfranco Poddighe makes his salame with *cosce* (thigh); he says it's the best part of the pig. He cuts long "sticks" of *lardo* (see right) like thin *grissini* and inserts three or four in each salame—when sliced, you see little identical shapes of fat. He also adds whole black peppercorns, salt, and garlic soaked in white wine.

It may not be the finest, but Milano is one of the best-known salami. Look out also for *salame di Varzi* from Piedmont, which has its own PDO. *Salame di Felino* is seasoned with peppercorns and salt, while salame di Napoli contains wine, garlic, and chile, the Tuscan *salame finocchiona* is made with fennel seeds, and the small *salame cacciatori* is designed to fit a hunter's pocket. Our supplier, Fabio Antoniazzi of La Credenza, introduced us to *n'duja*, a soft salame from Calabria—in a region that grows chiles, it is only natural that they appear in salami.

Prosciutto

see page 86.

Culatello

Properly known as *culatello di zibello*, this pear-shaped 'little rump' of the pig is the king of prosciutto. Fabio buys us one made by the Spigaroli family, who inherited a castle between the cities of Parma, Piacenza and Cremona. The composer Verdi used to live nearby and the great grandfather of the current Spigaroli generation was a sharecropper on the Verdi farm. The area is depressing and foggy, but the climate and the castle's cellars are the perfect environment for curing the *culatello* with salt, whole and cracked peppercorns, garlic and white wine. The hams are tied up to mature for 16–17 months. Such is their value that the family has a super alarm system to prevent the hams from being stolen.

Pancetta

Cured pork belly may be rubbed with red wine, and seasoned with salt and pepper, garlic and herbs before being matured. It might be smoked (*affumicata*) or unsmoked, flat (most typical in Tuscany) or round (usually unsmoked and for eating as it is). In Tuscany round pancetta is known as *steccata*. It is matured in marble containers then hung between two pieces of wood. Flat pancetta is used in cooking as we might use bacon, for example in pasta dishes, and also for barding—wrapping meat to add flavor and prevent it from drying out during cooking.

Pancetta coppata

Made with pork belly and back neck, and less fatty than regular pancetta.

Speck

A smoked prosciutto traditional in Alto Adige, the area close to the border with Austria and in particular in the Tyrol.

Mortadella

The speciality of Bologna, this is made with pork ground to a paste, spices, and sometimes pistachio nuts. It is cooked rather than cured and has a smooth texture.

Prosciutto cotto

Cooked ham; currently there is a trend for cooked hams studded with truffles.

Bresaola

Raw meat (*di cinghiale*: wild boar) marinated in wine and spices before curing; a speciality of Lombardy.

Lardo di Colonnata

This is pork fat cured in marble vats with salt and herbs and aged for a minimum of six months and up to a year. The most famous *lardo* comes from Colonnata, near Massa-Carrara in the marble hills of northern Tuscany. I know that many people are often terrified of eating fat, but it is delicious once you get over any inhibitions! Federica Manconi, who produces *lardo* in Colonnata and is really proud of her product, insisted that I try her *lardo* cold, as it should be served. It was not at all chewy, but melted instantly in my mouth, releasing its wonderful herby, salty flavor. Lardo is also great to cook with—once you get used to it, you will wonder how you managed without it. We use it liberally in our restaurants when we roast meat, to stop it from drying out.

Guanciale

The cured cheek of the pig, this is mainly made in Tuscany and Lazio, and is the essential ingredient in Roman carbonara and amatriciana sauces (see pages 196 and 168).

Sopressata

Here, every bit of a pig's head, including the ears and tongue, are cooked with lemon and spices, pressed in a casing and put inside a hessian coat.

Coppa

The back of neck of pork, cured and air-dried in a sausage casing. Large veins of fat run through it.

Salsiccia

Salame di Napoli

Salame di Milano

Larda

Prosciutto cotto

Pancetta coppata

Porchetta

Pancetta arrotolata

Soppressata

Mortadella

Pancetta affumicata

Bresaola

Prosciutto cruda

inghiale

San Daniele

Bresaola
Cured Beef

This recipe is adapted from Ann and Franco Taruschio's *Leaves from The Walnut Tree*. Franco showed us how to make our own bresaola for one of our restaurants; it is far superior to the shop-bought variety and so we have continued making it ever since. Franco was given the recipe from the restaurant Piperno in the Jewish quarter of Rome, where bresaola was made as an alternative to prosciutto, the popular air-cured ham. You need to use a non-metallic dish or bowl to marinate this dish; I use an old ceramic bread bowl.

Trim the beef, removing the fat and sinews. If the beef has silverskin around it, leave this on to help keep the meat together (it will be trimmed later).

Put all the ingredients for the marinade in a large non-metallic bowl. Add the trimmed meat, cover completely, and leave in a cool place for 7–10 days, or until the meat feels firm. The time this takes is dependent on the thickness of the meat; a long, thin piece will take less time than a fat piece.

Remove the meat from the marinade and pat dry. Wrap it in a layer of thin muslin or cheesecloth so that the air can get to it but flies cannot. Hang the meat in a dry, airy place for another week or two, until it feels firm enough to slice thinly; it should feel solid, and not give at all as you press with your fingers.

Unwrap the bresaola. If mold has appeared, don't worry; moisten a piece of paper towel with some oil and rub the meat clean. If there are any very hard areas, trim these away with a sharp knife. Coat the bresaola in olive oil, wrap in parchment paper and refrigerate until needed. The oil and paper will prevent it from drying out. To serve, slice thinly and follow the recipe idea on page 85.

Makes 2kg

4½ lb boneless beef, top round
  or rump roast
olive oil, for coating

FOR THE MARINADE
1 bottle of dry red wine
1 bottle of dry white wine
12 oz coarse sea salt
a large bunch of rosemary
24 cloves
10 bay leaves
2 garlic cloves, crushed
3 short cinnamon sticks
3 strips of orange zest
6 dried chiles
1 heaping tablespoon black
  peppercorns

Bresaola con rucola e limone
Bresaola with Arugula and Lemon

If you are not using your own homemade bresaola, buy it freshly sliced at a deli.

Serves 4

16 slices of bresaola
a handful of arugula leaves
1 oz Parmesan shavings
2 tablespoons extra virgin
  olive oil
juice of ½ lemon
freshly ground black pepper

Arrange the bresaola slices on a plate and top with the arugula and the Parmesan. Drizzle with the olive oil and lemon juice and season with the pepper, to taste.

Also try serving slices of bresaola rolled around spoonfuls of ricotta or mascarpone mixed with chopped walnuts and a little salt and pepper.

prosciutto crudo

HAM

Parma ham is so famous around the world that I think outside Italy people often don't realize there is any other kind of prosciutto crudo. The word *prosciutto* simply means "ham." *Crudo* means raw, referring to the fact that these hams are salted and dried rather than cooked. However, most non-Italians tend to drop the *crudo* and talk of prosciutto and Parma ham as if they were one and the same. Mention *prosciutto crudo* to an Italian however, and you start a big debate.

Everyone has an opinion in Italy as to which is the superior of the two big-name hams found all over the country: Parma, or the more expensive San Daniele (from Friuli). But air-cured hams are also produced in Piedmont, in the Berico-Euganean part of the Veneto region, in the Marches (*prosciutto di Carpegna*) and in Umbria and Tuscany, where there is a small production of ham from the Cinta Senese pig, an old black breed with a white belt or *cinta* around its middle. Recently, there has been increased breeding of these pigs—they had become extremely rare following the introduction in the 1950s of breeds from which it was easier to make profit. The flavor of the Cinta Senese hams is intense and highly regarded in Tuscany. The *prosciutto di Norcia* ham made in a tiny area of Umbria is also from traditional breeds of pig. At a very local level, hams are also produced by a single farmer—raising his own pigs and doing his own preserving as many people in the countryside would have done at one time in Italy.

All these hams are produced in a similar way: first a dry-curing with salt, followed by air-drying, and then ageing. These processes intensify the natural flavors of the ham, resulting in a salty but sweet meat that, when cut correctly, melts in the mouth. However, the breed of pigs and the diet they are fed, together with the air temperature and altitude at which the hams are cured also help to determine the taste, aroma and quality of the final product. While San Daniele and Parma ham are known as *dolce* for their sweet flavor, the hams of Tuscany and Umbria are known as *salato* for their saltier, more savory taste—extra salt and pepper and sometimes other spices or garlic are used in the curing process.

The process of preserving hams by salting and drying dates back at least to the 2nd century BC and is thought to have been used by the Romans and the Etruscans before them. Some say that the name *prosciutto* comes from the Latin *perexuctus*, meaning "deprived of all liquid." Others believe the name stems from the Italian *prosciugare*, which describes the process of salting to draw off moisture. It was the Gauls, however, living in the mountain regions, who became expert prosciutto-makers, the mountain air

and breezes supposedly giving their maturing ham its sweet flavor. They sold these hams to the Romans, and so their legacy continues to this day.

Returning to popular opinion on the two most famous hams, some say that *Prosciutto di Parma* has a more aged, subtly spicy flavor and a softer, more melting texture; others find San Daniele, which has the bone left in, sweeter with slightly firmer flesh and say it tastes more of the pig and its acorn diet. But this more intense flavor is too fresh, too "crude" perhaps, for others. Some of the Italians who work at our restaurants tell me there is a difference of opinion even within their own household. In one family, the mother prefers Parma ham and the father San Daniele, a bit like Jack Spratt and his wife.

Prosciutto di Parma (Parma ham)

The best known *prosciutto crudo* is, of course, Parma ham, which has its own PDO (Protected Designation of Origin). This means that in order to distinguish the high-quality, authentic product from its many imitators, it must be made to strict regulations in a defined geographic region, as dictated by the European Union.

I went to observe the making of Parma ham at one of the factories in the region and was amazed to see how many staff were working there. No wonder the ham is so costly—what huge sums they must spend on salaries! It was like a scene from *Charlie and the Chocolate Factory*, with such incredible attention given to these slabs of meat.

There is a proverb heard frequently in Parma: *grasso e magro non del tutto, ecco il pregio del prosciutto*. It tells of the important balance between lean and fat meat, and this is the essence of the best quality *prosciutto crudo*. The meat comes from the hind thighs of nine-month-old pigs which must weigh a minimum of 337½ lb. They have to have been bred in one of 11 northern and central Italian regions and fed on a carefully regulated blend of grains, cereals and leftover whey from the local Parmigiano-Reggiano cheese. Markings on the leg, applied at the farm, denote the origin of each pig. The legs are trimmed at the slaughterhouse, which adds its mark, and then they are sent to the curing house, where the date that curing begins is stamped on. All of this has to take place in the traditional production area near Parma, which centers around Langhirano.

At the curing house, the legs are salted (which also preserves the pink color). Salt is the only preservative used; no chemicals are allowed. Then the legs are hung for 6–7 days in a refrigerated chamber in 80 percent humidity. After this, they are given a second salt and hung in dry conditions for 15–18 days, when they start to dry out, losing up to 4 percent of their weight; they continue to lose weight through each of the processes that follow.

Buying, cutting and storing

Our Italian chefs are so snooty about pre-sliced and packaged *prosciutto crudo* that they absolutely refuse to taste it. For them, there is no substitute for freshly sliced ham.

If you eat a lot of prosciutto, it is worth considering buying a whole ham. If you do so, keep it hanging in a cool place rather than storing it in the fridge.

Many Italians have small domestic slicing machines. If you don't have one, ask your delicatessen to slice your prosciutto thinly. I couldn't believe what a difference it made to the flavor when I first tasted *prosciutto crudo* cut into paper-thin slices; it melts in the mouth.

Because it is on the bone, San Daniele should always be cut with a knife. The flavor of the prosciutto nearer to the bone will be more intense, though the slices are more difficult to make tidy and may be smaller.

Remember, the balance of fat and lean meat is all-important in prosciutto, so perish the thought of removing the fat.

If you are buying ham already cut, wrap it tightly to stop it drying out and store it in the fridge.

The next phase of the curing process is called "resting." The hams are put in another cold store room for 60–70 days at 75 percent humidity. After this, the hams are washed to remove excess salt and hung out to dry in large rooms with windows on either side. In these rooms, up to 20,000 hams hang at any one time on special wooden frames called *scalere*. The air-flow regulation is very important and the windows are only opened when the outside temperature and humidity are favorable, but connoisseurs believe that these moments—when the windows are open and the hams are wafted by aromatic breezes—are critical to the development of Parma ham's distinctive flavor. After about three months, the surface of the meat is hardened and dried, and in a scene that reminded me of one of Caravaggio's chiaroscuro (light and dark) paintings, the hams are slathered with *sugna*—a mixture of lard, salt, and pepper—by two ladies working under a heat lamp. The greasing softens the external layers, prevents the hams from drying too rapidly and also allows further humidity loss.

In the seventh month, the ham is transferred to the "cellars," rooms with less air and light, where they will remain for at least a year. At this point, the controller uses a long needle to determine the ham's level of maturity. Carved from the lower-leg bone of a horse, the needle is extremely porous and the controller plunges it into five different parts of the ham.

At the end of the minimum 12-month ageing period, the ham has shrunk by a third, making the flavor highly concentrated, and will have acquired its unique delicate aroma. Only then, once it has satisfied stringent criteria of color, flavor, and texture, is the ham ready for the official stamp of certification, the Ducal Crown, which is fire-branded onto it.

I came away from my visit to Parma with great respect for the *prosciuttai*, or ham-makers, and the feeling that we must support them, rather than buying cheaper and inferior products, if we don't want these fine, traditional ingredients to disappear.

Prosciutto di San Daniele

This ham has been made for centuries in San Daniele and Sauris in the northeastern region of Friuli Venezia-Giulia and is prized for its salty-sweet flavor. The pigs used for San Daniele hams are fed a diet high in acorns, which accounts for the particular taste of the finished product. While the ingredients and processes involved in making *Prosciutto di San Daniele* follow the same lines as other types of *prosciutto crudo*, aficionados believe that as well as the diet of the pigs, it is the unique climatic conditions of the Friuli region, with its higher altitudes and drier air, that give *Prosciutto di San Daniele* its special flavor and texture. *Prosciutto di San Daniele* also differs from other types of prosciutto in that the whole leg down to the trotter is cured, unlike Parma ham which uses only the thigh.

OLIVES

It wasn't until I began immersing myself in Italian cooking and travelling in Italy that I really began to appreciate how much a good olive affects a finished dish. Often a particular variety of olive gives a regional recipe its unique flavor.

There is a simple recipe on page 236 based on fish, olives, and potatoes. I mention in the introduction that you can murder the flavor by using cheap, canned pitted olives, or glorify it into something superb by pitting a handful of *taggiasche* olives yourself. A good olive makes that much difference.

As always with Italian ingredients, a huge variety of olives are found throughout the country, thanks to the diverse terrain of the peninsula. Differences in altitude, climate, and soil favour different cultivars. In this, olive-growing and the making of olive oil have much in common with the world of viticulture and wine-making. Both also involve labor-intensive harvesting, evoke true Italian passion and share a history dating back to the Greek and Roman civilizations.

Homer pronounced olive oil to be "liquid gold," and it still enjoys such reverence today. Italians talk about *unto d'olio*, which translates as "anointed with oil."

The main varieties from Puglia are *coratina, provenzale,* and *ogliarola*; here, too, grows the plum-sized *cerignola*, which is picked green. The largest olive in the world, it has a mild fruitiness. In contrast, some olives in Puglia are so small they are not worth pitting before cooking, which can be a bit of a shock mid-calzone! It can be difficult to source specific varieties of olive outside Italy, but the *cerignola* is found in good delicatessens, like the small aromatic *taggiasca* olive from northern Liguria, which adds a wonderful richness or spring note to dishes. Look out, too, for the purple-ish *gaeta* from Lazio, or *ascolane*, big green olives from Le Marche, often stuffed with meat, bread-crumbed and deep-fried, or the *Nocellara del Belice* from Sicily.

Time of harvest has a strong influence on the flavor of olives. Those picked fresh or green, early in the season, have a slightly bitter, tangy flavor and dense texture. When left on the tree to mature olives become softer and milder in flavor.

A busy time of year!

The olive harvest continues for several weeks from late autumn to early winter. Fine nets are placed around the tree trunk; in some regions, the olives are allowed to fall naturally onto the net when black and ripe. In other places, the olives are picked by hand, which often involves vigorously shaking the tree and using a large rake-like tool. Relatives travel from miles around to help their families at olive-picking time, and are often paid in bottles of oil. Olive trees do best in hot and dry climates with a long growing season, so more olive production is found in the southern part of the country. Puglia, the heel of Italy, is the most prolific olive-growing region.

Frittata di cipolle rosse e patate
Caramelized Red Onion and Potato Frittata

Serves 4

4 tablespoons extra virgin olive oil
1 red onion, sliced into thin circles
salt and pepper
2 medium potatoes, cooked, peeled, and cut into ⅛ inch cubes
6 eggs

Heat the oil in a medium non-stick frying pan over medium heat. When hot, add the onion and season with salt and pepper. Cook the onion for 5–7 minutes until well softened and lightly caramelized, taking care not to let it burn. Add the potatoes and stir through. Stir frequently with a wooden spoon or shake the pan from time to time. Add a little extra oil, if necessary, to prevent the potatoes from sticking.

Meanwhile, crack the eggs into a bowl and beat. Pour into the pan and cook over medium heat until the mixture has begun to come away from the sides of the pan, but the center is still a little runny. Put a plate bigger than the frying pan upside down over the pan. Wearing oven mitts, hold the plate over the pan and quickly invert so that the frittata drops onto it. Slide it back into the pan to cook on the other side until the egg is cooked but still soft. Serve warm or at room temperature.

Frittata estiva di Flavio con pomodorini e basilico
Flavio's Summer Cherry Tomato and Basil Frittata

Serves 2

2 tablespoons extra virgin olive oil
6 cherry tomatoes, halved
salt and pepper
3 eggs, beaten
1 cup mozzarella, shredded or cut into small cubes
10 basil leaves, roughly torn

Heat the oil in a large non-stick frying pan over high heat; when hot, add the tomatoes, season with salt and pepper, and cook for about 2 minutes.

Pour in the beaten eggs, mozzarella, and basil, and cook over medium heat until the mixture has begun to come away from the sides of the pan, but the center is still a little runny. Put a plate bigger than the frying pan upside down over the pan. Wearing oven mitts, hold the plate over the pan and quickly invert them so that the frittata drops onto the plate. Then slide it back into the pan to cook on the other side for a couple of minutes, until the egg is cooked but still soft. Serve either warm or at room temperature.

Serves 2 as main course or 4 as antipasti

3 tablespoons extra virgin olive oil

4 scallions, finely chopped

salt and pepper

3 eggs

a handful of fresh mint leaves, roughly shredded

a handful of flat-leaf parsley, roughly shredded

¼ cup Parmesan, finely grated

1½ cups fresh or frozen peas, cooked

Frittata di piselli e menta
Pea and Mint Frittata

Giancarlo often makes these as an antipasti or a quick lunch. Somebody always refers to it as a French omelette, but Giancarlo insists it's not because frittata should be thicker than an omelette (but thinner than a Spanish tortilla). So this is a delicious Italian frittata and nothing else!

Heat the oil in a large frying pan (non-stick is ideal) over medium heat. Cook the onions with a little salt and pepper until softened. Meanwhile, crack the eggs into a bowl and beat, then add the herbs and Parmesan and mix well. Add the peas to the pan and mix with the onions for a couple of minutes.

Pour the beaten egg into a pan and cook for about 5 minutes over low heat. When the frittata has begun to set and starts to brown underneath, put a plate bigger than the frying pan upside down over the pan. Wearing oven mitts, hold the plate over the pan and quickly invert so that the frittata drops onto the plate. Then slide the frittata back into the frying pan to cook on the other side for a couple of minutes.

Slide the frittata onto a warmed serving plate. Cut into slices and eat with hot bread and a green salad, or leave to cool to room temperature.

pomodori

TOMATOES

Whereas in Britain—until recently at least—we have tended to use round red tomatoes for everything, in Italy there is a tomato for every purpose. The number of varieties runs into thousands, with every region having its favorite and soil quality adding to their characteristic flavors. Italians can debate—at great length—the various properties of different tomatoes and why they should be used for a particular dish, and almost always someone in the family grows them. Even in cities, people find space for a few plants. What Italians want in a tomato is flavor, flavor, flavor: the kind of taste that allows you simply to crush the tomatoes with your hands, add a little oil and smear them over a pizza crust. Just as you can elevate a dish with wonderful ripe tomatoes, you can really spoil it with watery insipid tomatoes, which is why, out of season, Italians always used canned tomatoes.

Often our Italian staff talk wistfully of their childhood memories of picking tomatoes and taking part in the annual ritual of blanching, peeling, and canning the crop in big jars in their great grandmother's garage, or of making homemade passata... family occasions not to be missed.

The Italian seed company Franchi showed me an amazing range of tomatoes at their test gardens in Bergamo, where they are testing ever more new varieties as well as keeping alive lesser known species similar to the heirloom tomatoes now becoming popular in Britain and the United States.

We tend to think of cherry tomatoes playing a huge part in Italian cooking (see Pasta with Cherry Tomato Sauce, page 166), but although certain cherry varieties have been grown in Italy for a long time, they have only really been popular in the last 30 years—since the seeds began to be sold in packets rather than sacks.

Even so, the Italians have perfected the art of canning cherry tomatoes, just has they have the other varieties. Italian canned tomatoes are a revelation, because—as everyone in Italy will tell you—they know just when to pick them: when they are ripe and at the perfect point of sweetness for canning. Otherwise, what is the point?

KATIE'S TIPS

Buy tons of tomatoes when they are in season and ripe. Then make and can your own passata and sauces (see Gregorio's Tomato Passata on page 166).

Smash over-ripe tomatoes for bruschetta or to make _Acquasale_ (see page 99).

Keep tomatoes out of the fridge as the cold dulls their aroma and flavor. I keep mine in a bowl in the kitchen and the children eat them like apples.

If the skins are tough, drop tomatoes into boiling water for a minute, then score and peel. If making sauce, pass through a sieve to get rid of the skins.

To marinate sun-dried tomatoes, heat 1 gallon water with ⅓ cup red wine vinegar and 1 clove of garlic. When the water boils, drop in 8 oz dry-pack sun-dried tomatoes. Cook until soft, around 10 minutes. Drain and rinse the tomatoes under cold water for a couple of minutes, until cool. Then squeeze them and put into a container with 1 quart sunflower oil, 4 halved cloves of garlic, 4 bay leaves, another ⅓ cup vinegar, and a handful of coarsely chopped parsley. Cover and refrigerate. They are ready to eat after two days but last for a couple of weeks if always covered with oil.

In Naples I was shown the simplest dish: sticks of eggplant were fried in sunflower oil until crispy like chips. The oil was poured away and a little olive oil, garlic, and chile added followed by canned cherry tomatoes. What a quick pasta sauce!

Often I find non-Italian brands of canned tomatoes a little bitter. Adjust the flavor by adding a touch of sugar.

Preserved tomatoes

Passata
Peeled and puréed tomatoes are passed through a *passatutto* or sieve (hence the name). Sometimes it is flavored with *odori* such as basil and garlic. The purée is canned for using in sauces and stews.

Sun-dried tomatoes
San Marzano tomatoes are opened up, spread on racks, and dried in the Italian sun so that they dehydrate and then shrivel. They can be eaten as they are, included in cooking or preserved in oil.

Sun-blush or oven-dried tomatoes
These are left to dry in the sun for a shorter period than fully sun-dried tomatoes, so they stay soft and chewy. To make your own, preheat the oven to 225°F and arrange 12 oz of halved ripe cherry tomatoes cut-side up on a baking sheet. Combine 1 teaspoon each of sugar, salt and finely chopped fresh rosemary or thyme and sprinkle over the tomatoes. Bake for 1–1½ hours, depending on the size of the tomatoes, until shrivelled.

Salsa and conserva
The process for making these homemade sauces is similar to passata, but salsa and conserva are usually cooked twice or longer and flavored with *odori*. In Italian homes, these sauces are made at the peak of the season, then stored for the winter.

Polpa di pomodoro
This involves cutting tomatoes into small cubes, mixing them with a little concentrated tomato, then canning. As the chopped tomatoes are visible, they give an impression of freshness, which is useful in sauces.

Tomato purée and concentrate
Now found in any supermarket, but once these would be made at home every year. Purée is made by cooking tomatoes briefly, then straining to produce a thick liquid somewhere between crushed tomatoes and tomato. For concentrate (*concentrato*) or purée, tomatoes are cooked for several hours to reduce their moisture, strained to remove the seeds and skin, then cooked again until thick and rich. *Strattu* or *astrattu* is a super-concentrated tomato purée from southern Sicily. Its intensity is achieved by boiling tomatoes with salt for hours before baking them in the hot sun or an oven for a few more hours. Around 11 lb of tomatoes are required for just one jar of *strattu*.

Main varieties

San Marzano
This plum tomato is a favorite for sauces and stews, since it has more flesh than juice, giving a concentrated flavor. This variety is also the best for drying and canning.

Other plum tomatoes
Often grown specifically for making sauces, plum tomatoes have significantly fewer seed compartments than standard round tomatoes (usually only two) and are generally more solid, too, making them more suitable for processing. Today, lovely sweet baby plums are available.

Round tomatoes
The water content of round tomatoes tends to be higher than in plum varieties, making them lighter for eating raw. If you use round tomatoes in slower cooked dishes and sauces, allow a longer cooking time for all the water to evaporate and the flavor to develop entirely. The best are on the vine (*ramato*).

Green tomatoes
There are two types of green tomato: one is picked unripe and is quite tart but good for chutneys or fried. The other is a variety that stays green when ripe, has a tangy flavor and is good in salads or *sottaceto*—pickled in vinegar.

Cuore di bue
Literally translated as "ox heart," these are big tomatoes (see photo on page 97). On average they weigh 7–11 oz each, though some can reach 1 lb! The flesh is meaty, and when they are fully ripe they have the perfect sweet–sour balance, with few seeds and a soft skin. This makes a great tomato for eating raw as well as cooking (its shape makes it ideal for stuffing).

Cherry tomatoes
The popularity of these depends on the region. Our Tuscan and Sardinian chefs tell me that cherry tomatoes are not used much there, except for salads and decoration. But in Puglia, Naples, and Sicily, I saw them everywhere: in focaccia, fish dishes, open tarts... I use them all the time in pasta sauces, and they are wonderful for drying on a sunny day or roasting in the oven (see left). *Pachino*, *cieligini* or *pomodorini* have become generic names for cherry tomatoes, however *Pachino* tomatoes, which have been grown in Sicily since the 1920s at least, now have an IGP (*indicazione geografica protetta*), meaning that they must come from Pachino in Sicily.

Whole bottled and canned tomatoes
Pomodori pelati are peeled whole tomatoes in a can or jar. The homemade version, which evokes such fond memories among our young Italian staff, is well worth reviving when tomatoes are at their ripest. When you use these tomatoes for a sauce, first squash and break them up in a bowl using your hands, to help them break down during cooking. *Pelati* squashed in this way can also be used as a pizza topping with the addition of salt, oil, and oregano.

Gino!

Salsa di pomodori alla Gino
Gino's Tomato Salsa

Gino attributes the success of San Lorenzo restaurant in London to this recipe. He says it makes everything taste so good that it was used not only on toasted bread to make bruschetta, but added to chicken, fish, and pasta recipes—even to a wild-boar dish. It goes without saying that good tomatoes are vital. In Italy, Gino uses a mix of *San Marzano* and *Cuore di bue*, but we seek out Sicilian tomatoes or, better still, our own home-grown ones at the right time of year.

Makes enough for 6 (5–6 in) bruschette

1 lb tomatoes, the best-quality you can find
1 teaspoon fine sea salt
1 garlic clove, peeled, crushed and inside green shoot removed
3 large sprigs of basil (12 large leaves), coarsely chopped
1 large sprig of thyme, or 1 heaping teaspoon thyme leaves, stripped from the stems
⅓ cup extra virgin olive oil
2 heaping tablespoons coarsely chopped flat-leaf parsley
¾ red chile, coarsely chopped, including seeds (optional)

FOR THE BRUSCHETTA (SEE PHOTO ON PAGE 98)
crusty white loaf, cut into 8 x ¾ inch slices

Wash and halve the tomatoes, removing the coarse green cores. Chop the tomatoes coarsely into ½–¾ inch cubes and put into a sieve over a bowl for half an hour to drain.

Mix the rest of the ingredients with the tomatoes using a large spoon. Take care not to over-mix and turn them into a pulp. Season to taste; I cannot emphasize this enough as I don't know how hot your chiles will be or how tasty your tomatoes. Don't be afraid to add more thyme, chile and salt to achieve a full-flavored result. Store in a covered bowl in the fridge; this sauce keeps for up to 1 week. To make the bruschetta, toast the slices of bread and top with the tomato mixture.

Tip: Use as a pasta sauce: add to plain pasta with a few cubes of mozzarella and extra basil or topped with arugula salad; serve with seafood pasta, or make Pasta Arrabiata by adding more chile. This sauce is also good with grilled fish.

Insalata di tre pomodori
Three-Tomato Salad

Take a mixture of fresh, sun-blush (see page 91) and marinated sun-dried tomatoes (see page 91), cut into bite-size pieces, and toss with a little olive oil, salt and torn basil leaves.

Insalata Caprese
Mozzarella, Tomato, and Basil Salad

This is one of Italy's most famous salads, made in summer when tomatoes have maximum flavor. It originates from Capri, but is now served all over Italy (and the world), proudly displaying the colors of the Italian flag.

Lay slices of buffalo mozzarella and fresh ripe tomatoes onto a plate, alternating the colors. Tuck in some basil leaves and drizzle with a good extra-virgin olive oil. Season with salt and pepper and serve.

Crostini con purè di fave
Crostini with Fava Bean and Wild Garlic Dip

Franco Taruschio, the original owner of The Walnut Tree restaurant near Abergavenny in Wales, made me this vibrant green dip one spring when he taught our family to pick the long, green leaves of wild garlic. This pungent plant is often found by rivers and now our children recognize the smell and gather it when we are out walking. The leaves have a gentler flavor than garlic bulbs. The dip is very addictive and is also good with lamb chops, sausages, or spread on crostini.

If you are making crostini, preheat the oven to 400°F. Blanch the beans in boiling water for 1 minute, then plunge them into cold water. If the outer skins are tough and you have time, slip the beans out of their skins, though this is not essential as the whole dip is so finely chopped.

Put all the ingredients for the dip into a food processor and briefly process to a coarse paste. Taste and adjust the flavors of the garlic, salt, and pepper as necessary and feel free to add a little more olive oil to loosen the paste. If you are serving the dip with meat, spoon it into a bowl and serve at room temperature.

To make the crostini, put the bread slices on a baking sheet in the oven for 5–10 minutes, until golden brown and crisp. Remove from the oven and drizzle with olive oil. Spread with the dip and finish with another drizzle of olive oil and some coarsely chopped mint leaves.

Makes 24 (serves 12 as crostini or 6 as a side dish)

FOR THE DIP
1 lb young freshly shelled fava beans, or frozen fava beans
1–2 garlic cloves, finely chopped, or 10 wild garlic leaves
12–15 large fresh mint leaves
2 heaping tablespoons freshly grated *Pecorino Sardo* or Parmesan
6 tablespoons extra virgin olive oil, plus extra as needed
a good pinch of salt and freshly ground black pepper

FOR THE CROSTINI
white or brown country-style loaf, cut into 24 x thin slices
extra virgin olive oil, for drizzling
mint leaves, coarsely cut, to garnish

Serves 4

5 oz *friselle* or Danish
  wholewheat crispbreads
3–4 tablespoons olive oil
salt and freshly ground
  black pepper
12 oz ripe tomatoes
1 teaspoon dried oregano,
  or 2 teaspoons fresh
  basil (or both)

Crispbread and Tomato Salad with Oregano and Basil

The derivation of this dish and its name comes from sailors who would take the dry wholewheat bread known as *friselle* on voyages. Whenever they wanted to eat it, they would dip the bread into seawater (*acquasale*) to give it flavor and rehydrate it. It could then be dressed with oil and whatever topping they were lucky enough to have on board. Today, it is still the staple breakfast of the older generation in parts of Campania. My son Giorgio loves this dish, and after much practice has perfected the art of soaking so that the bread has just the right amount of contact with water. We have discovered that Danish crispbreads are the same as *friselle*. Most often, the crispbread is eaten with tomato and oregano or basil when in season (I like to use both the herbs) and plenty of good local olive oil, but celery or tuna and tomato make good variations.

Hold the crispbreads under running water for a few seconds; just long enough to coat all sides. Arrange the soaked pieces on a serving dish, drizzle with half the olive oil, and season with salt and pepper.

Break up the tomatoes with your fingers and arrange them over the crispbread. Dress with the remaining oil, more salt and pepper, scatter on top the herbs and serve.

OLIVE OIL

Most of us have heard about the health aspects of olive oil and the fact that its "good" monounsaturated fatty acids and antioxidants may help protect against heart disease and, some say, even delay the ageing process. However, let's be honest, most of us buy our olive oil from the supermarket, where the choice is usually between private-label blends and a few well-known names. So we can be forgiven for not being fully aware of the sheer variety and complexity of olive oils produced in a country like Italy.

You need to think about olive oil as you would wine: fine and expensive at one end of the scale and, at the other, the equivalent of everyday "plonk," with every oil varying in color, fragrance, and, most importantly, in flavor. A vast number of factors play a part in giving each oil its unique character, from the variety of olives grown and where they are grown to the quality of the soil and the weather during the growing season.

The process of making olive oil is all about separating the *sansa* and the *acqua* from the *olio*, that is, the solid matter (the skin and the pits) and the water from the oil. Around 11 lb of olives are needed for every quart of oil, so as few as four bottles may be produced from the fruit of one tree.

So what do virgins have to do with olive oil? Well, the term "virgin" refers to the purity of the first oil to be made from the olives using cold-pressing. In the days when larger scale production used steam and hot water processes to separate the oil, "cold pressing" using an old-fashioned mill and press made the best oils stand out from refined oils, since heat is the enemy of the olive's flavor. Today, cold pressing using modern technology is much more the norm, and so the words "first cold pressing" on a bottle have a more specific meaning. They indicate that the extra virgin olive oil has been produced at a temperature below 80°F, using a traditional granite millstone and a hydraulic press. If you see the words "cold extraction" the same applies, but this olive oil will have been produced using percolation or centrifugation systems.

People always ask me at our cooking school how to choose an olive oil. Price is a good guide. Be prepared to pay for a good bottle. Whenever possible, try to taste the oil—in good shops, this is often possible. To taste oil, pour a little into a small cup and cradle it in your hands. The warmth will gradually release the scent of the oil. Smell it first and then take a small sip. Swill the oil around, tasting it in all parts of your mouth, and finally swallow. Concentrate on the flavors: is it peppery, fruity (like tomatoes), robust, or light (like grass)? Does the flavor last after swallowing? Most important; do you like it?

Extra virgin olive oil has a low smoke point—the temperature at which it breaks down and begins to smoke—so we don't use it for deep-fat frying or when very high temperatures are required. For deep fat-frying we use sunflower oil, which has a higher smoke point.

We use three extra virgin oils in our kitchens. For sautéeing or roasting meat, fish, and vegetables and for salad dressings we use a good-quality extra virgin olive oil that is not too piquant. We save our most characterful oil for drizzling over cooked food, such as soup or meat. A robust fruity oil lends a lovely aroma and gloss. We use a lighter oil for a more delicate dish or the oil dominates the flavors.

Once a bottle of oil is open it starts to oxidize. To enjoy at its best, use within 6–8 weeks. Store oil in a cool dark place (not too cold or it will solidify) and away from direct sunlight: heat can change the flavor.

Even on a large scale there is something magnificent about olive-oil production. I went to the Filippo Berio plant in Lucca in Tuscany to watch the first oil of the season being made, and it was amazing to see the gleaming machinery go to work on a vat of fruit picked that morning. The olives, which had been harvested when they were on the turn from green to purple, were first washed and pressed to a paste. Next the liquids were separated from the solids by a centrifuge, then the oil and water separated by a second centrifuge in a continuous process. We tasted the first—absolutely luminous green—oil to be bottled. Although the flavor from the early-picked olives was strong (more so than the same variety picked and pressed at the end of the harvest), it was delicious. To celebrate, we drizzled it over *Ribollita* (see page 130) just as Tuscans have for centuries.

Flavors vary considerably from region to region, and within each region from oil to oil, but in general Tuscan oil is rich, fruity, and often peppery. Ligurian oil is usually more delicate, while Sicilian oil tends to have a spicy kick and Pugliese oil is robust and peppery. As with wine, you can detect a host of background flavors in an oil, from artichokes to tomatoes, hints of lemon, or even a tinge of grass. Don't be swayed too much by color when choosing oil—often Tuscan oils are deep green and Ligurian ones are lighter, but this has no connection with flavor or quality—green olives make green oil, riper black ones make golden oil. Professional olive-oil tasters use blue glasses so that the color doesn't distract them from the flavors.

The grading of virgin olive oil is based on acidity—the lower the better. Higher acidity compromises the flavor of the oil. According to the definition laid down by the International Olive Council, in order for a virgin oil to be classed "extra virgin" it must have an acidity of less than 0.8 percent, but the very best oils can have an acidity of 0.1 percent—though these are often difficult to find outside Italy. Bottles that are simply labelled "olive oil" contain a mixture of refined oil (which has gone through a chemical process) and virgin oil.

Crespelle di boraggine con sugo di pomodoro fresco
Herb Pancakes with Fresh Tomato Sauce

Borage is a pretty blue-flowered herb with a subtle flavor. It grows abundantly in Liguria, where our friend Giovanna makes this dish. If borage doesn't grow outside your back door like it does for lucky Giovanna, use marjoram, fresh oregano, or parsley instead.

Makes 8 pancakes (serves 6 as a starter or 4 as a main)

1 quantity of Fresh Tomato Sauce (see right)

FOR THE BATTER
2 eggs
1 cup "00" or all-purpose flour (see page 34)
1 tablespoon extra virgin olive oil
1 cup milk
½ teaspoon salt

2 tablespoons borage or other fresh herb, coarsely chopped
¾ cup Parmesan, freshly grated

Whisk the egg in a bowl by hand or with a mixer and gradually add the flour. Pour in the milk a little at a time. Make sure that no drifts of flour are visible and that the mixture is smooth and glossy—sieve it if necessary. Stir in the chopped borage or herbs and leave the batter to stand for 30 minutes.

Oil a small non-stick frying pan and place over medium heat. (Giovanna uses a saucer of oil and a cut potato stuck on a fork for this. She dips the cut side of the potato in oil, then wipes it over the pan.) Pour in a ladleful of batter, tilting the pan to spread it evenly. Cook for 2 minutes, then flip the pancake to cook the other side. Make eight pancakes in total in the same way and set aside, separated by squares of parchment paper.

Preheat the oven to 350°F. Pour a little of the tomato sauce into the bottom of a small roasting pan and lay a pancake on top. Pour a little more sauce over the pancake, then sprinkle with some of the Parmesan. Build up layers—pancake, sauce, cheese—until you have used all the pancakes. Finish with a layer of sauce and finally cheese. Put the pan in the oven for around 30 minutes until heated through. To serve, cut through the pancakes like a cake. Offer crusty bread to mop up the juices.

Sugo di pomodoro fresco
Fresh Tomato Sauce

As I watched Giovanna make this sauce (to accompany the herb pancakes, left) for the first time, I couldn't believe she didn't use any oil and yet the tomatoes didn't stick. The result was sweet, fresh, and seemed to radiate summer. This has become the only tomato sauce I make in summer. I save the canned tomato version (see page 166) for winter use.

Serves 6–8

2¼ lb fresh, ripe, and very red tomatoes, quartered
4 sprigs (10 leaves) of basil
1 medium red onion, peeled and quartered
5 tablespoons extra virgin olive oil
2 garlic cloves, peeled and lightly smashed using the flat side of a knife
salt and freshly ground black pepper
1 heaping teaspoon sugar (optional)

Put the tomatoes, 2 sprigs of basil, and the onion in a large heavy-bottomed saucepan over medium heat. Cover the pan with the lid and leave on the heat for about 45 minutes, shaking the pan frequently, until the tomatoes have released their juices and softened. Remove the basil sprigs.

Remove the pan from the heat and pass the sauce through a *passetutto*, food mill, or sieve, to remove the tomato skins and most of the seeds. Alternatively, use a hand blender and purée the tomatoes, skins and all.

Heat the oil in a pan and add the garlic cloves. After a couple of minutes add the tomatoes and the remaining basil. Adjust the seasoning to taste with salt and pepper and, if necessary, the sugar (if the tomatoes are very sweet, you might not need this). Bring to a boil, then lower the heat and simmer gently, uncovered, for 30–45 minutes, until the mixture has reduced and the flavor has become more concentrated.

Pallotte casc e ov
Parmesan and Parsley Fritters

This is Sabia Tortella's recipe from Abruzzo. The delicious little fried cheese balls are crunchy on the outside and soft inside. They are great served with a fresh tomato or pepper sauce—either as a vegetarian main course or on the side for dipping as antipasto. Try to find a coarse country loaf that has gone a little stale—the bread should bounce back to life after being soaked and squeezed.

Makes 25 fritters

5–7 oz stale bread, crust
 removed
¼ cup fresh parsley leaves
1 garlic clove
3 medium eggs
2 cups Parmesan, finely grated
salt and pepper
sunflower oil, for deep-frying

Soak the bread in water for a few minutes until soft. Squeeze out and crumble. If necessary, put in a food processor for a few seconds to break up larger lumps of bread. Finely chop the parsley and garlic together, then mix with the rest of the ingredients in a large bowl, adding about ¾ of the bread at first, then more if needed.

Test one ball first. Roll one 1½ inch ball from the mixture and fry in the hot oil. If the mixture seems wet, add more breadcrumbs, as necessary. If too dry, add more egg.

Roll out the rest of the mixture and fry the balls in hot oil until golden brown all round. Drain on paper towels and serve with Fresh Tomato Sauce (see left) or Roasted Red Pepper Sauce (see page 108).

Gianfranco

Gianmauro

Bagna cauda
Piedmontese Hot Anchovy Dip

This recipe is from Alba in Piedmont in northern Italy, where they use special *bagna cauda* dishes made from terracotta which look very pretty when kept warm with a glowing candle. A small fondue pot is equally suitable. The mixture of salty anchovies and garlic is incredibly addictive, particularly when enjoyed with a fine glass of the local Barbera wine. Traditionally, this dish is made with salted anchovies—they are first rinsed and any bones removed. However, it also works with the more familiar anchovies in oil. There are many recipes for *bagna cauda* including ones made with butter and oil. However my favourite is the simplest made with cream.

Serves 4

assorted vegetables for dipping or roasting, e.g. carrots, celery, and peppers (served raw or roasted), radicchio, endive, and cucumber (served raw)

FOR THE DIP
1 can of anchovies in olive oil (net weight 1oz)
1 fat garlic clove, peeled
1¼ cups heavy cream

Cut the vegetables into sticks for dipping into the hot sauce. If you want to eat them raw, store them beneath a dampened piece of paper towel. To roast them, follow the recipe for Grilled Vegetable Salad on page 384.

To make the dip, put the above ingredients (including the oil from the can) into a food processor and whizz together until smooth. Pour this into a small saucepan and heat through for around 10–15 minutes until it has thickened to a consistency suitable for dipping.

Serve the dip in a *bagna cauda* or fondue pot over low heat. Do not allow the mixture to become too hot or it will separate. If it does, remove from heat, let the dip cool, and stir together. Return to heat if necessary.

To serve as a dressing, arrange the roasted vegetables on a serving plate and drizzle with the sauce, serving any extra at the table.

Fritto misto di verdure
Deep-fried Artichokes, Cauliflower, and Sage Leaves

A *fritto misto* is an assortment of deep-fried vegetables, fish, or meats. It's all bite-size, intended to be eaten with fingers and a wedge of lemon. I like the idea of surprise: you don't know what is hidden beneath the batter until you have bitten into it. In Italy, sweetbreads are often prepared in this way, but that can be a bit too much of a surprise for some! We love *fritto misto* so much that we served this at our wedding as part of the antipasti. They were fried by a Tuscan lady outside in a huge vat of bubbling oil. When I make this, I tend to stick to vegetables or a mixture of seafood, such as shrimp, calamari rings, or white fish. Cut the fish into bite-size chunks, then follow the method for the vegetables below.

Heat the oil to 350°F, either in a deep-fat fryer or a large shallow frying pan. Test to see if it is hot enough by dropping in a small piece of bread; it should immediately sizzle and turn golden brown.

To prepare the sage leaves, place each of the anchovy fillets between two sage leaves and press them together. The oil from the anchovy should help them stick. Set aside. Prepare and cook the artichokes following the instructions in the masterclass on page 378. Allow to cool, then cut each one lengthwise into quarters.

To make the batter, beat the eggs in a bowl with a couple of tablespoons of the milk using a whisk or electric mixer. Add the flour little by little, making a thick paste before diluting with the remaining milk. Whisk in the rest of the ingredients. If there are any lumps, sieve the mixture. Coat the vegetables by dropping them into the batter by hand, retrieving them with a slotted spoon. Dip one piece at a time so that they do not stick together. Whisk the batter before each dip.

Use the slotted spoon to drop the coated vegetables carefully into the hot oil a few at a time. Fry for 5 minutes, shaking the basket regularly or moving them around in the pan to separate them. When the pieces are golden in color, remove with tongs and transfer to a plate covered with paper towels to soak up any excess oil. Sprinkle with a generous pinch of salt and serve with lemon wedges for squeezing.

Serves 6

24 medium–large sage leaves, each with
  a little stem left on
12 anchovies in oil
4 artichokes
½ cauliflower, cut into bite-size florets
2 cups sunflower oil, for deep-frying
lemon wedges, to serve

FOR THE BATTER
⅓ cup egg
1 cup all-purpose milk
¼ cup plain flour
¼ cup beer or sparkling water
½ teaspoon salt
½ teaspoon sugar

Peperonata
Slow-cooked Peppers

Peperonata is made all over Italy, but this variation is from Sicily, where breadcrumbs add crunch and texture.

Serves 6

4 large peppers, preferably a
  mixture of red and yellow,
  cut into 1-in dice
⅔ cup water
4 tablespoons extra virgin
  olive oil
2 red onions, thinly sliced
4 bay leaves
3 garlic cloves, sliced
salt
⅓ cup red wine
⅔ cup passata, or 6 fresh ripe
  plum tomatoes, chopped
salt and pepper

FOR THE BREADCRUMBS
1 garlic clove, finely chopped
1 red chile, finely chopped
¾ cup dry breadcrumbs
3 tablespoons extra virgin
  olive oil

Cook the peppers in a large pan with the water until it evaporates. Add the oil and cook for 15 minutes. Add the onions, bay leaves, and garlic, and cook for 10 minutes. Salt to taste. Pour in the wine, reduce a little, then add the passata. Cover and cook until soft, around 20–30 minutes.

Meanwhile, cook the garlic and chile in the oil, add the breadcrumbs and a generous pinch of salt and pepper and fry until golden and just crunchy. Allow to cool. Pour the peperonata into a serving dish and top with the breadcrumbs.

Polpettine di melanzane
Eggplant and Mint Fritters

Our diminutive Sicilian friend Dora first showed me these fritters. I thought they were delicious—and so did everyone around me. She threw together the recipe quickly from some leftover eggplant purée and I didn't have a chance to write it down. With a bit of adaptation from Ann and Franco Taruschio's recipe for the same thing, I am pleased to say that I can recreate Dora's delicious eggplant balls. Dora didn't put currants or pine nuts in hers, but I like the extra sweetness and texture. These fritters are a great party dish since they can be prepared ahead and frozen.

Makes 50 balls

FOR THE FRITTERS
2 eggplants (around 1½ lb)
¾ cup currants or raisins
5 cups fine fresh breadcrumbs
2 eggs
1 cup Parmesan, finely grated
6 tablespoons pine nuts, toasted
3 tablespoons chopped fresh mint
salt and freshly ground black pepper
1 teaspoon finely chopped fresh chile or dried red chile

sunflower oil, for deep-frying
2 eggs
½ cup flour, for dredging

Preheat the oven to 400°F. Put the whole eggplants on a baking sheet and put them in the hot oven. Roast for about 1 hour, or until soft. Remove from the oven and leave to cool.

Meanwhile, soak the currants or raisins in water. Scoop out the eggplant flesh and purée in a food processor or chop finely with a knife. Drain the currants or raisins. Transfer to a bowl and mix with ½ cup of the breadcrumbs, the eggs, and the rest of the ingredients for the fritters. The mixture should be soft but not wet. If the mixture is too dry, add a little more egg; if it is too soft, add extra breadcrumbs. Form the mixture into balls about 1½ inches in diameter.

Heat the oil in a large pan or deep-fat fryer to 350°F, or until hot enough that when you drop a small piece of bread into the oil it quickly becomes golden and bubbles. Beat the eggs in a bowl. Put the flour into another bowl and have the remaining breadcrumbs ready in a third bowl. Dip the balls first into the flour and then into the egg. Finally, roll them in the breadcrumbs, to coat. Deep-fry the balls until golden brown, around 5 minutes. Drain them on paper towels. Serve hot or at room temperature, with a tomato sauce for dipping or yogurt, cucumber, and mint.

Sugo di peperoni rossi
Roasted Red Pepper Sauce

This sauce goes with many dishes—try it with Baked Ricotta (see below), Franca's Roast Vegetables (see page 396), Parmesan and Parsley Fritters (see page 103), or with grilled chicken or fish. Once you discover how easy it is, you'll make it all the time.

Serves 6–8

4 red bell peppers
2 tablespoons olive oil
1 garlic clove, peeled and crushed
1 shallot, coarsely chopped
salt and pepper
½ cup vegetable stock or water
½–1 teaspoon sugar, to taste (optional)

Preheat the oven to 400°F. Put the whole peppers on a baking sheet; roast for 35–45 minutes turning once or twice, until blackened. Remove from the oven and put in a plastic bag to sweat. When cool, peel off the skins with your fingers. Slice the peppers open, discard the seeds and membrane, and coarsely chop the flesh.

Heat the oil in a frying pan. When hot, cook the garlic, shallot, and salt and pepper for a few minutes. Add the chopped peppers and cook for a few more minutes, stirring to combine. Add the stock, bring to a boil, then allow to reduce for a few minutes. Pour into a blender and process until smooth. Adjust the seasoning to taste. If the peppers are bitter, add sugar to taste. Serve hot or at room temperature.

Ricotta al forno
Baked Ricotta

This is embarrassingly simple and one of my favorite starters. Change the herbs according to availability and preference. I always use thyme as I feel it transforms the ricotta from bland to sublime but blend it with parsley, oregano, sage, or chives if you prefer.

Serves 4 as a starter or 2 for lunch

1 cup ricotta, drained
a little olive oil, for greasing
½ tablespoon freshly chopped oregano
½ tablespoon freshly chopped thyme
salt and pepper

Preheat the oven to 350°F. Turn out ricotta from its tub onto an oiled baking sheet. (If it has crumbled or become lop-sided, push it back into shape with your fingers.) Cover the entire surface of the ricotta with the herbs, salt and pepper, patting the herbs onto it and pushing them in slightly.

Put the sheet into the oven and bake for 45–60 minutes until a golden crust has formed over the cheese.

Serve in wedges with a portion of Roasted Red Pepper Sauce (see left) or Fresh Tomato Sauce (see page 98) on the side and a few salad leaves dressed in walnut oil.

Stuffed Zucchini Flowers

For every zucchini that grows, there are two flowers on the plant: a male flower with no fruit, and a female flower attached to the zucchini itself. The male flowers have long spiky stalks, which make for easy dipping into batter and hot oil, but when the zucchini are young they too can be fried along with the female flowers. This recipe is from Jo Hynes, who manages our cooking school. Jo used to work in Italy and loved this summery dish.

To prepare the zucchini, gently open out the flowers and remove the stamen—these contain a saffron-like substance that can taste bitter—and any lurking insects.

Prepare the stuffing by mixing all the ingredients together in a bowl and seasoning to taste. Use a piping bag or spoon to fill the flowers with the stuffing. Twist the flower at the top to close them over the stuffing.

To make the batter, beat the egg with a couple of tablespoons of the milk in a bowl using a whisk or electric mixer. Add the flour little by little, making a thick paste before diluting it with the remaining milk. Now whisk in the beer or water and the salt and sugar. If any lumps remain, sieve the mixture before dipping in the flowers.

Heat the oil in a large pan or deep-fat fryer to 350°C, or until hot enough that when you drop a small piece of bread into the oil it quickly becomes golden and bubbles.

Stir the batter (do this before dipping each time, to keep the batter at the right consistency). Dip a couple of flowers into the batter and then fry them for about 3 minutes, until golden brown. (Don't be tempted to squeeze in more flowers or the temperature of the oil will drop.) Remove the flowers from the oil, drain on paper towels, and keep warm. Make sure the oil returns to its original temperature before cooking the next batch of flowers, and scoop out any crispy bits from the oil that will spoil the look of your flowers. Serve two flowers per person, either on their own or with bread.

Variation: Put a small piece of mozzarella and an anchovy fillet inside each flower instead of the filling, then batter and fry as above.

Serves 4

8 zucchini flowers
sunflower oil, for deep-frying
lemon wedges, to serve

FOR THE STUFFING
½ cup fresh ricotta
1 cup mozzarella, finely chopped
⅓ cup Parmesan, freshly grated
1 oz Parma ham, finely
   chopped
a small handful of basil
   leaves, torn
a pinch of freshly grated nutmeg
zest of ½ lemon
salt and freshly ground
   black pepper

FOR THE BATTER
⅓ cup egg
1 cup milk
1 cup all-purpose flour
¼ cup beer or sparkling water
¼ teaspoon salt
¼ teaspoon sugar

Zucchini ripieni
Cheese-stuffed Zucchini

Stuffed vegetables are classic antipasti in Italy, but they also make a good vegetarian starter or main course. These zucchini go well with sliced meats, salads, and bread. They are usually served at room temperature and so are ideal to make in advance. This simple recipe is fun to make with children, who enjoy scraping out zucchini with a teaspoon. To save time, chop the ingredients in a food processor.

Serves 6 as a starter, 4 as a main

6 medium zucchini
5 tablespoons extra virgin olive oil
1 shallot or small white onion, very
  finely chopped
2 garlic cloves, finely chopped
1 cup Basic Tomato Sauce (see page 102) or
  Franca's Passata (see page 166)
6 tablespoons dry breadcrumbs
1 egg, beaten
¾ cup Parmesan, finely grated
1 tablespoon finely chopped flat-leaf parsley
salt and freshly ground black pepper

Preheat the oven to 350°F. Cut the zucchini lengthwise. Remove the soft fleshy center with a spoon and set aside, so that you are left with long canoe shapes. Put these onto a baking sheet and drizzle with 1 tablespoon of the oil. Bake for 10 minutes in the oven. Remove and set aside.

Meanwhile chop the zucchini flesh finely. Heat 3 tablespoons of the remaining oil in a frying pan and cook the zucchini flesh, the onion, and the garlic, stirring constantly, for 5 minutes, or until softened. Set aside.

Spread the tomato sauce over the bottom of an ovenproof dish large enough to hold all the zucchini. Add the breadcrumbs, the egg, the Parmesan and the parsley to the zucchini flesh, season with salt and pepper and mix together well. Stuff the zucchini with the mixture, pushing it down well to secure the stuffing inside each hollow. Place the stuffed zucchini on top of the tomato sauce. Season lightly again and drizzle over the remaining olive oil. Bake in the oven for 20 minutes, or until cooked through and golden brown.

Funghi ripieni di menta
e prezzemolo
Stuffed Mushrooms with Mint and Parsley

The favorite starter of Italian trattorias in the 1970s is a delicious classic, worthy, I felt, of a place in this book. As a former vegetarian, I would be happy to be offered this dish to replace meat at any meal.

Serves 6

6 large mushrooms or small portabella
  mushrooms
1 heaping teaspoon coarsely chopped
  fresh mint
2 heaping tablespoons coarsely chopped
  flat-leaf parsley
¼ cup Parmesan, finely grated
1 garlic clove, finely chopped
3 tablespoons dry breadcrumbs
⅓ cup olive oil

Preheat the oven to 350°F. Carefully remove and finely chop the stems of the mushrooms. Set aside. Place the mushrooms on a baking sheet, gills facing upwards.

Put the mushroom stems in a bowl with the rest of the ingredients except the oil and mix thoroughly. Divide the mixture into six even portions and spoon into the cavity of each mushroom, gently packing the mixture down with the back of the spoon.

Drizzle a little of the olive oil over each mushroom, then bake in the oven for 15 minutes, or until the tops are golden.

Variation: Omit the mint, Parmesan and 1 tablespoon of breadcrumbs and instead substitute 3 oz crumbled blue cheese, such as gorgonzola.

Insalata di fichi, caprino e miele
Fig, Goat Cheese, and Honey Salad

I have fallen in love with Italy's habit of eating honey with cheese. Honey is often served with the famous sheep cheese pecorino, but I have found that the combination works equally well with other cheeses too, the sweetness of the honey softening the sharpness of the cheese. This recipe builds the combination into a light lunch or starter. For a main course, bump up the quantities.

Serves 4 as a starter or 2 as a main

Cut the goat cheese into four discs, each about ¾ inch thick. (To slice them cleanly, wipe the knife between slices.) Put the nuts on a plate and roll the edges of the goat cheese in them. Set aside. Cut the figs into quarters. Toss the arugula leaves with the nut oil and season with the pepper, to taste. Arrange the salad on a plate, top it with the goat cheese and place the fig quarters around it. Drizzle the honey over the cheese and figs, and scatter over the pomegranate seeds, if using.

5 oz log of soft goat cheese
⅓ cup hazelnuts or almonds, toasted and finely chopped
4 figs
4 oz arugula leaves
2 tablespoons hazelnut oil or walnut oil
freshly ground black pepper
2 tablespoons acacia honey
a handful of pomegranate seeds (optional)

Crespelle ripiene di granchio e besciamella di spinaci
Crepes filled with Crab in Spinach Sauce

The tradition in Florence is to fill crepes with spinach and ricotta. Here is a variation on that theme, which has been adopted by our restaurant Caldesi Tuscan for many years now. When we tried to take it off the menu our customers complained, so it became a permanent fixture.

Makes 12 pancakes
(serves 6)

FOR THE FILLING
8 oz fresh white crab meat
⅔ cup Béchamel Sauce (from
  1 quart total, see page 175)
1 level tablespoon finely
  chopped flat-leaf parsley
salt and freshly ground
  black pepper

FOR THE CREPES
1½ cups "00" flour or
  all-purpose flour
a pinch of salt
3 medium eggs
2 tablespoons butter, melted
1 cup milk
butter, for frying

FOR THE SAUCE
4 oz spinach, cooked and
  squeezed dry
1⅓ cups béchamel (see above)
¼ cup Parmesan, finely grated

To prepare the filling, combine all the ingredients in a bowl, taste and adjust the seasoning, then set aside.

To make the pancakes, sift the flour and salt into a bowl and make a well in the center. Add the eggs and butter and whisk them, gradually incorporating the flour. Pour in the milk a little at a time, still whisking, or use a food processor. Heat a knob of butter in a small (8 inch) non-stick frying pan over a high heat. When it foams, pour in a pool of batter large enough to coat the base of the pan, swirling it around until the base is covered. Keep over the heat until the underside is golden brown. Now toss the crepe or flip with a fish slice and cook the other side until golden. Transfer to a warm plate while you cook 11 more crepes; interleave the crepes with parchment paper.

To stuff the crepes, put 1 heaping tablespoon of the crab filling onto each crepe and spread it out lengthwise. Roll the crepes up and place in an ovenproof dish. (I put mine into an oval lasagne dish, at an angle.) Make the sauce by combining the spinach and the béchamel, season to taste, and pour over the crepes. Sprinkle with the Parmesan and grill for 1 minute.

Variation: Substitute the filling from the Spinach and Ricotta Rolls (see page 46).

aceto balsamico

BALSAMIC VINEGAR

It's easy to see why balsamic vinegar became over-used once it was discovered outside Italy—it is just so delicious! Originally it was used as a medicine to give energy (after childbirth, for example) and as a digestive. The wonderful balance of sweet and sour, which is the essence of so much cooking, really hits the spot. However, some years ago, non-Italians rarely understood how or when to use it—the worst case I ever saw was balsamic vinegar poured over pasta; a definite no-no! Now, however, people have calmed down and reined-in their enthusiasm, and balsamic vinegar is finding its rightful place as an essential pantry ingredient to be used—sparingly—in a range of dishes.

Aceto Balsamico Tradizionale (the name originally means "health-giving") has its own PDO (Protected Designation of Origin), which means that it is made under strict guidelines in either Modena or Reggio in Emilia-Romagna.

The vinegar is made from cooked "must": the residual skins and juices left from wine-making. It is usually made from local grape varieties—mainly *Trebbiano*, but also *Occhio di Gatta, Spergola, Berzemino,* and *Lambrusco*. The must is cooked with sugar and a culture of bacteria, which break down the mixture and concentrate its flavor as it reduces.

The vinegar is aged for at least 12 years in a series of barrels made from different woods: oak, chestnut, cherry, acacia, juniper, ash, and mulberry. The water from the mixture evaporates over the years as the vinegar reduces in volume, and each barrel is topped up from the next one, starting with the smallest and working up to the largest. As the process goes on, the consistency thickens. Each barrel imparts a different flavor and you can taste this woodiness. Alberto Medici's family, who have been making balsamic for generations, still use barrels from the 18th century. After 12 years, the mixture can legally be called balsamic vinegar and the age is stated on the bottles.

Extra-aged vinegar is more than 12 years old and is extremely thick and viscous, incredibly expensive, and mouth-puckeringly good.

OTHER VINEGARS

The Italians could win prizes for their bureaucracy, and while the PDO system keeps their heritage alive and promotes respect for traditionally made produce, it can seem unfair to people who produce good quality food, but are outside the specified region of a PDO. *Aceto Balsamico di Modena* is an IGP product (Indication of Geographic Protection). There are good vinegars produced outside the designated *balsamico* region that have to be named "condimento balsamico" rather than balsamic vinegar. You might come across *salsa balsamica*, too, and other invented titles. There is also a very similar style of vinegar known as *vincotto* (cooked vinegar).

KATIE'S TIP

If you don't have an extra-aged vinegar, you can add sugar to regular balsamic vinegar and reduce it down over heat to make a balsamic reduction. Use 12–15-year-old vinegar for salads and *carpaccio*, use 18–25-year-old vinegar for steak, *frittata,* or Parmesan chunks, and use a few drops of 25-year plus for vanilla ice cream and strawberries and other woodland fruits.

Insalata di manzo
Beef Salad

Although this salad may strike some as more Thai than Italian, I did actually eat it in Tuscany. It was made for me by a lovely chef who whipped it up as his staff lunch. He was rather shy about giving it to me, preferring to give "La Signora" something rather more elaborate and professional. However, it was an absolute scorcher of a day and I was reluctant to be served piping hot gnocchi with ragù, especially as the coolness of the celery and the crunchy freshness of the lettuce paired with unctuous strips of beef was exactly what I craved. I'm so glad I made him let me try some, otherwise, I would not now have this marvellous recipe!

Serves 4 as a main or 6 as a side dish

2¼ lb boneless beef (top round or chuck roast)

FOR THE SALAD
1 large head lettuce (about 7 oz), preferably romaine for its crunchy texture
3 tomatoes, coarsely chopped
3 celery ribs, thinly sliced
2 large handfuls of flat-leaf parsley
½–1 red chile, depending on heat, finely chopped finely
2 tablespoons olive oil, plus extra for drizzling
1 tablespoon red wine vinegar
a generous pinch of salt and freshly ground black pepper

Boil the beef following the recipe for Beef Stock (see page 137). Once the beef is cooked, remove it from the liquid and place on a chopping board. Use your hands to pull the meat into thin shreds. Reserve the cooking liquid for soup or risotto.

Put all the ingredients for the salad in a large mixing bowl and toss delicately with your hands, ensuring that all the leaves get a thorough coating of oil and vinegar and that the chile and parsley are evenly distributed.

Transfer the tossed salad to a serving bowl and carefully place the shredded beef on top. Drizzle with a little more olive oil and serve.

Filetto alla Robespierre
Steak Robespierre

I have not been able to establish the link between Robespierre, the 18th-century French politician and writer, and this dish. But it is popular in Italy, nearly always made with balsamic, arugula, and Parmesan, and is absolutely addictive. If anyone can explain the name I would be most grateful!

Serves 4 as a starter

8 oz beef tenderloin or filet mignon
a handful of arugula leaves
1 oz Parmesan shavings

FOR THE DRESSING
6 tablespoons olive oil
3 tablespoons balsamic vinegar
1 large sprig of rosemary, leaves finely chopped
1 garlic clove, peeled and lightly crushed
salt and plenty of freshly ground black pepper

Preheat the grill to very hot or the oven to 450°F.

Trim the beef and discard the fat and silverskin. Slice it thinly, place the slices between two layers of plastic wrap and pound them with a meat tenderizer. Alternatively, press the slices down with the flat side of a knife; either way, make them as thin as possible. Arrange the slices on an ovenproof plate.

Mix all the dressing ingredients in a bowl. Sprinkle the meat with a little salt, then pour on top the dressing, ensuring the entire surface is covered. Place the plate under the broiler or in the oven for just 2 minutes. Top with the arugula and Parmesan shavings and serve immediately, warning people that the plate is hot!

Zuppe e

brodi

CHAPTER 3: SOUP AND STOCK

Zuppe e brodi

INTRODUCTION

Mention Italian soup and most people immediately think of minestrone, which means "big soup"—a mixture of whatever vegetables are in season, perhaps thickened with pulses, grains (such as barley), beans and pasta. The young Italians I know rarely make soups themselves, but all have heartwarming memories of their mother's and grandmother's minestrone, and know exactly how they would make a chicken stock or broth (the same word, *brodo*, applies to both) and serve it floating with tiny pasta shapes or filled pasta.

KATIE'S TIPS

A good stock is very important in the Italian kitchen. Not only is it essential for soups—often a good stock will be eaten just as it is with just some pasta floating in—but also for risottos and stews.

Save shrimp, crab, and lobster shells and keep them in the freezer ready to make Shellfish Stock (see page 138).

Ask the fishmonger for "fish racks," the leftover spine and head of filleted fish, which are essential for making fish stock (sometimes known as *fumetto*). See the recipe for White Fish Stock on page 138.

Use homemade stocks right away or cool, cover, and store them in the fridge for up to three days.

ur friend Francesca from Liguria still enjoys her mother's minestrone whenever she's at home. She says, "It is something Italian children grow up with; we love it more and more as we grow. It is typical in Liguria to add a large spoonful of pesto as well as the obligatory grated Parmesan or pecorino, and this thickens it further. In Liguria we say a good minestrone should be able to support a spoon standing vertically in it. Thick is good."

The term *zuppa* comes from the verb *inzuppare*, meaning to soak or dunk, and soups are often served with crostini, slices of toasted bread, either on the side or placed in the bowl with the soup poured over the top. This is one of the ingenious ways Italians use up stale bread: as a thickener or to bulk up a soup when there is nothing else to fill you up. Another way of thickening soups—known as *passato*, meaning "passed"—involves pushing the ingredients through a *passatutto*, or sieve. *Passato di verdure* (vegetable soup) is made in this way. Often you only purée a portion of the soup, reserving some whole beans or vegetables to add back in for texture. *Vellutata* is the word used to describe a soup that is creamed completely and has the texture of velvet.

Seasoning, seasoning, seasoning… this is one of the first things an Italian will say about any form of cooking, but where soups are concerned, it makes all the difference between a bland dish and wonderfully rich comfort food. The Italians are also experts at finishing off soups with a 'flavor enhancer' such as cheese, usually Parmesan or pecorino grated over the top. A thick soup such as *Zuppa di Farro* (Spelt Soup, see page 132) will be served with a really pungent olive oil drizzled over. When the oil takes up the soup's heat, the aroma is wonderful. I have seen many Italians pep up a bland soup by making a herb oil—heating a little olive oil with a clove of garlic and some sprigs of rosemary. Just before the herbs start to burn, they remove the oil from the heat, discard the herbs and garlic, then drizzle this oil over the soup, either while it is still in the pan or in the serving bowl.

Stracciatella is a thin broth made more substantial by the addition of a beaten egg, whipped in. The egg breaks into pieces, giving the soup more body and adding protein. In Puglia, I was shown how to make Fresh Pea, Parmesan and Egg Soup (see page 129); here, grated cheese is mixed into the egg before being added to the soup for extra flavor. From the Maremma area of Tuscany comes a soup called *Acquacotta*, which means 'cooked water' (see page 130). It uses whichever vegetables are available at the time, and is made more substantial not only by the placement of the ubiquitous crostini in the bottom of the bowl, but quite often with whole eggs, which are broken and cooked into the dish.

Teresa

Tuscany is the region with the most diverse repertoire of soups. It is famous for its bean soups—such as *Ribollita* (see page 130)—which are often eaten three times a week. Just as my husband Giancarlo has to have his daily pasta, there is a sense that bean soup, too, is vital to the Tuscan diet. In Tuscany, they say that the onion soup which the French have made their own is in fact Tuscan in origin; Catherine de Medici took it with her to France. *Zuppa di Pomodoro* or Rich Tomato Soup (see page 132), is another delicious Tuscan tradition. In Abruzzo, the speciality soup is cardoons in thin broth, with added meatballs and an omelette cut into pieces, while in the Alps they warm themselves with a hearty *zuppa di orzo*, barley soup. From the central regions of Italy come more soups made with pulses and grains, such as lentils, chickpeas, and rice; in the Abruzzo moutains, *minestra di farro*, made with the farro grain, is very typical.

Fish soups known as *brodetti* and *zuppe di pesce* are found up and down the coastal towns of Italy and, naturally, each region has its own version, of which it is fiercely proud. They were surely invented as a way to use up broken or unsellable fish, and typically are still made with small fish which give a great flavor, and usually (though not always) tomatoes.

KATIE'S TIPS

Ask the butcher for some bones to make a Beef Stock (see page 137), or after the Sunday roast make a stock from the chicken carcass using the Cooked Chicken Stock recipe on page 140.

Use up all your off-cuts and vegetable trimmings when you make stock—never throw away the base of a celery stalk, for example; throw it into the stockpot. Onion skin adds color, and parsley stems contribute a wonderful flavor.

Freeze concentrated stock in ice-cube trays or small plastic bags.

When you make soup from your stock, remember that good seasoning is crucial to the taste. When a recipe says "adjust the seasoning to taste," you need to do just that—taste the soup, add salt and pepper, taste again and, if necessary, add more until your soup has the wow factor.

Zuppa di fagioli
Bean Soup

Bean soups are popular all over Italy, but particularly in Tuscany—Tuscans are nicknamed *i mangiafagioli*, "the bean-eaters." For ease I have used canned beans but feel free to substitute soaked and cooked beans. You can use other beans, too, such as borlotti or small white haricots.

Add the stock to the pan of *soffritto* and bring it to a boil. Reduce to a gentle simmer for about 10 minutes and then add the drained beans. Stir well and continue to cook for a few minutes until the beans are heated through. Season to taste. Serve in warm bowls with crusty bread.

Variation: *Pasta e fagioli*—Pasta and Bean Soup
To make the soup more substantial, follow the recipe above, but add 12 oz short dried pasta (such as *ditalini*) to the pan when the stock is boiling. Simmer for 10–15 minutes, or until the pasta is cooked, stirring frequently. The pasta will absorb water from the stock, so if you prefer a thinner soup add extra stock by the ladleful, as necessary. For a thicker soup, before adding the pasta, blend one third of the soup then stir it back into the pan.

Serves 4

- 1 quantity of Soffritto with garlic and herbs (see opposite)
- 2 garlic cloves, peeled and lightly crushed with the flat side of a knife
- 3 cups vegetable stock (see page 136) or chicken stock (see page 140, you may need around 1 cup more if adding pasta)
- 3 cups canned cannellini beans, drained

Soffritto
Base Recipe

Also known as *battuto*, this is the essential base for Italian stews and soups, some sauces and ragú. The recipe varies by region, but most versions contain the "holy trinity" of Italian vegetables: celery, onion, and carrot. In summer, make batches to freeze for winter, including some without garlic.

Makes about 1½ cups

6 oz carrot (about 2–3)
6 oz celery (2–3 ribs)
1 medium onion (red or white)
⅓ cup olive oil
2 garlic cloves (optional)
salt and pepper
2 large sprigs of rosemary
  and/or thyme
2 bay leaves

Finely chop the vegetables by hand or in a food processor. If using a machine, cut them separately as carrots need to be processed longer than celery and onion.

Heat the oil in a large frying pan over medium-hot heat. Add the garlic, if using, and season with salt and pepper. Cook for 1 minute before adding the remaining ingredients. Keep cooking, stirring frequently, for 15–20 minutes, or until the vegetables have softened. The colors will change from bright and sharp to soft and golden. Use at once or freeze.

Freezing Soffritto
Divide into four portions and freeze in suitable containers. I use leftover yogurt or ricotta pots. Once frozen, turn out and store in a plastic bag in the freezer.

Tuoni e lampi
Thunder and Lightning Soup

This soup comes in many forms all over Italy but my favorite is the Pugliese version. I first ate it at Pasha in Conversano served in a Mason jar which was delivered to the table sealed. Each diner opened their own jar and the aroma was released... aaah!

Serves 4

1 quantity of Fresh Pasta, made with 1 egg and 1 cup "00" flour (see pages 148–149)

⅔ cup extra virgin olive oil
1 medium onion, finely chopped
2 sprigs of rosemary
1 teaspoon salt
1 x 15 oz can chickpeas (garbanzo beans), drained
2 cups and 2 tablespoons warm vegetable stock or chicken stock (see pages 136 or 140)

First make the fresh pasta following the instructions on pages 148–149. Let it rest, covered with plastic wrap, in the refrigerator.

Heat 2 tablespoons oil in a large frying pan and cook the onion with the rosemary and salt until soft. Stir in the chickpeas. Add the stock, bring to a boil, then reduce to a simmer for 15–20 minutes while you finish the pasta.

Roll out the fresh pasta until the sheet is so thin you can see your hand through it. Cut it into roughly shaped pieces about 1 x 1½ inches. Divide them into two piles. Heat the remaining oil in a large frying pan and fry half the pasta shapes. When puffy and golden, drain them on paper towels and sprinkle with a little salt. Set aside. Using a slotted spoon, lift out roughly one third of the chickpeas and blend with a stick blender or a *passatutto*. Put the rest of the pasta shapes into the soup and cook for about 3 minutes until done. Add the blended chickpeas and stir through. If very thick add a little hot water or stock. Pour the soup into warmed bowls (or try the Mason jar idea), remove the rosemary and top the soup with the reserved fried pasta shapes.

Variation:
With fresh basil: Sprinkle a small handful of basil leaves, roughly torn, over the soup just before serving. In summer this gives a lovely fresh taste.

Zuppa di pollo e verdure
Chicken and Vegetable Soup

This is a great way to use up a leftover roast chicken and create wonderful comfort food at the same time. In order to maximize the flavor, do ensure you have enough time to let the stock cook. This is crucial. If you use a fresh chicken, you will have more meat for the soup, but add in as much chicken as you have available and vary the vegetables according to the season. During the summer months I omit some of the potato and add asparagus and peas—delicious!

Serves 6–8

4 tablespoons extra virgin olive oil, plus extra
    for drizzling
8 oz zucchini, diced
3 large celery ribs, chopped
3 large carrots, diced, or 8 oz baby carrots
12 oz potatoes, diced
2 sprigs of thyme or 8 leaves of wild garlic
¼ cup flat-leaf parsley, coarsely chopped
1–1½ quarts chicken stock (see page 140)
12–14 oz chicken meat, picked off the bone
a generous pinch of salt and freshly
    ground pepper

Heat the oil in a large saucepan, add the vegetables and herbs, and cook for 20–25 minutes over medium heat until the vegetables soften.

Add 4 cups of the stock, season with salt and pepper to taste, and simmer for 30–40 minutes. At this point the soup is ready and can be served with the vegetables left whole, or you can purée one-third of it using a food processor, hand blender, or *passatutto* sieve. For ease, I put a hand blender down one side of the pan and process quickly. Stir in the chicken pieces and heat through. Add the rest of the stock if necessary. Serve in warm bowls with a drizzle of good olive oil.

Stufato di lenticchie, pomodori e spinaci
Lentil, Tomato, and Spinach Stew

I first tasted this dish in Rome, in Franca Leonardi's restaurant, da Sabatino a Sant' Ignazio. It makes a rich soup, but is also great as a side dish with roast meats. Castelluccio lentils grown on the plains of Umbria retain their shape and nutty flavor after cooking, but you can use good-quality small brown lentils.

Serves 6–8

1 quart Franca's Tomato Passata (see page 166)

8 oz brown lentils (preferably *Castelluccio*)
3 tablespoons extra virgin olive oil
2 garlic cloves, peeled and coarsely chopped
½–1 red chile (depending on heat),
    finely chopped
8 oz spinach, stemmed and rinsed

FOR THE VEGETABLE SOUP
5 tablespoons extra virgin olive oil
1 medium onion, coarsely chopped
2 garlic cloves, peeled and crushed
4 celery ribs or 2 celery hearts (leaves
    included), coarsely chopped
3 medium carrots, coarsely chopped
2 medium potatoes, coarsely chopped
salt
1 quart hot water

First, make the Tomato Sauce following the instructions on page 166. Then make the soup: heat the oil in a large saucepan and cook the onion and garlic over medium heat, until softened. Add the rest of the vegetables, except for the spinach and salt to taste, and cook for 5–10 minutes, stirring frequently. Add ¾ cup of the tomato sauce and the hot water and stir well to combine. Bring it to a boil and simmer for 1 hour before puréeing in a blender.

Cook the lentils in plenty of salted water for 45–60 minutes, according to package instructions, skimming off the foam regularly.

Heat the oil in a pan. When hot, cook the garlic and chile for a couple of minutes, taking care not to burn. Add the remaining tomato sauce and heat through. Then add the cooked, drained lentils, the soup, and spinach and stir well. Heat through, season and serve.

Zuppa di piselli freschi, Parmigiano e uova
Fresh Pea, Parmesan, and Egg Soup

This is one of those multi-use recipes that could be a soup, a pasta sauce, or a side dish. I was taught it by a firm but patient lady named Anna in Monopoli, Puglia. During this lesson, an Inglese/Pugliese debate started concerning how long to cook fresh peas. To me, they are deliciously sweet with a little bite and green as green can be after about 10 minutes. To our Pugliese friend, fresh peas should be cooked for *un'orettta*! My goodness, an hour of boiling freshly picked beauties to death. I decided on diplomacy and agreed to try the Pugliese way. Once I'd tasted the result I admitted defeat: the peas were green and deliciously sweet.

Serves 4

3 tablespoons extra virgin olive oil
1 small white onion or shallot, finely chopped
salt and pepper
1 lb fresh shelled peas
1 quart water
1 egg
¼ cup Parmesan, finely grated

Heat the oil in a saucepan and, when hot, add the onion, season with salt and pepper, and cook until softened. Stir in the peas, then add the water and cook for about 1 hour. Beat the egg in a small bowl, add the Parmesan, and mix together. Pour into the peas, stirring rapidly. The egg will set in strands and the peas are then ready to serve as a soup. If you prefer this as a sauce for pasta, allow the water to evaporate further and stir into freshly cooked ditalini or penne. To serve as a side dish, drain most of the water from the peas.

Ribollita
Tuscan Layered Bean and Bread Soup

I have often eaten this thick soup at local fairs in Tuscany, where it is served in a plastic dish with a plastic fork. If you are lucky there is a spring onion sticking out of the top to be dipped in and eaten. The soup is always dressed with some gorgeous local oil and despite its container is always delicious! This traditional Tuscan recipe relies on Tuscan bread, which is made without salt and quickly goes stale. The bread is layered between a thick vegetable and bean soup, and as it soaks up the juices from the soup it bounces back to life and becomes spongy but not soggy. Do be careful with your choice of bread: a stale white crusty loaf with plenty of holes, a sourdough, or a French Poilâne loaf (available at some delis) work well. As with minestrone, the vegetables for this hearty dish vary through the year, although as it is eaten in winter particularly, cavolo nero is frequently used.

Serves 8–10

1 quantity of Winter Minestrone (see page 134), without the rice

1 medium crusty white or sourdough loaf (about 12 oz)
1 fat garlic clove, peeled
extra virgin olive oil, to drizzle
scallions or chopped red onion, to garnish (optional)

Prepare the soup. Choose an ovenproof dish (a 9 x 13-inch lasagne dish is ideal) and preheat the oven to 350°F. Cut the bread in slices roughly ¾ inch thick and make sure you have enough to make two layers of bread in the dish. Toast the bread on both sides and rub with the garlic clove.

Pour one third of the soup into the dish. Cover with a layer of bread, then pour over another third of soup and another layer of bread. Finish with the remaining soup. Drizzle a little oil over the top and put into the oven for 30 minutes, or until bubbling hot. Remove from the oven and leave to cool a little before serving in warm bowls garnished with another drizzle of your best olive oil and, if you like, a little scallion or red onion.

Acquacotta
Pepper and Mushroom Soup with Eggs and Cheese

This is a poor man's dish from the Maremma area of Tuscany. The ingredients traditionally change according to what is plentiful, so peppers, basil, and fresh tomatoes would be used in summer and canned tomatoes, rosemary, and potatoes in winter. Freshly picked mushrooms could be used, or dried porcini in any season other than autumn when fresh ones are available. To eke out the soup during hard times, so much water was added that it ended up like its name, "cooked water." This version is enriched with eggs and cheese.

Serves 6

5 tablespoons olive oil
2 onions, finely chopped
6 celery ribs, finely chopped
1 large red bell pepper, chopped into ¾-inch squares
12 oz mushrooms, thinly sliced
3 garlic cloves, peeled and lightly crushed
2 sprigs of thyme
salt and freshly ground black pepper
14 oz canned plum tomatoes, plus 3 tablespoons water to rinse out the can
1 quart chicken stock or vegetable stock (see pages 136 or 140), or water
6 slices of country-style bread, plus extra to serve
6 eggs
½ cup Parmesan, finely grated
a small handful of basil, roughly shredded

Heat the oil in a large saucepan and cook the onion, celery, pepper, mushrooms, garlic, thyme, salt and pepper for about 20 minutes, stirring occasionally, until the vegetables are soft. Stir in the tomatoes and 3 tablespoons of water and cook for another 20 minutes. Add the stock or water and allow the soup to simmer gently for another 20 minutes. Season to taste.

Meanwhile toast the bread and put in the bottom of a casserole or saucepan suitable for serving. Pour the hot soup over the bread. Crack the eggs into the soup and add the grated Parmesan. Cover and cook for 8–10 minutes over medium heat, or until the eggs are set to your liking. Serve in warm bowls with a little basil and a slice of bread.

Zuppa di orzo e frutti di mare
Barley Soup with Seafood

Our wonderful Sicilian chef Gregorio Piazza showed me this rich dish. He believes it originates in Puglia, where the grain from the fields is often mixed with the catch from the sea. Please don't cheat and use bouillon cubes: the stock is the soup and the two should never be separated.

Serves 8–10 as a main

2 cups pearl barley
⅓ cup white wine
2 quarts shellfish stock (see page 138)
2 cups water
4 jumbo shrimp
6 langoustines
15 live clams, cleaned and checked (discard any that are broken or do not close)
15 live mussels, beards pulled off, cleaned, and checked (discard any that are broken or do not close)

FOR THE SOFFRITTO
⅓ cup extra virgin olive oil
1 carrot, finely chopped
1 celery rib, finely chopped
2 medium white onions, finely chopped
½ fresh red chile
1 garlic clove, peeled and crushed
3 parsley stems
4 teaspoons salt
freshly ground black pepper

First make the *soffritto*. Heat the oil in a large saucepan and, when hot, add the vegetables, chile, garlic, and parsley stems, and season with salt and pepper. Fry for 10–15 minutes, stirring frequently with a wooden spoon, until the vegetables have softened.

Add the pearl barley and continue to stir frequently for another 10 minutes as it absorbs the juices from the soffritto. Add the wine and reduce for a few minutes until the strong smell of wine has dissipated, then add the stock and water and bring it to a boil. Reduce it to a simmer for 20–25 minutes, or until the barley is cooked.

Meanwhile prepare the shellfish. Remove the heads from the shrimp and langoustines and peel off the shells (freeze the shells to make the next batch of Shellfish Stock). Cut the bodies in half along the backs and remove the black veins. Coarsely chop the flesh into bite-sized pieces.

Put one quarter of the soup in a blender or through a *passatutto* sieve and return it to the pan. Add the shrimp and langoustines along with the clams and mussels, and simmer for about 15 minutes or until the shellfish is cooked through. Serve in warmed bowls with toasted garlic bread.

Zuppa di farro
Spelt Soup

It is said that the Romans achieved their empire because of the nutritional properties of the mighty spelt grain. Apparently, feeding their soldiers a *puls* or mash of this grain kept them fighting for longer than enemy soldiers—all that slowly released carbohydrate must have given them energy. I love this Tuscan soup on a cold day, drizzled with a good olive oil and served with plenty of salty focaccia. It is typical in Tuscany to add the end piece of a cut of salumi or Parma ham that wouldn't go through the slicer. But you can substitute a piece of unsmoked pancetta or bacon. Vegetarians can of course omit this, in which case you could replace the meat with a Parmesan rind for extra flavor. Spelt is available at good delis and health food shops as well as online.

Serves 8 as a starter, 6 as a main

1 quantity of Soffritto (see page 125), made with
 2 garlic cloves and a sprig of rosemary

1 lb spelt
8 oz Parma ham, salumi, or unsmoked pancetta (optional)
2 bay leaves
3 cups canned plum tomatoes, squeezed through your hands to
 break them up
5–6 cups warm chicken or vegetable stock
 (see pages 136 or 140)
salt and freshly ground black pepper
extra virgin olive oil, for drizzling

In a large pot, combine the *soffritto*, Parma ham, if using, and the bay leaves. Cook over medium heat, stirring occasionally, until heated through. Add the spelt grains and "toast" them. They will start to stick and look as if they are about to burn; keep stirring with a wooden spoon and be brave for 3–4 minutes. The grains will start to break down a little at this stage and will absorb the flavors and oil from the *soffritto*.

Add the tomatoes and 1 quart of the stock, bring it to a boil then reduce to a simmer. Season to taste. Cook for 1 hour, stirring frequently, and adding more stock if the soup looks too thick. Taste the grains to check if they are soft; when they are, your soup is done. If you are making the soup in advance, the grains will continue to swell, so when you reheat, add more hot stock as necessary to achieve a thick soup-like consistency. To serve, drizzle a swirl of good extra virgin oil on top.

Variation:
To create a sausage and spelt casserole, brown some Italian sausages or homemade meatballs in a large frying pan and add these to the soup as you finish cooking.

Zuppa di pomodoro
Rich Tomato Soup

This relies on full-flavored tomatoes. If they are hard to find, add sun-dried tomatoes for concentrated flavor.

Serves 8–10

⅓ cup olive oil
1 white onion, finely chopped
1 celery rib, cut in half
1 carrot, cut in half
 lengthwise
1 fat garlic clove, peeled
 and smashed
salt and pepper
2¼ lb best-quality ripe
 tomatoes, quartered
1 teaspoon fresh oregano
1 handful of basil leaves, plus
 a few torn leaves to garnish
1 tablespoon tomato paste
1 quart water or vegetable
 stock (see page 136)
4 oz sun-dried tomatoes,
 oil-packed
1–2 teaspoons sugar (optional)

In a large pot, heat the oil over medium heat. Add the onion, celery, carrot, and garlic, seasoned with salt and pepper. Cook for a few minutes, stirring until the onion is softened. Add the tomatoes, herbs, and tomato paste and cook for 10–15 minutes. Add the water or stock and bring to a boil. Simmer for 20–30 minutes.

Stir in the sun-dried tomatoes. Discard the garlic, carrot, and celery. Purée the soup with a hand blender or using a *passatutto* sieve, and return it to the heat. Taste and adjust the seasoning if necessary with salt, pepper, and sugar. Serve in warm bowls with some torn basil leaves and crusty bread.

Zuppa di verdure arrosto
Roasted Vegetable Soup

This is a great way to use up leftover roasted vegetables as long as they are not dressed with oil and vinegar. Carolina, who teaches in our school showed me this recipe. She recommends roasting the vegetables well to give a lovely richness, and including a squash of some kind for its nutty flavor.

Serves 8 as a starter, 6 as a main

1 red onion, coarsely chopped
1 red bell pepper, coarsely chopped
1 small eggplant, coarsely chopped
2 zucchini, coarsely chopped
½ butternut squash, peeled and coarsely chopped
1 whole garlic head
1 large leek, coarsely chopped
2 celery ribs, coarsely chopped
salt and pepper
2 tablespoons fresh thyme leaves
⅓ cup olive oil, plus extra to serve
1–1½ quarts water
grated Parmesan or pecorino, to serve

Preheat the oven to 400°F. Put the onion, pepper, eggplant, zucchini, and squash on a baking sheet, season, sprinkle with the thyme and drizzle with half of the olive oil. Wrap the garlic head in foil and put it in the oven. Roast everything for 30–35 minutes.

In a large saucepan, heat the remaining oil, add the leek and celery, and cook over very low heat until very soft. Add the roasted vegetables, squeeze the garlic cloves out of their skins and add to the pot, then cover with the water. Bring to a boil and reduce to a simmer for 40–50 minutes. Purée using a *passatutto* sieve or hand blender and serve with grated cheese and a drizzle of olive oil.

Tip: I once had two soups served in one bowl in a restaurant and thought it was such a good idea. This soup combines really well with the Rich Tomato Soup (see opposite), so I now serve them next to one another, ladling a large spoonful of each into the bowl. Because they are both thick soups, they don't blend together. I dress them differently: one side with cheese and the other with basil leaves. Then I swirl olive oil over the top in a circular motion. A twist of black pepper and, hey presto, you have a beautifully presented dish!

This soup freezes really well, so I pour any leftovers into small plastic containers to keep for a rainy day.

Minestrone invernale
Winter Minestrone

Giancarlo's father used to say "*Che minestrone hai fatto*," meaning "What a mess you've made," referring to the mish-mash of ingredients you put into this soup. Minestrone is just the name of a type of soup made with vegetables, not a definitive recipe. It varies hugely from region to region and according to the time of year. Generally, chopped vegetables are cooked in flavorsome stock, sometimes with beans, rice, or pasta added, but the result is always a hearty bowl of soup designed to fill you up at low expense. Should you have an old rind of Parmesan, this can be added to give extra flavor.

Serves 6–8

1 quantity of Soffritto, made with garlic and herbs (see page 125)

1 lb carrots, diced into ½ in cubes
1 lb celery, chopped into ⅕ in pieces
1 lb potatoes, diced into 1½ in cubes
4 oz leeks, quartered then chopped finely
8 oz cabbage, coarsely chopped
1 oz Parmesan rind (optional)
2 oz pancetta (optional)
2 quarts warm vegetable stock (see page 136)
a pinch of salt and pepper
1 cup Arborio rice

Heat the *soffritto* in a large heavy-bottomed saucepan. Add all the vegetables except the cabbage, the Parmesan rind and the pancetta, if using. Cook for 10–15 minutes to soften the vegetables, stirring frequently and adding a little more oil if necessary. Add the cabbage and cook for 5 minutes, stirring again. Then add the stock, bring it to a boil and reduce to a simmer for about 1 hour, until the vegetables are cooked through.

Adjust the seasoning to taste and then add the rice and cook for another 20 minutes until tender. Serve in warmed bowls with plenty of crusty bread.

Minestrone estivo
Summer Minestrone

This Ligurian summer soup is much lighter and more delicate in flavor than its winter counterpart. Liguria is famous for its abundant use of locally grown herbs and vegetables. Choose the freshest, youngest vegetables you can and blend up some fresh pesto to swirl in.

Serves 4–6

½ quantity of Soffritto (see page 125), made without garlic
4 tablespoons Pesto (see page 164)

8 oz new potatoes, scrubbed and quartered
2 celery ribs, finely chopped
1 bunch of scallions, thinly sliced
8 oz baby carrots, left whole
12 oz baby zucchini, halved lengthwise then cut into half-moons 2 in thick
8 oz green beans, cut into fourths
8 oz fresh or frozen peas
8 oz asparagus, woody ends discarded, spears cut in half and tips separated
salt and freshly ground black pepper
6 cups hot water
a handful of flat-leaf parsley, coarsely chopped, stems reserved
4 oz lettuce, preferably romaine, shredded
4 oz baby spinach leaves
8 oz small pasta, such as ditalini (optional)

Prepare the vegetables, then heat the *soffritto* in a large saucepan. Begin by cooking the potatoes, celery, onions, and carrots in the *soffritto* for 5 minutes, stirring frequently. Next add the zucchini, green beans, peas, and asparagus spears and cook for 10–15 minutes, stirring frequently to prevent them from sticking to the pan (adding a little oil if necessary).

Season the vegetables well, then add the hot water and parsley stems. Bring it to a boil, then reduce to a simmer for 1 hour or until the vegetables are cooked through and have softened, but not to a mush. If you are using pasta, add it 10–12 minutes before the end of the cooking time, depending on your chosen pasta. Add the asparagus tips, parsley, lettuce, and spinach five minutes before serving. Serve in warm bowls with a swirl of the Pesto.

Brodo di verdure
Vegetable Stock

This has to be the simplest and cheapest stock to make: nothing is fried and no oil is added. I've never bought another bouillon cube after learning this recipe! It is essential for vegetable risottos, soups, and many vegetarian dishes. If you prefer, tie the peppercorns and herbs in a muslin bag, which makes them easier to remove.

Makes 3 quarts

1 small onion, unpeeled, cut in half
1 carrot, quartered lengthwise
1 large tomato, the top skin scored with the
  tip of a sharp knife
1 bay leaf
a handful of parsley stems
1 celery heart and 2 celery ribs, or
  4 celery ribs
12 peppercorns
1 teaspoon salt
3 quarts water

Put all the ingredients into a very large stockpot and add the water. Bring to a boil and reduce to a simmer for 30–60 minutes. Strain and use immediately, or leave to cool and refrigerate for up. Freeze for longer storage.

Brodo di verdure ed erbe
Vegetable and Herb Stock

This method produces a rich, herb-flavored stock. It entails first making a *soffritto*—by "underfrying" vegetables—to give a base flavor to the dish. Although this adds a little oil to the stock, sautéed vegetables also give a wonderful flavor.

Makes 3 quarts

1½ tablespoons olive oil
1 large tomato, the top skin scored with the
  tip of a sharp knife
1 celery rib, coarsely chopped
1 carrot, coarsely chopped
2 onions, coarsely chopped
a small handful of parsley stems
10 black peppercorns
4 bay leaves
a sprig of sage
a sprig of thyme
2 garlic cloves, peeled and lightly crushed
3 quarts water

Pour the oil into a very large stockpot and add everything except the water. Cook for about 5 minutes, stirring occasionally, and then add the water. Reduce to a gentle simmer for 45–60 minutes. Strain and use immediately, or leave to cool and refrigerate for up to 3 days. Freeze for longer storage.

Brodo di carne di Zia Maria
Zia Maria's Beef and Chicken Stock

This is a full-flavored beef and chicken stock for soups, stews, or risottos. It can also be served as a broth for pasta shapes such as cappelletti—a traditional Italian Christmas dish.

Makes 1–1.5 quarts/serves 8–10

1 quantity of Cappelletti (see page 187), optional

1 lb beef bones, roasted
1 chicken carcass, cooked or uncooked
2 celery ribs, quartered
1 small onion, unpeeled, cut in half
1 garlic clove, peeled
1 carrot, cut in half
1 tomato, the top scored with the tip of a sharp knife
4 bay leaves
a handful of parsley stems
2 tablespoons olive oil
black peppercorns
3 quarts water

First roast the beef bones and chicken carcass in the oven at 350°F for 30 minutes.

Meanwhile, cook the vegetables in the olive oil for 5 minutes, then combine all the ingredients in a large pan. Bring to a boil and then reduce to a gentle simmer for about 2 hours, skimming off any foam from the surface, as necessary.

Strain the broth through a fine sieve to remove the bones and vegetables. Use immediately or leave to cool completely and refrigerate for up to 3 days. Freeze for longer storage. If cooking the *cappelletti*, cook them in the broth for 10 minutes (if fresh) or around 12 minutes (if frozen).

Brodo di carne
Beef Stock

Use the beef itself to make Meatballs (see page 304) or slice it for a salad.

Makes 4 quarts

2 lb boneless beef roast (blade, chuck, or top round)
4 quarts water
1 onion, unpeeled, cut in half
10 cloves
3 celery ribs
2 tomatoes, the top scored with the tip of a sharp knife
1 carrot, unpeeled, cut in half
4 bay leaves
scant teaspoon salt
2 tablespoons brandy

Rinse the beef in cold water. Put it into a very large stockpot with the water, bring it to a boil and reduce to a simmer for about 30 minutes, regularly skimming off the foam. When foam has stopped forming, stud each onion half with 5 cloves. Add to the pot with the rest of the vegetables, bay leaves, salt, and brandy. Simmer gently for 2–2½ hours, until the beef is tender.

Set aside the beef to eat cold or to use in another dish. Discard the vegetables. Use the stock immediately, or leave to cool completely and refrigerate for up to 3 days.

Fumetto di pesce
White Fish Stock

Fish heads give lots of flavor: I keep a stock of fish heads and bones in the freezer.

Makes 1¾ quarts

2 tablespoons olive oil
1 fish head and the bones from 2 fish
1 celery heart and 1 celery rib, chopped
1 carrot, coarsely chopped
1 white onion, cut in half
1 fat garlic clove, lightly crushed
1 lemon, cut in half
10 black peppercorns
2 tomatoes
2 bay leaves
a small bunch of parsley
3 quarts water

Heat the oil in a large stockpot, add the fish heads and bones, celery, carrot, onion, and garlic. Cook for 5 minutes. Add the remaining ingredients, squeezing in the lemon juice and adding the skins. Bring to a boil, then reduce to a simmer for 1 hour, skimming off the foam regularly. Strain through muslin or a fine sieve, then leave to rest for 1 hour until the sediment settles. Ladle out the stock, discarding the sediment. Use immediately or leave to cool.

Fumetto di pesce fritto
Fried Fish Stock

A simple stock for tons of flavor in fish dishes.

Makes 1¾ quarts

⅓ cup olive oil
1 red chile, coarsely chopped
7 garlic cloves, unpeeled and crushed
5 anchovies, coarsely chopped
1 fish head and the bones from 2 fish
3 tablespoons brandy
⅓ cup tomato paste
3 quarts water

Heat the oil in a large heavy-bottomed stockpot, cook the chile and garlic for 2 minutes then add the anchovies and fish. Cook for 10 minutes to brown the fish head well on both sides (turn only once). Pour in the brandy and reduce for 3–4 minutes. Stir in the paste and water. Bring to a boil and simmer for 1 hour. Strain and use immediately, or leave to cool and refrigerate.

Brodo di gamberi
Shellfish Stock

Of all the experiences in my 12-year total immersion into Italian cooking, the "shellfish-stock moment" stands out. I had always enjoyed the combination of shrimp and pasta, fish stews and soups, but had never managed to achieve the intense flavor I was looking for. One day I walked in to find our Sicilian chef with an empty bottle of wine in one hand and a pan full of lobsters in the other. Not an unusual sight for a stressed out chef, but it seemed unusual that he was hitting the lobster shells with the bottle. His explanation was that he was making a shellfish *brodo* (a bisque-like stock) and this was the secret ingredient that gave his fish dishes the wow factor. So now I save lobster, crab, and shrimp shells in the freezer until I have enough shells and time to make a big batch of this amazing stock. I use it in nearly all my fish dishes, including risotto, pasta, soups, and even Thai fish curry.

Makes 2½ quarts

5 tablespoons olive oil
2 lb frozen shrimp shells and heads
1 lb mixed crab and lobster shells
2 carrots, coarsely chopped
2 celery ribs, coarsely chopped
2 onions, coarsely chopped
1⅓ cups dry white wine
⅔ cup tomato paste
a small handful of parsley stems
2½ quarts water
2 generous pinches of salt

Heat the olive oil in the biggest stockpot you have with the shrimp shells and heads. Allow them almost to burn, then add all the vegetables and cook for a couple of minutes. Using a rolling pin or potato masher bash the heads and vegetables down into the pan, then add the white wine. Allow it to reduce and add the tomato paste and the parsley stems. Next add the water and the salt to the stock. Bring to a boil, then reduce to a simmer for 1½ hours.

Pass the stock through a fine sieve a little at a time, pressing down on the shells with the back of a large spoon to release the juices. Use immediately or leave to cool completely and refrigerate.

Brodo di pollo
Chicken Stock

This stock can either be made with a fresh chicken or with a leftover carcass, with the cooked meat picked off and reserved. I remember my mother frequently doing this on a Monday after the Sunday roast. This stock is good for risotto.

Makes 1 gallon (4 quarts)

3 lb free-range chicken, cut in half, or a
  cooked chicken carcass
1 medium white onion, unpeeled, cut in half
10 cloves
1 celery heart and 2 celery ribs
1 medium carrot, cut in half lengthwise
12 peppercorns
1 bay leaf
4 quarts water

If using fresh chicken, wash the bird in cold water and put it in a very large stockpot. If using a cooked chicken carcass, pick off any flesh and reserve for other dishes. Put the carcass in the pot.

Stud each onion half with 5 cloves. Add to the pot with the celery, carrot, peppercorns, and bay leaf, and pour in enough water to cover the bird. Bring to a boil and then reduce to a simmer for 3 hours. Skim the surface frequently to remove the foam, particularly at the beginning. Add a little more water if the level becomes too low for the bird to cook through.

Reserve the whole chicken, if using, to eat cold or to use in other recipes. Strain the vegetables from the stock and discard. Use immediately or leave to cool completely and refrigerate for up to 3 days. Freeze for longer storage.

Brodo di pollo cotto
Cooked Chicken Stock

There is something so homey and comforting about the smell of chicken stock emanating from the kitchen. Forget perfumed candles and room sprays, give me steaming chicken stock any day to make a house feel like a home! My mother was forever bubbling up the leftover chicken bones from the Sunday roast and turning it into delicious soups. Now I use mine for risottos and stews as well.

Makes 2 quarts

1 cooked chicken carcass and bones (12 oz to 1 lb)
3 quarts water
1 small white onion, unpeeled, cut in half
10 cloves
1 celery rib, quartered
1 carrot, cut in half lengthwise
1 large tomato, the top scored with the tip
  of a sharp knife
10 black peppercorns
1 bay leaf
6 parsley stems

Pick off any flesh from the chicken and reserve to make a pie, meatballs, or soup. Put the carcass, bones and any leftover juices into a large stockpot and pour in the water.

Stud each onion half with 5 cloves and add to the pot with the celery, carrot, tomato, peppercorns, bay leaf, and parsley. Bring it to a boil and then reduce to a gentle simmer for at least 2 hours and up to 3 hours—the longer the better. Skim the surface if any scum appears and top up with a little hot water if the level becomes too low (around 2 cups water is lost every hour).

Strain the stock, discarding the bones and vegetables and use at once or allow to cool completely and refrigerate for up to 3 days. Freeze for longer storage.

For frozen stock, allow it to boil down to around 2 cups so that it is more concentrated and then freeze in small quantities.

CHAPTER 4: PASTA

Pasta

INTRODUCTION

remember the first time I took a piece of pasta from Giancarlo's plate with my fork; it was not long after we had met. I had never seen him so cross. He has gotten used to sharing with me now, but at the time he told me, "Two things you need to know about an Italian man: no one takes his woman, or his pasta!"—and he was only half joking!

Pasta (the word means "paste" or "dough") is, at its most basic, just flour mixed with water. One of the simplest of all foods, it has been an Italian staple since ancient times. It is accepted these days that while the Chinese were the first to perfect the art of making noodles from such a dough, it wasn't Marco Polo who first introduced the idea to Italy. Etruscan tombs apparently show people mixing flour and water to a paste, an Arab geographer, Idrisi, talked of a Sicilian semolina made into strands in the 12th century, and there are references to macaroni dating back to the 13th century.

Outside Italy, I often think there is a perception that fresh pasta is superior to dried, but in Italy they are treated as two entirely different things, each appropriate for certain dishes. There is a size and shape of pasta for every dish, too, from *stelline* (little stars), or *ditalini* (little fingers) that go into soups, through to linguine—good with light and seafood sauces, such as crab, and also tomato sauces—and short penne, fusilli, tagliatelle, and pappardelle (the latter is most traditional with ragù and porcini mushrooms). Spaghetti is never served with *ragù Bolognese* in Bologna, it is always ribbons of tagliatelle, though in Abruzzo it is normal to have ragù with *spaghetti alla chitarra*, since the shape of the squared-off spaghetti, traditionally made by pushing the pasta through a guitar-like stringed gadget, makes all the difference. Of course there are regional differences and variations all over Italy.

At one time, production of dried pasta as we know it today was concentrated around Naples, where most of the hard durum wheat variety needed to make pasta was grown. The climate was also perfect for drying the pasta naturally. These days, of course, durum wheat is also grown in other regions and commercial production has taken over from sunshine.

Fifty years ago, especially in the north, fresh pasta may well have been made on a daily basis, but these days it is more likely to be a weekly event, perhaps on Sundays, or even just something that is done on special occasions, such as Easter. Once made, though, leftover fresh pasta is never wasted. Giancarlo's mother had a drawer in a *madia* (cabinet) especially for scrap pieces of pasta, which would be cut into *maltagliati* (rough shapes),

My husband, Giancarlo, took packages of pasta in our suitcase when we went on our honeymoon to the Caribbean. That, for me, sums up the way Italians feel about pasta. Friends come to visit us in London and I say, "Why don't we go out and eat some Asian food?" Our cosmopolitan city offers every kind of cuisine, but no, they eat every night at our restaurant because they simply cannot be without pasta. Many Italians who work with us think nothing of eating pasta every day, and some of the men eat it twice a day!

and our chef, Stefano, told me that his grandmother would always grate leftover balls of pasta to make *grattini*—little dots of pasta which would go into broth and minestrone.

In Sardinia, I spent time making pasta with Anna Pino, the mother-in-law of our head chef Monserrato. She and her daughter would sit around the table making *Gnocchetti Sardi* together (see page 192), laughing and chatting, and they told me that it was an important tradition; something that brought a family together. They could easily have bought some factory-made *gnocchetti*, but not only did they prefer the flavor and texture of the homemade pasta, it gave them a chance to catch up on news, and sometimes female neighbors or other family members would join in. They make their pasta in the drier months —otherwise the humidity would affect it.

I remember when we first started eating spaghetti in the UK, on each plate there would be a neat nest of pasta with the sauce sitting on top. We've come a long way since then, but I still don't think we perceive pasta quite as the Italians do. Where we often still think of the sauce as an adornment, to an Italian, pasta and sauce must come together in the pan as one. In our cooking classes I teach people how to toss the pasta and sauce together, much as a Chinese person would toss noodles in a wok, but you can do it just as well with two forks, as long as you keep tossing everything together vigorously. As you do so, the starch from the pasta comes out into the sauce, thickening it (you can keep back some of the starchy cooking water to add if necessary). At the same time, the outside of the pasta breaks down a little, so the sauce clings to it—even more so, in the case of long pasta, such as spaghetti—if it has been made by a producer who extrudes the dough through a traditional *bronze die*. This will give the pasta a slightly rough surface, unlike the smooth, more slippery finish you find when it has been extruded through a *Teflon die*.

To Giancarlo, the most important thing is the flavor of the pasta so at home, if the boys and I would let him, he would eat the pasta straight from the saucepan—"Why waste time putting it in a bowl?" is Giancarlo's argument. He wants to eat the pasta right away, the moment it is prepared. In Italian homes there is no such thing as waiting for everyone to be served before starting to eat your pasta. And Italians, I notice, have none of our shyness and reservation about forking up spaghetti—the important thing is to enjoy it at its best and not let it get cold as you tentatively push it around the bowl or plate.

Cooking dried pasta

The secret to cooking dried pasta properly is to use the biggest pot you have, so you can put in plenty of water, salt it well, make sure it is bubbling hard when you put in the pasta, and then stir it regularly so that the pasta moves around. Italy is divided as to whether to add a dash of oil to the cooking. As far as I am concerned, as long as it has enough space, you don't need any oil in the water to stop it from sticking together, which some people suggest. The more important thing is to add oil to the pasta after it is drained, and particularly if it is not immediately going into a sauce.

The rule of thumb for cooking pasta is around 1 lb of pasta to 6 quarts of water and 4 tablespoons of salt. Enough salt is important, otherwise your pasta won't have enough flavor. I know immediately when I eat pasta whether the water has been salted enough. If you taste the water, it should taste like the sea, and the pasta, provided it is seasoned enough, should be tasty enough to eat on its own.

Just before the suggested cooking time stated on the package, remove a strand of pasta to test. If it is just tender, but still has some resistance, then it is ready—*al dente*, literally "to the tooth".

Reginette

Ziti, twisted and plain

Pappardelle

Fusilli lunghi

DRIED PASTA CHART

Penne Lisce

Stelline

Grattini

Malloreddus

Farfalline

Lasagne

Farfalle

Paccheri

Lumaconi

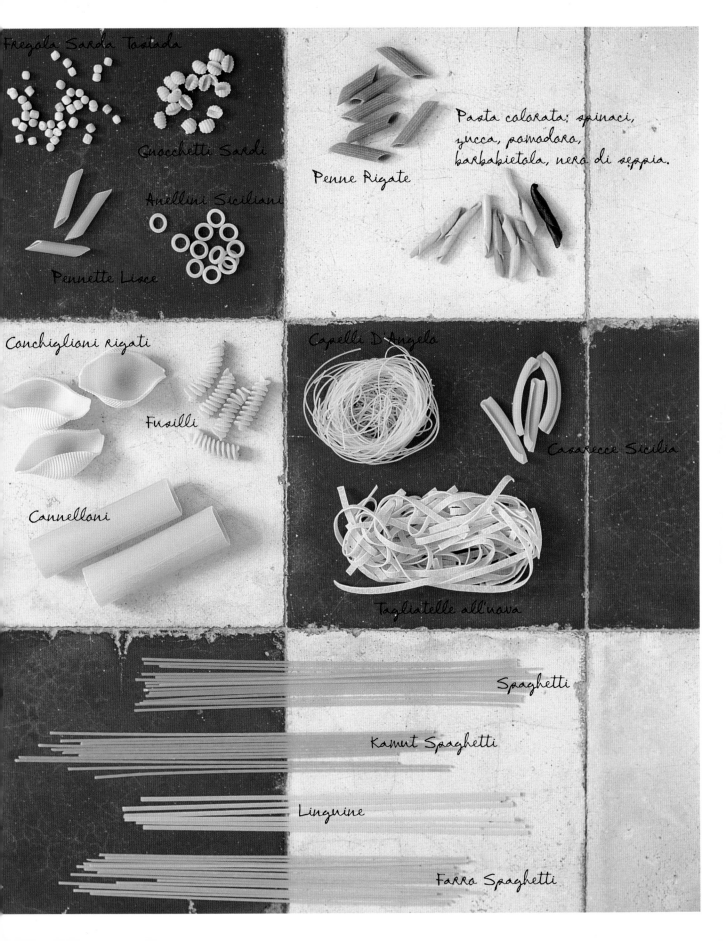

Fregola Sarda Tostada

Gnocchetti Sardi

Penne Rigate

Pasta colorata: spinaci, zucca, pomodoro, barbabietola, nera di seppia.

Anellini Siciliani

Pennette Lisce

Conchiglioni rigati

Capelli D'Angelo

Fusilli

Casarecce Sicilia

Cannelloni

Tagliatelle all'uova

Spaghetti

Kamut Spaghetti

Linguine

Farro Spaghetti

How to Make Fresh Pasta

This is the general guide to making fresh pasta: 1 egg to every 1 cup of "00" flour. However, as egg sizes differ, a little bending of the rules is sometimes necessary. Ideally, pasta is made and rolled on a wooden surface because the tiny particles of wood that project from the surface add to the texture, helping the pasta to absorb the sauce that will eventually coat it. Many Italians use a tablecloth for the same purpose.

The texture of pasta rolled on a metal work surface or through a pasta machine is completely smooth and less absorbent. This means that dried pasta, which is normally put through metal rollers, has a smooth, harder exterior, and is better designed for liquid sauces such as seafood or tomato. Its lack of absorbency prevents it from becoming soggy.

This masterclass shows how to make fresh pasta by hand, but the flour and eggs can be put into a food processor together if you prefer. Use the plastic "knife" attachment (dough blade) if your machine has one. When a dough is formed, take it out of the machine and continue to knead by hand for a few minutes, following the instructions opposite.

2 cups "00" flour or pasta flour, plus a little extra if necessary
2 medium free-range eggs, preferably corn-fed for color

Pour the flour onto a flat surface or into a bowl and make a well in the center of the mound. The walls around the edge of the mound should be high enough to contain the eggs. Crack the eggs into the well in the center.

Using a table knife, gradually mix the egg into the flour. Keep mixing until they form a thick paste.

Use the fingertips of one hand to incorporate the rest of the flour. If working on a flat surface, when the dough forms a ball but lots of smaller, drier crumbs remain, put the ball of dough to one side and sieve the crumbs and flour. Add the large wetter crumbs and the sifted flour to the dough and knead to blend them in. Discard the small dry crumbs. (If working in a bowl, this isn't necessary).

The dough should form a soft but firm, flexible ball. If it is still sticking to the palm of your hand, add a little more flour until it stops sticking, but be cautious: stop adding flour as soon as it stops sticking. If the dough is really dry and has many cracks, add a drop or two of water—do this in a bowl. Knead the pasta for 5–10 minutes, or until it springs back to the touch.

If you cut the ball of dough open it should be full of small air bubbles; this means that you have kneaded it for long enough.

Leave the pasta to rest on a floured work surface or kitchen towel for 20 minutes with a bowl inverted over it. Alternatively, lightly dust the pasta with flour and wrap it in plastic wrap to prevent it from drying out while it rests.

Meanwhile, clean the work surface. Scrape off the stuck pasta with a dough scraper or the dull side of a knife and use a damp cloth to clean the rest.

To cut the pasta, see the master-class on pages 152–153.

Pasta ricca all'uovo
Rich Egg Pasta

This variation on the fresh pasta recipe makes a richer pasta dough. This type of dough is used more in the north of Italy. Recipes for pasta containing no egg were born out of strife. But at the other extreme, I once ate pasta made with 2 lb of flour to 30 egg yolks in Piedmont. It was served with butter and fresh white truffle; the egg flavor married perfectly with the truffle.

3 cups "00" flour or pasta flour, plus a little extra if necessary
2 whole free-range eggs
4 egg yolks

Follow the same method as for the fresh pasta recipe (see left), adding a little more flour if necessary to compensate for the extra eggs.

GIANCARLO'S TIPS

If you think you have added too much flour and the pasta is hard and lumpy, wrap it in plastic wrap and leave it for around 30 minutes. Miraculously, it will become soft and the lumps of flour will blend into the egg.

I always precook my pasta at home because I find it then stores better and becomes more robust. The minute it is made, I drop it into boiling salted water for just a couple of minutes so it is nearly cooked. Then I drain it and spread out the pasta strands. Stuffed pasta should be in a single layer so that it does not stick together. Toss in sunflower oil (rather than wasting precious olive oil). If too much water comes out with the pasta, drain it off. When cold, cover each layer with a sheet of plastic wrap and then repeat as before. This way, the pasta can be stored in the fridge for up to 5 hours, until you are ready to complete the cooking.

To serve, drop the pasta into salted boiling water for just a minute or two until it is cooked but still al dente. Drain, toss with the sauce, and serve.

To freeze fresh pasta, do not precook it, but spread it out in a single layer on trays covered with baking parchment and flash-freeze it. Once frozen, pile the pasta into freezer bags.

To dry pasta, spread it out in sheets or ribbons onto a clean tablecloth. Alternatively, hang the pasta ribbons to dry over a broom handle suspended between two chairs. The best situation for drying pasta is a well ventilated area so that plenty of air circulates between the pasta. Once dry, the pasta can be gathered together; do it carefully, as as it is very brittle in this state. Open-weave baskets are good for storage to prevent any humidity from softening the pasta. Dried pasta will keep for a few days like this. Cook it as if it were fresh.

After cutting or stuffing pasta, lay it onto a tray, scattered with semolina to prevent it from sticking.

Pasta

MASTERCLASS

How to Make Spinach Pasta

Spinach loses half its weight when cooked and squeezed, so you will need 7 oz fresh spinach for 4 oz cooked, squeezed spinach.

Enough to make 35 ravioli (serves 6 as a main or 8 as a starter)

4 oz spinach, cooked from fresh or frozen and thoroughly squeezed dry
3 cups "00" flour, all-purpose flour, or pasta flour, plus a little extra
2 free-range eggs

To make the pasta a smooth green color, purée the spinach after squeezing dry with the eggs in a blender.

Pour the flour onto a flat surface or into a bowl and make a well in the center of the mound. The walls around the edge of the mound should be high enough to contain the egg mixture.

Pour the egg mixture into the well and use a table knife to combine, gradually forming a thick paste.

Use the fingertips of one hand to incorporate the rest of the flour. When most of the dough forms a ball, but lots of smaller, drier crumbs remain, put the ball of dough to one side and sieve the crumbs and flour.

Add the large wetter crumbs and the sifted flour to the dough and knead to blend them in. Discard the dry small crumbs. The dough should form a soft but firm flexible ball. If it is still sticking to the palm of your hand, add a little more flour until it stops sticking, but be cautious: stop adding flour as soon as it stops sticking. If it is really dry and has many cracks, add a drop of two of water—do this in a bowl. Knead the pasta for 5–10 minutes, or until it springs back to the touch.

If you cut the ball of dough open it should be full of small air bubbles; this means that you have kneaded it for long enough. Leave the pasta to rest on the work surface for 20 minutes with a bowl inverted over it or lightly dust it with flour and wrap in plastic wrap to prevent it from drying out while it rests. Meanwhile, clean the work surface. Scrape off all the stuck pasta with the blade of a knife and use a damp cloth to clean the rest.

To cut the pasta, follow the instructions in the masterclass on pages 152–153.

It is hard to give a precise recipe for black pasta as squid ink varies in consistency from the real thing—from the ink sac of a squid or cuttlefish—to a jar or sachet.

Variations: colored pasta

Pasta al nero di seppia
Black Pasta

8 oz "00" flour, pasta flour, or all-purpose flour
3 tablespoons cuttlefish ink (see page 272)
2 eggs

Follow the instructions for making fresh pasta on pages 148–149, adding the cuttlefish ink with the eggs. If you need to add more ink to achieve a really black pasta, add a little more flour to compensate for the extra liquid.

Pasta ai pomodori
Red Pasta

8 oz "00" flour, pasta flour, or all-purpose flour
2 eggs
¼ cup tomato paste

Follow the instructions for making fresh pasta on pages 148–149, adding the tomato paste with the eggs.

Pasta alla barbabietola rossa
Beet Pasta

2 whole eggs plus 1 egg yolk
3 oz cooked beet
3 cups "00" flour, pasta flour, or all-purpose flour

Blend the eggs with the beet in a food processor until the beet is puréed. Put the flour into a bowl to avoid staining the work surface and make a well in the center of the mound. Pour in the egg and beet mixture and then follow the instructions for making fresh pasta on pages 148–149.

How to Cut Fresh Pasta by Hand

1 quantity of fresh pasta, rested for 20 minutes (for recipes see pages 148–149)
flour, for dusting

Remove the pasta from the inverted bowl or the plastic wrap. Lightly flour the work surface and rolling pin. Begin rolling out the pasta, giving it a quarter turn between each roll.

Continue to roll it until the pasta is around 1mm thick. When using uncolored pasta you should be able to see the color of your hand or the work surface showing through the sheet of pasta.

When it is 1mm thick, lightly dust the surface of the pasta with flour. Now fold up each side a few times until they meet in the middle.

Using a long, sharp knife, cut the pasta into even strips of the desired width.

Slide the knife beneath the pasta, lining up the edge of the knife with the center of the folds.

Lift up the knife and the pasta ribbons will fall down over each side.

Drape the ribbons over a cane or broomstick to dry, or use right away.

Pasta
MASTERCLASS

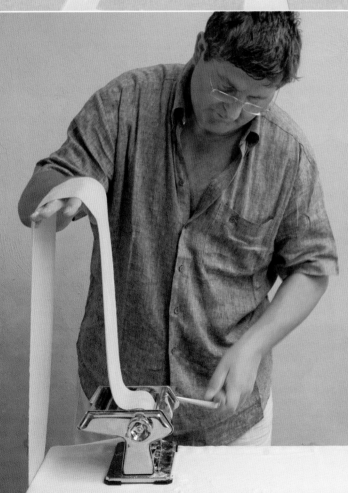

How to Cut Fresh Pasta by Machine

1 quantity of fresh pasta, rested for 20 minutes (for recipes see pages 148–149)
flour, for dusting

Roll out the pasta using a rolling pin or simply flatten it with your hands so that it can fit through the rollers of the pasta machine. Flour the pasta lightly on both sides.

Set the machine to its widest setting and roll the pasta through.

Dust the pasta with flour a second time and roll it through again, this time on no. 4 or an equivalent notch. Repeat this process twice more, until the machine is on its thinnest setting, cutting the pasta into more manageable lengths as it gets longer.

Keep the pasta dusted at all times with flour. If you would like to cut pasta such as *tagliolini* or fettucine use the appropriate cutting attachment. For lasagne, cut the pasta into rectangles roughly 6 x 8 inches in size.

Ravioli di spinaci ripieni di mozzarella affumicata con sugo di pomodoro frescho
Spinach Pasta Stuffed with Smoked Mozzarella with Fresh Tomato Sauce

I ate this one blissful evening in an outdoor restaurant in Ravenna, watching well-dressed Italians on their evening *passeggiata*. Like any typical foodie tourist I can wander for ages, dragging my complaining family behind me until I find the "right" place to eat. As it is often impossible to tell what a restaurant will be like merely from the décor and menu, I have often been mistaken. However, this was a good night and as a couple of locals had recommended this restaurant and a table was available, we stayed. The food was great, made with love and care by the family, and we were served by the proud daughter. I had never eaten anything so simple yet so lovely but was amazed to see, when I came back home, the winner of Masterchef cooking the same dish. No such thing as an original recipe, eh? Maybe he had been to the same restaurant in Ravenna! Smoked mozzarella or *scamorza* is perfect for this dish, but I have experimented with smoked applewood and was happily surprised by the result.

Makes 50–60 small ravioli or 35–40 large ravioli (serves 6 as a main or 8 as a starter)

1 quantity of spinach pasta (see page 150)
semolina flour, for dusting (optional)
1 ravioli cutter, about 2½ in wide, or a glass of the same diameter, or a wavy-edged pastry wheel

FOR THE FILLING (double the amount for large ravioli)
8 oz smoked *scamorza*, smoked mozzarella, or smoked applewood, finely chopped in a blender
4 oz ricotta (preferably cow's milk)
a good pinch of freshly grated nutmeg
salt, to taste

TO SERVE
1 quantity of Giovanna's Fresh Tomato Sauce (see page 102) or, if fresh tomatoes are not in season, make any of the tomato sauce recipes using canned Italian plum tomatoes
¼ cup Parmesan, finely grated

First make the pasta according to the instructions on page 148–149. While the pasta dough rests, make the tomato sauce in a frying pan or large saucepan.

To make the filling, thoroughly mix together the chopped smoked cheese, ricotta, and nutmeg in a mixing bowl. Season to taste, but go easy on the salt as the cheese is already salty; add extra nutmeg if needed.

Remove the pasta from the fridge and roll it out, a little at a time (or it will dry out) to a thickness of about 1mm or using the thinnest setting on a pasta machine. Lightly dust the work surface, the pasta, and the rolling pin with flour to prevent them from sticking. Cut long lengths in half for ease of handling. If you are using a pasta machine, dust the underside of the dough only, not the top, which needs to stick to another piece of dough.

Place heaping teaspoons of stuffing onto one of the lengths of pasta, spacing them far-enough apart to allow for the shape you want to cut, but not so much that you waste pasta. Aim for around 1 inch between the mound of stuffing and the edge of the *raviolo*.

Lay a second piece of pasta face-down (with the non-floured side downward) over the stuffing and press gently around the mound to expel the air. You can either do this mound by mound to make individual ravioli (as shown in the photos) or make several ravioli at a time by placing a longer top sheet of pasta over the bottom sheet containing the mounds of stuffing.

Now cut the pasta into ravioli using the cutter or a glass, or make square shapes using a pastry wheel.

Put the ravioli on a floured baking sheet (dust with a little semolina flour, if you have it), spaced apart in a single layer. Set aside until ready to use, but for no longer than one hour or they will stick to the surface. If you need to make the ravioli in advance, either freeze them at this stage, or blanch them and toss in oil.

Bring a large pot of salted water to a boil and cook the ravioli for 3–5 minutes, or until the pasta is al dente, then drain in a colander. Add the pasta to the sauce in the frying pan and gently toss or stir to combine the pasta and the sauce. Serve on warmed plates and sprinkle with the grated Parmesan.

Ravioli di barbabietola con radicchio, speck cipolla rossa e salsa di pinoli, burro e salvia

Beet Pasta stuffed with Radicchio, Red Onion, and Speck, with Pine Nut, Butter, and Sage Sauce

This recipe was inspired by chef Dino at La Colonna restaurant in Milan. The pasta, stained a deep pinky-purple by the beet, looks beautiful arranged on the plate, dressed delicately with a drizzle of sage butter and scattered with toasted pine nuts. In his recipe, Dino uses speck, a local smoked ham, but for a vegetarian alternative use a little more ricotta and a soft herb like fresh thyme or parsley. In Milan, black pepper is not widely used but a little is optional.

Serves 4–6

1 quantity of beet pasta
(see page 151)

FOR THE STUFFING
4 tablespoons olive oil
½ large red onion, finely
  chopped
1 garlic clove, peeled and
  smashed into 2 pieces
3 sprigs of thyme
4 oz radicchio, finely
  chopped
3 oz speck or smoked bacon,
  cut into juliennes
8 oz ricotta
salt, to taste
black pepper (optional)

FOR THE PINE NUT, BUTTER,
AND SAGE SAUCE
8 tablespoons butter
10 sage leaves
salt, to taste
black pepper (optional)
¼ cup pine nuts, toasted
grated Parmesan, to serve

To make the stuffing, heat the oil in a frying pan. When hot, add the onion, garlic, and thyme, and cook for 3–4 minutes. Add the radicchio and speck, and cook for another 5 minutes over medium heat until the radicchio wilts. Remove the garlic and leave the mixture to cool in a bowl. When cool, remove the thyme stems, mix in the ricotta, and season to taste.

Lightly dust the work surface, the pasta, and the rolling pin with flour to prevent sticking. Roll out the pasta to about 1mm—it should be thin enough to see your fingers through the dough. Using a teaspoon, place little mounds of stuffing onto the pasta 2 inches from the edge. Fold the edge over the mounds and, using a glass, press out *mezzaluna* or half-moon shapes, expelling the air as you do. Put them on a floured baking sheet, spaced apart in a single layer. Set aside, but not for longer than one hour or they will stick.

Cook for 5–6 minutes in boiling salted water, or until the pasta is al dente. Meanwhile, make the sauce by melting the butter in a large frying pan. Add the sage leaves, salt and pepper, if using, and the toasted pine nuts, then cook for a few minutes. Add a ladleful of the pasta cooking water and stir well.

Drain the *mezzaluna* through a colander, add the sauce and toss to combine. Serve on warmed plates with grated Parmesan.

Ravioli di zucca
Pumpkin Ravioli

This is Emilio Cappelli's version of the classic ravioli from the Veneto. The Parmesan on the bottom of the dish is used to prevent the pasta from moving when serving!

Serves 6

1 quantity of fresh pasta (see pages 148–149)

FOR THE STUFFING
1 butternut squash (approximately 1½ lb)
1 teaspoon syrup of Mustard Fruits (optional)
10 amaretti cookies
2 tablespoons finely grated Parmesan
salt and freshly ground pepper
a sprinkling of ground cinnamon

TO SERVE
1 quantity of Pine Nut, Butter, and Sage Sauce
   (see recipe left), minus the pine nuts

To make the stuffing, preheat the oven to 400°F. Peel the squash and cut into 6 even pieces. Lay them on a piece of aluminum foil and bake for around 1½ hours. Allow to cool, then remove from the foil and put through a ricer or food mill. Mix in the syrup, 6 of the cookies, and Parmesan. Season to taste. Use this to stuff the ravioli, following the masterclass on page 155. Sprinkle Parmesan over the warm plates, then top with the cooked ravioli. Drizzle with the sauce. Combine the remaining Parmesan, amaretti, and cinnamon and scatter over the top.

Erbette con pasta di semola di grano duro
Pasta with Semola Flour for Spinach and Ricotta Ravioli

In this speciality from Parma, Swiss chard is often used instead of spinach. In Italy's south, pasta is often made with *semola*, or semolina flour. An unusually self-effacing northerner once told me that she copied the southerners' way of making *erbette*: "In the south they use a lot of *semola* in the pasta, but they know what they are doing down there!" Using *semola* makes the pasta smoother and more resistant to heat so that the *erbette* are less likely to open.

Makes 50–60 erbette (serves 8 as a main or 10 as a starter)

FOR THE PASTA
3 eggs
1½ cups "00" flour or all-purpose flour
1½ cups *semola* flour or fine semolina

FOR THE SPINACH AND RICOTTA FILLING
6 oz spinach, cooked and squeezed dry
12 oz ricotta, drained if very wet
5 tablespoons Parmesan, finely grated
nutmeg, freshly grated
salt and pepper

TO SERVE
1 quantity of Pine Nut, Butter, and Sage Sauce
   (see recipe left), or 1 quantity of Franca's
   Tomato Passata (see page 166)
grated Parmesan or pecorino

Make the *erbette* by following the ravioli masterclass on page 154–155. To make the spinach and ricotta filling, mix the ingredients together in a bowl and season to taste. Serve with the sauce and grated cheese.

Tortelloni al nero di seppia ripieni di salmone affumicato e gamberetti con sugo alle cozze Black Pasta Tortelloni Stuffed with Smoked Salmon and Shrimp in Mussel Sauce

On a freezing March day in Santa Maria di Castellabate, two hours south of Naples, we dived into the restaurant Archelino to escape the winds. The owner gave us little choice of what to eat, but we were so grateful to be inside that we agreed to try whatever he suggested. The pasta dishes were great, but the most outstanding was the special of the day. It looked so impressive that there were wows of delight as it arrived at the table. The huge mound of black pasta was indistinguishable from the mussel shells until the tortelloni were cut open to reveal their pink and white filling (for photo, see page 269). Squid ink varies in consistency, so add enough to make the pasta really black. If this makes the pasta too soft, add more flour.

Serves 8 as a first course and 10 as a starter

1 quantity of black pasta (see page 151)

FOR THE FILLING
2 tablespoons olive oil
6 oz shrimp, peeled and coarsely chopped
salt and freshly ground black pepper
4 oz smoked salmon
1½ tablespoons brandy
8 oz ricotta
sunflower oil or vegetable oil, to dress the pasta

FOR THE SAUCE
2 tablespoons extra virgin olive oil
2 lb mussels, cleaned of barnacles and debearded (see page 269)
2 garlic cloves, peeled and lightly crushed
parsley stems
½ dried or fresh red chile, finely chopped
¼ cup dry white wine
8 oz cherry tomatoes, quartered
salt, to taste

First make the filling. Heat the oil in a frying pan and, when hot, add the shrimp and cook for about 5 minutes seasoned with salt and pepper. Stir the salmon and then add the brandy and flambé or cook to reduce briefly. Remove from the heat and allow to cool before stirring in the ricotta.

Next make the pasta, following the instructions in the masterclass on pages 148–149, carefully adding the squid ink to the flour with the eggs. Do be careful not to get the ink in your eyes as it can temporarily blind you (it is designed as a defense against predator fish).

Using a rolling pin or a pasta machine on its thinnest setting, roll out the pasta until it is 1mm thick. Then on a floured work surface, cut into 2½ inch squares. Dot a heaping teaspoon of the filling onto each square and fold the square into a triangle. Press the pasta together around the filling, then hold the triangle and fold the edges inward so that it resembles a bonnet. Bring the ends of the bonnet together and pinch them around your finger but nip off a piece of the pasta where it joins or this area will be too thick to cook through.

Set the tortellono aside on a floured board and repeat with the remaining squares. Don't worry about the white flour showing; when the tortelloni are cooked they turn deepest, darkest black again and look really impressive with a pink filling inside.

Bring a large pot of salted water to a boil and drop in the tortelloni in 2 or 3 batches—they will take about 5 minutes to cook until al dente. Drain, set aside in a warm bowl and dress with the sunflower oil to stop them from sticking to each other. (If you have more tortelloni than you need right now, see page 149 for freezing techniques.)

To make the mussel sauce, heat the oil until hot, add the mussels, garlic, parsley stems, and chile, and cook for a couple of minutes, shaking the pan frequently. Add the white wine and cover the pan. Cook for 5–8 minutes, then discard any mussels that haven't opened. Add the cherry tomatoes and cook for just 2 minutes. Pick most of the mussels out of their shells, but leave a few on the shell for garnish. Discard the parsley, then toss everything together in a frying pan or large serving bowl. Garnish with the reserved mussels in their shells and serve right away.

Anna

Pasta
MASTERCLASS

MAKING
TORTELLONI

Ravioli ripieni di stracchino in brodo di pollo
Nicoletta's Stuffed Pasta with Stracchino Cooked in Chicken Broth

Nicoletta is mother to one of our managers, Marco Sani. During our Italian Mammas Week, six mothers brought their sons' favorite recipes over to show us real home cooking. We were so impressed that most of the recipes are in this book! This is Nicoletta's fresh pasta stuffed with *stracchino* cheese, (available in some delis and online). If you cannot find this wonderful soft, creamy cheese, look for *crescenza*. I asked Nicoletta if there was another cheese people could use. She simply answered "No!" I experimented and she is right, of course, so please persevere. Nicoletta made her broth using a whole fresh chicken. She served the bird with mashed potatoes and *salsa verde*, saving the delicious broth for cooking the pasta.

Makes 32 ravioli (serves 6 as a main or 8 as a starter)

FOR THE PASTA

2 cups "00" flour or all-purpose flour, plus a little extra if necessary
2 medium free-range eggs, preferably corn-fed for color

FOR THE FILLING

12 oz *stracchino* or *crescenza*
1 egg
½ cup grated Parmesan
grated nutmeg, to taste

2 quarts Chicken Stock or Cooked Chicken Stock (see page 140), heated
8 tablespoons butter
¼ cup Parmesan

To make the pasta, follow the instructions for the masterclass on pages 148–149. Roll out into 2 sheets.

Mix all the ingredients for the filling, and make the ravioli following the masterclass on pages 154–155. Cook the ravioli for 3–4 minutes in the hot chicken stock.

Melt the butter and toss with the cooked pasta in it. Serve in warmed bowls sprinkled with the Parmesan.

Ravioli di branzino con burro e limone
Seabass Ravioli with Lemon Butter Sauce

A classic recipe from our restaurants which never ceases to impress and took a long time to perfect. It works well with egg pasta or spinach.

Makes approximately 30–36 ravioli (serves 8 as a starter, 6 as a main course)

1 quantity of egg pasta (see page 149) or spinach pasta (see page 150)

FOR THE FILLING

2 whole sea bass or 4 sea bass fillets
4 sprigs of thyme
4 garlic cloves, skin left on and lightly crushed
2 tablespoons flat-leaf parsley, coarsely chopped
approximately ½ cup prepared Béchamel Sauce, (follow the 1 quart recipe on page 175, halving the quantities accordingly)
salt and freshly ground black pepper

FOR THE LEMON BUTTER SAUCE

8 tablespoons unsalted butter, melted
zest and juice of 1 lemon
8 tomatoes
2 tablespoons flat-leaf parsley, stemmed for the sauce, plus a little extra for serving

Preheat the oven to 350°F. Lay the sea bass, thyme, and garlic onto an oiled tray and season well. Cook for 20 minutes (for a whole fish) or 10–15 minutes (for fillets). Remove from the oven. Remove the skin and flake the flesh into a bowl, ensuring all bones are removed, add parsley and enough béchamel sauce to bind the mixture together. Season and set aside.

Make a small cross in the top of each tomato. Then drop into very hot water for a minute to split the skins. Remove right away and peel them. Chop the flesh into ½ inch cubes. Make the sauce by heating the butter in a medium pan. When hot and foaming add lemon zest and juice, then the tomatoes. Gently stir in the parsley. Reduce the heat, cook for 2 minutes and then turn off, allowing the flavors to blend. Make the ravioli following the masterclass on pages 154–155.

Bring a large pot of salted water to a boil. Working in batches, cook the ravioli for 3 minutes. Remove with a slotted spoon and add to the pan with the sauce. Toss to coat and sprinkle with the extra parsley.

Rotolo di pasta
Pasta Spirals with Mushroom, Mascarpone and Walnut Filling

Our good friend Valentina Harris gave us this recipe. She cooks her wonderful food at our school and this is one of the staff's favorite dishes. This is great for vegetarians but also satisfies carnivores because the filling is crunchy and substantial. Valentina told me the important thing to remember is NOT to overfill the roll because it will simply fall apart and not be sliceable. Also, make sure the mushrooms are completely cold before adding them to the mascarpone mix, otherwise it becomes a soup rather than a filling. You need to cook this in a fish kettle or a wide pan.

Serves 6

FOR THE FILLING

1 lb wild fresh mushrooms, cleaned and chopped

2 oz dried porcini mushrooms, soaked in warm water for 3 minutes, then drained and chopped, liquid reserved

8 tablespoons unsalted butter

10 oz freshest possible mascarpone

2½ oz walnuts, finely chopped

2 cups freshly grated Parmesan

2 eggs, beaten

2 tablespoons freshly chopped flat-leaf parsley

sea salt and freshly ground black pepper

FOR THE PASTA

2 eggs

4 oz *semola* flour or fine semolina

4 oz plain flour

TO SERVE

1 quantity of Franca's Tomato Passata (see recipe page 166), or butter

grated Parmesan

Gently sauté the fresh and dried mushrooms together with the butter, stirring frequently. Strain the reserved liquid and use this to baste the cooking mushrooms, if necessary. When the mushrooms are soft, dry, and thoroughly cooked, set aside to cool completely.

Chop or process them finely, then stir in the mascarpone, the walnuts, 1½ cups Parmesan, the eggs, the parsley, and seasoning. Set aside until required.

Make the pasta following the instructions for the masterclass on pages 148–149 and, once rested, place the dough on a large clean kitchen towel or a piece of muslin on a work surface. Roll into a wide sheet with a rolling pin. The size of the sheet will depend on how large the cloth is—allow enough fabric at each end of the roll that you can tie the cloth securely in place—and also on the size of your fish kettle or pan.

Spread the filling evenly and not too thickly over the sheet and then roll the pasta up like a Swiss roll, making sure there is no air trapped as you make each turn. Keep within 1½ inches of the edges of the cloth. Now wrap the roll tightly in a clean muslin cloth (see tip below). Tie the ends tightly with string and make a couple of ties along the length; don't pull them too tight.

Bring a fish kettle or wide pan of salted water to a boil. Slide the wrapped roll into the water carefully and boil gently for about 45 minutes. Very importantly, do not let it sag in the center.

Remove the roll from the pan very carefully and drain. Unwrap the roll, place it on a board and cut into slices with a very sharp knife.

Arrange the slices of roll on a plate and spoon over a little of Franco's Tomato Passata or melted butter and a little Parmesan. Valentina serves the plates as they are, but I like then to flash them beneath a hot broiler until the cheese is bubbling and the edges of the pasta become a little crunchy.

Tips: Do make sure the cloth is not saturated in fabric conditioner as this really affects the flavor of the dish. Once cooked, the roll will sit quite happily in the hot water until you are ready to serve—for up to about 30 minutes. Toss any leftover filling through freshly cooked pasta; it makes a simple but rich and effective sauce.

Corzetti
Ligurian Pasta Coins with Marjoram, Parmesan, and Pine Nuts

Corzetti are discs of pasta that bear the emblem or name of the house or restaurant where they are made. Traditional *corzetti* stamps are made of wood and usually have the name on one side and a flower design on the other. Each stamp cuts the pasta into discs and makes the patterns. As they are unavailable in Britain, you could be inventive and use a glass to cut the discs and then a rubber stamp, fork, teaspoon end, or knitting needle to create patterns in the pasta. Alternatively, serve any short dried pasta, such as penne, with the same sauce.

Serves 6

FOR THE PASTA
3 cups "00" flour, pasta flour, or all-purpose flour, plus a little extra if necessary
2 whole eggs
4–5 tablespoons white wine

FOR THE SAUCE
1¼ cups half-and-half cream
6 tablespoons pine nuts
2 tablespoons butter
2 heaping tablespoons marjoram leaves
¼ cup Parmesan, finely grated

TO SERVE
1 oz Parmesan
white pepper (or black, if you prefer)

Sift the flour into a mound on a work surface or into a bowl. Make a well in the center of the mound and add the eggs. Start to mix the two together using a fork, adding the wine little by little until a soft pliable dough is obtained. Knead the dough to ensure it is well-blended and smooth. Wrap the dough in plastic wrap and leave to rest for around 20 minutes.

Lightly dust the work surface, the pasta, and the rolling pin with flour to prevent sticking. If the pasta is too wet it will stick to the stamp so use a little more flour on the work surface and over the pasta, if necessary. Roll out the pasta to a thickness of about 1mm—it should be thin enough to see your fingers through it. Use a *corzetti* stamp, cookie cutter, or small drinking glass to cut out disc shapes. Traditionally they are 2 inches across. Then use a wooden *corzetti* stamp or improvise to create patterns on the pasta coins. As you finish each coin, place it in a single layer on a large, well-floured tray.

Bring a large, wide saucepan of salted water to a rolling boil and cook the *corzetti* for about 10–12 minutes. They need to be cooked through, but still al dente.

Meanwhile, make the sauce. Gently heat together all the ingredients in a large frying pan until the cheese melts into the cream. Adjust the seasoning as necessary but bear in mind that the Parmesan will add saltiness. When the *corzetti* are cooked through, drain and add to the sauce. Toss well and serve immediately.

Pesto Genovese
Genoese Pesto

Originally pesto was a sauce made from basil leaves during summer that, when sealed with oil, would last until winter. Over the years, chefs have adapted the recipe to use different ingredients. Even within Liguria, where *Pesto Genovese* originated, Ligurians argue over the best way to make it. My version is, I believe, the nearest one can get to the definitive Ligurian without growing your own Ligurian basil! Purists use a pestle and mortar, but if your kitchen doesn't have one, use a food processor or blender instead. I prefer to lightly toast the pine nuts to make their presence stronger, although it's fine to leave them raw.

Makes about 8 ounces (serves 6 as a main or 10 as a starter)

½ cup basil leaves, torn from their stems
1 small garlic clove, peeled
6 tablespoons pine nuts, lightly toasted
½ cup extra virgin olive oil
¼ cup Parmesan, finely grated
salt, to taste

Put the basil leaves into a mortar and crush them with the pestle until they become a pulp. Add the garlic and nuts and crush repeatedly. Using a metal spoon, stir in the olive oil, followed by the cheese. Add salt if required, but remember that Parmesan is salty.

Use immediately or, to store, pour into a sterile jar and top with a little olive oil to seal. This way it will last for up to 3 weeks in a covered container in the fridge.

Tip: Don't heat pesto; just stir into hot, drained pasta. In Liguria, pesto is served with with long green beans, chopped boiled potatoes, and *trofie*, a short dried pasta.

Pesto alle noci tostate
Toasted Walnut Pesto

Makes 12 ounces (serves 6 as a main or 10 as a starter)

1 cup walnuts (check they are not rancid)
1 cup finely chopped flat-leaf parsley, leaves stripped
½ garlic clove
½ cup grated Parmesan
⅔ cup olive oil
2 tablespoons ricotta
a generous pinch of salt and pepper

Preheat the oven to 400°F.

Spread the walnuts on a baking sheet and toast for 6 minutes or until fragrant. Once toasted, place the walnuts with the rest of the ingredients into a blender and process until the consistency is smooth.

Tip: Although it is delicious fresh, this is best left to stand for a day. To keep the pesto for 2–3 days, pour a layer of olive oil over the surface to act as a sealant and to stop it from drying out, cover, and refrigerate.

Pesto al limone e prezzemolo
Parsley and Lemon Pesto

This is a zingy, zesty summer sauce that can be enjoyed in many ways. Serve over hot or cold pasta with some cherry tomatoes, simply cooked fish, or seafood salad. Black pepper is rarely used in Liguria, the home of pesto, but a twist gives a little extra bite.

Serves 6

1 cup coarsely chopped parsley, either flat-leaf or curly
½ garlic clove, peeled
½ cup dried breadcrumbs (see page 30)
2 tablespoons lemon juice
⅔ cup olive oil
1 level teaspoon finely grated lemon zest
a pinch of salt
black pepper (optional)

If you have a food processor, simply put all the ingredients in it and process until a paste has formed. Alternatively, finely chop the parsley and garlic and mix in a bowl with the rest of the ingredients. Adjust the seasoning as necessary.

Use immediately or, to store, pour into a sterile jar (see page 482) and top with a little olive oil to seal. This way it will keep for up to 3 weeks, covered, in the fridge.

Passata di pomodorini di Gregorio
Gregorio's Cherry Tomato Passata

At the end of the tomato season in Italy, huge boxes of ripe and over-ripe tomatoes are sold off cheaply. In Sicily we made this delicious passata—a wonderful sauce to serve with pasta or to enhance other dishes where canned tomatoes are normally used. It can be stored in jars or frozen in portions for use throughout the winter and into the next season of fresh cherry tomatoes. Buy tomatoes at the end of summer when they are really ripe, dark red, and soft. Taste them to make sure you are happy with the sweetness. If you find your passata not sweet enough, add a little sugar to taste.

Makes 2½ lb

FOR THE FIRST STAGE
¾ cup olive oil
8 oz cherry tomatoes
1 cup diced carrots
1 cup diced celery
1 cup diced white onion
3 garlic cloves
2 teaspoons salt
1 teaspoon freshly ground
  black pepper

FOR THE SECOND STAGE
3 tablespoons olive oil
½ cup finely chopped
  white onion
1 fat garlic clove
salt and freshly ground black
  pepper
3 sprigs of basil
2 tablespoons sugar, as necessary

For the first stage, put the oil, tomatoes, carrots, celery, onion, garlic, and salt and pepper into a very large saucepan and cook over medium heat, stirring and breaking up the tomatoes. Bring to a boil and then reduce the heat to a simmer and cook for 50 minutes.

Pass the sauce through a food mill or *passetutto* to remove the skins. Alternatively, use a hand blender to create a purée.

For the second stage, heat the oil in a large pan and add the onion and garlic. Stir and season with salt and pepper. Cook for 7–10 minutes until soft, then add the basil.

Add the sieved tomatoes and cook for anywhere between 10 and 40 minutes. The variance in time allows for the water content of the tomatoes which differs from variety to variety. Just cook until the consistency becomes like a sauce: this may not take long, or you may have to wait patiently for it for reduce by half. Taste and adjust the seasoning with salt, pepper, and sugar, if necessary.

Pour into sterilized jam jars and boil again (follow the instructions on page 482) or freeze in batches.

Passata al pomodoro di Franca
Franca's Tomato Passata

The quintessential tomato passata is as much a part of the Italian kitchen as good stock. A ladleful is needed frequently to enrich a sauce or soup or to serve with pasta for a fast lunch. This is the simplest tomato passata I have come across in my travels. If you like garlic, add some and remove with the vegetables before processing.

Serves 6

3 tablespoons extra virgin
  olive oil
2 celery ribs, broken in half
1 carrot, cut in half lengthwise
1 red onion, peeled and cut
  in half
3 large sprigs of basil
2½ lb canned Italian plum
  tomatoes
½ teaspoon sugar
salt

Heat the oil in a large frying pan over medium heat. Briefly cook the vegetables and the basil in the hot oil, then add the tomatoes. Season with salt and bring to a boil. Reduce the heat and simmer for 30–60 minutes, depending on how much time you have: the longer it cooks, the more concentrated the flavor. Stir regularly, breaking up the tomatoes with a wooden spoon.

Discard the vegetables and basil and purée the tomatoes in a blender or food processor. (Or, if you prefer, leave the vegetables in the sauce and blend.)

Amatriciana
Tomato, Bacon, and Onion Sauce

Amatriciana is one of those classic Italian sauces made all over the world in various mutations. To be truly authentic it is made with *guanciale*, cured pig's cheek, but this is hard to find and quite fatty for my taste. I use pancetta, if I can get hold of it, or softly smoked bacon instead. The sauce hails from Amatrice in the mountains of Lazio. Apparently the dish, originally called *La Gricia*, came from the mountain people of the area, who simply fried *guanciale*, pasta, black pepper, and pecorino; tomatoes were a later addition by the wealthy.

Serves 4 as a main or 6 as a starter

6 tablespoons olive oil
1 medium white onion, finely chopped
a pinch of salt and a good pinch of black pepper
8 oz pancetta, or bacon, chopped
⅓ cup dry white wine
1 x 28 oz can Italian plum tomatoes, crushed with your hands
¼ cup finely grated *Pecorino Romano* or Parmesan

Heat the oil in a large pan, add the onion and season. Cook for a few minutes, then add the pancetta and cook, stirring, until lightly browned. Add the wine and allow to reduce. Add the crushed tomatoes and gently simmer for 1 hour, until reduced.

Adjust the seasoning and serve with hot pasta and grated cheese.

Salsa veloce di pomodorini
Quickest Tomato Sauce for Gnocchi Parmigiana and Meatballs

No excuses for store-bought sauces here! This sauce is *pronto* in 5 minutes, but if you can leave it for 15, it tastes even better.

Serves 2

1½ tablespoons extra virgin olive oil

1 garlic clove, peeled and lightly crushed with the flat of a knife

salt, to taste

1 large sprig of basil (about 4 big leaves)

1 x 14 oz can cherry tomatoes

2 teaspoons sugar, if necessary

Heat the oil in a pan and cook the garlic and salt for 1 minute. Add the basil and then the cherry tomatoes. Cook for a minimum of 5 minutes and a maximum of 20. Season and taste—if the sauce is a little bitter, add some sugar. Serve with hot pasta tossed into it.

Variation:
As with Gino's Tomato Salsa (see page 92), you can chop ½ chile in with the garlic at the beginning to produce a really quick *Arrabiata*—a tomato and chile sauce.

Salsa di noci e panna
Walnut and Cream Pasta Sauce

This recipe is from a mountain village outside Parma where my friend Stefano Borella's grandparents lived. Every year they would spend hours making the traditional *cappelletti* to serve on Christmas Eve (see page 187). This sauce would be made quickly to enjoy with the trimmings of leftover pasta. Always taste the walnuts first; rancid ones will ruin the sauce. That open bag in the back of your cupboard will have to be thrown out!

Serves 2–4

8 oz dried pasta (tagliatelle, penne, farfalle)
4 tablespoons salted butter
1 garlic clove, peeled and lightly crushed
1 cup walnuts, coarsely chopped
¾ cup heavy cream
¼ cup Parmesan, finely grated

Bring a large pot of salted water to a boil and cook the pasta according to the package instructions.

Meanwhile, melt the butter in a frying pan and add the garlic and nuts. Cook over a medium heat for a few minutes, until the garlic is softened and the nuts have taken on the flavor of the garlic and butter. Keep stirring so that the nuts and butter do not burn. Add the cream and stir well. Turn the heat down and let the sauce reduce and thicken. Remove the garlic.

When the pasta is cooked, drain it and add to the sauce in the frying pan. Toss the mixture together and serve in warmed bowls with the grated Parmesan.

Tip: If the sauce separates, add a drop of hot cooking water from the pasta.

Pasta al cartoccio con frutti di mare e pomodorini
Pasta with Seafood and Cherry Tomatoes "al Cartoccio"

Literally translated, *al cartoccio* means "cooked in a parcel." The incredible flavors of the seafood are contained inside, resulting in a wonderful aroma when the paper parcel is cut open. The pasta really soaks up all the juices for enhanced flavor.

Serves 4

4 tablespoons extra virgin olive oil
1 red chile, seeded and sliced
2 garlic cloves, peeled and lightly crushed
salt and freshly ground black pepper
1 lb assorted seafood (tuna, salmon, shrimp, monkfish, squid, clams, mussels)
12 oz vine-ripened cherry tomatoes, halved
1 sprig of flat-leaf parsley, leaves stripped and chopped
½ cup dry white wine
12 oz spaghetti or linguine
4 large sheets of parchment paper

Preheat the oven to 400°F and bring a large pot of salted water to a boil. Drop the pasta into the boiling water and cook for 2 minutes less than the package recommendations.

Put a large frying pan over medium heat and heat the oil. Add the chile, garlic, seasonings, and cook for 2 minutes. Add the seafood and continue cooking for another 2 minutes. Add the cherry tomatoes and parsley and cook for 2 minutes. Lastly, add the wine and simmer until its scent has dissipated, around 3–4 minutes. Drain the pasta and add to the seafood mixture in the pan. Toss everything together.

Spread the sheets of parchment onto a work surface and, using tongs, divide the pasta into four even portions. Wrap each parcel by pulling up the parchment from the front and back to the center. Fold the top edges over and over again, leaving the seam in the center. Turn the side ends inwards several times to seal in the juices. Place the parcels on a baking sheet and bake for 5 minutes. Remove, unwrap the center seam to let out the steam, and bring to the table still *al cartoccio*.

Tip: Extra ⅓ cup of shellfish stock adds a wonderful flavor to the sauce.

Penne con verdure arrosto e mandorle tostate
Penne with Roasted Vegetables and Toasted Almonds

Here, crunchy almonds contrast with roasted vegetables. Vary the ingredients with the season, for example, asparagus and pine nuts in spring, and mushrooms and chestnuts in autumn.

Serves 4 as a main or 6 as a starter

½ large eggplant, cut into bite-size sticks
1 red bell pepper, cut into bite-size sticks
1 zucchini, cut into bite-size sticks
1 medium red onion, cut in half, then each half cut into 6 segments
4 oz green beans, trimmed and cut in half
4 garlic cloves, unpeeled, crushed
1 red chile, sliced and seeded
salt and freshly ground black pepper
1 large sprig of thyme, leaves stripped
½ cup extra virgin olive oil, plus extra for drizzling
1 head broccoli (about 300g), broken into bite-size florets
12 oz penne, or any short pasta
½ cup sliced almonds
¼ cup grated Parmesan

Preheat the oven to 350°F and bring a large saucepan of salted water to the boil.

Put all the vegetables except the broccoli with the chile on a baking sheet. Generously sprinkle with salt, pepper and the thyme, and drizzle with the oil. Using your hands, toss the vegetables until well coated with oil. (Oil stops the vegetables from burning and is used in the sauce, so don't be stingy.) Put the baking sheet in the oven and bake for 20 minutes.

Halfway through cooking, add the broccoli and toss to combine with the other vegetables and oil. Return to the oven. Bring a large pan of water to a boil and cook the dried pasta, if using, according to the package instructions, or until al dente if using fresh.

Toast the almonds in a pan in the oven for about 5 minutes, checking regularly. When the pasta is cooked, drain and combine it with the roasted vegetables and almonds in a warm serving bowl. Drizzle with more olive oil to taste and serve topped with the Parmesan.

Trofie con piselli, pancetta, porri e panna
Bacon, Peas, and Leek with a Cream Sauce and Trofie

This is a classic Italian dish but using leek rather than the usual onion. Throughout the year this can be adapted according to the season and made with fresh or frozen peas and full grown or baby leeks. The sweetness of peas and leeks is delicious with the salty pancetta and makes it incredibly addictive. I cannot lie and say that this is a light dish, but it is so flavorsome that it is worth the indulgence. If you cannot get hold of pancetta, use smoked bacon instead.

Serves 4

12 oz *trofie* or similar pasta
8 oz frozen or shelled fresh peas
3 tablespoons extra virgin olive oil
1 large leek, finely chopped
12 oz pancetta
salt and freshly ground black pepper
⅓ cup heavy cream
¼ cup grated Parmesan

Bring a large saucepan of salted water to a boil and cook the pasta according to the package instructions. If you are using fresh peas, drop them into the water at the same time as the pasta; for frozen peas, drop them in 4 minutes before the end of the cooking time.

Meanwhile, pour the olive oil into a large frying pan over medium heat. Cook the leeks and pancetta together until golden. Add only a little salt (as the pancetta is already salty) and a good twist of black pepper.

When the pasta and peas are cooked, drain them and stir into the ingredients in the frying pan. Add the cream and toss or stir everything together until heated through. Stir in the Parmesan and serve immediately in warmed bowls.

Ragù alla Bolognese
Bolognese Ragù

On a mission to find the perfect Bolognese, I once ate ten in Bologna, all delicious and all quite different from one another in their ingredients and the shape of the pieces of meat. Each was delivered as the quintessential *ragù di Bologna*, so I was none the wiser; in fact I was more struck by the lightness and thinness of the pasta than by any mind-blowing difference in the sauce. Further research and speaking to as many Bolognese as possible has led me to conclude that there is no definitive recipe, so I have experimented with many and chosen the one I like most. The chicken livers and pancetta make this ragù really rich in flavor, and the milk softens and melds the flavors together. Don't be tempted to use smoked pancetta or bacon, though, because it will completely dominate the dish.

Serves 8 as a main or 10 as a starter

1 quantity of Soffritto (see page 125), omitting the garlic and rosemary

1¼ lb ground beef

8 oz unsmoked pancetta or unsmoked bacon or *lardo*, minced in a food processor or chopped finely by hand

8 oz chicken livers, finely chopped

¾ cup dry red wine

1 x 28 oz can Italian plum tomatoes

¾ cup water, to rinse out the tomato can

⅔ cup whole milk

1 teaspoon salt

Make the *soffritto*, frying the vegetables in hot oil for 15–20 minutes or until softened. Add the ground beef, pancetta, and chicken livers and cook for 10–15 minutes over medium heat, stirring frequently until the meat is browned and the water has been released and evaporated. The mixture should sizzle as it is stirred. Add the wine and cook over high heat for 5 minutes until it has separated from the oil. Then add the tomatoes; rinse out the can with the water, and add this too. Reduce the heat to a simmer and leave to cook for 1 hour. Stir in the milk, and leave to cook for another 30 minutes. Adjust the seasoning to taste.

Ragù di lepre
Hare Ragù

Very Tuscan, this is traditionally served with pappardelle. Hare is strongly flavored and tough; it needs the marinade to tenderize it.

Serves 8–10

1 large hare, jointed

FOR THE MARINADE
1 bottle of dry red wine
1 medium carrot, cut into ¾ in chunks
1 large celery rib, cut into ¾ in chunks
1 small onion, cut into 8 pieces
2 sprigs of rosemary
10 black peppercorns
10 juniper berries
10 cloves
6 bay leaves

FOR THE CASSEROLE
⅓ cup olive oil
2 bay leaves
3 tablespoons chopped fresh rosemary
2 garlic cloves, lightly crushed
4 oz chicken livers or calf's liver
1 cup dry red wine
1 cup dry white wine
5 tablespoons tomato purée
1 x 14 oz can Italian plum tomatoes
1½ quarts meat, game, or chicken stock

Put the hare into a large container with all the ingredients for the marinade. Cover and refrigerate overnight.

The following day, strain the hare, herbs, and vegetables through a colander, discarding the wine. Remove the pieces of hare and set aside.

To make a *soffritto*, finely chop the vegetables by hand or using a food processor. Heat the oil in a large frying pan and cook the vegetables with bay leaves, stirring frequently, for around 15–20 minutes or until they have softened and changed in color from bright and sharp to soft and golden.

Finely chop the rosemary with the garlic and liver, then add to the *soffritto*. Continue to cook for 5 minutes. Add the hare and cook for another 5 minutes, until it starts to stick to the pan, then add the wine. Reduce for a few minutes, then add the purée, tomatoes, and stock. Cook for about 3 hours, or until the meat is tender and falling off the bones. Allow to cool, then remove the hare pieces and pull off the meat, discarding the bones. Return the meat to the pot and allow it to warm through. Serve with pappardelle or polenta.

Ragù di agnello
Lamb Ragù

This is from Abruzzo, where Sabia makes a ragù typical of the region. She serves it with pasta made using a *chitarra*—wood with strings stretched over it to cut the pasta.

Serves 8 as a main or 10 as a starter

1 quantity of fresh pasta (see pages 148–149) made with 3 eggs and 3 cups flour, or 1 lb dried pasta, such as spaghetti

1 red or white onion, finely chopped
1 carrot, finely chopped
1 red bell pepper, finely chopped
1 cup olive oil
salt and freshly ground black pepper
1 lb lean lamb, coarsely cut into ¾ in cubes
1 lb minced pork
¾ cup white wine
1 x 28 oz can Italian plum tomatoes
¼ cup pecorino, finely grated

Make a *soffritto* from the onion, carrot, and pepper by chopping them finely and cooking them in the olive oil. Season generously with salt and pepper. After about 10 minutes, when the vegetables have softened, add the meat and brown thoroughly. Allow any water to evaporate and, when the meat is dry and sizzling, pour in the wine. Reduce for a few minutes and then add the tomatoes. If the sauce looks a little dry before the meat is cooked through, add a little hot water. Simmer the sauce, stirring frequently, for around 1–1½ hours. Serve with the hot pasta stirred into it and pecorino on top.

Ragù alla Toscana
Tuscan Ragù

A Tuscan ragù is usually made with a mixture of ground pork and beef and flavored with rosemary or thyme as well as a good local red wine. This is the recipe my husband Giancarlo grew up with. His father made it every 2 weeks and stored it in jars in the fridge until he made the next batch. At exactly one o'clock every day he would eat a little bowl of ragù, served quite dry, tossed into short pasta with a sprinkling of Tuscan pecorino.

Serves 8 as a main or 10 as a starter

1 quantity of Soffritto (see recipe page 125), including the garlic and rosemary

1 lb ground beef
1 lb ground pork
1 cup dry red wine
1 x 28 oz can Italian plum tomatoes
¼ cup tomato paste
salt and freshly ground black pepper

Make the *soffritto*, cooking the vegetables in hot oil for 15–20 minutes or until softened. Add the ground meats and cook for 10–15 minutes over medium heat, stirring frequently, until the meat is browned and the water has been released and evaporated. The mixture should be sizzling as it is stirred. Add the wine and cook over a high heat for 5 minutes, until the wine has separated from the oil. At this point add the tomatoes; rinse out the can with a little water and add this too, along with the paste. Turn down to a simmer and leave to cook for 1½ hours, stirring frequently, until the sauce is darker in color and rich in taste. Adjust the seasoning to taste.

Besciamella
Béchamel Sauce

The Italians and French will forever argue as to who invented béchamel sauce as we know it. The Florentines claim it is their recipe, taken to France by Catherine de Medici and her cooks when she married Henry II of France in 1533. The sauce is now made all over the world and is essential to many Italian dishes. I was taught to make it the Italian way, by putting the roux (the butter and flour) into the milk all in one go. It works well and is quick and easy. When recipes call for 1 quart of béchamel, such as Seafood Lasagne (see page 183), follow the same method, but use the second list of ingredients. Season the sauce well with pepper, salt and plenty of nutmeg—the final dish will be much better for it.

Makes 1½ quarts

1½ quarts milk
1 small onion, peeled and
  cut in half
2 bay leaves
¼ nutmeg, finely grated
salt and black pepper, to taste
10 tablespoons butter
1¼ cups all-purpose flour

Makes 1 quart

1 quart milk
1 small onion, peeled and cut
  in half
1 bay leaf
a good pinch each of nutmeg
salt and black pepper
8 tablespoons butter
½ cup all-purpose flour

Put the milk, onion, bay leaves, nutmeg, salt and black pepper into a medium saucepan over the heat and bring to a gentle boil.

Meanwhile, make a roux: melt the butter in a small saucepan and stir in the flour. Cook the butter and flour for a few minutes over a medium heat, stirring constantly. Remove the bay leaves and onion from the milk, then add the roux, whisking furiously. Cook until it thickens, adjust the seasoning to taste and remove from the heat. Cover the surface of the béchamel with plastic wrap or a circle of dampened parchment paper to prevent a skin from forming.

Tip: If, when you come to use the béchamel, you find it too thick, add a little milk to thin it out. Reheating it also helps.

Rigatoni al ragù bianco
White Ragù with Rigatoni

This is a simple dish that is quick to prepare and cook. My children like the big tube pasta, which they fill up with meat sauce. Leftovers can be reheated in an ovenproof dish with extra cream and Parmesan for delicious baked pasta. You can use leftover meat from a roast —leftover Roast Pork (see page 316) with all its herby stuffing is great. Simply pop chunks of cooked meat into a food processor and process to mince. Brown the meat in hot oil; and then add the sage leaves and wine.

Serves 4

4 tablespoons olive oil
1 small white onion, finely chopped
1 large garlic clove, finely chopped
salt and freshly ground black pepper
1 lb ground turkey, veal, pork, or chicken,
  raw or cooked
8 sage leaves, coarsely chopped
⅓ cup dry white wine
1 cup chicken stock
12 oz rigatoni
⅓ cup cream

TO SERVE
olive oil
¼ cup grated Parmesan

Bring a large saucepan of salted water to a boil. Heat the oil in a pan over medium heat and add the onion, garlic, and salt and pepper. Cook for about 2 minutes, then add the ground meat and reduce the heat. If using raw meat, allow the water to evaporate from it. Once the meat is browned, add half the sage leaves.

Next add the wine and allow to reduce for a couple of minutes. Add the stock, stir well, reduce the heat, and allow to simmer. Adjust the seasoning as necessary.

Meanwhile, put the pasta in the boiling water and cook until al dente. After 5 minutes, add the cream to the ragù and simmer gently, stirring frequently. When the pasta is cooked, drain, add to the ragù, and toss to combine. Serve with a drizzle of olive oil, the remaining sage, and a generous sprinkling of Parmesan.

Penne con gamberoni e zucchini
Jumbo Shrimp and Zucchini Pasta

This dish has always flown out of the door whenever it is on the menu at our restaurants. The color combination alone is lovely: plump pink shrimp with pale green zucchini. If you don't have penne, a cut pasta such as linguine or tagliatelle will also work. Homemade stock is not difficult to make and really brings this dish to life. Save a little in the fridge for another time; it is well worth it.

Serves 4 as a main or 6 as a starter

20 jumbo shrimp
⅓ cup shellfish stock (see page 138)
12 oz penne
4 tablespoons olive oil
2 zucchini, cut into sticks about 1½ in long
  and ¼ in thick
½–1 dried chile, thinly sliced
2 garlic cloves
salt and freshly ground black pepper
3 tablespoons Prosecco or other dry white wine
2 tablespoons heavy cream (optional)

Shell the shrimp, reserving the shells for stock, and remove the black vein along the back. Make the shellfish stock using the shells or, if you already have stock prepared, freeze these shells to make another batch in the future.

Bring a large saucepan of salted water to a boil. Drop in the pasta and cook until al dente.

Meanwhile heat the oil and sauté the zucchini, chile, garlic, and salt and pepper until softened slightly. Add the shrimp and, when just cooked, add the wine. Allow to reduce for a couple of minutes, then add the stock. Allow to reduce for a further couple of minutes and then add the cream, if using. Keep warm over low heat until the pasta is cooked, then drain and toss into the sauce. Serve right away in warmed bowls.

Vincisgrassi
Layered Pasta with Porcini and Parma Ham

Franco and Ann Taruschio are famous for having served this as their signature dish at The Walnut Tree Inn in Abergavenny, renowned as the first ever gastro pub. *Vincisgrassi* is a speciality of Le Marche, which is Franco's region. Apparently, this dish was named after an Austrian general, Windisch Graetz, who spent time with his troops in Ancona in 1799 during the Napoleonic war. This recipe is based on the Taruschio's version.

Serves 6

1 quantity of pasta made from 2 eggs and 2 cups flour (see page 149)
1½ quarts Béchamel Sauce (see page 175)

2 oz dried porcini mushrooms
2 tablespoons olive oil
8 oz Parma ham, thinly sliced
⅔ cup half and half cream
1 garlic clove, lightly crushed
3 tablespoons finely chopped flat-leaf parsley
1 cup freshly grated Parmesan
2 tablespoons butter
salt and freshly ground black pepper

truffle oil or white truffle shavings, to finish

Make the pasta as on page 149 and let it rest. Soak the mushrooms in hot water for 30 minutes, then strain through a sieve. Heat the oil in a pan over high heat and cook the mushrooms and garlic for 5 minutes, then set aside.

Meanwhile, make the béchamel and stir in the ham, cream, mushrooms, and parsley. Preheat the oven to 425°F. Roll out the pasta to 1mm thick, cut into 6 inch squares and cook in boiling salted water until al dente, then drain on dry kitchen towels.

Butter an ovenproof dish measuring 9 x 13 inches and cover the bottom with a layer of pasta sheets, tearing them to fit and allowing them to wrinkle. Pour in a layer of béchamel and then a sprinkling of Parmesan and a few dots of butter. Add another layer of pasta and continue until the sauce and pasta are used up. Finish with Parmesan and a few drops of truffle oil or shavings of white truffle. Bake for 20 minutes or until bubbling hot.

Pasta al forno
Neapolitan Baked Pasta

One evening I was taken high into the Cilento mountains—so high our ears popped. We ran in the wind and rain to the warmth of Fabio's restaurant perched on a cliff and ate *pasta al forno*—probably the best pasta dish I have ever eaten. Fabio was guarded about his recipes but luckily my friend Maria's aunt, who is from the same area, was with us and told us how it was made.

Serves 6 as a main

FOR THE TOMATO SAUCE
5 tablespoons olive oil
1 large red onion, finely chopped
2 garlic cloves, crushed
salt and pepper
2½ lb canned Italian plum tomatoes
2 sprigs of basil
1 teaspoon sugar (optional)

FOR THE MEATBALLS
4 oz ground pork
4 oz ground beef
3 oz salami, diced (optional)
2 medium eggs, beaten
¼ cup fresh white breadcrumbs
salt, to taste
flour, for dredging
3 tablespoons olive oil

3 medium eggs
8 oz penne
1½ tablespoons olive oil or sunflower oil
4 oz Parmesan, finely grated
4 oz Parma ham, cut into bite-size strips
8 oz mozzarella, torn into bite-size pieces

Preheat the oven to 350°F. First make the tomato sauce by heating the olive oil in a large pot and cook the onion, garlic, and salt and pepper until soft. Then add the tomatoes and basil. Bring to a boil, then simmer for 30–40 minutes, stirring frequently with a wooden spoon to break up the tomatoes. Adjust the seasoning to taste and, if necessary, add a little sugar.

Meanwhile, make the meatballs. Mix together the ground meat, salami, if using, eggs, and breadcrumbs in a bowl. Roll into balls the size of marbles (with wet hands is easiest), coat lightly in flour, tapping off the excess. Heat the oil in a frying pan and lightly fry the meatballs, turning to seal on all sides.

Boil the eggs for 8 minutes. Drain, crack the shells, and drop the eggs into cold water to prevent dark rings from forming around the yolk.

Cook the pasta in boiling salted water until al dente, drain, and leave to cool, tossed with a little olive or sunflower oil. Shell the eggs and chop them coarsely. Combine the tomato sauce with the pasta and meatballs.

Put a layer of the pasta mixture in the bottom of a 9 x 13 inch lasagne dish. Scatter over some of the chopped eggs, grated Parmesan, Parma ham, and mozzarella over the top. Continue to layer until the dish is full, ending with a layer of pasta topped with mozzarella and Parmesan. Bake for 20–30 minutes, or until golden brown and bubbling.

Conchiglioni ripieni di manzo, piselli e Parmigiano
Conchiglioni Stuffed with Beef, Peas, and Parmesan

Conchiglioni are large, ridged pasta shells that are perfect for stuffing. Although I love fresh vegetables, for this recipe I like to use canned peas for their sweetness.

Serves 8

1 quantity of Franca's Tomato
 Passata (see page 166)
1 lb *conchiglione*

FOR THE BÉCHAMEL
1 quart milk
freshly grated nutmeg
1 small onion or 1 shallot,
 peeled
salt and pepper
2 bay leaves
8 tablespoons butter
¾ cup flour

FOR THE STUFFING
2 lb ground beef
2 cups canned peas (or use
 frozen or fresh peas, cooked)
2 cups Parmesan, finely grated
1 egg
salt and pepper

olive oil or sunflower oil, for
 coating
freshly grated Parmesan

Preheat the oven to 350°F. Bring a large saucepan of salted water to a boil and, once boiling, add the pasta and cook until al dente.

Meanwhile, make the béchamel. Heat the milk in a saucepan with the nutmeg, onion or shallot, salt, pepper, and bay leaves. At the same time, melt the butter in another saucepan and stir in the flour to make a roux. Cook for 1–2 minutes, stirring all the time. Add this roux to the milk all at once as the milk is coming to a boil. Now whisk furiously until the sauce has thickened. Remove from the heat, check the seasoning, and cover the surface with plastic wrap to prevent a skin from forming.

When the pasta is cooked, drain it and toss with a little sunflower or olive oil. Lay out the *conchiglioni* on 1 or 2 large baking sheets, spaced apart so that they do not stick together and set aside.

Put the ingredients for the stuffing in a large bowl and mix everything together with 1⅓ cups of the béchamel to bind it, using either your hands or a spoon. Then use a small spoon to stuff each *conchiglione* with the filling. Place each filled shell back on the sheet, face down. Once you have filled all the *conchiglioni*, pour the tomato passata evenly over the surface of the pasta. Top with the remaining béchamel. Sprinkle with Parmesan and bake in the oven for 30–40 minutes, or until the surface is brown and bubbling.

Traditional Lasagne

It is almost impossible to say which is the traditional lasagne in Italy—there are just so many varieties—but here is a recipe that will fit the bill, serve a large family, and taste really good. Use this as your basic recipe; we often add porcini mushrooms, either dried and rehydrated or frozen, and adding sliced mozzarella and extra Parmesan between the layers will enrich your lasagne. I have chosen Giancarlo's Tuscan Ragù as the meat component but that's purely personal—the other ragùs are equally good.

Serves 10 as a main or 12 as a starter

FOR THE FRESH PASTA
2 cups "00" flour, pasta flour, or all-purpose flour
2 medium free-range eggs

FOR THE LASAGNE
1½ quarts Béchamel Sauce (see recipe page 175)
1 quantity of Tuscan Ragù (see recipe page 174)
18–20 sheets of fresh or dried pasta
¼ cup finely grated Parmesan

First make the fresh pasta, following the instructions in the masterclass on pages 148–149. After it has rested, put the pasta through a pasta machine on the thinnest setting (about 1mm thick) or roll it out thinly with a rolling pin until you can see your hand through it. Cut into rectangles, roughly 3½ x 7 inches—you will get between 18 and 20 sheets. Put these, a few at a time, into boiling salted water for a couple of minutes, until cooked al dente. Remove using a pair of tongs and plunge into cold water to stop the cooking while you boil the next batch. When the pasta sheets are cool to the touch, lay them on a clean kitchen towel to dry.

If using dried pasta, precook as required, following the package instructions. Preheat the oven to 350°F.

Select a lasagne dish measuring 9 x 13 inches and spread a little béchamel over the bottom. Next make a layer of the ragù (don't worry if it is not too even; the odd bump of ragù is fine). Top with a layer of cooked lasagne, without letting the sheets overlap too much. Repeat the layers of béchamel, ragù, and pasta and build up about four layers in this way, finishing with a layer of béchamel. Sprinkle with Parmesan and transfer to the oven for 30–40 minutes, or until golden brown on top and bubbling at the edges.

Variations:
Add 1 oz rehydrated porcini mushrooms (dry weight) to the ragù.

Shred 1 or 2 balls of mozzarella and add to the layers.

Instead of Tuscan Ragù, use double the quantity of Tomato, Sausage, and Fennel Seed Ragù (see page 201).

Green Lasagne

Lasagne from Bologna is frequently made with green pasta flavored with spinach. It has many layers to it and, of course, contains the famous Ragù Bolognese.

Serves 10 as a main or 12 as a starter

FOR THE FRESH PASTA
2 cups "00" flour or pasta flour
2 egg yolks
4 oz spinach, cooked from fresh or frozen and thoroughly squeezed dry

FOR THE LASAGNE
1½ quarts Béchamel Sauce (see page 175)
1 quantity of Bolognese Ragù (see page 172)
18–20 sheets fresh or dried pasta sheets
¼ cup finely grated Parmesan

Make the pasta according to the Spinach Pasta Masterclass on page 150.

Follow the instructions for the Traditional Lasagne on the left.

For extra richness, add another ½ cup of finely grated Parmesan or mozzarella between the layers.

Giancarlo's lasagne

Lasagne di verdure al forno
Roasted Vegetable Lasagne

We have so many requests from people to know how to make a vegetarian lasagne, so here it is. Roasting the vegetables first concentrates their flavors, giving more impact to the final dish. Vary your choice according to the season so that you are always buying vegetables with maximum flavor. This is also a great way to use up extra vegetables; there is no need to stick to the list and quantities below; for example 1 pepper and 3 zucchini or a roasted fennel bulb would make a marvellous alternative. Be inventive, and let the contents of your fridge inspire you!

Serves 10 as a main or 12 as a starter

FOR THE TOMATO SAUCE

1 x 28 oz can Italian plum tomatoes
5 tablespoons olive oil
½ red onion, finely chopped
1 garlic clove, peeled and lightly crushed
salt and freshly ground black pepper
1 sprig of basil
2 heaping teaspoons sugar

FOR THE ROASTED VEGETABLES

1 medium eggplant, cut into slices ½ inch thick
5 tablespoons olive oil
1 zucchini, cut into slices ¼ inch thick
2 red bell peppers, trimmed, seeded, and cut into roughly 10 pieces each
12 oz cultivated button or other mushrooms, sliced
salt and freshly ground black pepper
4 sprigs of thyme
2 garlic cloves, crushed in their skins

FOR THE LASAGNE

20 fresh or dried pasta sheets (see page 149), cooked
1½ quarts Béchamel Sauce (see page 175)
1 x 4 oz mozzarella ball
¾ cup finely grated Parmesan

First make the tomato sauce by tipping the canned tomatoes into a bowl. Rinse out the tins with about ⅓ cup water and add this to the bowl, too. Crush the tomatoes with your hands to break them up. Heat the olive oil over a medium heat and cook the onion and garlic with salt and pepper for 7–10 minutes, or until soft, then add the tomatoes and basil. Bring to a boil, then simmer for 30–40 minutes, stirring frequently with a wooden spoon to break up the tomatoes. Adjust the seasoning and, if necessary, add sugar to taste.

Meanwhile, preheat the oven to 400°F. Lay the eggplant slices on a baking tray lined with parchment paper and brush with 2 tablespoons of the olive oil. Bake for 20 minutes. Remove from the oven and tip into a bowl.

Lay the zucchini and peppers in a single layer in a roasting pan and brush with 2 tablespoons of the oil. Season with the salt, tuck the thyme sprigs under the peppers, and put the garlic between the vegetables. Bake for 20 minutes. Remove from the oven and turn into the bowl with the eggplant.

Cook the mushrooms in the remaining oil with plenty of salt and pepper, until softened. Remove from the heat and mix with the roasted vegetables.

Select a lasagne dish measuring 9 x 13 inches and spread a little of the béchamel over the bottom. Next, make a layer of vegetables, tomato sauce and top with the cooked lasagne, without allowing the sheets to overlap too much. Slice and layer in the mozzarella, along with ½ cup of the Parmesan. Repeat the layers of béchamel, vegetables, tomato sauce, pasta, and cheeses and build up about four layers in this way, finishing with a layer of béchamel. Scatter with the remaining Parmesan and transfer to the oven for around 30–40 minutes, or until the lasagne is golden brown on top and bubbling at the edges.

Variation:
Add some circles of goat's cheese to the top before baking as above.

Lasagne ai frutti di mare
Seafood Lasagne

The fantastic flavor of this dish is due to its shellfish stock. Seafood has a subtle flavor, so it always needs the help of a good stock. The shellfish can be altered according to the season and availability. Try a mixture of clams, squid, mussels, large and small shrimp, and meaty fish, such as tuna, cod, or salmon.

Serves 8

FOR THE FISH SAUCE
2 lb mixed shellfish and fish (raw shell-on shrimp, well-scrubbed clams and mussels, cubed salmon and seabass)
1¼ cups water
6 tablespoons extra virgin olive oil
1 white onion, finely chopped
⅓ cup dry white wine
¼–½ red chile, depending on heat, finely chopped
1 garlic clove, finely chopped
salt and freshly ground black pepper
a handful of flat-leaf parsley, finely chopped
1 tablespoon tomato paste

FOR THE LASAGNE
1 quart Béchamel Sauce (see page 175)
1 quantity of fresh pasta made with 2 cups flour and 2 eggs (see page 149) or pre-cooked, dried lasagna sheets
½ cup finely grated Parmesan (optional)

Remove the heads and shells from the shrimp, keeping them for stock. Keep the shrimp in the fridge until later. Put the clams and mussels in a pan with half the water, cover and bring to a boil. Simmer until the shells open, 5–10 minutes. Discard any that remain closed. Strain and reserve the cooking liquor. Remove the meat from the shells and set aside, discarding the shells.

To make the stock: Heat half the olive oil over medium–high heat and add half the onion. Smash the prawn shells and heads with a rolling pin and add them to the pan. Cook, stirring, for 5 minutes. Add the wine and allow to reduce for 5 minutes. Add the remaining water and leave to simmer until reduced by half.

Cook the remaining onion in a large frying pan over medium heat for 5 minutes, or until soft. Add the chile, garlic, and salt and pepper, and cook for 1 minute more. Add the shrimp and fish and carefully stir together, coating the fish without breaking it up. Strain the stock into the pan, discarding the heads and shells. Add the paste, mussels, clams and their cooking liquor and simmer for 5–10 minutes, until the fish is cooked. Remove from the heat and stir in the parsley.

Preheat the oven to 350°F. Spread 2 ladlefuls of the béchamel over the bottom of a 9 x 13 inch lasagne dish. Next make a layer of seafood with some of its liquid. Top with a layer of pasta, without allowing the sheets to overlap. Repeat the layers of béchamel, seafood, and pasta; building up to 4 layers and finishing with béchamel. Scatter with the Parmesan, if using, and bake for 30–40 minutes, until bubbling.

Gregorio likes the combination of Parmesan and fish, whereas most Italians raise their eyes to heaven when you ask for cheese with seafood dishes! I will leave the decision up to you.

Cannelloni alle erbette estive
Summer Herb Cannelloni

Often cannelloni is simply stuffed with spinach and ricotta but, to give more impact after the effort to make the dish, I bump up the flavor with soft-leaf herbs, such as basil, chives, parsley, and oregano. Be generous with them, and keep tasting the filling to make sure you are happy with the flavor. Fresh pasta is best for perfect cooking but, when short on time, dried pasta tubes are a good compromise. Usually these are pre-cooked as fresh pasta and then filled with a pastry bag, but it is best to follow the instructions on the packet. A bit of advance planning when cutting pasta is a good idea, but knowledge comes with practice. The pasta expands by around 20 percent during cooking, making it difficult to judge the size beforehand. For this recipe, I have trimmed the sheets of pasta to make two rows in two layers to fit inside the dish. Giancarlo and I had a massive fight over this: he told me cannelloni should *never* be piled more than two high, but I once successfully made a pyramid from them and each one became crispy along the edge. It looked triumphant! Giancarlo had to eat his words—and my cannelloni—afterwards. So experiment as much as you wish, but don't invite an Italian to lunch that day.

Serves 8

FOR THE CANNELLONI

1 quantity of fresh pasta made from 3 cups "00" flour or all-purpose flour and 3 eggs (see page 149)
1 quart of Béchamel Sauce (see page 175)
1 quart of Tomato Passata (Franca's or Gregorio's, see page 166)
¼ cup Parmesan, finely grated

FOR THE FILLING

8 oz cooked spinach, squeezed of water (the pre-cooked weight of fresh spinach would be 1 lb)
1 lb ricotta, drained
1 cup herbs (parsley, basil, chives, marjoram, and oregano), finely chopped
½ cup Parmesan, finely grated
½ teaspoon nutmeg, to taste
salt and freshly ground black pepper

Preheat the oven to 350°F.

First prepare the filling: making sure the spinach is well squeezed of water, then mix all the filling ingredients together in a bowl and season to taste.

Roll out the pasta to roughly 2mm thick—using the setting before last on a pasta machine. The pasta should not be too thin for cannelloni. Cut the pasta into rectangles. The pasta machine is 6 inches wide, so I get two rectangles out of one width. For this dish I used 24 sheets of pasta measuring 3 x 6 inches. When cooked, they expand to around 4 x 6½ inches. Cook the sheets in batches in salted boiling water for 3 minutes, then remove with tongs and drop into ice water. After a minute in the cold water, lift the sheets out and stretch them onto clean kitchen towels. Trim the pasta sheets to size, if necessary, and use right away.

Select a lasagne dish measuring 9 x 13 inches and spoon a layer of the béchamel into the dish.

Put a heaping tablespoon of filling onto each pasta sheet.

Roll up the pasta leaving an overlap of about 1 inch— no more or it will be chewy and undercooked.

Place the cannelloni onto the béchamel layer seam-side down.

Spoon on a layer of the tomato and the béchamel sauces. I don't like to cover the pasta completely with sauce, as I like the crispy edges where it is uncovered.

Now build up the second layer and spoon on the sauces as before. Finish by sprinkling with Parmesan. Bake the cannelloni for 30 minutes, or until browned and crispy at the edges.

Variation:
Other filling ideas are endless, but one that is popular in our house is chicken and cheese. I mince leftover cooked chicken with a handful of parsley in a food processor and then stir in ricotta, nutmeg, grated Parmesan, and season with salt and pepper to taste. Cook in the same way as the Summer Herb Cannelloni.

Pasta
MASTERCLASS

MAKING
CANNELLONI

Pasta

MASTERCLASS

MAKING CAPPELLETTI

Cappelletti di Maria
Zia Maria's Cappelletti Stuffed with Stracotto

Like so many Italian women, Maria learnt her wonderful cooking from her mother and mother-in-law. Zia Maria is my great friend Stefano's aunt. She makes a large batch of cappelletti and freezes them. The word *cappelletti* means "little hats," and this pasta is typical of the Parma region. The *cappelletti* are stuffed with *stracotto*, beef stewed for hours until beautifully tender. Maria told us of a similar recipe, *cappelletti alla povera*, with a filling of breadcrumbs soaked in broth. I tried them, but the flavor is much more subtle than the ones made with *stracotto*. Maria uses a little oil in her pasta to make it stronger and more flexible. It is also less likely to dry out while you are stuffing and making the *cappelletti*.

Makes about 80 cappelletti (serves 10)

FOR THE CAPPELLETTI

2 cups "00" flour, pasta flour, or all-purpose flour
2 tablespoons olive oil
2 eggs
1½-in pasta cutter (or cookie cutter or shot glass)

FOR THE FILLING

1 lb *stracotto*, pureed in a blender (see page 292)
¼ cup fresh breadcrumbs
¼ nutmeg, finely grated
1 egg
1 cup Parmesan cheese, finely grated, or use ½ cup Parmesan and ½ cup pecorino

To make the pasta, make a well of flour and into it pour the oil and the eggs. Maria uses her hands to blend it all together, whereas we use a fork or knife. (See the pasta making masterclass on pages 148–149).

Maria's tip is to add a drop of water to the drier crumbs to bind them together, then blend with the others. Knead until smooth, until the flour is no longer visibly white and the pasta springs back to the touch.

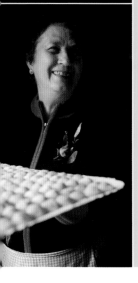

Pasta
MASTERCLASS
MAKING CAPPELLETTI

To make the filling, mix the puréed *stracotto* with the breadcrumbs, the nutmeg, the egg, and the cheese.

Using a rolling pin or a pasta machine, roll out the pasta into a long thin piece, 1mm thick.

Continue to put the pasta through the machine at progressively thinner settings, taking it right through to the last setting. The oil in the pasta makes it very flexible so it doesn't need to be covered to stop it from drying out.

Lay the long thin piece of pasta on a work surface and dot teaspoonfuls of the filling about 2 inches apart and 1 inch from the edges. This amount works for a 1½-inch cutter or glass; if you use a larger one, increase the amount of filling.

Fold the pasta over to cover the mounds, then cup your fingers around each mound of stuffing, as in the photo on page 186.

Press the cutter onto the pasta to cut out the *cappelletti*. Leave a little flat edge so the shape looks somewhere between a full circle and a half-moon. Leave the pasta shapes on a floured board to dry a little. Then put them in the fridge to firm up. Unless using right away freeze for another occasion.

To cook the *cappelletti*, bring a beef or chicken stock to a boil and cook for 5–6 minutes if fresh and 6–8 minutes if frozen.

Tip: When rolling the pasta, keep adding flour to the underside of the pasta lengths to stop them from sticking to the pasta machine. Don't add it to the top or it won't stick together when you fold it over.

Stefano's grandmother used to grate any leftover pasta onto a board and leave it to dry. This she called grattini. The dry grattini could then be wrapped in paper and kept until needed to make a quick meal, cooked in broth with Parmesan grated on top.

Timballo di Melanzane di Gregorio
Timballo of Eggplant and Pasta

This is one of those elaborate masterpieces you see in Sicilian restaurants. However, despite their splendid appearance, they are not that difficult to make. I was shown how to make one in Sicily, where our head chef, Gregorio Piazza, comes from. He used rings of pasta, which my children said reminded them of the spaghetti loops they sometimes have at school. "Humph," said Gregorio, "I bet they don't use homemade cherry tomato passata with theirs." In winter, I add canned peas as they are so sweet and delicious; just imagine them in jars preserved by someone's aunt in Sicily and not at half-price in a supermarket and you will have discovered a much-maligned vegetable.

Preheat the oven to 350°F. Butter an ovenproof dish, bowl, or pan measuring 8–10 inches wide and about 2–3½ inches deep. This will be your mould: its dimensions are not critical—see what you have. Even a saucepan with curved sides would do, as long as it fits in the oven.

Cut off a thick slice from the side of one of the eggplants so that it sits flat on a chopping board. Trim off the stem and the very tip. Cut lengthwise slices around ¼ inch thick. Repeat with the second eggplant. Pour flour onto a plate and dredge the eggplant slices. Tap off the excess.

In 1 or 2 large frying pans, heat about ⅓ inch of oil until very hot. Fry the eggplant slices in batches until golden, turning halfway through. Drain the eggplants on layers of paper towels on a plate to absorb the oil. Discard the oil in the pan after every 3 or 4 batches—or when you see burnt flour on the bottom—and heat again before cooking a fresh batch. Scatter both sides of the cooked eggplants with a little salt.

Meanwhile bring a large saucepan of salted water to a boil. Drop in the pasta and cook until al dente. Drain and transfer to a large mixing bowl to cool. Mix in some olive oil to prevent the pasta from sticking.

Now line the edges of the greased dish with overlapping eggplant slices, allowing them to hang over the sides of the dish. Line the bottom with smaller slices.

Mix the passata, mozzarella cubes, Parmesan, peas, and pepper and salt with the pasta in the bowl. Pour this into the lined dish and then lay over the remaining slices of eggplants in the center. Fold the eggplant slices around the edge into the center so that the pasta is completely enclosed and bake for around 45 minutes. Allow to cool and set before serving warm or at room temperature.

To invert the *timballo*, hold a board or serving plate over the top of it and quickly invert. Serve cut into wedges.

Pasta
MASTERCLASS
MAKING TIMBALLO

Serves 8–10

1 tablespoon butter, for greasing
2 eggplants
flour, for dredging
⅔–¾ cup sunflower oil, for frying
salt and freshly ground black pepper
12 oz short pasta, such as short penne
olive oil, for coating
3 cups Tomato Passata (Gregorio's or Franca's see page 166)
1 x 4 oz ball mozzarella, cut into ½-in cubes
¾ cup Parmesan, finely grated
10 oz canned or cooked frozen peas (optional)

Pasta senza uova
Egg-free Pasta

Mainly for reasons of poverty and scarcity of eggs, there are many recipes from all over Italy that call for eggless pasta. Montepulciano in Tuscany has *pici* or *pinci*, long hand-rolled strands of pasta made simply from flour and water. South of Naples, in the area of Cilento, there are *fusilli*, lengths of pasta wound around thin metal skewers. In Sardinia, *malloreddus* pasta is made from flour, water, and saffron, rolled over strings to achieve the ridged effect so effective at trapping sauce. This recipe, also from Sardinia, uses flour and water without saffron, and the shapes are rolled over a grater-like piece of metal.

Serves 8

Gnocchetti Sardi
Sardinian Pasta Shells
(see photos to the right)

1 lb *semola di grano duro* or "00" flour
a good pinch of salt
1–1¼ cups tepid water

Pour the *semola* or flour into a mound on a flat surface, add the salt and make a well in the center. This can also be done in a bowl. Add the warm water little by little into the well in the center and use a table knife to mix it together. When it is too stiff for the knife, use your hands to bring the dough together. Add slightly less or more water as necessary to make a soft, pliable dough. If the dough becomes too soft, add a little more *semola* or flour.

Roll the dough into strips as big as a little finger and make the *gnocchetti* by shaping the dough into kidney-bean sized pieces.

Using your thumb, push each piece of pasta onto a grater (the side used for grating lemon zest) so that the imprint makes little nodules on the *gnocchetti*. This helps to collect the delicious sauce they are served with. Reserve in a single layer on a floured tray until you are ready to cook them.

Bring a large pan of salted water to a boil. Drop in the *gnocchetti* and cook until they float, then drain and add them to a sauce. Serve with any meat ragù or tomato sauce.

Variation (see photos to the left):
Gnocculi Siciliani
Sicilian Pasta Frills

Follow the instructions for making the *gnocchetti sardi* above, but roll the pasta flat with a rolling pin, then cut it into strips.

Roll each of the strips into a thin strand, then use your fingertips to squash the strands down to make a soft frilly edge.

Dry the *gnocculi* on a kitchen towel for an hour or so. Boil in salted water until soft. They will take around 10 minutes until al dente. Serve with the Cuttlefish Sauce on page 273.

Pasta
MASTERCLASS
MAKING
GNOCCHETTI

Pasta con le vongole di Sabia
Sabia's Pasta with Clams

Sabia is the mother of Matteo, manager of one of our restaurants. Matteo claimed that his mother's pasta with clams was the best-ever example of this popular dish, which is made all along Italy's coasts. I jokingly told him he should ask her over to show us, so he rang and asked her, just like that. She instantly agreed, much to my surprise, at which point he told me I knew nothing of the bond between Italian mothers and their sons: all they have to do is pick up the phone and their mother will come to them.

His claim about his mother's wondrous cooking skills began a debate in our restaurant Caffè Caldesi in London, which resulted in the mothers of six of our staff flying over to show us their cooking. Of course, Sabia's son was right about his mother's method of cooking this dish. Her way is very simple, quick to prepare, and mouth-wateringly good. My only tweak would be half a finely chopped chile, added with the garlic.

Serves 4

12 oz spaghetti or linguine
3 tablespoons extra virgin olive oil
1½ lb fresh clams, cleaned and purged (see page 269)
1 garlic clove, finely chopped
a handful of chopped flat-leaf parsley
3 tablespoons dry white wine
3 tablespoons halved cherry tomatoes
1 teaspoon salt

Bring a large saucepan of salted water to a boil, drop in the pasta and cook until al dente.

Meanwhile, heat the oil in a saucepan and, when it is hot, add the clams. Add the garlic and parsley and cover the pan. The clam shells will start to open in just a few minutes. When they are all open, add the wine and let it reduce. Then add the cherry tomatoes and the salt. Drain the pasta and toss in the sauce, then serve right away on hot plates.

Pasta con fugo ai funghi porcini e panna
Porcini and Cream Pasta Sauce

One of my best quick pasta dishes results in an impressive rich dish that no one will believe was just ingredients in the back of the cupboard 15 minutes previously! Try to buy good quality porcini mushrooms; I always put some in my suitcase before returning to England. If you are lucky enough to find them at home, oven-dry your own (see pages 392–393). Many Italians scorn having cheese with porcini—they feel its taste is too strong and you should savor every morsel of mushroom. However, in my opinion, a little cheese makes this dish all the more glorious.

Serves 4 as a main or 6 as a starter

2 oz dried porcini mushrooms
2 tablespoons olive oil
salt and freshly ground black pepper
2 garlic cloves, lightly crushed
½–1 chile, finely chopped (optional)
2 sprigs of rosemary
3 sprigs of thyme
⅓ cup white wine
9–12 oz spaghetti (depending how hungry you are!)
⅓ cup heavy cream
¼ cup Parmesan or pecorino, grated

Soak the mushrooms in 2 cups cold water for 20–30 minutes. Toward the end of this time, bring a large pot of salted water to a boil. Lift out the mushrooms with a slotted spoon and set aside in a colander placed over a bowl. Strain the soaking water through a sieve into a measuring cup to use as stock. If needed, chop the mushrooms into bite-size pieces.

Heat the oil, salt and pepper in a large frying pan, add the garlic, chile (if using), and herbs, and cook briefly. Add the drained mushrooms, cook for 3–5 minutes, then pour in the wine and allow to reduce for a minute or two. Measure off ¾ cup of the mushroom stock, add to the pan, and reduce again for 10 minutes over a medium heat.

Add the pasta to a pot of salted boiling water. Add the cream to the sauce and stir well. Taste and adjust the seasoning. Heat through and, when the pasta is al dente, drain and toss it into the sauce in the frying pan. Serve in warm bowls sprinkled with the Parmesan or pecorino.

Spaghetti con acciughe e cipolle
Spaghetti with Anchovy and Red Onion

This is one of my über-quick pasta recipes, shown to me by friends from the south of Italy where it is regularly eaten—they couldn't believe I hadn't had it before. The flavor of the anchovy is softened by the sweet onions, and it is a great recipe to make out of store pantry ingredients.

Serves 4

9–12 oz spaghetti (depending how hungry you are!)
⅓ cup extra virgin olive oil
1 red onion, finely chopped
salt and freshly ground black pepper
7 anchovies, drained and finely chopped
¼ cup Parmesan, finely grated

Bring a pot of salted water to a boil. Add the spaghetti and cook until al dente.

Meanwhile, pour the oil into a large saucepan over medium heat. Cook the onion with pepper and only a dash of salt (the anchovies are salty) for about 10 minutes, or until soft, then stir in the anchovies.

Drain the cooked pasta and add to the sauce with the Parmesan. Serve right away in warm bowls.

Spaghetti al limone con panna e basilico
Spaghetti with Lemon, Basil, and Cream Sauce

I love this simple, quick pasta. It is a perfect girls' lunch: quick, fresh-tasting, and zesty. Normally it is served without basil along the Amalfi coast in southern Italy, where the lemons are full flavored and often sweet. Try to buy the best lemons you can—organic and unwaxed. Do be generous with the salt or the dish will lack flavor, and don't skimp on the cream, otherwise the end result will be sticky pasta. I have included ½ cup Parmesan, double what I would normally recommend for dressing pasta, as the lemon needs the cheese to counteract its sharpness, so scatter liberally and encourage your fellow diners to do the same.

Serves 4 as a main or 6 as a starter

12 oz spaghetti, linguine, or *tagliolini*
2 cups heavy cream
2 tablespoons juice and zest of 1 lemon
20 basil leaves, torn
a generous pinch each of salt and pepper
½ cup Parmesan, finely grated

Bring a pot of salted water to a boil. Add the pasta and cook until al dente.

Meanwhile combine the cream, lemon juice and zest, half the basil, salt and pepper in a large frying pan over medium-high heat. Let the mixture bubble for a couple of minutes until slightly thickened. The cream is now ready for the pasta, but if the pasta isn't ready for the cream, remove the cream from the heat and wait!

After the pasta is cooked, drain and pour it into the frying pan. Return the pan to medium heat and toss the pasta with the sauce. Serve immediately, topped with Parmesan and the remaining basil.

Carbonara
Coal Miners' Pasta

This recipe is named after the coal miners from around Rome—the black specks of pepper are a reference to the coal dust. From my research in Rome, wading through tons of *bucantini* pasta dressed with a rich egg sauce, I discovered that a traditional carbonara should contain *guanciale*—the cheek of a pig—black pepper and egg yolks. However, *guanciale* is harder to find outside of Italy, so I usually use bacon or pancetta, and I prefer the lighter flavor of a whole egg rather than just the yolk. I also like to add a dash of white wine but no cream—I find that the egg is rich enough—but by all means make your own adjustments and enjoy this satisfying Italian version of bacon and eggs.

Serves 6

2 tablespoons olive oil
12 oz smoked bacon, pancetta, or *guanciale*, thinly sliced
⅓ cup dry white wine
1 lb dried pasta (bucatini or penne)
5 eggs
2 teaspoons black peppercorns, crushed in a pestle and mortar or coarsely ground in a mill
1 cup pecorino, freshly grated

Bring a pot of salted water to a boil for the pasta.

Meanwhile, heat the oil in a large frying pan and, when hot, add the bacon and cook until crispy. Add the wine and allow to reduce for a couple of minutes. Set aside.

Now boil the pasta until al dente. Beat the eggs and black pepper together. Drain the cooked pasta in a colander, return it to the pan off the heat, and add the beaten egg, bacon, and ¾ cup of the pecorino; stir well to combine. Serve in warm bowls with the rest of the pecorino scattered over the top.

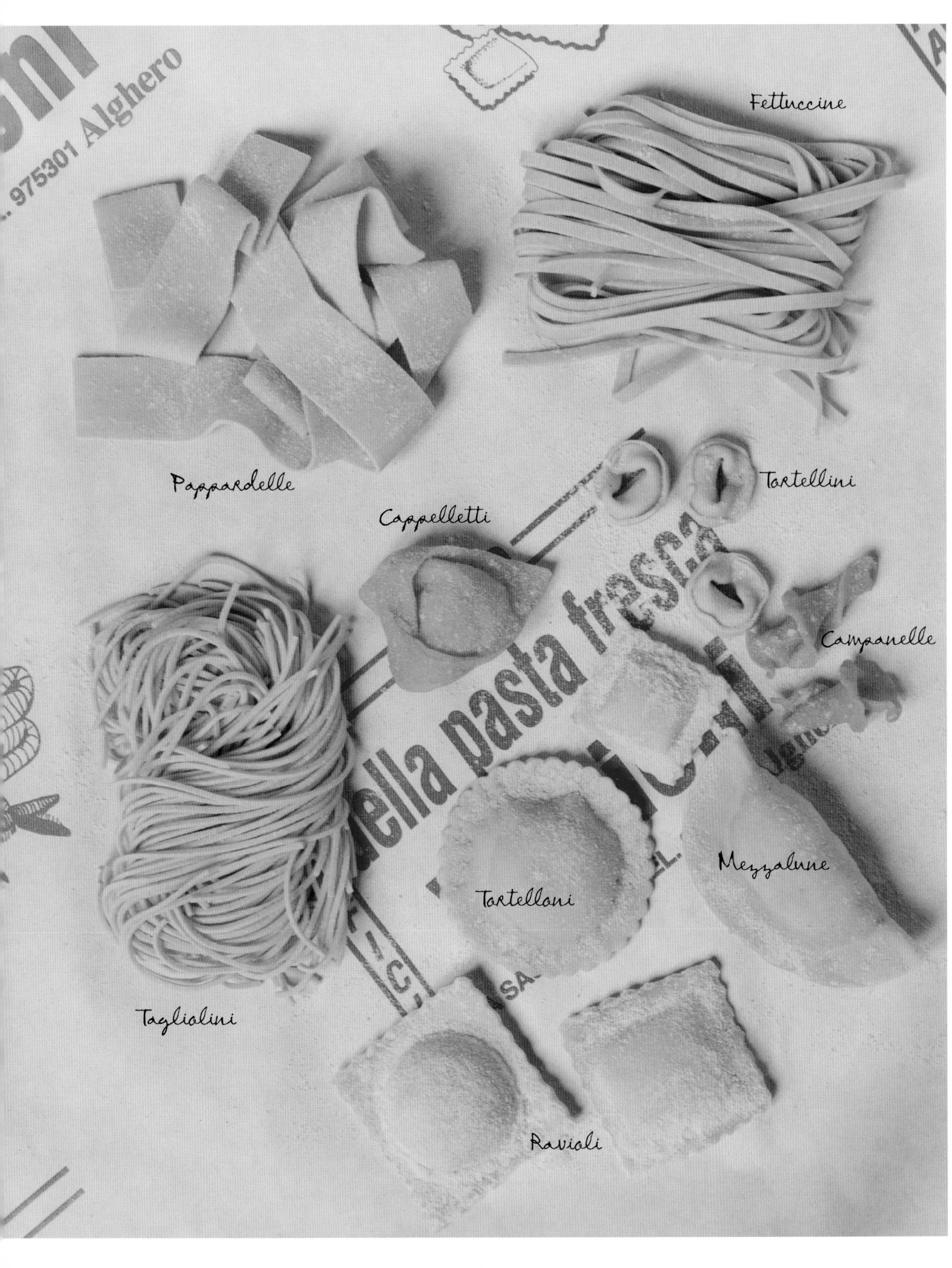

Fettuccine

Pappardelle

Tortellini

Cappelletti

Campanelle

Mezzalune

Tortelloni

Tagliolini

Ravioli

Gnocchi di patate
Potato Gnocchi

There is nothing as comforting as soft pillows of potato gnocchi coated in a creamy or meaty sauce to banish woes. Both are satisfying and welcoming. Gnocchi are best made with potatoes that are not too waxy, such as Yukon gold or russet. The Italians say they should be boiled in their skins so that the water doesn't penetrate. I am not sure I believe this, although I do think the flavor is better when potatoes are cooked in their skins. The secret of light gnocchi is to trap as much air inside as you can, and rubbing the cooked potatoes through a *passatutto* foodmill or ricer will achieve this, but otherwise you can mash them. Freezing gnocchi before they are cooked can give even better results than cooking from fresh; they tend to hold their shape better.

Serves 8

2¼ lb potatoes (Yukon gold or russet), unpeeled

1 egg

2¼ cups "00" flour or pasta flour, plus up to 1 cup extra, depending on water content of potatoes

1 heaping teaspoon salt

a generous twist of pepper

Pasta
MASTERCLASS

MAKING GNOCCHI

Cook the potatoes in a large pot of boiling salted water until tender—this could take up to an hour, depending on their size. Drain and peel them while they are still hot, either by holding them in one hand on a fork or with a cloth, and peeling the skin away with a knife in the other hand.

Pass the potatoes through a *passatutto* foodmill or ricer and into a bowl.

Stir in the egg using a wooden spoon and add the salt and pepper.

Add one third of the flour to form a soft, pliable dough.

Pour the remaining flour onto the work surface in a mound and turn out the dough onto the flour. Knead the flour in with the dough, adding a little more if the dough still sticks to your hands. (The more flour you add at this stage, the heavier the gnocchi will be, so only add up to the extra 1 cup if the dough is really sticky).

You need to decide how big to make the gnocchi. The trick is to keep them the same size so that they all have the same cooking time. Roll out the dough into long sausages and chop between 1 and 1½ inches in length.

Flick the gnocchi with the blade of the knife onto a well-floured cloth. You can then roll them over the tines of a fork for texture or make an indentation in the top with your finger—this means more sauce will stick to them—or you could simply leave them pillow shaped and plain.

If you plan to eat the gnocchi right away, bring a large pot of salted water to a boil and drop in the gnocchi. They are cooked when they float to the surface—this takes about 2–4 minutes. Drain well and toss in your chosen sauce.

To freeze gnocchi before cooking them, spread them on a well-floured baking sheet, making sure they don't touch each other, and put them in the freezer. When frozen, shake off any excess flour and transfer to a freezer bag. Use within 3 months. To cook from frozen, allow an extra 1–2 minutes cooking time.

Variation: Gnocchi with Giancarlo's Mushrooms
Gnocchi are delicious served with Giancarlo's Mushrooms (see page 395), made into a sauce using ⅔ cup heavy cream instead of the water or stock. Simply cook 12 oz gnocchi as before, drain and toss them into the mushroom sauce. Combine gently and serve topped with ¼ cup freshly grated Parmesan.

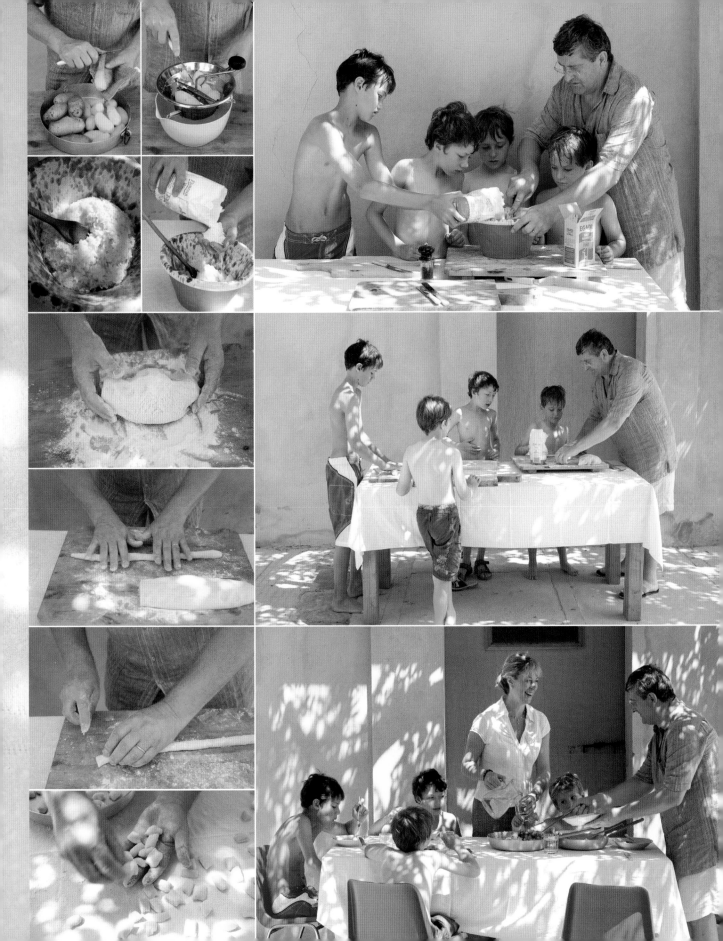

Gnocchi alla Monserrato
Monserrato's Gnocchi with Clams and Bottarga

Monserrato is Sardinian and loves to use *bottarga*, the roe or eggs of grey mullet, tuna or swordfish, which is dried, cured in sea salt and then coated in wax to preserve it. It can be eaten in slices with the wax removed or grated over fish or pasta. Used in small quantities, it adds a wonderful zing to a fish recipe like a natural flavor enhancer, but go easy—the flavor is strong and can overpower other ingredients. Most of Italy's *bottarga* comes from Sardinia—you should be able to buy it from Italian delis or order it online. I once had some amazing fried fish in a Sardinian restaurant and I asked the owner what made it taste so good. Giancarlo was becoming embarrassed at my persistence, claiming that it was due to the freshness of the fish. No, this was something else: I'm from Eastbourne and I know my fresh fish! The owner eventually indicated his wife, the chef, who was grating tiny shavings of *bottarga* over her grilled fish to give them that extra wow. Ah! Great food, coupled with the fact that I had discovered something made me extra pleased with myself, much to Giancarlo's annoyance!

Serves 2

1 quantity of Gnocchi (see recipe page 198)

2 tablespoons olive oil
1 garlic clove
1 red chile, fresh or dried, thinly sliced
a small handful of flat-leaf parsley,
  coarsely chopped
18 live clams (discard any that refuse to close)
2 teaspoons *bottarga*, finely grated
1½ tablespoons white wine
1 tablespoon butter, cut into two pieces

Put a pot of salted water on to boil for the gnocchi. Meanwhile, heat the oil in a large frying pan. When hot, add the garlic, chile and most of the parsley and cook for just 1 minute. Then add the clams and half the *bottarga*. Place a lid over the frying pan to steam open the clams and leave covered for about 2 minutes, until the clams have opened (discard any that remain closed). Add the wine and reduce for a couple of minutes. Add half the butter and mix well with the sauce, followed by the other half and mix well again.

Cook the gnocchi in the boiling water for 2–4 minutes. As soon as they float to the surface, remove with a slotted spoon, add to the sauce in the pan and toss well to combine. Add the remaining *bottarga* and parsley and serve right away on hot plates. *Buon appetito!*

Gnocchi al pomodoro, salsiccia e semi di finocchio
Tomato, Sausage and Fennel Seed Ragù with Gnocchi

This is my version of a ragù I tasted in a *lasagnetta* in a restaurant, Il Divo, in a cave in Siena. The inclusion of fennel seeds is typically Tuscan. Instead of buying ground pork or sausage, Italians often split sausages open and use the meat. The contents are generally just ground pork, garlic, and salt so, if possible, buy Italian sausages or go for the best-quality lean ones you can find with little (or no) bread filler.

Serves 4

6 lean best-quality pork sausages
6 tablespoons olive oil
2 whole garlic cloves, lightly crushed
salt and freshly ground black pepper
½ white onion, finely chopped
1 tablespoon fennel seeds
2 bay leaves
½ cup dry red wine
1 x 14 oz can Italian plum tomatoes
3 heaping tablespoons tomato paste
¼ cup finely grated Parmesan
½ quantity of Gnocchi (see recipe page 198)

Put a large pot of salted water on to boil. Meanwhile, remove the sausages from their casings and chop the meat to break it up.

Put the olive oil in a frying pan over medium heat and add the garlic and salt and pepper. Cook for about 2 minutes, until the garlic becomes light gold. Then add the onion and cook for a few minutes, until translucent. Stir in the fennel seeds and bay leaves. Add the meat to the pan and cook for 6–7 minutes, or until cooked through. Using a wooden spoon, break the meat into bits and scrape the bottom of the pan to prevent sticking. If the sausages release a lot of fat, drain off most of it.

Add the wine and allow to reduce for a couple of minutes, then add the tomatoes and tomato paste and stir well. Leave the ragù to simmer for 10 minutes while you cook the gnocchi in the boiling water. When the gnocchi are cooked, drain and toss into the ragù. Serve in warm bowls and scatter Parmesan over the top.

Gnocchi alla Romana
Roman Gnocchi

This type of gnocchi is made from semolina, which is cooked and then allowed to set. It is an ancient Roman speciality and still popular today. Often it is made with coarse semolina, which is harder to buy outside of Italy but I prefer it with the smooth version. It is comforting and delicious.

Makes 35–40 gnocchi (Serves 4 as a main or 6 as a starter)

1 quart milk
¼ nutmeg, grated
salt and freshly ground black pepper
2¼ cups semolina
8 oz Parmesan, finely grated
8 tablespoons butter, plus extra for greasing
3 egg yolks
oil, for greasing

Heat the milk, nutmeg, and salt and pepper to just under the boiling point, then add the semolina, stirring with a whisk to prevent lumps from forming. When the mixture becomes stiff, change to a wooden spoon and beat well for about 15 minutes, until it pulls away from the sides of the pan. (This stage is much like making choux pastry or polenta.) When the mixture is really thick, add ¾ of the butter and beat until melted, then remove the pan from the heat and beat in 1½ cups of the Parmesan. Pour in the yolks, whisking continuously.

Pour the mixture ½ inch deep into an oiled baking sheet and leave to set. This could take up to 2 hours but, to speed up the process, once the gnocchi have cooled to room temperature, put them in the fridge.

When set, use a 2½ inch cutter or the rim of a glass to cut out circles. Lay them slightly overlapping in a buttered ovenproof dish and dot with the remaining butter and Parmesan. Broil for 12–15 minutes, until golden brown and bubbling. Serve with a twist of black pepper.

Gnocchi gnudi di spinaci con salsa burro e salvia
Spinach Gnocchi Nude in Butter and Sage Sauce

The name of these gnocchi literally means "nude"—they are like the spinach and ricotta stuffing you find in ravioli or *tortelli*, only without their pasta covering.

Makes 30 (serves 4 as a main or 6 as a starter)

FOR THE GNOCCHI
12 oz cooked spinach
8 oz cow's milk ricotta
1 egg yolk
½ cup Parmesan, finely grated
½ cup "00" flour or all-purpose flour
salt and pepper, to taste
½ teaspoon grated nutmeg

FOR THE SAUCE
oil, for coating
4 tablespoons salted butter
6 large sage leaves
¼ cup Parmesan, finely grated

Thoroughly squeeze the spinach dry of water. Chop it in a food processor or with a sharp knife. Mix together all the remaining ingredients for the gnocchi in a bowl.

Form "quenelles" between two teaspoons by pressing small spoonfuls of the mixture together firmly to pack it into oval shapes. Make sure you tightly pack the mixture between the spoons so that it won't break up in the water. As you make each quenelle, leave it, not touching another one, on a floured surface.

Bring a large pot of salted water to a boil and add the gnocchi to the water, working in batches. Let them float to the surface and bounce around for around 3–4 minutes, until cooked through. Lift them out with a slotted spoon and leave on a warm serving dish coated with a little oil to stop them from sticking together. Meanwhile, melt the butter with the sage leaves in a large frying pan. When all the gnocchi are cooked, toss them in the butter sauce and serve with a little Parmesan sprinkled on top.

Riso e Polenta

CHAPTER 5: RICE AND POLENTA

Riso e Polenta

Every Italian has strong views on risotto, and what the "perfect" one should be like. I have eaten beautiful *risotti* all over Italy, but also I have had dishes served to me by famous risotto makers in Milan, one of the heartlands of risotto, in which, to my mind, the grains have been too crunchy and undercooked. At other times in the same city I have eaten soupy-wet mounds of seemingly overcooked rice and been told that this too was the perfect dish. So who knows what perfect means? Actually, I don't think it matters. Everyone should make risotto according to what gives them the most pleasure. Whether the grains have a slight crunch or are soft enough to squash against the roof of your mouth with your tongue is really up to you.

The origins of rice-growing in Italy probably go back to the days of the crusaders returning from the East or the merchants of Venice peddling spices and possibly rice at the same time. Whatever the exact history, by the end of the 15th century, rice was commonly grown in the north of Italy, often by monks, and even earlier there had been rice growing around Naples, possibly introduced from Spain, since Naples came under the rule of the conquering House of Aragon in the middle of the 15th century.

These days, most rice-growing is in the *risaie*, the large paddy fields of the northern wetlands in the provinces of Vercelli in Piemonte and Pavia in Lombardy, where it grows in constant flowing water at a stable temperature, called a thermal blanket. As the young shoots develop, the fields here take on a soft, emerald look. Women used to do most of the work in the rice fields until machines replaced them in the 1950s. Harvest is in September or October, when the plants dry out and become brown, and the grains are milled carefully to make sure they remain whole and perfect.

The food writer and cook Valentina Harris, whom I call the queen of risotto because she has made this wonderful dish so much a part of our diet here in Britain, told me that as a child growing up in Tuscany she remembers that there were 30–40 different types of rice available. Her cousins in Tuscany grew their own rice and in September they would send over whichever variety was good. When the sacks were delivered, Valentina would help pick them over, to discard shrivelled or discolored grains or the odd stone or rice husk. One variety she remembers in particular was called Rosina; it was a pale pink and very pretty to look at.

Today, the three varieties most people use are *Vialone Nano, Carnaroli,* or Arborio. Arborio is the one that everyone recognizes, and it is used in homes throughout Italy—which is odd in a way, because it is probably the least forgiving in terms of cooking a risotto for the right amount of time. *Carnaroli*, which is the favorite in Piemonte, and *Vialone Nano*, which is preferred in the Veneto, allow you a little more leeway before becoming too soft.

Risotto rice is different to any other kind of rice, such as the Indian basmati or Thai jasmine rice. If you put a risotto rice grain under the microscope, you will see two shells: an outer shell that is fragile and soft, and an inner one that is harder. It is the relationship between the starches

in these two shells and the way in which they break down and absorb liquid that makes each rice variety slightly different. When you "toast" the grains—stir them into the sautéed onions to warm them up—as you begin to make a risotto, you are loosening the outside shell to release fifty percent of the starch into the risotto. This starch will make it creamy, and this is why stirring is important throughout the cooking of a risotto. If you are not stirring, you aren't breaking down the rice grains.

You will find rice called *ordinario* in the shops in Italy, which is used for making soups and puddings, but the three grades of rice used for risotto are *semifino*, *fino,* and *superfino*. The grades are not to do with the quality but the look of the rice, which varies from small and round to long and pointed. Many people say *superfino*, the largest grain, is the perfect risotto rice. However *semifino Vialone Nano*, which is a smaller round grain, is often used too, especially in the Veneto, where most of it is produced. This may be because in the Veneto they typically make fish risotto and Rice and Peas (see page 216), which are better eaten soupy and made with a smaller, harder rice grain. In Piemonte, however, the most famous risotti are *al tartufo* (mushroom) and *alla Milanese* (saffron), and these would usually be made with the local *Carnaroli* or Arborio rice.

In Italy, risotto tends to be a much more simple affair than the sophisticated versions often made in restaurants elsewhere. Sometimes when I make a risotto *alla Milanese*, just flavored with saffron, or *al Parmigiano*, with Parmesan, I worry that people might not like it because it is too plain. But every time I make these classic dishes I realize how right the Italians are to stick to such simple, really lovely flavors.

If I am honest, I avoided making risotto for a long time, as, like most people, I was a bit scared of it. I thought it would be too complicated to make, especially when friends came around, but then I came to realize that actually, in these days when everyone has moved out of the dining room and into the kitchen, it is a very sociable process to have people around you and enjoy a glass of wine while you stand at the stove and stir. These days, I make risotto for my two sons a couple of times a week, often with whatever leftovers I have in the fridge, but, like all good Italians, they like nothing better than a simple risotto with *Parmigiano Reggiano*.

KATIE'S TIPS

Have everything you need for your risotto ready and within reach so that you can keep stirring without interruption.

A risotto is only as good as the stock you make it with. Homemade stock is really easy (see pages 136–140) and makes such a difference. Failing that, there are some very good fresh ones you can buy—but please don't use a bouillon cube. I can't bear the smell, let alone the taste of them, and there is no disguising it in a risotto.

Keep the stock warm on the stove, next to the pot in which you are making your risotto, so as each ladleful is absorbed into the rice, you can add the next without affecting the temperature.

Riso e Polenta
MASTERCLASS

Risotto ai funghi e zafferano
Mushroom and Saffron Risotto

Having spent a few years watching various chefs cook risotto, I realize that there are plenty of variations in their methods. However, this way appears to be foolproof. There are two things a risotto needs: the effort of stirring with a solid wooden spoon and a good hot stock. It's worth the effort of toasting the rice grains and stirring constantly as the rice cooks in the hot stock, as this breaks down the outer shell of the rice grains and creates a creamy consistency. If you are using store-bought stock or bouillon cubes, go easy with the salt since often these contain salt already. In this recipe, we use fresh porcini mushrooms, but a mixture of wild mushrooms is also good. If you want to use dried porcini, follow the recipe for Porcini Mushroom Risotto on page 218.

Serves 6

5–6 cups beef stock, chicken stock, or
  vegetable stock, warm
3 tablespoons olive oil
4 oz shallots or red onion, finely chopped
12 oz mixed fresh mushrooms, roughly sliced
2 garlic cloves, finely chopped
1 small red chile
a good pinch of salt and freshly ground
  black pepper
8 tablespoons butter
2 cups risotto rice (Arborio or *Carnaroli*)
¾ cup dry white wine
a pinch of good-quality saffron mixed with
  3 tablespoons of the hot stock (optional)
½ cup Parmesan, finely grated

Pour the stock into a large saucepan and place over medium heat. Heat the olive oil in another large pot and, when hot, cook the onion for around 7–10 minutes, until softened.

In a frying pan, cook the mushrooms, garlic, chile, and salt and pepper in half of the butter until softened. Keep them over high heat and stir frequently until all the water has, excluded from the mushrooms and evaporated.

Add the rice to the onion and "toast" it for a few minutes so that it absorbs the flavors of the other ingredients and starts to become translucent. Keep stirring with a large wooden spoon so it doesn't burn.

When the rice is toasted, stir in the wine and allow it to evaporate for a few minutes while stirring.

Add the saffron-infused stock, if using. Hold the pot with one hand and stir the rice with a folding action, as if making a cake. As the rice cooks, this stirring will break down the outer shell of the rice grains and create a creamy risotto. Make sure you scrape any grains of rice from the sides of the pot down into the risotto or you will have the odd hard, uncooked grain of rice in your finished risotto.

When most of the stock has been absorbed, you will see a crescent-moon shape appearing at the bottom of the pan while you stir; this indicates that you need to add more stock from the saucepan, a ladleful at a time. Repeat this process until you think the rice is done—it will take between 20–25 minutes—you may or may not need to add all the stock.

Halfway through the cooking time, stir in the mushrooms. Adjust the seasoning to taste. When the rice grains have only the merest hint of crunch in the center, it is time to stop adding stock.

Remove from the heat and add the remaining butter and the cheese; stir well. Cover the pan for no more than 3 minutes while you prepare warmed bowls. Serve right away.

Risotto al formaggio
Cheese Risotto

From this basic recipe, use your imagination to add ingredients—try pancetta or bacon, mushrooms, asparagus, or radicchio. Most additions are made at the start with the onions to get the most out of their flavor. Always use cooking or soaking water, such as mushroom stock from dried porcini or the asparagus cooking water, again to maximize flavor.

Serves 4 as a main or 6 as a starter

6 tablespoons butter
1 quart good-quality vegetable stock, chicken
  stock, or meat stock
½ medium white onion, chopped
salt and pepper
2 cups risotto rice (Arborio)
½ cup finely grated Parmesan

Melt 4 tablespoons of the butter in a large saucepan. Have the stock simmering next to you over medium heat. Add the onion and salt and pepper to the butter, and cook for about 10 minutes, stirring constantly with a wooden spoon. Add the rice and "toast" it for 3–5 minutes, stirring constantly until all the grains are covered in the butter and have become very hot but not burnt. Add 2 cups of the hot stock and stir quickly into the rice. When a crescent-moon shape appears in the bottom of the pan while you stir, add more stock, a ladleful at a time.

After about 20–25 minutes and when you have used almost all the stock, taste the rice to see whether it is done. Stop cooking when the rice grains retain the merest hint of crunch in the center. Adjust the seasoning to taste.

To finish, remove from the heat and stir in the remaining butter and the Parmesan. Cover the pan and allow the risotto to rest while you get out warmed bowls, but no longer than a few minutes or it will become too thick.

Variations:
Risotto al Barolo: Substitute Barolo or other red wine for 2 cups of the stock and reduce the cheese to ¼ cup.

Risotto al tartufo: For a wonderful truffle risotto from Piemonte, drizzle over a little truffle oil. If you have a black or white truffle, grate a few shavings on top. This is excellent topped with Parmesan Ice Cream (see page 473).

suppli al telefono alla Daniela
Daniela's Risotto Balls Stuffed with Mozzarella

These hot balls of rice are named after the telephone lines of Rome because the melting strings of mozzarella that ooze out when you bite into them resemble wires. Daniela is a great friend of ours who used to make these with her mother and grandmother from leftover risotto cooked the day before. If you have no leftover risotto, this recipe gives a quick way of making some.

Makes 10 large or 15 small suppli'

¾ cup Franca's Tomato Passata (see page 166)

2¾ cups cold water
½ white onion, finely chopped
2 sprigs of flat-leaf parsley, coarsely chopped
a large pinch of salt
1½ cups risotto rice (Arborio or *Carnaroli*)
1 medium egg, lightly beaten
1 x 4 oz mozzarella ball (buffalo's or cow's
  milk), diced into small cubes
1 cup fine dry breadcrumbs (see page 30)
sunflower oil, for deep-frying

Put the water in a large saucepan and add the onion, parsley and salt to add flavor. Bring to the boil, then add the rice and cook until tender, about 20 minutes.

Drain the rice and spread in a large shallow dish to cool. Add the passata (it can be cold) and stir in the beaten egg, a little at a time. You will probably need all of it—you are looking to achieve the consistency of a risotto, though not too liquid a mixture.

Use your hands to form oblong-shaped rice balls, each the size of a large egg. Make a hole in the center of each ball with your finger and stuff a small cube of mozzarella into it. Close the hole over and squeeze the balls tightly between your hands.

Put the breadcrumbs into a shallow bowl and dip and gently roll the rice balls in them to coat them on all sides. Heat enough oil in a saucepan or deep-sided frying pan to deep-fry the *suppli'*. Give the *suppli'* one more squeeze before gently lowering them into the hot oil in small batches. Fry until golden brown. Drain on paper towels and serve immediately.

Flavia

Risotto con fagioli e salsiccia
Borlotti Bean and Sausage Risotto

This is a dish from Padua in the Veneto, one of the heartlands of risotto. Oretta, who lives in Padua, gave me this, one of her favorite risotto recipes. It uses the bean cooking water to give a wonderful nutty flavor to the risotto, so don't throw it away! For the best borlotti beans, look for those from Lamon, another town of the Veneto; these beans are more velvety than others and soften deliciously in the mouth. Italians frequently use sausages for ground sausage in their cooking; the skins are split open and the meat is used for ragù and so forth. So try to buy Italian sausages if you can, because they are normally made with coarse ground pork, garlic, salt and black pepper—and no bread.

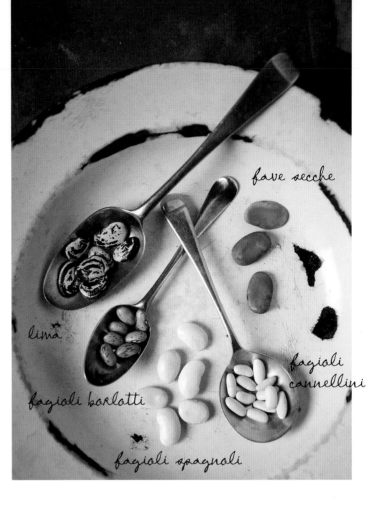

fave secche

lima

fagioli cannellini

fagioli borlotti

fagioli spagnoli

Serves 6 (or 8 as a starter)

If you are using fresh or rehydrated borlotti beans, put them in a large pan with the sage, tomato, and garlic. Cover with plenty of fresh cold water, bring to a boil and cook for about 1 hour, until soft. Drain the beans and reserve 5 cups of the cooking water. Keep this liquid warm while you make the risotto. If you are using canned beans, rinse them, drain and set aside, then heat the vegetable stock because it needs to be added warm.

Heat half of the oil in a large saucepan and, when hot, add half the onion. Cook until lightly golden, then add the ground sausage. Brown the meat and continue to cook until any liquid has evaporated. Remove from the heat and use a slotted spoon to remove the sausage and onion. Set aside in a bowl.

Heat the remaining oil in the pan. When hot, add the rest of the onion and cook until soft. Add the rice to the pan and toast it for a few minutes, until the grains are covered in the oil and onions are slightly translucent. Pour in the wine and let it reduce. Continue to make the risotto following the instructions in the masterclass on page 208, adding the hot bean water or stock a ladleful at a time.

When the risotto is almost ready, stir in the beans and the sausage and onion mixture. Once the rice is cooked but the grains retain a little bite, stir in the butter and cheese. Cover the pan, switch off the heat, and leave to rest for 3 minutes before serving drizzled with your best olive oil.

8 oz borlotti beans, fresh or dried and soaked overnight, or canned and drained
a handful of sage leaves
1 large tomato
4 garlic cloves, skins on
5 cups bean cooking water or vegetable stock
6 tablespoons olive oil
1 medium red or white onion, finely chopped
12 oz Italian sausages (about 3, skins split and meat removed
⅔ cup white wine
1½ cups risotto rice
2 tablespoons butter
3 tablespoons finely grated Parmesan or *Grana Padano*
best-quality olive oil, for drizzling

Risotto alla pescatora di Valentina Harris
Risotto with Seafood a la Valentina Harris

Valentina is known as the queen of risotto, and rightly so. She was the one who demystified the risotto-making process for me years ago. She teaches regularly at our cooking school and is passionate about passing on her knowledge of Italian food and particularly about promoting the cooking of risotto in the UK. This is how Valentina describes a risotto: first you have the *tentazione*, the temptation like the siren in Ulysses, then the *sospiri* or sighs of relief that you have given in and finally added the wine. This recipe is all about preserving the cooking liquid from the shellfish: as Valentina will tell you, a risotto is only as good as the stock it is made from. She taught me to turn the heat up and down as necessary when making a risotto. She also told me not to over-stir the risotto, leaving the spoon every now and again. Remember too, to push the rice grains down from the sides of the pan or they won't cook. A variety of seafood is best for this dish, but if you can't find clams, for example, use twice the amount of mussels instead.

Serves 4 as a main course or 6 as a starter

12 oz uncooked shrimp, large or small, with shells
5 tablespoons olive oil
6 garlic cloves, 1 whole, 3 peeled and crushed, 2 finely chopped
a good handful of parsley (about ¼ cup), finely chopped and stems reserved
2¼ lb seafood (mussels and/or clams)
1¼ cups dry white wine
salt and freshly ground black pepper
½–1 small dried or fresh red chile (depending on strength), finely chopped
1½ cups risotto rice (Arborio)

Remove and reserve the heads, tails, and shells from the shrimp. Peel away and discard the black vein from the back of each shrimp. Cut large shrimp into ¾ inch pieces. Leave small ones whole. Set aside, covered, in the fridge.

Put the shrimp shells, tails, and heads into a large saucepan with 2 tablespoons of the oil, 1 whole clove of garlic and one third of the parsley stems. Cook until pink and almost burning—until a brown residue appears in the bottom of the pan. Now add 1 quart of water and bring to the boil. Allow to simmer while you cook the rest of the seafood; this is the basis of a shellfish stock.

Scrub the mussels of barnacles with a metal scouring pad or brush. Hold the mussel with the pointed end towards you, and pull the beard off the mussel towards you. Put the cleaned mussels into a saucepan with ⅓ cup of the white wine, salt, another third of the parsley stems and 1 crushed clove of garlic. Cover and cook for 8–10 minutes. Discard any mussels that hasn't opened after this time. Reserve the cooking liquor and shell all the mussels unless they are very pretty, in which case set aside some of the mussels in their shells to use as a garnish. Set the shelled mussels aside. Strain the cooking liquor into the saucepan with the shrimp shells.

Cook the clams in the same way as the mussels, if using, and add another ⅓ cup of the white wine with the remaining crushed garlic clove and parsley stems, for 8–10 minutes. Discard any clams that don't open. Pick the clams from their shells and add them to the reserved shrimp and mussels. Strain the liquor and add to the shellfish stock. Strain this stock through a sieve into a saucepan, pressing the liquid out of the shrimp shells and heads to get as much flavor out of them as you can. Keep the stock warm and have a ladle nearby.

Heat the remaining oil in a large, heavy bottomed pot and cook the chopped garlic and chile together for 2 minutes. After a couple of minutes add the rice and "toast" it for 3 minutes, until it crackles. The heat should be hot but not burning; if the rice starts to burn, turn the heat down. Add the remaining wine and let it reduce, stirring. It will already appear creamy on the bottom of the pan. Then add around 1¼ cups of the stock and stir well with a wooden spoon. When the risotto starts to look dry, add more stock. Don't be afraid to reduce or increase the heat as necessary, but work mainly over a medium-high heat. Continue in this way until the rice has only a slight crunch in the center of the grain. Five minutes before the end of cooking, add the reserved seafood and the chopped parsley. Season to taste with salt and pepper. Remove from the heat, put the lid on for 3 minutes and serve in warmed bowls.

Tip: If you run out of stock, simply add hot water.

Risotto al limone e gamberoni
Lemon Risotto with Chile Shrimp

For this refreshing summer risotto, try to find Sicilian unwaxed lemons for the extra zing they give and, if you have time, make your own shrimp stock from the shrimp shells and heads: it is not difficult and the flavor is amazing. If you are using store-bought stock or bouillon cubes, go easy on the extra salt as they usually contain enough already.

Serves 4 as a main or 6 as a starter.

4 jumbo shrimp or 16 tiger shrimp with shells

FOR THE SHRIMP STOCK
heads and shells of the shrimp
2 tablespoons olive oil
1 small carrot, cut into ½ in chunks
1 small celery rib, cut into ½ in pieces
½ white onion or 1 shallot, coarsely chopped
salt and freshly ground black pepper
3 quarts cold water

FOR THE RISOTTO
5–6 cups warm fish stock (see recipe page 138), if not making the shrimp stock
3 tablespoons olive oil
6 tablespoons butter
½ cup white onions or shallots, finely chopped
½ small red chile, finely chopped
a good pinch of salt and freshly ground black pepper
2 cups risotto rice (Arborio or Carnaroli)
¾ cup dry white wine
finely grated zest of 1 lemon and its juice (about 3 tablespoons)
1 teaspoon finely chopped flat-leaf parsley

Remove the heads and shells from the shrimp and reserve. Peel away the black vein from the back of the shrimp and chop them roughly into 1cm pieces. Keep the shrimp in the fridge while you prepare the stock.

To make the stock, put the heads and shells of the shrimp into a medium saucepan with the olive oil, carrot, celery, onion, and salt and pepper. Cook the ingredients over high heat for 10 minutes, stirring frequently to prevent them from sticking to the bottom of the pan. Use the end of a bottle or a wooden rolling pin to crush the shrimp heads to release their juices and add to the flavor. When a dark orange residue appears on the bottom of the pan, pour in the water. Bring to the boil and then reduce to a simmer for at least 1 hour and up to 2 if you have time. Strain the stock; if you prefer a whiter risotto, skim the pink oil from surface of the stock. Personally, I like the color and the flavor of the oil so I leave it.

When you are ready to make the risotto, unless you have just prepared your own shrimp stock, put the fish stock into a large saucepan over medium heat. Taste the stock so that you know whether or not it is salty; this will dictate how much salt to add with the rice.

Heat the oil and 1½ tablespoons of the butter in another large saucepan. Add the onions and cook for 5 minutes over high heat, until softened. Next add the chile, a little salt and some ground pepper, and cook for a minute. Add the rice and "toast" it for 3–4 minutes so that it absorbs the flavors of the other ingredients. It will start to crackle, but keep stirring with a large wooden spoon so that it doesn't burn. When toasted, add the wine and let it evaporate. Add the lemon zest and juice and stir through. Then add about ⅓ cup of the warm stock, holding the pan with one hand and folding the rice into the stock with the other. As the rice cooks, this stirring will break down the outer shell of the rice grains and create a creamy risotto. Make sure you scrape any grains of rice from the sides of the pan down into the risotto or you will have the odd uncooked grain of rice in your finished risotto.

When most of the stock has been absorbed you will see a crescent-moon shape appearing in the bottom of the pan while you stir; this is a sign to add more stock, a ladleful at a time. Do not add the next ladleful until the last one has been absorbed. After 15 minutes, add the shrimp and stir through to cook them. Taste the rice when you think it is done—after about 20–25 minutes. When the grains are left with only a hint of crunch in the center, it is time to stop. You may have stock left over. Adjust the seasoning to taste.

Remove from the heat and add the parsley and the remaining butter, and stir well. Cover the pan with the lid for no more than 3 minutes while you get warmed bowls ready. Serve right away.

Risotto al topinambour Jerusalem Artichoke Risotto

This risotto is a great vegetarian dish and enhances and celebrates the deep smoky flavor of this humble tuber. Jerusalem artichokes are actually the root of a type of sunflower, not artichokes at all. The name is thought to have derived from the Italian word for sunflower, *girasole*.

Serves 4 as a main or 6 as a starter

12 oz Jerusalem artichokes
salt
2 quarts water
1½ tablespoons extra virgin olive oil
3 tablespoons butter
½ white onion, finely chopped
2 cups risotto rice (Arborio)
⅔ cup white wine
¼ cup finely grated Parmesan, plus extra for sprinkling

FOR THE STOCK
1 medium onion, peeled and halved
6 cloves, pressed into the onion halves
1 bay leaf
1 carrot, cut in half lengthwise
2 celery ribs, cut in half

Rinse the artichokes under cold water to remove any dirt from the skins. Boil them in the salted water for 10–20 minutes, depending on size, until tender. Remove the artichokes with a slotted spoon, reserving the cooking water, and leave them to cool.

To make the stock, add the clove-studded onion, bay leaf, carrot, and celery to the reserved cooking water. Bring to a boil, then leave to simmer. Meanwhile, remove the artichoke skins with a small knife (they come off easily once boiled). Mash or purée the artichoke flesh and set aside.

Put the oil and half of the butter in a saucepan over medium heat. When hot, add the onion and cook for a few minutes. Add the rice and allow it to "toast" for 4–5 minutes, stirring constantly, until all the grains are covered in oil and are very hot, but not burnt. This helps to break them down.

Pour in the wine and simmer to allow the alcohol to evaporate. Now start adding the hot stock, a ladleful at a time, stirring constantly. You will know when to add more stock because a crescent-moon shape will appear in the bottom of the pan. Remember, the constant stirring will give you a creamy risotto, which makes it worth all the effort!

After about 20 minutes, when you have used about 1 quart of the stock, taste the rice. Once the grains retain only the merest hint of a crunch, add the artichokes, stir well and adjust the seasoning. Remove from the heat and stir in the remaining butter and the Parmesan. Cover and allow to rest for a few minutes while you warm bowls. Serve sprinkled with Parmesan.

Risotto di porri e Taleggio con pesto di noci
Leek and Taleggio Risotto with Walnut Pesto

Taleggio is soft, buttery cheese that melts easily, giving a nutty flavor to the sweetness of the leeks. The walnut pesto is milder than the Ligurian version with basil. The walnuts offer crunch and a variation of texture to the risotto. Using vegetable stock will help the flavor of your recipe, but for speed at home I have used water, which works provided the rest of the ingredients are strong.

Serves 6

1 quantity of Toasted Walnut Pesto (see recipe page 164)

8 oz leeks
8 tablespoons butter
⅓ cup olive oil
leaves from 3 sprigs of thyme
2 cups risotto rice (*Carnaroli*)
⅔ cup dry white wine
1½–2 quarts vegetable stock, hot
8 oz Taleggio, chopped coarsely, including the rind

Chop the leeks finely and fry them over a gentle heat in the butter and oil taking care not to burn them. Stir in the thyme leaves. When the leeks have softened, add the rice and "toast" it for a few minutes, stirring constantly. Add the wine and allow it to reduce for a few minutes.

Now start adding the hot stock a ladleful at a time, stirring constantly and waiting until a crescent-moon shape appears at the bottom of the pan before adding the next ladleful. Continue stirring ladlefuls of stock into the rice until the rice is almost cooked, but the grains are slightly al dente in the center. Don't worry if there is stock left over; you will probably need around 5 cups in total. Now stir in the cheese, then immediately remove from the heat and put a lid on the pan while you warm the serving bowls. Spoon into the bowls, stir in the pesto and serve.

Variation:
If you like radicchio, add half a bulb, finely shredded, with the leeks. The sweetness of the leeks balances beautifully with the bitterness of radicchio.

Risi e bisi
Rice and Peas

This old Venetian dish was traditionally served to the Doge, the head of the Serenissima (most serene) Venetian Republic at the Feast of Venice's patron saint, St. Mark, on 25th April. This feast coincided with the start of spring and peas were welcomed as the first sign of warmer weather. The consistency of this risotto is quite soupy, so be generous with the stock and provide spoons as well as forks at table.

2 lb fresh peas in their pods, or 1 lb frozen petits pois
2 quarts water for the stock made from the pods of the peas, or 1½ quarts warm vegetable stock
1 tablespoon olive oil
6 tablespoons butter
1 small white onion, finely chopped
4 oz pancetta, finely chopped
2 tablespoons finely chopped flat-leaf parsley
1½ cups risotto rice (*Vialone Nano*)
salt and freshly ground black pepper
½ cup finely grated Parmesan

If using fresh peas, shell them and drop the pods into 2 quarts of salted water to make the stock. Boil for 20 minutes, then drain off the pods and discard. Keep the stock warm in a pan. If you are using vegetable stock instead, heat gently and keep warm in a pan.

Heat the olive oil and 4 tablespoons of the butter in a large saucepan and cook the onion and pancetta until soft, then add the parsley. Stir in the peas and two ladlefuls of warm stock. Simmer, uncovered, for about 10 minutes, until the peas are cooked through and the water has evaporated.

Add the rice and stir gently with a wooden spoon for a couple of minutes. Add 2 cups of stock and leave to cook, stirring frequently. As soon as the water has been absorbed, add more stock a ladleful at a time. Continue to cook for 20–25 minutes, or until the rice has a trace of crunch in the center and the risotto has a soupy consistency. Don't worry about using up all the stock.

Remove from the heat and stir in the Parmesan and the remaining butter. Cover the pan, turn off the heat, and leave to rest for a few minutes before serving in warmed bowls.

Risotto primavera
Spring Risotto

This is fantastic made using spring vegetables at their best. Try to find baby leeks if you can as they have a delicious sweetness to them. You can make this risotto with frozen beans and peas, but it won't have that same marvelous freshness.

Serves 6

4 oz fresh shelled fava beans

8 oz fresh shelled peas

1 lb asparagus

8 oz leeks, preferably baby ones

⅓ cup olive oil

8 tablespoons butter

3 heaping tablespoons mint, chopped

3 heaping tablespoons parsley, chopped

2 cups risotto rice (*Carnaroli*)

⅔ cup dry white wine

½ cup Parmesan or *Grana Padano*, finely grated, plus extra for serving

Drop the fava beans and peas into 2 quarts of boiling salted water in a large saucepan and cook until just tender. Lift them out using a sieve or slotted spoon and set aside, reserving the water in the saucepan for the stock. Trim off the woody stems from the asparagus and any tough green parts from the leeks and add the trimmings to the stock. Bring the water back to a boil and simmer while you prepare the rest of the ingredients.

Cut the tips from the asparagus and set aside. Chop the stems finely and add to the drained peas and beans. Chop the leeks finely. Melt the butter with the oil in another large saucepan and cook the leeks for about 10 minutes until translucent, stirring regularly. Now add the peas, beans, chopped asparagus spears (not tips), and herbs and stir well to combine. Add the rice and "toast" it for a few minutes, stirring constantly, ensuring that all the grains become covered in oil. After 3 or 4 minutes add the wine and stir again until it has evaporated (about 3 minutes).

Now start adding the hot stock a ladleful at a time, stirring constantly. Wait until a crescent-moon shape appears at the bottom of the pan before adding the next ladleful. Meanwhile, steam or lightly boil the asparagus tips. When just cooked, set aside. Continue stirring ladlefuls of stock into the rice until the rice is almost cooked but the grains are slightly al dente in the center. Now stir in the cheese, then immediately remove the pan from the heat and put a lid on while you warm the serving bowls. Pour the risotto into the bowls, top with extra cheese and the asparagus tips and serve.

Risotto ai funghi porcini
Quick Porcini Mushroom Risotto

This recipe uses a partially-cooked quick method which is often employed in restaurant kitchens to save on cooking time when a customer orders risotto. Done properly, it doesn't spoil the flavor or texture in the slightest and is a good method of cooking risotto at home for a special occasion when you don't want to be segregated from your guests. If you do want to make the risotto in one go, follow the masterclass on page 208.

Serves 6

2 oz dried sliced porcini mushrooms

4 cups warm water

3¼ cups vegetable stock (see recipe page 136), warm

2 tablespoons olive oil

10 tablespoons butter

4 oz shallots or red onions, finely chopped

2 garlic cloves, peeled and lightly crushed

½ fresh or dried chile

a good pinch of salt and freshly ground black pepper

2 cups risotto rice (Arborio or Carnaroli)

¾ cup white wine

½ cup finely grated Parmesan

Put the mushrooms in a bowl with the warm water to soak for about 30 minutes. Then strain the water into a bowl through the finest sieve you have—or a piece of muslin or a tea-towel—to remove any grit. Set aside the mushrooms and reserve the soaking water.

Put the stock into a saucepan over medium heat and keep it warm. Heat the oil and 8 tablespoons of the butter in another large saucepan and, when hot, add the shallots and cook for a few minutes. Add half the mushrooms, the garlic, chile, and salt and pepper, and cook until everything has softened. Add the rice and "toast" it for a few minutes so that it absorbs the flavors of the other ingredients. Keep stirring with a large wooden spoon to prevent burning. When the rice has toasted, add the wine and allow it to evaporate. Then add 3 cups of the mushroom water (and a little of the vegetable stock, if necessary). Stir it into the rice, holding the pan with one hand and folding the rice into the stock with the other. As the rice cooks, this stirring will break down the outer shell of the rice grains and create a creamy risotto. Make sure you scrape any grains of rice from the sides of the pan down into the risotto or you will have the odd uncooked grain of rice in your finished risotto.

When most of the stock has been absorbed—around 8–10 minutes—you will see a crescent-moon shape appearing in the bottom of the pan while you stir; this is a sign to stop and remove the risotto from the heat. Pour the rice onto a baking sheet to cool. Make little holes on the surface; don't leave it flat and smooth or the heat will be unable to escape. Stir the rice a few times to help release the heat. Leave to cool. Cover and keep in the fridge for up to 24 hours.

When you are ready to resume making the risotto, turn the rice and the remaining mushrooms back into a medium saucepan and add 2 cups of warm stock (use any remaining mushroom soaking water made up to 2 cups with the vegetable stock). Add more stock as necessary, ladleful by ladleful. Taste the rice when you think it is done—around 8–10 minutes. It is ready when the grains have only a trace of crunch in the center. (You may have stock left; don't expect to finish it all.) Adjust the seasoning to taste.

Remove from the heat and add the remaining butter and half the cheese. Stir vigorously to cream the risotto, then cover the pan with the lid for no more than 3 minutes before serving in warmed bowls. Top each serving with a sprinkle of the remaining cheese.

Tip: This is a popular risotto and the flavor of the mushrooms really sings. It is deliciously warming and satisfying on a cold day and can be given the Parmesan Ice Cream treatment (see page 473) to impress still further.

Riso e Polenta
MASTERCLASS

Arancini dell'Etna
Rice Volcanoes

These little hot rice pyramids (or other shapes) are sold as snacks in bakeries around Sicily. I travelled near Etna and there they were made in the shape of its famous volcano. Fillings vary from tomato sauce to mozzarella to, in this case, ragù with peas and Fontina cheese. "The worse the rice, the better the *arancini*," goes the saying in Sicily. Arborio rice is usually used for this dish, but any rice that sticks when well cooked will work.

Makes 8

FOR THE VOLCANOES
1½ quarts vegetable stock
2¾ cups risotto rice (Arborio)
1 teaspoon saffron
1 teaspoon salt
4 tablespoons butter
sunflower oil, for frying
¾ cup fine dry breadcrumbs

FOR THE FILLING
¼ cup shelled and cooked peas
8 oz ragú (see page 172)
3 oz Fontina cheese

FOR THE BATTER
1¾ cups "00" flour or all-purpose flour
2 cups cold water

Put the stock into a large saucepan over medium heat and, when hot, add the rice, saffron, and salt. Cook without stirring (although you can shake the pan from time to time) for around 20–25 minutes, until cooked through. If necessary, add a little more stock or hot water. When the water has evaporated and the rice is cooked through, add the butter and stir in, until melted. Remove from the heat, put a lid on the pan and leave for 10 minutes.

Meanwhile, prepare the batter. Put the flour into a bowl and then add the water little by little until it is all used up. The batter will be very runny, but smooth and without any lumps of flour; whisk it if necessary.

To make the filling, stir the peas into the ragù. Cut the cheese into small pieces and divide into 8 equal portions. Heat the sunflower oil in a high-sided pan or deep fat fryer to 350°F.

Spoon the rice onto a flat work surface and work through it with your hands for around 5 minutes to break down the grains. Dip your hands into tepid water so that the rice does not stick to you.

Divide the rice into 8 equal portions. Cooking one at a time, flatten it a little into the palm of your hand.

Put around 2 tablespoons of the ragù mixture and 1 tablespoon of the cheese into the hollow in the rice.

Close the rice around the filling, squeezing and pushing the rice together with the point facing down towards you. Flatten the end away from you.

Dip the volcano into the batter and, as you bring it out, let the batter drain off.

Now roll the volcano in the breadcrumbs. Pick up more breadcrumbs and scatter them over the surface, pressing them in. Repeat to make 8 *arancini*. Drop a small piece of bread into the hot oil; if it turns brown and sizzles within a couple of minutes, the oil is ready for frying. Fry the *arancini* in batches in the hot oil until golden brown, around 7–10 minutes. Drain on the kitchen towels and serve warm.

POLENTA

Often, polenta leaves the British wondering, but ask most British people what they feel about mashed potatoes and their likely answer will be, "Mmm… melting butter… sausages and mash… the Sunday lunch my mother made…," and so on. Just as mashed potatoes conjures up homey images for us, so polenta does the same for Italians. Instantly, northern Italians think of their grandmothers lovingly stirring the huge copper pot, or *paiolo,* in their houses in the mountains. They have an emotional link with polenta; so much so that they are often called the *polentoni* by mocking southerners!

Polenta is cornmeal ground from the delicately flavored white maize or the more common yellow maize. It can be coarse (*grezza*) or fine (*fina*), depending on the desired texture. As usual, different regions prefer their polenta in different ways, and Italians can be quite divided on whether they favor white or yellow, though in general fish dishes, such as *baccalà,* are usually served with white polenta.

It is thought that the word *polenta* originates from the Etruscan *puls*, which the Romans later called *pulmentum* and which referred to a "mash" of any type of grain, from spelt to buckwheat, which had been boiled and mashed. Maize, or *mais* as it is known in Italian, wasn't brought to Italy until the sixteenth century, when it arrived in Venice from Turkey. The Venetians called it *grano turco*, "Turkish grain," and within a hundred years of its arrival maize was being grown all over the land then known as Venetia, where it brought relief from hunger to thousands of people who made it into polenta. Unfortunately, everyone was so charmed by maize that they often ate nothing else during harsh winters, and soon a new disease arose known as *Pellagra*, meaning bad skin, cause by a lack of any other food in the diet. It became such a problem that polenta was banned and famine returned to Venezia. Finally, it was recognized that a balanced diet of a variety of foods was necessary for health, and polenta was welcomed back into the diet.

Once cooked in water or milk or both, soft polenta might be mixed with a cheese such as gorgonzola, or it is often left to cool and set; then it can be cut into slices and fried for *polenta fritta* or grilled to make *crostini di polenta*, perhaps topped with mushrooms. Other famous polenta dishes include *Polenta Concia* (see page 224), where the polenta is sliced, then layered with either ragù, sausages, mushrooms or cheese, and baked. If you go to the pretty town of Bergamo you will see strange little birds made of polenta, which look very sweet but hark back to a traditional dish of songbirds cooked inside a polenta crust, known as *polenta e osei*.

These days you can buy instant polenta, but it doesn't have the feel and flavor of traditional polenta, stirred clockwise over the heat for 45 minutes (see recipe, right) or for real devotees, up to three hours—many an Italian *nonna* will tell you that the longer you cook polenta, the better the texture.

Traditional Polenta

Depending on the region you are from, polenta is made with water, milk, or as I suggest here, with a mixture of the two.

Serves 6

salt
1 bay leaf
3¼ cups of water, or half milk and half water
¾ cup uncooked polenta

Put a good pinch of salt and the bay leaf in the water or milk and water mixture in a large saucepan. Bring it to a boil and then gradually pour in the polenta, whisking to prevent lumps from forming. Keep stirring (traditionally clockwise, but I can't see the point in this!) over a low heat for 40–45 minutes, until the consistency of hot cereal.

Eat right away as it is or with 4 ounces of cubed gorgonzola or grated Parmesan stirred in.

For firm polenta, pour onto a baking sheet or glass dish and allow to cool until set, 1–1½ hours.

Polenta Concia
Layered Mushroom, Mascarpone, and Polenta Bake

This is utterly delicious comfort food based on the tradition of the mountain dwellers from areas such as Val d'Aosta and Lombardy in the north of Italy. Our friend Stefano's aunt Maria came from here and showed me her traditional use of firm polenta. She said *"Più si mette, più si trova,"* meaning the more you put in the more you find, which I thought was a great way of describing this dish. It is a baked polenta layered with whatever needs using up. Her special tip was to add Kraft cheese slices! I decided to miss these out, so try this mushroom version.

Serves 6

FOR THE POLENTA
¾ cup uncooked polenta, or 1 lb 8 oz cooked polenta
salt
2 bay leaves

1 white onion (8 oz) sliced in rings
salt and freshly ground black pepper
8 tablespoons butter
12 oz mushrooms (mixed or one type only)
2 garlic cloves
2 sprigs of rosemary
8 oz mascarpone
1 cup milk
a good pinch of grated nutmeg
2 cups finely grated Parmesan

Follow the cooking instructions on the package for the uncooked polenta, using half water, half milk if desired and adding salt and the bay leaves for extra flavor. Bring the liquid to a boil in a large saucepan, then gradually whisk in the polenta. Keep stirring until all the polenta is incorporated, keeping it over a low heat for 40–45 minutes. Pour onto a baking sheet or glass dish and allow to cool until set. This will take 1–1½ hours.

Preheat the oven to 350°F. Cook the onion rings with a little salt and pepper in half the butter until soft. In another frying pan cook the mushrooms, garlic, and rosemary in the rest of the butter over high heat, adding salt and pepper to taste. Meanwhile, mix the mascarpone and milk together with the nutmeg.

Slice the set polenta into ¼ inch slices. Butter a medium lasagne or other ovenproof dish. Lay half the polenta slices in the bottom, scatter the fried onions over the top, followed by the mushrooms; sprinkle with pepper and add half of the Parmesan. Pour over half the mascarpone sauce and arrange the remaining polenta slices on top. Pour over the remaining sauce and finish with the remaining Parmesan. Transfer the dish to the oven and bake for 30 minutes, or until bubbling and browned.

Polenta al forno alla Anna del Conte
Baked Polenta á la Anna del Conte

In her book *The Painter, the Cook and the Art of Cucina*, Anna del Conte gives a simple but delicious version of baked polenta.

Serves 4–8

1½ quarts water
2 teaspoons sea salt
1½ cups coarse yellow polenta
unsalted butter

Heat the oven to 375°F. Bring the water to a boil. Turn down the heat and add the salt. Now add the polenta in a very slow stream while beating with a balloon whisk to prevent lumps from forming. When you have added all the polenta, turn the heat up, take a long-handled wooden spoon or stick and continue cooking and stirring for 8–10 minutes.

Butter a deep ovenproof dish, pour in the mixture and bake for 45 minutes.

Tip: If you like a stiffer texture, add more polenta and if you like it softer, add less.

Insalata di mozzarella, pomodori e cetriolo
Farro Salad with Mozzarella, Tomato, and Cucumber

Salads such as these are made all over Italy with rice, farro, barley, or couscous. In Tuscany I watched our friend Livia using two types of Pecorino, the local sheep's cheese. if you find this hard to buy try Emmental or Gouda as well as Parmesan or omit the cheese and add tuna and sundried tomatoes instead.

Serves 8

8 oz *farro* (emmer wheat or spelt)
8 oz ripe tomatoes, cut into ½ in cubes
4 oz young pecorino, cut into ½ in cubes
4 oz ball buffalo mozzarella, roughly torn
 into bite-sized pieces
2 celery ribs, finely diced
4 oz cucumber, cut into ½ in cubes
20 basil leaves, shredded
small handful of parsley, roughly chopped
⅔ cup extra virgin olive oil
2–3 tablespoons red wine vinegar
salt and freshly ground black pepper

Wash the farro grains in a sieve under cold running water. Drop the farro into salted boiling water for 15 to 20 minutes or until cooked through but still al dente. (There are different varieties of farro, some of which need a lot more cooking time). Cool the farro under cold running water in a colander. Prepare the rest of the ingredients and mix together with the farro in a large bowl. Season to taste with salt and pepper.

Insalata di couscous al limone
Lemon Couscous Salad

Franco Taruschio taught me this dish. He serves it with Poussin Stuffed with Grapes (see page 337), which lends it a Middle Eastern feel, even though a lot of couscous is eaten in the east of Sicily. I particularly like the flavor of lemon, so I have added a little more than in his recipe. Franco uses sage in his recipe, but you could substitute parsley. Try this as a buffet dish with Roasted Vegetables and Peperonata (see page 106).

Serves 4

1 lb couscous
2½ cups boiling chicken stock or water
½ cup olive oil
zest of 2 small lemons, finely grated
juice of 3 lemons
4 tablespoons salted capers, rinsed
6 tablespoons finely shredded sage leaves
⅓ cup pine nuts

Pour the couscous into a bowl and cover with the stock or water. Cover tightly with plastic wrap and let it stand for 5 minutes, or until the liquid has been absorbed. Use a fork to fluff up the couscous, separating the grains.

Heat half the oil in a large frying pan over medium heat. Add the lemon zest, capers, sage leaves, and pine nuts and cook for 7 minutes, or until the nuts are lightly toasted. Add the contents of the pan to the couscous with the rest of the oil and the lemon juice, and toss to combine. Serve at room temperature.

Pesce

CHAPTER 6: FISH

Pesce

Italians always seem to have a fishing story. When Giancarlo was growing up, he used to catch eels by hand—he would wrap his hands in burlap first, to get a good grip—while our head chef at Caffé Caldesi, Monserrato, and his dad used to catch carp and perch from the river bed (also with their hands) as they fed on the bamboo shoots at the water's edge. Both families needed to supplement their diet with whatever they could catch around them, but they enjoyed the experience, too. Giancarlo and his brother also used to go out catching frogs, which they would stun with the light from their flashlights!

iancarlo and Monserrato are inland Italians and so only ate freshwater or lake fish—*pesce d'acqua dolce*—when they were young. Such fish would usually have to be purged before eating, to get rid of the 'muddy' flavor that often characterises lake fish. Gone are the days when wealthy Romans had channels built from the sea to their ponds so that they could have a fresh supply of sea water. As a result, Roman lake fish wouldn't have tasted that dissimilar to a seabass.

Only four of Italy's twenty regions do not have a coastline. And each of those four regions has lakes and rivers that provide a good source of fish. After the Roman era, monasteries continued to keep fish ponds—full of carp, trout, and eels—so it's not surprising that fish has been an important source of food for Italians since earliest times, regardless of where they lived. Bartolomeo Scappi, the Renaissance cook and writer, who cooked for six popes, wrote down many of the recipes for the fish dishes he cooked at banquets, including for stockfish and *pottaggi*, forerunners of the fish soup beloved by Italians in countless forms all over the country.

It is only really in the last decade that fish has been transported around Italy so that now you can find a range beyond the local catch in supermarkets, and inland Italians, especially, have more access to different species of sea fish. Tuna is a perfect example of that change: while fresh tuna has always been cooked in a variety of ways in the south, the idea of a tuna steak in northern Italy would have been unheard of until the 1990s. Before then, in the north it was only available in cans. Confusingly, though, the names of fish differ the length and breadth of Italy—for example a seabass is known as *branzino* in the north but in the south is referred to as *spigola*, and anchovies are either called *alici* or *acciughe*, depending on where you come from.

Fishermen who go out to sea can have dangerous lives and many coastal towns have local patron saints to protect them. You often see shrines around their statues or carved names or plaques telling of storms and the loss of life. When you see the small wooden fishing boats that are often still in use today, it seems that life hasn't changed that much around Italy's coastal communities, despite the advent of supermarkets. The fish markets are full of hustle and bustle and usually there is a plentiful supply of fish, especially the small ones that are essential for the many fish stews and soups enjoyed all around Italy's coast (see pages 256–258)—unless, of

course, the sea is so stormy that the fishermen can't go out. Or it is festival time. When we were in Sicily shooting photographs for this book, I managed to pick the one day of the year when the local fish auction was closed, and there was only a handful of sardines and crustaceans in the market. It turned out that this was the day after the annual *festa*, when all the fishermen had terrible hangovers!

Another thing to remember about Italy and fish is that certain fish are only caught in the appropriate season—again, I found this out to my cost while shooting photographs in Sardinia for the masterclasses in this book. I was told very firmly, "*Non è il periodo Signora*" (it is not the season) for monkfish, calamari, tuna, and many of the other varieties of fish I had hoped to photograph being landed.

Even though the market for different varieties of fresh fish has opened up so much more recently—and there are even laws stating that frozen fish has to be declared on Italian menus—the tradition of preserving fish to eat when they are out of season is as alive now as it has always been during the last 8,000 years. The Romans preserved fish and used garum, a fish sauce made from decaying fish. They were fond of anchovies, which play a big role in Italian cooking, adding flavor and saltiness to a dish, often in ways we wouldn't think of elsewhere—for example in the old Roman dish *abbacchio*, lamb is combined with anchovies to delicious effect. Salted anchovies are sold from massive brightly colored cans in the markets and are wonderful when rinsed and marinated in olive oil and lemon or vinegar (see page 249). And then, of course, there is *baccalà* (salted and dried cod) and *stoccafisso*, which is similar, except that the cod is air-dried but not salted. I also love tuna *sott„olio* (packed in olive oil), which has a delicacy to it that lifts it above the canned tuna that we have at home. While trout have long been smoked around the lakes in the north of Italy, it is only in recent years that other smoked fish have been found on restaurant menus—smoked tuna, swordfish, and salmon are also popular today.

When I was in Puglia, I noticed just how many restaurants serve raw fish (see the *carpaccio* recipes on page 261). These days, many Italians, the young especially, are familiar with sushi, but in Puglia and a few other regions, raw fish has been popular for centuries, so it is strange to think that the Japanese have probably re-introduced Italian people to a way of eating that their predecessors had followed for a very long time.

KATIE'S TIPS PREPARING FISH:

A good pair of kitchen scissors is essential for cutting away fins and tails.

A fish filleting knife is very flexible; being made from thin metal, it bends easily when pressed against fish bones. This helps you to separate the flesh from the bones without cutting into it.

Always make sure that knives are sharp: you are more likely to hurt yourself with a dull knife.

If the fish is slippery use a dry kitchen towel or paper towel to hold it in place.

Keep the cutting board in place by placing a damp cloth underneath it.

A pair of pin-bone tweezers, available at cook shops, will help you to pull out any remaining bones from a fillet.

KNOWING WHEN FISH IS FRESH:

The gills should be bright reddish pink and when you smell behind them there should be no taint of ammonia. If the fish is from the sea, there should be a pleasant aroma of the sea.

The eyes should be clear and bright; if they are sunken and opaque, the fish has been out of the water for too long.

The flesh should be firm to the touch and should not leave an imprint when poked with a finger.

If possible, buy live shellfish to be sure of their freshness.

If the shells of live mussels, clams, and other shellfish stay open when tapped, they are dead and should be discarded.

Pesce
MASTERCLASS

How to Clean and Gut a Round Fish

Using scissors or a knife, remove all the fins from the fish.

Remove the scales from the fish with a table knife or blade, using the blunt side to scrape. This is more easily done under running water, otherwise the scales "ping" around the room!

If you want to keep the fish intact for cooking whole, make a short cut—around 3 inches long—from the middle of the fish to the small hole at the end of the belly. If filleting the fish, you can make a longer cut, to open up the whole fish from head to tail.

Use your fingers to pull out the guts, and discard. Hold the fish under cold running water to clean it and wash away the blood. If the blood is in clots around the spine and you want to cook the fish whole, use the tip of the knife to scrape them away. Wash the fish well under cold running water.

Use the tip of the knife or scissors to cut the gills loose at the two points where they attach to the body; pull away and discard. Wash the fish again and dry with paper towels. It is now ready to cook whole.

How to Fillet a Round Fish

Remove the head from behind the gills, including the triangle of flesh where the fin was attached. Discard or use for a fish stock.

Slide the knife just above the spine, keeping the blade as close as possible to the bones. Hold the fish down firmly with the other hand.

Continue sliding the knife to the tail, lifting the fillet away with the other hand.

Now repeat on the other side.

Cut away the remaining rib cage and any fat from inside the fish. Trim away the skin to form a neat edge around the fillets.

Trota lessa con finocchio al vapore e salsa di timo e limone
Poached Salmon Trout with Lemon and Thyme Dressing on Steamed Fennel

This is a very healthy way to cook fish and it is full of flavor and easy to prepare. I have used salmon trout because I like the color and flavor, but ordinary trout, sea bass, or salmon would work equally well—just adjust the cooking times according to the size of the fish. The stock can be prepared in advance, but if you do this, remove the lemon zest after it is cooked or the flavor will be too strong. The rest of the ingredients can remain in the stock to further infuse.

Serves 2

2 medium salmon trout, scaled
  and cleaned (see opposite)
1 fennel bulb
1 tablespoon extra virgin olive
oil or butter
black pepper

FOR THE STOCK
2 or 3 tops from the fennel bulb
2 quarts water
zest of 1 lemon, peeled in long
  strips
3 bay leaves

10 black peppercorns
salt, to taste

FOR THE SAUCE
¼ cup olive oil
1 small garlic clove, peeled and
  finely chopped
juice from 1 lemon
2 sprigs of thyme, leaves
  stripped
salt
2 tablespoons finely chopped
  flat-leaf parsley

First prepare the stock. Cut the long green stems and fronds from the fennel bulb and put them into a frying pan wide enough to allow the fish to lie horizontally or in a fish poacher. Add the remaining stock ingredients and bring to a boil. Taste for salt and adjust as necessary. Let it simmer for 30 minutes.

Meanwhile, prepare the sauce by mixing the ingredients together. Adjust the seasoning to taste.

Poach the trout in the stock over medium heat, allowing the water to just bubble gently. Cover the pan with a circle of parchment paper to keep the fish within the water and steam them. They will take about 10 minutes, depending on the size of the fish.

Meanwhile, thinly slice the fennel bulb and cook it in a steamer for a few minutes, until tender. Remove from the heat, dress with a little olive oil, salt, butter, and plenty of black pepper, then arrange on a warm serving dish.

To test if the fish are done, push down on their backs. If the flesh is firm to the touch, remove the fish from the stock and place on a warmed serving dish. Serve the fish on the steamed fennel, either with boiled new potatoes or a Lemon Couscous Salad (see page 225) with the dressing on the side.

Filetto di branzino o orata con purè di cannellini e salsa verde
Pan-fried Sea bass or Sea bream Fillets on Cannellini Bean Mash with Salsa Verde

This is one of the best sellers in our restaurants. It is quick and easy to prepare and good for entertaining because the bean mash and salsa verde can be prepared in advance, leaving just the fish to cook. I like to get the skin of the fillets crispy so that it contrasts perfectly with the soft bean mash.

Serves 4

4 sea bass or sea bream fillets (see page 230), skin on
salt and freshly ground black pepper
¼ cup all-purpose flour, for dusting
2 tablespoons olive oil, plus extra for drizzling

FOR THE SALSA VERDE
½ cup olive oil
⅓ cup flat-leaf parsley
1 tablespoon capers, drained and rinsed
5 anchovy fillets
1 tablespoon lemon juice
1 garlic clove
salt and freshly ground black pepper, to taste

FOR THE CANNELLINI MASH
5 tablespoons extra virgin olive oil
2 sprigs of rosemary
1 garlic clove, crushed with the flat side of a knife
2 x 14 oz cans cannellini beans, drained and rinsed
¾ cup vegetable stock or water (if required)

First prepare the salsa verde by combining and blending all the ingredients in a food processor. Adjust the seasoning to taste and set aside.

Next prepare the mash. Heat the oil in a frying pan, add the rosemary and garlic and cook gently for 3 minutes, taking care that they do not burn. Add the beans and cook for 10 minutes, stirring occasionally, until they are soft enough to mash in the pan. If the mixture appears too dry, add a little stock or water. Remove the rosemary sprigs and garlic and use a potato masher to gently crush the beans, but retain some of the texture. Cover and keep warm.

Cut each fish fillet into thirds, season with salt and pepper and flour lightly, tapping off the excess. Heat the oil in a large frying pan over medium heat and place the fillets in the pan, skin-side down. Cook for 3 minutes, until the skin is crispy. You may need to press each fillet down slightly as the skin contracts upon cooking. Carefully turn each fillet over and cook for another 2 minutes. You may need to extend the cooking time for thicker fillets, but take care not to overcook them; the fish should be firm to the touch but not dry.

Place a portion of cannellini mash in the center of warmed plates, layer three pieces of fillet on top and drizzle with the salsa verde and a little olive oil. Serve right away.

Orata con semi di finocchio e brandy
Sea bream with Fennel Seeds and Brandy

This is a dish with real punch. I love the brandy and chile as well as the spice of the seeds. The sauce works with most white fish with enough flavor to stand up to it—try cod, coley, or hake.

Serves 4

2 sea bream fillets (see page 230), cut in half
flour, for dredging
⅓ cup sunflower oil
¼ cup extra virgin olive oil
2 teaspoons crushed fennel seeds
2 anchovy fillets
½ red chile, including seeds
2 garlic cloves, peeled
a good pinch of salt
¼ cup brandy
¼ cup dry white wine
½ cup fish stock (see page 138) or water

Season and flour the fish, tapping off the excess. Heat the sunflower oil and fry the fish pieces until golden brown on both sides. Meanwhile, chop the anchovy, chile, and garlic very finely together. Remove the fish and set aside on a warm plate. Pour off the leftover oil and any browned bits, and wipe out the pan.

Pour the olive oil into the pan and, when hot, add the fennel seeds, anchovy, chile, and garlic. Cook gently until softened, then return the fish to the pan, pour in the brandy and ignite. Carefully pour in the wine and reduce for a couple of minutes. Add the stock and cook for 5 minutes or until the fish is cooked through. Serve with mashed potatoes.

1 whole sea bass, cleaned (see page 230),
  or 2 fillets, skin on
salt and freshly ground black pepper
3 tablespoons olive oil
1 garlic clove, finely sliced
1 sprig of thyme
10 cherry tomatoes, halved
1 sprig of basil
½ cup dry white wine
¾ cup water or fish stock (see page 138)

Spigola all' acquapazza
Sea bass in Crazy Water

"Ma, sei pazza?"—"Are you mad?" is often shouted by one Italian to another (or to me when I even think about changing a recipe!). *Pazza* in this sense means "mad" or "crazy." It is applied to the cooking liquid in this dish because it should bubble and foam furiously as the fish cooks quickly in it. The recipe is from Naples, but this method of cooking fish is used all over Italy. Monkfish, scorpion fish and many others are also good cooked in this way. *Spigola* is the name for sea bass in the south; in the north it is often referred to as *branzino*.

Serves 2

Season the sea bass with salt and use the tip of a knife to make 3 slits in each side to allow the sauce to flavor the fish. Set aside.

Heat the oil and cook the garlic with salt and pepper for a minute or two, then add the thyme, tomatoes, and basil. Cook for 1 minute and then add the fish, skin-side down if using fillets. Let it cook briefly on either side, then add the white wine and the water or stock. Bring to a boil and let it bubble furiously for 10 minutes or until the fish is cooked through.

Season the sauce to taste. Serve on warm plates with bread to mop up the sauce.

Sgombro con piselli e pancetta
Mackerel with Peas and Pancetta

Sometimes known as *lacerti*, mackerel are not as common in Italy as they are in the UK, but I have seen these beautifully mottled fish in the markets of Liguria and Sardinia. For some bizarre reason they remind me of the actor David Niven: long, lean, and elegantly dressed. Now that is in my head, I cannot look at a mackerel without thinking of him! Mackerel are usually cooked with peas, but I like the twist in this recipe, in which pancetta adds a pleasant saltiness. You need enough pancetta to wrap around 18 pieces of mackerel—if in doubt or the pancetta slices are short, buy extra.

Serves 6

3 medium mackerel
9 slices of pancetta, each one halved lengthwise
2 cups frozen, fresh, or canned peas
flour, for dusting
6 tablespoons olive oil
1 onion, finely choppped
2 anchovy fillets
½ red chile
1 tablespoon finely chopped parsley
2 tablespoons tomato paste
⅓ cup white wine
salt and freshly ground black pepper
2 teaspoons sugar (optional)

18 toothpicks, to secure the pancetta

Clean the mackerel by cutting them through just behind the heads and pulling out the guts with your fingers, keeping the bodies intact. Cut off the fins and tails and discard. Cut each fish crosswise into 6 pieces, each one about 1½ inches long. Wrap each piece of mackerel, skin in tact, in a slice of pancetta and secure with a toothpick.

Boil the peas in 2 cups salted water for 5–10 minutes, until done. Then drain, reserving the cooking water.

Season the mackerel and dust with flour. Heat 2 tablespoons of the oil in a large frying pan and add the mackerel pieces. Cook for a couple of minutes on each side until lightly browned and the pancetta is slightly crispy. Remove the pieces from the pan and set aside.

Clean the pan, discarding the oil, then heat the remaining oil. Cook the onion, anchovies, chile, and parsley over a medium-high heat for 1 minute. Stir in the tomato paste until combined, then add the mackerel pieces and white wine. Allow to reduce for a couple of minutes and then add the peas and 1 cup of the reserved cooking water. Cook for 15–20 minutes, until the mackerel is tender. Season to taste and, if necessary, add sugar (this may not be necessary with canned peas, which often contain sugar in the preserving water). Remove the toothpicks from the mackerel and serve 3 pieces per person on a spoonful of peas.

Orata al forno all' isolana
Baked Sea bream with Crispy Potatoes and Tomatoes

This is an easy dish that epitomizes much of Italy's great cooking: a few perfect ingredients simply prepared. Of course, you could murder this recipe with cheap, pitted canned olives and a fish that has seen a few days on shore. But you could also choose your fish or fishmonger wisely, pit the best-quality little black olives you can find (preferably *taggiasche*), only use perfectly ripe tomatoes and drizzle with a peppery, pungent olive oil. Hey presto! You have wondrous Italian cooking on a plate which celebrates the star ingredient—the fish.

Serves 4–6

12 oz potatoes, peeled
⅔ cup white wine
⅓ cup olive oil
salt and freshly ground black pepper
1 teaspoon dried oregano
2 whole sea bass or sea bream, scaled and gutted,
  gills and fins removed but head and tail intact
  (see page 230 or ask your fishmonger to do this)
a handful of flat-leaf parsley
4 oz cherry tomatoes, halved
15 good black olives, pitted (optional)

Preheat the oven to 400°F. Slice the potatoes as thinly as possible—around 1–2mm thick—put in a pile on a baking sheet and pour in half the wine and half the oil. Season and sprinkle with the oregano. Gently toss the potatoes with the wine and oil to mix, then spread in a single layer. Put in the oven for 15 minutes.

Meanwhile, season the fish cavity with salt and pepper and fill with a generous amount of parsley. Season the outside of the fish also.

Remove the tray from the oven; reduce the temperature to 350°F. Baste the potatoes with the juices and move any crispy ones to the center. Place the fish on the layered potatoes and scatter the tomatoes and olives, if using, over the top. Drizzle the fish with the remaining olive oil and wine. Return to the oven for 15–20 minutes, until the fish is cooked through (put the point of a knife into the back of the fish and twist; flesh should come easily away from the bone). Remove and serve immediately, pouring the cooking juices over the fish.

Spiedini di pesce e gamberoni con arance e alloro
Salmon, Shrimp, and Tuna Skewers with Orange and Bay Leaves

The combination of salmon marinated with orange occurs frequently in Italian cuisine. However fish skewers—found mainly in the south of Italy—traditionally contain lemon slices. By all means try this, but I often think the sharpness of the lemons overpowers the delicate fish, whereas orange gives an amazing sweet contrast without the acidity.

Serves 4

4 jumbo shrimp, head and tail intact, vein and
  shell removed
1 tuna steak (about 4 oz), cut into 1 in cubes
1 salmon fillet (about 8 oz), cut into 1 in cubes
1 monkfish fillet (about 4 oz), cut into 1 in cubes
zest and juice of 1 orange
1 orange, peeled and cut into 4 thick slices
12 bay leaves
3 tablespoons olive oil
salt

4 wooden or metal skewers

If you are using wooden skewers, soak them in water for at least 30 minutes to prevent them from burning.

Put the prepared shrimp and fish, the orange zest, orange slices and bay leaves into a 9 x 13 inch lasagne or other shallow ovenproof dish and pour in the olive oil and the orange juice. Season with a good pinch of salt and toss the ingredients together gently with your fingers. Leave to marinate for at least 30 minutes, or up to 1 day in the fridge, if necessary.

When you are ready to cook, preheat the broiler while you make up the skewers. Thread the fish and shrimp onto the skewers, interspersing them evenly with the bay leaves and pieces of sliced orange. Strain and discard the orange zest from the marinade and reserve for basting. Put the skewers under the broiler for around 10 minutes, or until done. Turn them halfway through and baste with the reserved marinade.

Serve with crusty bread, a glass of good rosé and a salad of lettuce and mint leaves, or with Lemon Couscous Salad (see page 225).

These skewers also work really well if you
have a steamer oven or if your skewers will
fit in a steamer placed on the stove for
about 10–15 minutes or until cooked through.

Salmone al forno in crosta di pistacchi e miele
Oven-baked Salmon with Pistachio and Honey Crust

I was shown this slightly unusual combination of salmon and parsnips by two Italian chefs. One of them, Cristiano, suggested it for our *Caffè*. Muttering about weird combinations and modern cooking, I sat down to try it and had to eat my words—and the whole plate of fish—it was delicious! It's a modern fusion of ingredients because, except in the far north, parsnips are not common in Italy. However, the sweetness of the parsnips and honey is perfect with the strong-flavored salmon, and the bright green crust contrasts impressively with the pink. The parsnips are a great partner in winter, but in summer I would serve a side of salmon as part of a buffet by doubling or tripling this recipe and serving with Gino's Tomato Salsa (see page 96) or Lemon Couscous Salad (see page 225) and a crisp green salad.

Serves 4

½ cup shelled pistachios
1 slice stale bread
1 tablespoon rosemary leaves
1 tablespoon thyme leaves
salt and freshly ground black pepper
4 salmon steaks, or one piece of salmon
  (about 1¼ lb)
4 teaspoons honey
4 teaspoons olive oil

FOR THE PARSNIP PURÉE
1 lb parsnips, cut into large chunks
2 tablespoons butter
2–4 tablespoons milk
salt and freshly ground black pepper

Preheat the oven to 350°F. If time allows, drop the pistachios into boiling water for 3–4 minutes, drain, then slip off the skins. This gives a much greener, brighter color to contrast with the salmon. It also gives the nuts a little more moisture, making them less likely to dry out in the oven. If time is short, though, you can leave them unskinned; the flavor is equally satisfying, even if they are not so pretty on the plate.

Boil the parsnips in salted water for 20–25 minutes, or until cooked through.

Meanwhile, prepare the crust for the salmon steaks. Chop the nuts by hand or in a food processor until they are the size of peppercorns. Set aside in a mixing bowl. Do the same with the bread and herbs to make herb breadcrumbs, then mix thoroughly with the nuts and salt and pepper.

Season the salmon all over with a little salt and, if using steaks, place them against one another in a roasting tin. Drizzle the honey over the salmon, spreading it out with your finger. Now coat with the breadcrumb mixture, patting it down so that it sticks to the honey. Drizzle with the oil. If using steaks, separate them to allow even cooking. Transfer to the oven for 15–25 minutes, or until cooked through. Check the thickest part in the center by piercing it with a knife and twisting gently to see if it's done.

When the parsnips are cooked, drain them in a colander then return them to the pan and mash with the butter, milk, and salt and pepper, until smooth. Set aside. Serve the salmon on a bed of parsnip mash.

Trota ripiena di gamberi e brandy
Trout with Shrimp and Brandy Stuffing

Inland Italy has many recipes for freshwater fish because, until relatively recently, fish and seafood were available only to coastal communities, unless salted or dried. This recipe is packed with flavor from the shrimp, anchovies, and brandy. The dish also looks impressive when served: the shape of the fish is maintained because the head and tail are intact and the stuffing is inserted into the belly.

Serves 2

2 trout, gutted and spines
   removed (see page 230)

FOR THE STUFFING
2 tablespoons olive oil
1 garlic clove, finely chopped
3 anchovy fillets, finely
   chopped
1 small red chile, finely
   chopped
8 oz peeled shrimp, coarsely
   chopped
2 tablespoons brandy
2 tablespoons dry white wine
¼ cup flat-leaf parsley,
   chopped
3 tablespoons breadcrumbs
1 egg
a few sprigs of thyme

Preheat the oven to 350°F. To make the stuffing, heat the oil in a medium saucepan and cook the garlic, anchovies and chilli for 2–3 minutes until golden brown in color, taking care not to burn them. Add the chopped shrimp and cook for 5 minutes. When the shrimp start to stick, add the brandy and flambé, or allow to reduce.

Add the white wine and allow to reduce for a couple of minutes. Remove from the heat, leave the mixture to cool, then add the parsley, breadcrumbs, and egg. Mix thoroughly. Divide the stuffing in half. Stuff both trout with half the mixture and place them on a baking sheet with the thyme sprigs between them. Transfer to the oven and bake for 20–25 minutes, depending on the size of the fish. Serve with a simple green salad and roast potatoes.

Pesce
MASTERCLASS

How to Clean a Fish Through the Gills

Put the tip of the scissors through the small hole at the lower end of the fish's belly and snip the intestine which lies beneath this hole without making the hole any bigger.

Pull out and discard the frilly red gills on each side of the fish's head. Most of the guts will come out with this. Use your finger to pull out the rest.

Rinse the fish well by running plenty of cold water through the fish until the water runs clear. If you are planning to cook the fish in salt it does not need to be de-scaled.

How to Fillet a Cooked Round Fish

Crack the salt crust with a spoon and lift away any large pieces of salt. Use a pastry brush or spoon to push away any remaining pieces.

Cut the skin on either side of the fish by pulling it away with a fork.

Use the tines of the fork to loosen the skin just above the tail. Lift the skin under the first two tines and then turn the fork to trap the skin.

Continue turning the skin so that it wraps around the fork, revealing the fish underneath. Discard the skin.

Run the tip of the fork down the center of the fish, just to one side of the spine. Use the spoon and fork to lift the first fillet onto a warm serving plate. Do the same on the other side. Now turn the fish over and repeat on the other side.

When all four fillets are on the serving plate, drizzle with a little olive oil and serve right away.

You can also use this method to fillet a round fish that has been cooked whole in the oven without a salt crust.

Spigola in crosta di sale
Sea bass in a Salt Crust

Our children love to help with this dish,
patting the salt into a mound over the fish
and then cracking open the baked crust
with the back of a spoon. There are many
variations on this recipe: chefs will tell you to
mix egg white into the salt, to add or not to
add water, to make a dough crust, etc, etc,
but for me, the simpler the better. There's
no need to scale the fish since the skin
peels off with the salt crust.

Serves 4–6

1 whole sea bass, (about 2¼ lb), gutted (see
  page 230)
2¼ lb large-grain salt
cold water, as necessary

FOR THE LEMON AND PARSLEY OIL
⅓ cup extra virgin olive oil
juice of 1 lemon
a handful of flat-leaf parsley, coarsely chopped
salt

Preheat the oven to 400°F. Rinse and clean the fish
thoroughly (there is no need to remove the scales).

Distribute a ½ inch-thick layer of the salt over a baking
sheet or ovenproof dish. Pour the rest of the salt into a
bowl and mix in enough water to moisten but not
overwet the salt—you need a stiff slush that can be
patted into shape. Place the fish on the salt on the
pan/dish and cover completely with the remaining salt;
it should be completely encased. Put the pan/dish
in the oven and bake for 25 minutes.

To serve, crack open the salt, crush the casing with a
spoon and follow the instructions opposite. It is often
served just as it is, with no seasoning. However, I like
it with a lemon and parsley oil. To make this, simply
combine the ingredients in a cup and serve with the fish.

How to Fillet a Flat Fish

The trickiest part is removing the skin, but once you have a good grip you are on your way. Some people cut the frilly edges from the sides of the fish with scissors to help the skin come free. You can drop only the tail of the fish into very hot water to loosen the skin, or make a small cut to loosen the skin just above the tail. Then use the tip of a sharp knife to scrape the skin upwards from this point. Work your fingers up under the skin and above the flesh to loosen the skin on either side. You will be able to push your fingers between the skin and the flesh to each frilly edge at the base of the tail.

With a cloth or paper towel, grab the tail in one hand and skin in the other. Pull the skin up to the top. Repeat on the other side.

Cut down the middle of the fish on one side of the spine. Slide the knife to one side between the bones and flesh; keep the knife at a 45° angle.

Loosen the flesh from the spine all along the fish, keeping the knife close to the bone at all times, then remove the fillet. Repeat on the other side of the spine; remove the other fillet.

Turn the fish over. Remove the skin and cut away the two fillets from the back of the fish.

Razza al burro nero e capperi
Skate with Black Butter and Capers

The sharp acidity of capers mellowed out by lightly burnt butter makes a perfect sauce with which to anoint a fish as magnificent as skate. This recipe has become an Italian restaurant classic, and rightly so. It is quick and easy, yet has the air of a sophisticated restaurant dish.

Serves 2

½ large skate wing, cut in half
salt and freshly ground black pepper
flour, for dusting
3 tablespoons extra virgin olive oil
2 tablespoons butter
1 anchovy fillet, coarsely chopped
1 tablespoon capers, rinsed and drained
3 tablespoons white wine

Preheat the oven to 400°F. Lightly season and flour the skate on both sides. Heat the oil in a large frying pan or a roasting pan and cook the skate until just lightly brown on both sides. Transfer the skate to a roasting pan (if needed) and roast in the oven for 15 minutes.

Meanwhile, make the black butter. Melt the butter until it foams and turns golden, then add the anchovy, capers and wine, and cook for a few minutes, breaking it up with a wooden spoon. Remove from the heat and set aside in a warm place. Transfer the skate to a warm plate, pour the sauce over the top and serve.

Sogliola alla mugnaia
Sole with Lemon and Parsley

This classic dish has lasted through the years because the gentle sauce complements the delicate flavor of the fish. *Mugnaia* means a girl who worked in a mill making flour. Maybe the leftover flour was used to thicken sauces!

Serves 4

4 lemon sole or 2 Dover sole, filleted (see opposite)
salt and pepper
sunflower oil, for frying
⅓ cup white wine
¾ cup fish stock (see page 138)
zest and juice of 1 lemon
a handful of parsley, chopped
2 tablespoons butter
2 tablespoons flour

Take the fish fillets, season and flour them on both sides. Heat the oil in a frying pan and cook the fillets for 1 minute on each side, using an offset spatula to turn them. Set the fillets aside and pour away the leftover oil. Pour in the wine and let it reduce for 2 minutes. Pass the liquid through a sieve into a bowl.

Wipe the pan with a paper towel, put it back on the heat and add the fillets. Pour in the stock, lemon juice and zest, white wine reduction, and parsley. Squeeze the butter and flour into a lump in your hand and add to the sauce to thicken it, stirring carefully with a wooden spoon or small whisk (do not break up the fish). When the sauce has thickened, serve the fish on heated plates, drizzled with the sauce.

Brodetto di San Pietro con patate e zafferano
John Dory Stew with Potatoes and Saffron

This is an example of a fish stew without tomato. The color and flavor of saffron is wonderful with the John Dory. Fillet the fish yourself (see page 242) or ask your fishmonger to do it, but keep the bones because you will need them for the stock.

Serves 4

2 carrots, coarsely chopped
top and green fronds of a fennel bulb (optional)
½ fresh red chile, finely sliced
2 celery ribs, coarsely chopped
⅓ cup olive oil
salt and freshly ground black pepper
1 tablespoon parsley, finely chopped
4 small John Dory (or 2 large), or 2 sea bream, filleted with bones reserved
1 tablespoon white wine vinegar
¼ cup brandy
2 bay leaves
½ teaspoon saffron
1 quart vegetable stock
juice of 1 lemon
2 fresh purple or green artichokes, thinly sliced, fried in a pan (optional)
1 tablespoon butter
1 fat garlic clove, crushed and peeled
1 lb new potatoes or 3 medium potatoes, peeled and cooked a few sprigs of dill, finely chopped

Cook the carrot, fennel, chile, and celery in half of the oil and season. Add the parsley and cook for 7–10 minutes, then add the fish bones. After a few minutes stir the vinegar, brandy, bay leaves, and saffron. Add the stock or water and bring to a boil. Boil gently (do not simmer) for 20–30 minutes. Strain the stock and discard the bones and vegetables. Allow the stock to boil and reduce for 15 minutes, until half its original volume. Add the lemon juice, taste and season. Season and flour the fish fillets and artichokes and cook in the remaining oil until cooked through. Whisk the butter into the sauce and add the potatoes. Put the fish onto serving plates. Mix in the dill and serve the scrape the sauce and potatoes over the fish. Serve with thinly sliced steamed and buttered fennel.

Pesce spada alla griglia con salmoriglio
Grilled or Barbecued Swordfish with Salmoriglio Sauce

This summery sauce comes from Sicily and certain parts of Calabria. Half of the sauce is used to marinate the fish and the remainder to dress it after cooking. This sauce works well on more or less any type of fish. Try it with grilled shrimp, roast whole sea bass, or tuna steaks—and with grilled lamb, too.

Serves 4

4 swordfish steaks

FOR THE SAUCE
6 tablespoons extra virgin olive oil
¼ cup lemon juice
finely grated zest of ½ lemon
6 tablespoons coarsely chopped flat-leaf parsley
2 tablespoons fresh oregano or marjoram leaves or 2 teaspoons dried oregano
salt and freshly ground black pepper

Make the sauce by combining all the ingredients in a bowl and adjust the seasoning to taste. Marinate the fish in half of the sauce for 30 minutes. Do not leave it in the marinade for longer than 1 hour or the fish will start to 'cook' in the acidity of the lemon.

Cook the steaks under a preheated broiler grill or on a grill for 1–2 minutes on each side, or until just cooked. If you can, turn the fish by 180° mid-way through cooking on each side so that it has the appearance of grill marks on the outside. Dress with the remaining sauce and serve with Lemon Couscous Salad (see page 225) and Giorgio's Salad (see page 403) and plenty of crusty bread.

Baccalà e Stoccafisso

SALT COD AND DRIED COD

Baccalà, which is popular in the south of Italy, is cod which has been gutted and had its backbone removed. It is then salted and dried. *Stoccafisso* is air-dried—but not salted—cod, and is found mainly in the north, especially in Liguria and the Veneto. However, just to be confusing, it is also often referred to as *baccalà*! Both were popular on Fridays and other meatless days in the Catholic calender, and they made good foods for travellers since they would keep for a long time.

Before cooking, both *baccalà* and *stoccafisso* need to be soaked (whole or filleted) in water for 48 hours, with the water changed every 12 hours. After soaking, fillets need only to be rinsed and patted dry. Whole fish should be taken off the bone and the pin bones removed with tweezers. Again, wash and pat dry. In Italy many grocers sell ready-soaked *baccalà*.

Baccalà mantecato is typical in Venice; the fish is pounded in a mortar and oil is then added to it, together with parsley and garlic, so that it becomes creamy. It has a delicious flavor. I also love the *Polpettine* (see opposite) that I ate in Sardegna in which the fish was cooked, flaked and mixed with parsley and breadcrumbs to make fishballs. I have made this recipe successfully using freshly cooked coley instead of *baccalà*.

Baccalà alla Siciliana con porri
Sicilian Salt Cod with Leeks

This is typically Sicilian. The sweet leeks are delicious with the salty cod, and potatoes make it a one-pot meal.

Serves 6

3 potatoes, peeled and cut into 1 in cubes
1¼ lb salt cod, soaked for 48 hours (see left), or 1¼ lb fresh cod or pollack
flour, for dredging
3 tablespoons sunflower oil
3 tablespoons olive oil
1 fat garlic clove, lightly crushed
1 shallot or small onion, finely chopped
1 leek (about 4 oz), finely chopped
3 tablespoons dry white wine
1 x 14 oz can Italian tomatoes
¼ cup olives (*Taggiasche* or *Gaeta*)
salt and freshly ground pepper

Boil the potatoes in salted water until only barely tender, about 10 minutes, then drain and set aside.

Cut the fish into 6 equal portions and dredge in flour, topping off the excess. Heat the sunflower oil in a large frying pan or heavy-bottomed casserole and cook the fish pieces for about 5 minutes, until lightly browned. Remove and drain on paper towels.

Wipe the pan clean with another paper towel and heat the olive oil. Cook the garlic, shallot, and leek for 5–10 minutes, until soft. Add the wine and allow to reduce for a couple of minutes over medium-high heat. Pour the tomatoes into a bowl and squash with your hands to break them up before adding to the pan along with ¾ cup water. Stir through, then add the cooked potatoes, olives with the sauce and fish. Baste to cover the fish and potatoes, but take care not to break up the fish. Lightly season with salt and pepper (remember the fish is salty). Cover and leave to cook for 30 minutes. Serve in warm bowls.

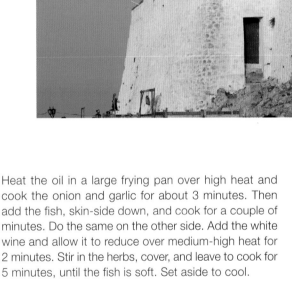

Polpettine di Baccalà di Ristorante Angedras
Salt Cod Patties from Ristorante Angedras

I loved these delicious little morsels of fish so much I persuaded Marco Coronzu, the restaurant's owner, to give me his recipe. He serves them as antipasti in the hot Sardinian summer months on the terrace overlooking the sea in Alghero. In case you're wondering about the name of his restaurant, it spells Sardegna backwards!

Makes 15 balls (about 1–2 inches wide)

1 lb salt cod fillets, soaked for 48 hours
 (see opposite), or coley or cod
3 tablespoons olive oil
1 small white onion, finely chopped
2 garlic cloves, finely sliced
⅓ cup white wine
1 heaping tablespoon fresh thyme leaves
1 heaping tablespoon chopped parsley
1 heaping tablespoon torn basil leaves
¼ cup fresh breadcrumbs
flour, for dredging
1 egg, beaten
6 tablespoons fine dry breadcrumbs
 (see page 30), sieved
sunflower oil, for frying

Heat the oil in a large frying pan over high heat and cook the onion and garlic for about 3 minutes. Then add the fish, skin-side down, and cook for a couple of minutes. Do the same on the other side. Add the white wine and allow it to reduce over medium-high heat for 2 minutes. Stir in the herbs, cover, and leave to cook for 5 minutes, until the fish is soft. Set aside to cool.

Heat the sunflower oil to 350°F in a deep-fat fryer or heavy-bottomed saucepan. When the fish is cool, peel off the skin and mash the flesh and the contents of the pan in a bowl with a fork. Now add the fresh breadcrumbs and mix together with your hands. Form the fish mixture into little balls, then flatten them lightly into patties. Dip them first into flour, then egg, and lastly dry breadcrumbs. Fry in the hot oil until golden brown and then drain on paper towels. Marco serves them with battered and fried red peppers, zucchini, and a wedge of lemon to squeeze over.

Pesce
MASTERCLASS

How to Clean an Anchovy or Sardine

If the fish has scales, scrape them away from the tail towards the head using a table knife or the back of a sharp knife. This is best done under cold running water. Use scissors to cut away the dorsal fin at the top of the back. Then make a cut from the tail to the head with your finger or with a knife. Pull away the guts and discard.

Cut off the head and discard.

Open out the fish and put it down on a board. Push the spine with your thumb. This helps to loosen it from the flesh.

Use your fingers to work under the spine and loosen it from the flesh. Pull the spine away.

Cut the spine on the chopping board and discard. The tail can be left on or discarded. Gently rinse the fish under cold water and dry on a kitchen towel or paper towel.

Acciughe marinate sotto sale
Marinated Salted Anchovies

Available at good Italian delis, salted anchovies are a great alternative to fresh ones.

Serves 8

1 lb anchovies in salt
coarse sea salt, to cover
juice of 2 lemons
¾ cup white wine vinegar
1 red onion, finely chopped
1 fat garlic clove, thinly sliced
½ chile, thinly sliced
⅓ cup extra virgin olive oil
1 tablespoon coarsely chopped
  flat-leaf parsley

Remove the spines from the anchovies with your fingers, gently easing them out.

Rinse the anchovies in cold water. Lay them in a bath made from the juice of 1 lemon and the vinegar for 30 minutes. Rinse them again and squeeze gently between sheets of paper towels or in a clean kitchen towel. Lay them on a serving dish and dress with the onion, garlic, chile, the remaining lemon juice, oil, and parsley. Leave them to marinate for 3 hours or up to overnight. If the oil sets in the fridge, wait for them to reach room temperature before eating. Serve with toasted bread.

Acciughe all' ammiraglia
Marinated Anchovies

This is a classic antipasto served throughout Italy. Anchovies are available either fresh or salted in Italy, from markets and fishmongers. On the cookery holidays we run in Tuscany, our lovely Sicilian assistant Dora makes these using fresh anchovies.

Serves 8

1 lb fresh anchovies, cleaned (see opposite)
2–3 glasses white wine vinegar
1 red onion, chopped into thin strips
salt and freshly ground black pepper
extra virgin olive oil, to serve

Rinse the anchovies well and halve them lengthwise. Clean according to the masterclass opposite, then place the fillets side by side on a non-metallic dish and cover them completely with white wine vinegar. Cover with plastic wrap and leave to marinate in the fridge, overnight if possible, or for as long as it takes for them to become clear with white flesh.

Soak the onion strips in water for 30 minutes to remove some of their strength, drain, then mix in a bowl with salt and pepper.

Drain the anchovies completely and scatter the seasoned onion all over them. Drizzle with olive oil and serve right away, or refrigerate overnight.

Gamberoni al Cognac
Jumbo Shrimp in Cognac

This has been an Italian classic for years—and yet whenever it appears on one of our menus it sells and sells.

Serve 4 as a starter or 2 as a main

3 tablespoons extra virgin olive oil
3 garlic cloves, crushed
1 fresh red serrano or jalapeño chiles, coarsely chopped
8 raw jumbo shrimp, heads on, peeled and deveined
2 tablespoons brandy
⅔ cup fish stock or vegetable stock
1 tablespoon butter
1 tablespoon coarsely chopped flat-leaf parsley

Heat the oil in a large frying pan and cook the garlic and chile for 1 minute over a high heat, taking care that they don't burn. Add the shrimp and shake the pan. Turn them over when pink on the underside. Add the brandy and allow it to reduce for a couple of minutes, then add ⅓ cup of the stock and reduce for 3–5 minutes.

Add the butter and stir or shake the pan to combine. Transfer the shrimp to a warmed plate and return the sauce to the heat. Add the remaining stock and allow the sauce to reduce over the heat for just 1 minute. Pour the sauce over the shrimp and serve with hunks of crusty bread to mop up the juices.

Tip: Freeze the shrimp shells to make a stock, see page 138.

Sarde a beccafico
Stuffed Sardines in Tomato Sauce

Beccafico is the Sicilian word for two people who are having an argument and are face to face in conflict, just as the sardines lie in the roasting dish. This is Teresa's way of doing them from the east of the island. On the west side, they stuff the sardines with a mixture of spinach, pine nuts and raisins and instead of the tomato sauce, they are served with lemon. I have used 13 small sardines in this recipe, 12 to eat whole, and one to break up for the sauce. However, if the sardines are large, use 7 and cut 6 of them in half.

Serves 6

13 sardines (12 oz), cleaned and scaled (see page 248), heads and tails off
⅓ cup sunflower oil, for frying
flour, for dredging

FOR THE STUFFING
¼ cup fresh breadcrumbs
¼ cup Parmesan, finely grated
a small handful of parsley
2 eggs
1 garlic clove, finely chopped
salt and freshly ground black pepper

FOR THE SAUCE
¼ cup olive oil
½ red or white onion, finely chopped
1 sardine, cleaned and cut into 2 fillets
2 anchovy fillets
1 fat garlic clove, finely chopped
¼ cup white wine
1 x 28 oz can Italian plum tomatoes, crushed with your hands
salt and freshly ground black pepper

Put the dry ingredients for the stuffing into a blender and blitz. Pour the ingredients into a bowl and mix in the eggs.

For the sauce, heat the oil in a large frying pan and, when hot, add the onion and fry until soft. Add the sardine, anchovies, and garlic and fry together for a few minutes. Break up the sardine and anchovies with a wooden spoon. Then add the white wine and reduce. After a few minutes add the tomatoes, bring to a boil, and simmer for 20–25 minutes. Season and set aside when cooked.

Clean the sardines. Lay 1 sardine skin-side down and put on a tablespoon of stuffing mixture. Spread the stuffing out a little and lay over another sardine, this time skin-side up. Press down. Stuff the rest of the sardines and set aside. Dip in flour and tap off the excess. Heat the sunflower oil and when hot fry the fish until the skin starts to brown. Turn over gently using a fish slice and a fork and brown on the other side. Add to the sauce and cook for 15–20 minutes with the lid on, shaking the pan frequently. You may need a little more water if it starts to dry out. Serve hot or at room temperature with focaccia (see pages 58–63), followed by salad.

Sarde al forno con finocchio e agrumi
Oven-baked Sardines with Fennel and Citrus Fruits

This recipe was developed in our school during "Slow Fish week." It uses the classic *soffritto* (see page 125), but with a citrus twist to balance the oily fish. If you can't find fresh baby fennel, use a teaspoon of fennel seeds. Mackerel can also be cooked in this way.

Serves 4

juice of ½ lemon
¾ cup fish stock, plus extra as necessary
2 lb sardines, cleaned and trimmed
 (see page 138)
3 tablespoons extra virgin olive oil
handful of flat-leaf parsley, leaves stripped and
 coarsely chopped

FOR THE SOFFRITTO
⅔ cup extra virgin olive oil
1 red onion, very finely chopped
2 celery ribs, very finely chopped
1 medium carrot, very finely chopped
salt and freshly ground black pepper
2 sprigs of fresh rosemary
3 bay leaves
2 x 2-in lengths of orange zest
4 baby fennel bulbs, finely chopped
2 garlic cloves, lightly crushed

Preheat the oven to 350°F. To make the *soffritto*, heat the oil in a frying pan and add the onions, celery, and carrot. Season. Add the herbs, zest, fennel, and garlic and cook over low heat, stirring regularly, for 15 minutes. Remove and discard the herbs.

Add the lemon juice to the *soffritto* and cook for a few minutes. Then add the stock and simmer gently for 10 minutes. Season to taste. If the *soffritto* looks dry, add a little more stock or water. Stir in the parsley and set aside.

Lay each sardine skin-side down on a board. Spread a little *soffritto* on each one and roll up. Arrange in an ovenproof dish and pour in any leftover *soffritto* or oil. Put into the oven for 10–15 minutes, or until the sardines are cooked through. Serve with Lemon Roast Potatoes (see page 390) and sautéed spinach.

Sarde in saor
Marinated Sardines with Onions, Pine Nuts and Raisins

This is a dish from medieval days when shepherds away from home for days at a time took their food with them. Soused fish and vegetables travelled well and provided the protein necessary for a hard life. This is a good entertaining dish: it keeps for a couple of days and the flavors are the better for it. The dish is *agrodolce*, sweet and sour, from the vinegar and sugar. I love this balance and whenever I see the word on a menu, I order the dish.

Serves 8 as a starter

1 lb fresh sardines (about 8), cleaned and
 gutted (see page 248), heads and tails off
salt and freshly ground black pepper
flour, for dredging
6 tablespoons olive oil
1 white onion, thinly sliced
¼ cup raisins
3 tablespoons pine nuts, toasted
⅓ cup dry white wine
⅓ cup white wine vinegar
2 tablespoons caster sugar

Season the sardines with salt and pepper and lightly dredge them in flour. Tap off the excess flour, then fry them in a non-stick pan in half the hot oil for 1–2 minutes on each side. When cooked, drain the sardines on paper towels, and discard the oil.

Pour the rest of the oil into the pan and fry the onion with up to 6 tablespoons of water over medium heat. Season with salt and pepper. The onion should be softened and still completely white, so fry it slowly and add water as necessary to ensure that it doesn't stick.

After 10 minutes, stir in the raisins and cook until softened. Then add the pine nuts, wine, vinegar and sugar. Continue to cook for 5 minutes, then remove from the heat. Allow to cool. Place the sardines in a shallow non-metallic dish, pour in the marinade, cover with plastic wrap, and leave to marinate overnight or for up to 2 days in the fridge.

Variation: Our Sicilian chef, Gregorio can't help but add a little shredded mint to the marinade. He likes mint everywhere and always holds it under my nose so that I can breathe in the aroma.

Anguilla in umido
Eel Stew

Our chef Monserrato's uncle Salvatore used to prepare this on Sundays on his barbecue at home in Sardinia. At the same time, he would cook onions, peppers, and zucchini *alla brace*, on the grill. Eels are sold widely in Italy, kept alive in bowls of water for a day or two before being eaten. This purges the eels and removes the muddy taste they often have.

Serves 6

1 eel
salt and freshly ground black pepper
flour, for dusting
3 tablespoons olive oil
1 carrot, finely chopped
1 onion, finely chopped
2 celery ribs, finely chopped
1 garlic clove, lightly crushed
2 bay leaves
1 cup dry white wine
4 oz tomato paste
¾ cup fish stock (see page 138) or water

You can get the fishmonger to dress the eel; otherwise remove the guts by slitting it along the length of the belly. Loosen the skin around the head and then pull the skin away from the body. You will need to do this with two people, and it is better if you both hold the eel using paper towels or kitchen towels to get a good grip. Peel off the skin entirely and discard. Remove the head. Cut the eel into 8 pieces and season lightly and dust with flour.

Heat the oil in a large frying pan and add the eel pieces. Cook for about 5 minutes, until lightly browned, and then add the carrot, onion, celery, garlic, and bay leaves. Cook for about 10 minutes until the vegetables have softened, then pour in the wine. Allow to reduce for a few minutes, then stir in the tomato paste. Top up with the stock, cover the pan, and simmer for 20 minutes, or until the eel is cooked through—the meat should fall easily off the bone. Season to taste and serve with polenta or bread.

Pesce
MASTERCLASS

How to Prepare a Monkfish

Using scissors or a sharp knife, remove the spiny fins from the top of the fish.

Cut away the thin flaps on either side of the fish.

Use the tip of the knife to divide the body of the fish from the skin and the thick membrane attached to it. Now turn the fish over; grab the skin in one hand and the fish in the other and pull away. Use the knife to help divide the skin from the fish.

Pull away the skin and discard.

Insert the knife between the membrane and the flesh, pulling it away in strips until the monkfish is clean of membrane.

Now either finish filleting the monkfish using this method, or make medallions (see below). Slide the knife down one side of the bone to divide the fillets from the spine.

Using a sharp cook's knife, divide the monkfish tail into medallions around 1 inch wide, cutting through the spine. Discard the tail.

Coda di rospo con gin e ginepro
Monkfish with Gin and Juniper Berries

Gino Borella cooked this for me after observing my seven o'clock gin and tonic habit! I love the crunch of the juniper berries that release their flavor into the dish. If you haven't got any fish stock you can use water, although the flavor will be less intense. It's a good idea to keep small containers of stock in the freezer for such occasions.

Serves 4

1½ lb monkfish tail, cut into 8 pieces
salt
flour, for coating
⅓ cup sunflower oil
4 anchovy fillets
1 small chile, seeds removed
1 garlic clove
5 tablespoons extra virgin olive oil
⅓ cup gin
⅔ cup fish stock (see page 138)
1 heaping teaspoon tomato paste
20 juniper berries, lightly crushed
2 tablespoons butter

Take the fish pieces, season lightly all over with salt and drop them into flour in a shallow dish, coating all sides. Tap off the excess. Heat the sunflower oil in a large frying pan and, when hot, fry the fish for 7–10 minutes, until golden. Meanwhile, finely chop the anchovies, chile, and garlic together on a board. Remove the fish from the pan and set aside in a warm serving dish.

Pour away the excess oil and clean the pan. Return it to the heat and pour in the olive oil. Cook the anchovies, chile, and garlic for a couple of minutes, making sure that they don't burn, then pour in the gin. Let it cook for just 2 minutes before adding the fish stock or water and tomato paste. Bring to a boil and then reduce to a simmer.

After a few minutes, when the sauce has reduced slightly, add the juniper berries and put the fish back into the pan to cook through. Adjust the seasoning as necessary. Stir in the butter, crushing the berries with the tip of a wooden spoon to release their flavor. Serve with spinach and mashed potatoes.

Zuppa di Pesce
FISH SOUP

Up and down the long shorelines of Italy, there are countless recipes for fish soups and stews. Anyone who has visited a coastal town will probably have enjoyed a regional version at some point. The Italians would never admit it since they are so fiercely proud of their local specialities, but there are strong similarities between these dishes because they usually contain local fish, shellfish, and tomatoes. Often they are flavored with a local ingredient and either left as a soup or thickened with pasta, couscous, or *fregola*, which resembles large couscous.

To give some examples, a *buridda* in Liguria contains pine nuts and sometimes mushrooms; a *brodetto* from le Marche may have the local saffron to give it color and flavor or be made into a sweet and sour dish with the addition of sweet red peppers and white wine vinegar. *Cacciucco* in Livorno, west Tuscany, is made with as many types of fish as there are c's in its name. In Puglia, I ate a flavorsome *zuppa di pesce* simply made by infusing tomato sauce with the spine of a scorpion fish. Later, we ate the sauce with the fillets of the fish and *ditalini* pasta. Further south still, I made couscous with a group of women in Sicily, which we ate with the tomato sauce that the fish had been cooked in. This time, the dish was followed by the fish itself, not eaten at the same time. In Sardinia, I was treated to *fregola* in a fish and tomato broth made with tiny crabs.

Fish and tomatoes seems a peculiarly Mediterranean combination. Since we have perfectly good fish, lobsters, and crabs from our own shores and good tomatoes in season, it is easy to recreate the flavors. The trick is to get the flavor—and that relies on flavorful fish and a good stock.

Brodetto di San Benedetto
San Benedetto Fish Stew

The Adriatic sea off the coast of Le Marche is rich with fish and shellfish. *Brodetto* is a type of soup made originally from the leftovers and damaged fish that couldn't be sold at market. There are four main types of *brodetti* in the region: Ancona, Porto Recanati, Fano, and San Benedetto del Tronto. They differ in their use of saffron and tomatoes (which may be green, red, or omitted altogether), and also in the inclusion of local fish. I have chosen to include this one from San Benedetto as I loved the flavor of the sweet red peppers with the vinegar. Often this is made with green tomatoes in Le Marche, from where this dish originates. However, as these are difficult to get, I have made it instead with red tomatoes.

Serves 6

1 red bell pepper, cut into ¾-in cubes
½ cup olive oil
1 medium white or red onion, finely chopped
3 garlic cloves, crushed
½ red chile, finely sliced
1 lb squid, cut into small pieces
2 lb red or green tomatoes, coarsely cubed
⅓ cup white wine vinegar
⅔ cup fish stock or shellfish stock (see page 138), or water
1 lb sea bream, filleted (see page 230) and cubed into bite-size pieces
12 oz halibut, filleted and cubed into bite-size pieces
1 lb clams

Cook the pepper in a frying pan with 6 tablespoons water for 10 minutes. When the water has evaporated, add the oil and continue to cook for 5 minutes over medium heat before adding the onion, garlic, and chile. Cook for 5 minutes or so, until the onion has become translucent.

Turn up the heat and add the squid and tomatoes. Stir well to combine. Pour in the vinegar and allow it to evaporate for a couple of minutes. Pour in the stock or water and then add the fish and clams. Reduce the heat to a simmer, cover, and leave to cook for 10 minutes, until the fish is cooked through and the clams have opened. Discard any clams that haven't opened. Serve right away with crusty bread.

Cacciucco
Tuscan Fish Stew

This is a fish stew from Livorno, a port on the coast of Tuscany. It is said that *Cacciucco* should contain five types of fish—as many c's as there are in its name. This dish resembles many fish stews cooked with tomatoes. In Liguria, a similar stew called *buridda* sometimes also contains pine nuts and mushrooms.

Serves 6

6 tablespoons extra virgin olive oil

1 small red onion, finely chopped

2 garlic cloves, whole and lightly crushed

salt and freshly ground black pepper

4 small squid, cleaned and chopped into bite-size pieces

12 oz monkfish, cleaned (see page 254) and chopped into bite-size pieces

¾ cup dry white wine

1 x 14 oz can Italian chopped tomatoes

12 oz live clams, cleaned

12 oz mussels, cleaned

12 jumbo or tiger shrimp, shells on

3 cups fish stock (see page 138)

parsley, to garnish

crusty white or sourdough bread, thickly sliced and toasted

Heat the oil in a large frying pan or saucepan with a lid. Cook the onion until softened—around 5–7 minutes. Add the garlic and salt and pepper, and cook for a couple of minutes. Add the squid and monkfish and put the lid on the pan. Continue to cook for a few minutes, shaking the pan frequently.

Remove the cover from the pan and add the wine. Leaving the lid off, let the wine reduce for a couple of minutes. Add the tomatoes; crush them with a wooden spoon to break them up a bit (they will also break down during cooking) and cook for 10 minutes. Add the clams, mussels, shrimp, and stock, and bring to a boil.

Reduce the heat and simmer, uncovered, for about 20 minutes. At this point discard any closed clams and mussels—do not force them open. Taste and adjust the seasoning, then serve in warmed bowls, garnished with parsley and accompanied by toasted crusty bread.

Brodo di pesce della Nonna Giovanna
Fish soup with Couscous á la Giovanna

This is a typical Italian fish soup: simple and full of flavor. Usually, small local fish are used, but in the UK these are harder to find, so I use a mixture of sea bass, bream, John Dory, gurnard or red mullet. The fish are cleaned and scaled, but left whole so that the flavor comes out of the bones, too. The whole shrimp are also cooked in the sauce, with their shells. In Sicily, they serve the couscous with the sauce and then eat the fish later. Without offending the traditions of the Sicilians, I like to serve the fish and shrimp over the couscous. The whole fish can be removed and taken off the bone, but the shrimp are best eaten with your fingers—the Sicilians will tell you that the best part of eating shrimp cooked like this is sucking the heads! Finger bowls are therefore a good idea. In Sicily a *soffritto*—the base flavor of the dish—is frequently made from large quantities of garlic, onions, and parsley. I watched the Sicilian women whiz up garlic and parsley in a mini-food processor and asked them how their grandmothers would have made it before these handy little machines were invented: "With pestle and mortars," they answered. Their grandmothers used to pound and pound the pestle against the mortar to crush the garlic and parsley together, which reminded me of the pastes made in Thai cooking.

Serves 6–8

Variation: I worked with the head chef of Nonna Maria in Monopoli, a charming fishing village in Puglia, and he showed me a similar fish and tomato soup that had pasta cooked in it. He used *scorfano*, or scorpion fish, as it is full of the flavor of his beloved Adriatic sea. Apparently, the high levels of salt in the sea bring a fantastic flavor to the seafood. However, far more obtainable in the UK are red mullet, John Dory, or gurnard, which in this instance make a perfectly suitable alternative. Instead of couscous, the chef used small pasta shapes called *ditalini* to make the soup more substantial.

FOR THE COUSCOUS
2 cups couscous, homemade or store-bought
⅓ cup olive oil
½ onion, finely chopped
a good pinch of salt

FOR THE FISH SOUP
1 medium white or red onion
½ bunch flat-leaf parsley, stems reserved
5 garlic cloves
½–1 red chile (depending on its strength and your taste), thinly sliced
⅓ cup olive oil
salt and freshly ground black pepper
⅓ cup dry white wine
1 x 28 oz can Italian plum tomatoes, lightly squeezed between your fingers
2 quarts fish stock, (see page 138), or hot water
2–4 whole fish (depending in size), cleaned and scaled
20 whole tiger shrimp, shell-on

To start the soup, put the onion, parsley, and garlic and chile into a food processor and process until it becomes a paste, or finely chop them together by hand. Pour the oil into a large saucepan and, when hot, fry the paste from the food processor with plenty of salt and pepper for around 10 minutes, stirring frequently. Add the wine and cook for a couple of minutes to let it evaporate. Add the tomatoes and stock or water and bring to a boil.

Once boiling, add the fish and shrimp and reduce the heat. Leave to simmer for around 20–30 minutes, or until the fish is cooked through and is just starting to come away from the bone. Remove the soup from the heat.

Meanwhile, prepare the couscous according to the instructions on the package, if bought; if homemade, follow the instructions on page 260. When the couscous is cooked, heat the oil and cook the onion until soft, then toss in the cooked couscous and salt to taste. Stir well to combine. When ready to serve, move the fish to the side of the pot, take out a couple of ladlefuls of tomato sauce and mix with the couscous. Put the couscous in bowls and top with fish from the pot, or serve the fish after with bread, like the Sicilians.

Couscous

In the Trapani area of Sicily, couscous is very popular, clearly demonstrating the legacy left by invading Arabs many centuries ago. The locals frequently make couscous at home. It is a job mainly carried out by women, and I was lucky enough to join in one hot summer Sunday. "*Gira, gira, gira,*" Nonna Giovanna told me as I stirred the water, salt and pepper into the *semola* flour. She cooked her couscous in a *couschiera*, an old yellow earthenware pot with a lid with small holes in it. Once the couscous went into the top, the edges were sealed with a length of dough. This stops the steam escaping from the edge and forces it through the couscous instead.

Serves 8

TO MAKE THE COUSCOUS
2 lb *semola rimacinato*
salt and ground white pepper
tepid water, as required

TO COOK THE COUSCOUS
2 quarts water
¼ cup olive oil

Pour the semolina flour into a bowl and mix in the salt and pepper. Add a little water, make your fingers into a claw shape and use them to stir the flour and water together (Giovanna always worked in a clockwise direction), adding a little water at a time until small grains appear. Then divide the couscous into two bowls so that you can work one while the other rests.

Add a little more tepid water to one bowl and, using your fingers again, stir the grains round and round. Let this bowl rest as you do the same in the other bowl. Then add a little more water to the first bowl and *gira, gira*, stir, stir, again. The constant movement of the grains stops them from sticking together. Only stop when the grains in one bowl are the size of grains of demerara (raw) sugar. Rest that bowl and repeat with the other bowl.

To cook the couscous, put the water and the olive oil in a large saucepan. Rest a colander over the pan, making sure that the water does not touch the colander. Put a muslin cloth or very thin kitchen towel into the colander and pour in the couscous. Put the lid on and tie another cloth around the lid to stop the steam from escaping. Steam for 1¼ hours, or until cooked through.

Pesce Crudo
RAW FISH DISHES

Long before fashionable Japanese sushi restaurants opened in Italy's larger towns, the habit of eating raw fish and shellfish existed in many regions. I have watched a group of Pugliese men munching on freshly caught shrimp that were still twitching in a market! Here, there are also many restaurants proudly advertising their *pesce crudo* (raw fish) dishes. I too have enjoyed (to my surprise) a plate of raw baby whitebait-like fish: quite deliciously fresh and salty. Now raw fish dishes with either Italian- or Japanese-inspired sauces abound in modern restaurants.

Carpaccio di merluzzo con limone e timo
Carpaccio of Cod with Lemon and Thyme Dressing

A *carpaccio* (which these days refers to any dish served in ultra-thin slices) is best made with a fish with enough flavor to stand up to the marinade that it "cooks" in. Made with a really fresh catch, this is a wonderfully pure and healthy way to get more fish into your diet.

Serves 4 as a starter

12 oz cod or other white fish fillets

FOR THE MARINADE
½ cup light extra virgin olive oil
2 tablespoons lemon juice (about ½ lemon)
1 tablespoon finely chopped thyme
1 tablespoon finely chopped flat-leaf parsley
a good pinch of salt

Slice the cod as thinly as possible (before slicing it helps to chill it in the freezer until firm). Lay the slices onto a board and cover with plastic wrap. Use a meat tenderizer to pound out the slices until they are around 2mm thick. Lay the pieces of fish over a plate in a single layer. Mix together the ingredients for the marinade and pour over the fish. Serve right away with crusty bread.

Carpaccio di tonno
Carpaccio of Tuna

To my mind, the flavor of tuna has a delicate spicy note that can stand up to this sweet marinade.

Serves 4

1 cup finely chopped flat-leaf parsley
1 lb tuna (loin fillet if possible)

FOR THE MARINADE
4 teaspoons acacia or other honey
3 tablespoons balsamic vinegar
6 tablespoons olive oil

Lay a sheet of plastic wrap on a board and scatter the parsley over the surface. Roll the tuna in the parsley-flecked plastic wrap so that it is tightly encased in plastic, like a sausage. Put in the freezer until you are ready to cut it. Cut into wafer-thin slices on a slicing machine or using a very sharp knife. Mix together all the ingredients for the marinade and pour over the fish.

Pesce

MASTERCLASS

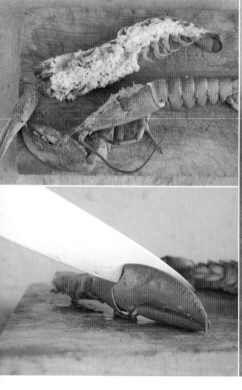

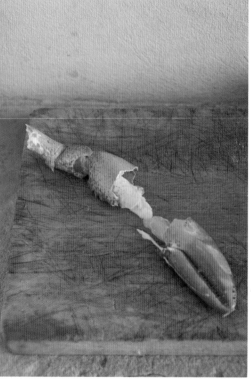

How to Prepare a Lobster

There are several ways of killing and cooking lobsters. They can be brought slowly to a boil in salted water, frozen for a couple of hours to lull them into a sleep or cut through the head with a sharp knife. I prefer to handle lobsters as little as possible, so I drop them live into boiling water.

Plunge the lobster into well-salted boiling water for 8–10 minutes, depending on the size. Gregorio, our chef, cooks lobster until it is completely pink and no more, particularly if the flesh will be cooked again, as in all our recipes here. Remove from the water with tongs and drop into a bowl of iced water for 2 minutes. Place the lobster on a board and, holding it steady with one hand, with the other hand cut from the top of the tail straight down to the end of the tail. Divide the tail in half.

Now turn the lobster and cut the top in half, again holding the lobster firmly in place.

The lobster is now in two separate halves. Scoop out the flesh from each half and use as required, or simply drizzle with lemon juice, oil, salt and pepper and eat right away.

Twist the claws away from the body and use a sharp chef's knife to cut the shell. This is best done by holding the knife in place and banging the top of it down with the other hand. Pick out the flesh using a small fork or the end of a spoon.

Crack open the rest of the legs in the same way and remove the flesh. Reserve the shells to make Shellfish Stock (see page 138).

Spaghetti all' aragosta
Lobster Spaghetti

This is a quick dish to prepare once the lobster is cooked, so my advice is to have everything ready and at hand so that you can assemble the dish easily. This dish was one Giancarlo cooked for me when we first met and he was trying to impress me—it worked, particularly served after a glass of pink vintage champagne; what an old romantic he is!

Serves 4 as a main or 6 as a starter

2 live lobsters
¾ cup extra virgin olive oil (½ cup for the stock and ¼ cup for the sauce)
1 carrot, coarsely chopped
2 medium red or white onions, coarsely chopped
1 celery rib, coarsely chopped
¾ cup brandy (½ cup for the stock and ¼ cup for the sauce)
1 heaping tablespoon tomato paste
4 tomatoes
1 garlic clove, lightly crushed
12–14 oz spaghetti (depending on how hungry you are)

Plunge the lobsters into salted boiling water and cook for 8 minutes. Remove from the water and allow to cool, reserving the cooking water. When cool enough to handle, remove the flesh from the body and claws (see page 262). Set the flesh aside in a covered bowl in the fridge and use the rest to make the stock.

Heat the ½ cup oil in a large saucepan and, when hot, cook the vegetables, shells and heads for around 10 minutes. Crush with a wooden spoon to break the shells. Pour in the ½ cup brandy and ignite or continue to heat for a few minutes until the strong smell of alcohol has dissipated. Stir in the tomato paste.

Add 6 cups hot water from the lobster and bring to a boil. Leave to bubble and reduce for about 1 hour or until it has reduced by two-thirds. Sieve the stock, pressing down on the heads of the lobster with a wooden spoon to extract as much flavor as possible. Discard the shells and vegetables. Put the pan over medium heat and reduce the stock to approximately 1 cup.

Chop the lobster flesh into 1-inch chunks. Make a small cross in the top of each tomato and then plunge them into boiling water for a minute to loosen their skins. Peel away the skin and chop into small ½-inch cubes. Cook the spaghetti in plenty of salted boiling water while you finish the sauce.

Heat the remaining oil in a large frying pan and, when hot, cook the onions and garlic together for a few minutes until softened. Stir in the tomatoes, then add the lobster flesh followed by the remaining brandy. Allow it to evaporate for a couple of minutes and then add 1 cup stock. Any leftover stock can be frozen for another time. Bring to the boil and taste to adjust the seasoning. Toss the cooked pasta into the sauce and serve right away.

Mezzelune con ripieno di aragosta
Lobster Mezzelune

This is one of those impressive restaurant dishes that I cannot say is quick and easy, but oh how satisfying it is when you serve it to loved ones, guests, and customers. I have designed ours with a parsley leaf on top. The leaves are rolled between two sheets of pasta, which has the effect of stretching each leaf and letting it show between the layers.

Makes 4 (serves 6 as a main or 8 as a starter)

1 live medium lobster
⅔ cup Béchamel Sauce (see page 175)

FOR THE PASTA
4 medium eggs
4 cups "00" flour
a large handful of flat-leaf parsley

FOR THE STOCK AND SAUCE
4 teaspoons olive oil
1 celery rib, coarsely chopped
1 carrot, coarsely chopped
1 shallot or ½ onion, peeled and cut in half
shells from the shrimp
shell and legs from the lobster
5 black peppercorns
1 quart water
1 tablespoon butter

FOR THE FILLING
4 teaspoons olive oil
½ celery rib (add the rest to the stock)
1 small carrot or ½ large carrot (add the rest to the stock)
1 shallot, finely chopped
salt and freshly ground black pepper
6 tiger or jumbo shrimp (about 4 oz shelled), shelled and finely chopped, shells reserved
4 teaspoons dry white wine
1 heaping teaspoon chopped flat-leaf parsley

Make the pasta according to the instructions in the masterclass on page 148 and let it rest in the fridge. Cook and clean the lobster following the instructions in the masterclass on page 262. Finely chop the meat and set aside in the fridge, and reserve the shell and legs.

Prepare the stock: heat the oil in a large saucepan, then cook the celery, carrot, and shallot in the oil until softened. Add the shrimp and lobster shells and the small legs, and drop in the peppercorns. Allow everything to cook for about 10 minutes, occasionally crushing the shells with a wooden spoon to release the juices. When browned and sizzling hot, add the water and bring to a boil. Allow the stock to bubble gently while you prepare the rest of the ingredients, around 1 hour. Strain through a fine sieve into a large frying pan and set aside, off the heat.

Make the béchamel as shown on page 175 and leave, covered with plastic wrap, to cool.

To make the filling, heat the oil in a large frying pan and sauté the celery, carrot, shallot, and salt and pepper. Add the shelled shrimp and cook for a few minutes, until cooked through. Add the white wine and allow to reduce for 2 minutes, or until the strong smell of wine has dissipated. Add the reserved lobster meat, béchamel, chopped parsley and stir through. Check the seasoning and leave to cool.

Bring a large pan of salted water to a boil for the pasta.

Remove the pasta from the fridge and roll out two strips 6 inches wide (the standard width for a hand-worked pasta machine). When you have reached the thinnest setting or rolled it out by hand to 1mm thick, cut into approximately 16 inch lengths. Lay the parsley leaves on one piece of the pasta 1 inch apart and 1 inch from the edge. Put another length of pasta on top and press down, sealing the parsley between the layers. Roll through the machine again on the thinnest setting, or roll by hand. Dot a fully heaping teaspoonful of the filling on top of each leaf. Put another strip of pasta on top. Press around the outside of the filling to exclude any air. Trim the pasta mounds with a pasta cutter or glass into *mezzaluna* (half moon) shapes about 3 inches by 2 inches. Set aside in a single layer on a floured baking sheet. Don't leave for any longer than 30 minutes or they will stick to the pan. The ravioli can be frozen, partially-cooked or cooked to eat right away (see page 149).

For the sauce, reduce the stock in the pan for 10 minutes or so, until slightly thickened. Add the butter and stir through. Taste, adjust the seasoning and remove from the heat. Boil the pasta for 3 minutes, or until cooked through. Drain, toss gently with the sauce, and serve in warmed bowls.

Fregola ai frutti di mare
Seafood Fregola

Fregola from Sardinia are tiny pasta shapes which were originally made by hand from *semola*, semolina flour. In this way it is similar to, although larger than, couscous, but *fregola* is toasted which gives it a more interesting, nutty flavor. Commercial and homemade versions are available in delis and from online stores. *Fregola* can be stirred into soups or boiled and dressed with oil and mixed with other ingredients for a salad. It cooks in less than 10 minutes.

Serves 6

2 tablespoons olive oil
2 garlic cloves, lightly crushed
½ red chile, finely chopped
3 anchovy fillets
salt and freshly ground black pepper
6 oz squid rings, fresh or frozen
1 lb clams (discard any that refuse to close)
1 lb mussels, scrubbed and debearded (discard
  any that refuse to close; see page 269)
12 jumbo shrimp, shell on for maximum flavor
⅓ cup dry white wine
1 lb small grain *fregola*
1–1½ quarts shellfish stock or fish stock
  (see page 138)
2 tablespoons tomato paste
8 oz cherry tomatoes
¼ cup coarsely chopped flat-leaf parsley
2 tablespoons butter

Heat the oil in a non-stick frying pan and cook the garlic, chile, and anchovy fillets for 1 minute. Give it a stir and add a good pinch of salt and pepper. Add the squid first and leave to cook for 5 minutes, then add the clams, mussels, and shrimp. Add the wine and cover with a lid and cook for 5 minutes or until the shellfish have opened. Discard any that do not open.

Using a slotted spoon, remove the shellfish from the pan and set aside, covered. Add the *fregola* and cover with half the fish stock. Stir for a few minutes, then add the tomato paste. Keep adding fish stock as necessary until the *fregola* is al dente. If you run out of stock, add hot water. The *fregola* will take around 10–12 minutes to cook depending on their size.

When the *fregola* are al dente, return the clams and mussels and add the cherry tomatoes and chopped parsley. Taste and season with more salt and pepper if necessary. Stir in the butter and serve.

Cozze ripiene
Stuffed Mussels

This popular antipasti dish can be prepared in advance and then slipped under a hot broiler before serving. Once you start eating these garlicky morsels, it is impossible to stop. I ate tons in Puglia where they have been cooking with mussels for centuries. There is even a seaside village called Cozze, which means 'mussels' in Italian. The mussels of Puglia are quite big and therefore perfect for this dish. Try to buy large, evenly sized ones and enlist the help of someone for the task of separating the mussels from their shells.

Serves 4 as a starter

FOR THE MUSSELS
¼ cup white wine
2 lb mussels, scrubbed and debearded (see opposite page)

FOR THE STUFFING
3 tablespoons fresh breadcrumbs
1 medium garlic clove
a handful of flat-leaf parsley
¼ cup extra virgin olive oil
salt

First select a large frying pan or saucepan with a lid. Heat the wine for a couple of minutes over high heat and then add the mussels and cover with the lid. Cook for about 5 minutes, shaking the pan frequently. When the mussels have all opened (discard any that remain closed), uncover the pan, remove from the heat and allow to cool a little so that they are not too hot to touch.

Pick the mussels out of their shells and reserve. Pull the shells apart and reserve the half without the white part where the mussel had been attached. Arrange the reserved shells on a heatproof plate, either in rows on a square plate or concentric circles on a round one. At this point I would also swap any small shells for big ones (even if they have the white part) so that you end up with similar-sized shells. Reserve the unwanted shells until you finish the recipe (in case you need any more) and then discard. Reserve the cooking liquid and freeze for another recipe (such as risotto) or discard.

Preheat the broiler to high.

Process the breadcrumbs, garlic, and parsley together in a food processor and scrape into a bowl. Add the mussels, olive oil and salt to taste, and mix together so that the mussels are coated with the breadcrumbs. Now put the mussels back into the shells arranged on the plate. At this point, either cover the plate with plastic wrap and keep in the fridge for a couple of hours or broil right away for around 5 minutes, or until the breadcrumbs look golden brown and crunchy. Leave the plates to stand for 5 minutes (they will be piping hot) then serve to be eaten with fingers, straight from the shells.

Preparation of Mussels and Clams

When you buy fresh mussels or clams, check them carefully and discard any with cracked or broken shells. Purge them by putting them into a bowl covered with cold water containing sea salt. Allow 2 tablespoons salt per quart of water. Stir them around and leave for a couple of hours. This way they will open and close as if they are in sea water and it should rid them of any grit and other debris. Rinse the shellfish well in the bowl and change the water several times. Then use a knife or metal scouring pad to remove any barnacles from the shells and give them a good scrub. For mussels, you also need to pull off the beards: hold the mussel, pointed end facing you, and pull the beard towards you. Live mussels or clams should close if tapped on a hard surface; if any remain open, they should be discarded. If you are using the cooking liquor from the mussels, strain it well through a fine sieve to remove any lingering grit.

Tartelloni al nera di seppia ripieni di salmone affumicato e gamberetti con sugo alle cozze (for recipe, see page 158)

Tiella di Antonietta
Rice, Potato, and Mussels Baked in Terracotta

This is a typical Pugliese dish that changes its name from *tiella* to *tiadedda*—and its contents slightly—up and down the coast of Puglia. It is thought to have the same origins as the Spanish dish paella and therefore could be a legacy of the Bourbons who, centuries ago, inhabited Puglia. This is traditionally cooked in a *tiella* dish. These are small, lidded terracotta pots about 8 inches wide and 3 inches high which are sold in the local markets, but if you don't have one, use a small lidded casserole instead. Antonietta's husband, Vito, explained that his favorite part of this dish is the rice that collects in the open mussel shells. This can be served hot or eaten cold next day as an antipasto.

Serves 4

15–20 live mussels, depending on size
⅓ cup olive oil
1 lb potatoes (about 5 in total), cut into ¼-in slices
8 oz tomatoes (about 5 medium), cut into ¼-in slices
1 heaping tablespoon roughly chopped flat-leaf parsley
2 teaspoons salt
1¼ cups pecorino, finely grated
1½ cups risotto rice (Arborio)
1 small onion or 1 shallot, finely chopped
½ garlic clove, coarsely chopped
⅔ cup dry white wine
2–2½ cups fish stock (see page 138)
2 teaspoons salt

Preheat the oven to 400°C. Prepare the mussels as explained on page 269.

Pour one third of the oil into a casserole and lay over one third of the potato slices, followed by one third of the tomatoes. Add the parsley, one third of the salt and one third of the pecorino. Now lay the raw mussels on top, checking again that they are all closed. Then pour the rice over the top.

Add another third of the potatoes and tomatoes, along with the onion and garlic. Pour another third of the oil over the top, scatter over another third of salt and another third of the cheese.

Slowly pour in the wine through one spot in the rice rather than all over so that it goes down to the bottom. Then layer the final third of the potatoes, tomatoes, and the rest of the salt. Finish by pouring the fish stock over the contents of the dish, adding enough to cover the vegetables to the top, depending on the size of your casserole. Finish with the last of the cheese and oil, put a lid on and bake for 30–40 minutes, or until the rice is cooked through. Serve on its own or with some crusty bread—the Italians would eat a salad after this rather than with it.

Stufato di calamari con pomodoro e peperocino
Slow-cooked Squid in Tomato and Chile Sauce

Calamari has to be cooked either very quickly or very, very slowly. Here, slow cooking transforms squid into soft, melting mouthfuls.

Serves 4

1 lb squid
⅓ cup olive oil
4 garlic cloves, crushed
2 onions, finely sliced
1 hot fresh red chile
salt and pepper
⅔ cup dry white wine
1 x 14 oz can Italian plum tomatoes, crushed

First prepare the squid following the instructions in the masterclass on page 272. Take care to remove the gray membrane. Then cut the tentacles into rings about ½ inch wide.

Heat the olive oil in a frying pan and add the garlic, onions, chile, and salt and pepper. Cook over high heat for around 7–10 minutes, stirring to prevent it from burning, until the onion is golden and soft.

Add the squid to the pan and let it cook so that the water is released. After about 10 minutes, when the squid has a "bouncy" appearance, add the white wine, return to a simmer and reduce the wine for 2 minutes, then add the tomatoes. Bring to a boil, stirring occasionally and breaking up the tomatoes. Then lower the heat and simmer for at least 1 hour. Serve on warm plates with hot, crusty bread.

Pesce
MASTERCLASS

How to Prepare a Squid

Pull away the tentacles from the body. Remove the quill (it looks like a long piece of clear plastic).

Pinch the wings together and pull them away from the body.

Peel away the wings completely and reserve.

Peel away the thin purple membrane coating the body and the wings.

Now turn the squid inside out and wash under cold running water. Leave it like this if you are going to stuff the squid or cut it open to lay flat.

Cut the tentacles away from the head just behind the eyes.

Pull up the hard beak and pinch it away from the body, then discard.

The body, wings, and tentacles are ready for cooking.

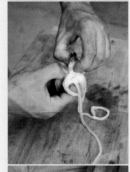

How to Prepare a Cuttlefish

Pull away the tentacles from the body.

Cut the tentacles away from the head just in front of the eyes.

Push out the hard mouth part, pinch it away and discard.

Cut the thin skin to one side of the hard white oval bone using a knife and pull the bone away; this is often dried and used as bird food. Cut down the flesh carefully using scissors and avoiding the silver pouch, which contains ink. Discard the guts. Cut around the ink sac with a knife or scissors. Since the ink is used as a defense, it can cause temporary blindness, so be careful not to get any ink in your eyes. Carefully remove the ink sac if it is still intact. This can be used to die pasta black (see page 151).

Wash the cuttlefish and peel away the thin grayish purple membrane around the body and on the legs. Discard this, but save the white fleshy wings if they are large enough. Remove the membrane from the wings before using the flesh.

The body, tentacles, and ink sac are ready for cooking.

Gnocculi con le seppie
Teresa's Gnocculi with Cuttlefish Stew

This is a delicious cuttlefish stew from the Marsala area of Sicily that is served as a sauce for homemade pasta strips known as *gnocculi*. The pasta is made without egg, and is similar to *pici* from Tuscany and *fusilli* from Naples. *Gnocculi* are lengths which are squeezed under the fingers to form a tube with a frilly edge. They can be fun to make and I give the method below, but unless you have a Sicilian grandmother permanently installed in your kitchen, use linguine or spaghetti instead. These days, the paste made from onion, garlic, and parsley is made in a food processor. When I asked the Sicilian women how this was done before these gadgets were invented, they told me that every household had a pestle and mortar for this purpose. Teresa added a couple of teaspoons of sugar to her sauce, which is very typical in Sicily, but I don't generally find that this needs it.

Serves 4

FOR THE PASTA

1 quantity of *semola* pasta (*gnocculi*, see
  page 192) or 12 oz linguine or spaghetti
½ cup water, or more as necessary
salt and freshly ground black pepper

FOR THE CUTTLEFISH SAUCE

1 small onion
2 garlic cloves
a handful of flat-leaf parsley
6 tablespoons olive oil
1½ lb cuttlefish (2–3, depending on size), cleaned
  (see opposite) and chopped into bite-size pieces
¾ cup dry white wine
1 x 14 oz can Italian plum tomatoes
salt and freshly ground black pepper

FOR THE GREEN BREADCRUMBS

2 thick slices white bread from a country-style
  loaf, torn into pieces
3 tablespoons coarsely chopped flat-leaf parsley
1 medium garlic clove (optional)
2 tablespoons olive oil

To make the sauce, first put the onion, garlic, and half the parsley into a food processor and pulse until a paste is formed. Heat the olive oil and, when hot, cook the paste for a couple of minutes and then add the cuttlefish pieces. Cook for about 15 minutes then add the wine. Let it reduce for another few minutes and then add the tomatoes. Bring to a boil and simmer for 20–30 minutes, or until the cuttlefish is tender. Add salt and pepper to taste. Make the pasta (see *gnocculi* page 192).

Meanwhile make the breadcrumbs by pulsing the bread in a food processor with the parsley and garlic, if using. If you do not have a food processor, use a grater to reduce the bread to crumbs, then finely chop the parsley and garlic and mix in. Stir in the olive oil and put into a serving bowl. Serve the cuttlefish mixed with hot cooked pasta in bowls with the breadcrumbs on top.

Calamari ripieni di granchio
Stuffed Squid with Crab in Tomato Sauce

I was first shown this dish in Castellabate al Mare in Cilento, south of Naples. We were dining in the quirky and charming hotel La Mola, perched on a cliff looking out to sea. On this day there was a howling gale blowing across the sea, hammering on the windows as if wanting to be let in to join our feast of fat calamari bobbing and bubbling in the tomato sauce. Giuseppina, the cook, didn't use crab in her stuffing, but I have since found that the addition of crab and anchovy gives a wonderful fishy flavor that, sadly, calamari often lack. Stuffed calamari are typically eaten at room temperature as part of an array of antipasti. However, I like them hot with rice—which is not very Italian but is great for soaking up the juices. The other way is to eat the tomato sauce, which has a gorgeous flavor, with pasta first and then serve the calamari afterwards with bread and a lightly dressed salad of shredded lettuce.

6 medium squid, cleaned (see page 272)
6 tablespoons olive oil
1 white onion, finely chopped
2 garlic cloves, finely chopped
2 heaping tablespoons finely chopped parsley
6 anchovy fillets, finely chopped
1 tablespoon salted capers, well rinsed
salt and freshly ground black pepper
4 tablespoons dry white wine
2 cups fish stock (see page 138), or water
¼ cup fresh breadcrumbs
3 tablespoons milk
4 oz fresh or canned crab meat
2 heaping tablespoons finely grated Parmesan
½ red chile, thinly sliced
⅓ cup white wine
4 oz tomato paste

6 toothpicks, to secure the stuffing

Separate the tentacles from the bodies of the squid and set the bodies aside. Finely chop the tentacles and cook in half the oil with half the onion, 1 of the garlic cloves, half the parsley, all 6 anchovies, the capers and salt and pepper. As you cook, scrape the bottom and sides of the pan to get every scrap of flavor into the dish. After about 10 minutes, pour in the white wine and let it reduce for a couple of minutes, then add ⅓ cup of the fish stock or water. Bring to a boil and then remove it from the heat. Pour into a bowl and allow to cool for a few minutes.

Soak the breadcrumbs in the milk for a couple of minutes and then add to the squid mixture in the bowl. Stir in the crab and the Parmesan. Blend the mixture well with your fingers and adjust the seasoning to taste.

Use a pastry bag or your fingers to fill the squid cavities two-thirds full. Weave a toothpick in and out of the top of each squid to secure them closed.

Heat the remaining olive oil in a frying pan over medium high heat and cook the squid on all sides for 5 minutes, or until lightly golden. Add the rest of the onion, garlic, parsley and the sliced chile. Season with salt and pepper and continue to cook. When softened, after about 5 minutes, add the white wine and allow it to reduce for a couple of minutes, then add the tomato paste. Stir through and then add the remaining fish stock. Bring to a boil and simmer, covered, for 30 minutes. Adjust the seasoning to taste and serve with crusty bread.

Capesante avvolte nella pancetta con salsa di avocado Scallops Wrapped in Pancetta with Avocado Sauce

Avocados are not commonly used in Italy but are available in supermarkets. Monserrato, my chef friend, made the observation that his British customers loved the combination of avocado, spinach, and bacon and while looking for a way to serve scallops, he came up with this. So a modern recipe it is, using an ingredient not so common in Italy but with the age-old combination of pancetta and scallops. The avocado takes on a completely different flavor when cooked.

Serves 4

FOR THE SAUCE
2 tablespoons olive oil
1 tablespoon butter
1 medium avocado, peeled and cut into
   ¾-in cubes
½ garlic clove, finely chopped
1 sprig of thyme, leaves stripped
6 tablespoons vegetable stock or water, optional
salt and freshly ground black pepper
2 teaspoons sugar, optional

TO SERVE
24 spinach leaves
12 scallops
12 slices of very thinly sliced smoked pancetta,
   guanciale or bacon
2 tablespoons extra virgin olive oil

Melt the olive oil and butter in a frying pan and cook the avocado pieces with the garlic and thyme. Cook for 3–4 minutes, stirring until the avocado breaks down.

Remove from the heat and process in a blender to make a purée. Spoon into a medium saucepan and use a little stock to rinse out the blender; then add the stock to the pan to make a sauce. Season with salt and pepper and add a little sugar if necessary.

Arrange spinach leaves in 3 pairs to a plate. Drizzle with a little olive oil. Wrap the scallops in a thin slice of pancetta and pan-fry them over high heat for around 2 minutes, turning once. Turn the heat down and continue to cook, turning once again for another 3–4 minutes, until the pancetta is lightly browned and the scallop is cooked but still soft in the center. Arrange a scallop on each pair of spinach leaves. Pour the hot avocado sauce around the edge of the plate and serve.

How to Cook and Prepare an Octopus

In Italy, it is common to place the octopus on a cutting board before cooking and to beat the body and legs with a rolling pin a few times. This tenderizes the flesh. Remove the eyes of the octopus using scissors or a sharp knife and pinch out the hard mouth with your fingers from the center of the tentacles. Another way to make the octopus more tender is to hold it over a pan of boiling salted water and dip it in and out 3 times.

To cook the octopus, drop it in salted boiling water for around 1 hour, depending on the size. The cooking water can be flavored with a lemon cut in half, 2 bay leaves, 5 black peppercorns, a dash of white wine vinegar, and 1 garlic clove (see page 278). When cooked, the octopus should be so tender that you can pass a fork or skewer easily through the thickest part of a tentacle. Remove the pot from the heat and leave the octopus to cool in the cooking water, which can be used as a stock.

Alternatively, to cook an octopus, put it in a saucepan with ½ cup cold water. Put the lid on the pan and wrap foil over the top, sealing it around the edges so no steam can escape. Put the pan over the heat and cook slowly for 1 hour, or until the flesh is tender when pierced with a sharp knife or skewer. When it is soft, remove the octopus from the heat and remove from the water. The cooking water can be used as a stock.

Cut away the head of the octopus—this can be cleaned, cut into pieces and eaten. Using a cloth or paper towel, pull the colored membrane away from the back of the tentacles. This is tough to eat if left on. If the suckers fall away easily, remove them; this often happens when an octopus has been previously frozen.

Separate the tentacles from one another.

Chop the tentacles as needed.

Insalata di Mare
Seafood Salad

This delicious combination of vibrant color and flavor is found all over Italy, with regional differences according to taste and the availability of seafood. It is best eaten the day after it is made with crusty bread to dip into the oily dressing. This version was made for me in Sardinia by Monserrato, our Head Chef from Caffè Caldesi. He used the local seafood available and says his secret is to adjust the seasoning the day after making the salad, adding more vinegar, salt, and a dash of best olive oil at the end to get the balance right.

Serves 6

TO COOK THE OCTOPUS

½ lemon

5 black peppercorns

2 bay leaves

1 tablespoon white wine vinegar

salt

FOR THE SALAD

1 octopus

2 medium squid, cleaned (see page 272)

12 medium tiger shrimp

3 tablespoons extra virgin olive oil

12 oz clams

24 mussels

1 garlic clove, lightly crushed

½ red fresh chile, finely chopped

salt and freshly ground black pepper

2 celery ribs, cut into matchstick-size pieces

juice of 2 lemons

1 carrot, cut into matchstick-size pieces

6 tablespoons white wine vinegar

1 quart sunflower oil

TO SERVE

¼ cup extra virgin olive oil

flat-leaf parsley

Put the flavoring ingredients for cooking the octopus in a large pan with enough salted water to cover it. Bring to a boil. Meanwhile wash the octopus under cold running water, then place it on a board and bash it 3 times with a rolling pin along its length, working from the head to the end of its tentacles, to tenderize the flesh.

When the water is boiling fiercely, hold the octopus by its head and plunge it in and out of the water 3 times. Cook the octopus for about 1 hour and leave it to cool in the cooking water. When it has cooled to room temperature, remove from the water. Using paper towels, grip the octopus tentacles and pull off the membrane following the masterclass instructions on page 276. Cut the flesh into pieces about ¾ inch wide. Set aside in a large bowl.

Next boil the squid in the salted water as you did with the octopus. They are cooked when a fork enters the thickest part easily—allow around 20 minutes. Remove the squid and set aside, reserving the water. Drop the shrimp into the water for a few minutes; when they are completely pink they are cooked. Remove from the water and set aside.

Cut the squid into rings about ½ inch wide and add these and the octopus pieces to the shrimp. Heat the olive oil in a large frying pan and cook the clams, mussels, garlic, and chile with salt and pepper over high heat with the lid on for 8–10 minutes.

Mix with the rest of the ingredients in a large bowl so they are coated with the sunflower oil. Leave, covered, to marinate overnight in the fridge. The day, remove the seafood from the oil with your hands, allowing the oil to drain away, and place on a serving platter. Drizzle the olive oil over the top and sprinkle with a little parsley. Serve with crusty bread.

Variation
Sardine marinate
Marinated Sardines

Brush some cleaned and opened fresh sardines (see page 248) with sunflower oil and season with pepper and salt. Broil them briefly until just cooked through on both sides, then set aside on paper towels to cool. Put these with the marinating ingredients for the salad, covered with oil, and keep in the fridge for up to 4 days. On day 2, adjust the flavor to taste, adding more vinegar, lemon juice, or salt as necessary. Drain and serve.

How to Prepare a Crab

Female crabs have bigger carapaces and contain more meat. They can be identified because they have a larger flap of soft shell on the underside than the male. Normally, the white flesh only is used for pasta and other dishes—see Crab-stuffed Squid on page 274 and Crab Pancakes on page 115—but the brown meat is good, too, spread on toasted bread. Usually the Italians I have worked with drop live crabs into boiling water to kill and cook them at the same time, but some prefer to pop them into tepid salted water and bring them up to the boil. However, many cooks prefer to kill crabs before boiling as they feel it is more humane and stops any possibility of the crabs shedding their limbs upon impact with the water. Personally, I drop lobsters and crabs into boiling water on a regular basis. But to kill them first, drive a sharp skewer through the small mouth hole and wiggle it back and forth a couple of times. Boil the crab in plenty of salted water—about 2 teaspoons salt per quart—allowing approximately 15 minutes for the first 2 lb then another 3 minutes for every extra pound.

Twist off the claws from the crab and set aside.

With the crab belly facing upwards, push up from the front flap until the underneath of the body, known as the carapace, lifts away.

Discard the "dead man's fingers" from around the edge of the body. These long, pale gray lengths of feathery filaments cannot be eaten.

Pick out any brown crab meat from inside the shell with a teaspoon and reserve. Cut the carapace in half with a sharp knife and pick out the white flesh with a skewer or small knife. Any brown crab meat can be added to the previous amount from the shell.

To cut the shell on the claws and legs, take a large knife, blunt edge facing down, and crack open the shell. Try to stop at the shell rather than break the flesh inside. The flesh within the large claws should come out in one piece. Repeat with the other leg pieces.

Pick out all the flesh inside with a skewer and reserve.

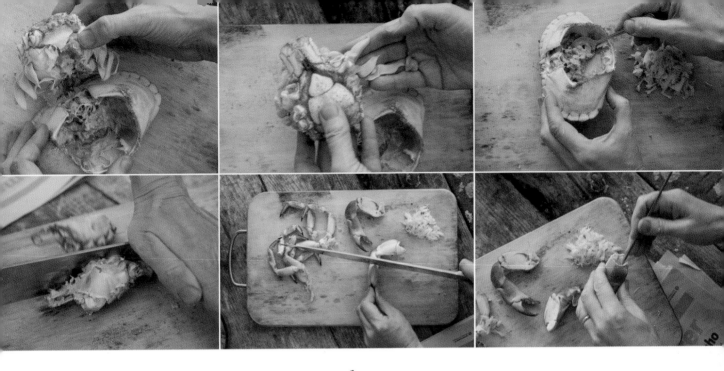

Pesce

MASTERCLASS

Carne

CHAPTER 7: MEAT

Carne

INTRODUCTION

I stopped being a vegetarian on a train travelling between Viareggio and Venice. After two and a half years of not eating meat, I was on holiday, travelling around Italy with a friend, and had just been reading in my student guide to Italy that the real Italian experience was sharing a picnic hamper with an Italian family on a train. We, of course, hadn't come prepared for our journey of several hours, there was nothing much to eat at the buffet and we were famished.

n Italian couple was sitting opposite us and, sure enough, down came their hamper from the luggage rack. But they had forgotten the bottle opener for their beer. Being a student, I had one handy and, in return for borrowing it, they offered each of us a *panino* stuffed full of prosciutto. I can remember the moment as if it was in slow motion. As my friend went to protest that I was vegetarian, one of my hands went over his mouth, the other grabbed the *panino*, and I greedily devoured the wonderful sweet, salty slivers of cured ham with their beautiful, tasty white fat. I should have known what an effect Italy would have on me. A Florentine friend, Dante, summed up the dedication that Italians in particular have to meat, when he told me his grandmother, when told a vegetarian was coming for dinner, said, "No matter; I will just do lamb."

In Tuscany, when you say *carne* (meat), you usually mean beef or veal. *Un pezzo di carne* offered to a child will usually be a piece of veal, breaded and pan-fried. All over Italy households will have their own recipe for *polpettone* (meat loaf), not to be confused with *polpettine*, or meatballs (see page 304); and while the pig is revered for everything it gives, from prosciutto to salame as well as fresh meat—Giancarlo calls it "the king of the table."

There is an idea that meat doesn't play such a major role in the Italian diet as it does in Britain, but most of my Italian friends are confirmed carnivores. Since the BSE scare, there has been quite a movement in Italy toward supporting traditional breeds, particularly of pigs, such as the Cinta senese, with a distinctive white band running around its black body, and cattle such as the famous and historic Chianina breed in Tuscany. Or the Podolica in Basilicata, which is a direct descendant of the *Bos primigenius*, the huge, ancient beasts imported by the barbarians on their way to Rome in classical times.

The respect accorded to meat and to butchers in Italy is wonderful. Invariably the *macellerie* (butchers' shops) are pristine, with imaginatively presented meat and salami and hams hanging up. Italian butchers fillet the meat into smaller pieces rather than leaving large joints. I remember waiting for half an hour to be served at a shop in Castellabate, south of Naples. In that time I learned three new recipes, because the women were talking

284

about what they were going to cook; the butcher would recommend which cut to use, then someone else would come in with a different idea.

There is an astoundingly beautiful butchers' shop named Angelo Feroci in central Rome, with marble counters, where you see elegant women buying lovely joints of the freshest looking meat ready to roast, including guinea fowl wrapped in parchment paper and then clay, which you bring from the oven to the table to crack open the casing.

In the summer you will see butchers' shops with their own open-air grills and barbecues over which they will roast their meat. I love this way of cooking and eating. Before I met Giancarlo I often used to grill skewers of meat, but it wasn't until he showed me how to do it the Tuscan way that I realized how dry the meat can be if you don't baste it enough. He smothers the meat in oil and uses plenty of sea salt, then, as the juices are released from the meat, he collects them in a pan underneath and pours them back over the top of the skewers. A delicious idea is to intersperse cubes of beef with chunks of crusty bread and pieces of pancetta, so that the bread absorbs the wonderful juices and flavors from the meat next to it.

On average, we eat one animal for every two that we kill as so many of us eat only the prime cuts. In Italy, only a generation ago, people ate every part of the animal, including offal and the tougher cuts, which they tenderized with longer cooking times.

TIPS ON KNIVES AND KNIFE SHARPENING

Grip the knife firmly in your dominant hand and stroke it at a 45-degree angle against the length of the sharpener held in your other hand. Do this on both sides of the blade for a few minutes. Sharpen it regularly: once a week is good practice, though this will depend on how often you use it.

When buying a knife ask to hold it first to feel the weight of it. Your strength and the size of your hands will make a difference to the knife you choose. It should feel well balanced and secure in your hand.

Point and face the knife away from you at all times, and hold knives pointing down when walking around.

Chefs seldom lend their knives to others as they get used to their own equipment and method of sharpening.

For meat, a boning knife is important: this is long, thin and not flexible. A chef's knife is important too, for cutting through small bones.

Abbacchio alla Romana
Roman Lamb with Anchovies and Rosemary

Lamb with anchovies: how strange, I thought, until someone told me that this was a perfectly normal way for Romans to flavor their dishes and that actually no taste of fish can be detected in the final dish. Of course, as I should have known, since it was cooked by Franco Taruschio, it is delicious, with that addictive salty taste that I yearn for in a roast. Traditionally this recipe is made with baby lamb but that is often hard to come by, so we are using cheap cuts like knuckle and shank. Trust me, you are going to love this dish.

Serves 6

4 knuckles and 4 shanks of lamb (about 4½ lb)
salt and freshly ground black pepper
2–3 tablespoons flour, for coating
4 tablespoons extra virgin olive oil
2 sprigs of rosemary, finely chopped
1 sprig of sage
2 garlic cloves, finely chopped
¼ cup white wine vinegar
4 anchovy fillets, preserved in oil
⅔ cup hot water

Trim the pieces of lamb, season and flour on all sides. Heat 2 tablespoons oil in a large lidded flameproof casserole. When hot, fry the lamb pieces until golden, turning frequently. Remove the lamb and drain on paper towels. Discard the oil and wipe the pan clean. Chop the herbs, garlic, and anchovies together on a board.

Heat the remaining oil and briefly fry the anchovies, herbs, and garlic. Return the lamb to the casserole and stir. Add the vinegar and hot water. Cover the casserole and cook over low heat for 1 hour or until the meat is tender. Preheat the oven to 350°F.

Remove the pieces of lamb from the casserole and place on a baking sheet. Roast in the oven for 10–15 minutes, until browned. Meanwhile, heat the sauce in the casserole and adjust the seasoning. If there isn't enough sauce, add a little water or, if it is quite watery, boil to reduce. Remove the meat from the oven and transfer to a serving dish. Pour the sauce over the top and serve with cannellini bean mash or with potato gnocchi and some grated Parmesan.

Agnello con piselli
Lamb and Pea Stew

This is a dish from the south of Italy where cheaper cuts of lamb are stewed slowly on the stove or in the oven. Ask your butcher for a cut such as middle neck, shoulder, or scrag end that will stand up to the long cooking time and contains some fat to flavor the stew. Although this stew is slow to cook, it is very quick to prepare and so makes a good supper dish.

Serves 4

1½ lb boneless stewing lamb, cut into 2 in cubes
salt and freshly ground black pepper
3 tablespoons oil
1 white onion, finely chopped
2 garlic cloves, sliced
4 sprigs of rosemary
⅔ cup dry white wine
10 oz frozen peas
1 cup stock or water

Season the lamb all over with salt and pepper. Heat the oil in a large lidded frying pan or heavy-bottomed flameproof casserole. When hot, add the onion and garlic. Cook until softened and then add the lamb and cook, turning the pieces, for about 10 minutes, until they are brown on all sides. Next pour in the wine and let it reduce for a couple of minutes. Then add the peas, stock or water and bring to a boil.

Cover the pan and let it simmer for 1–1½ hours, until the lamb is tender and the sauce has reduced. If you feel the stew is too watery, remove the lid and let the sauce bubble and reduce, as necessary.

Agnello alla brace con oregano e aglio
Barbecued Lamb with Oregano and Garlic

I was served this dish at Easter time in a restaurant in the region of Cilento, south of Naples. Oregano is a very popular herb in this area and it is the only herb that I would use dried. Whenever you are in Italy, buy some oregano in branches, as sold in markets: the flavor is intense and will remind you of your vacation.

Serves 6

4–5 lb leg of lamb, boned and butterflied
4 garlic cloves, coarsely chopped
2 tablespoons dried oregano or finely chopped rosemary
⅓ cup olive oil
salt and freshly ground black pepper

Put the lamb into a large bowl. Mix together all the other ingredients and rub all over the lamb, ensuring the marinade gets into all the crevices. Leave for at least 1 hour or cover and refrigerate for up to 24 hours to infuse.

Preheat the grill or barbecue to very hot and put the lamb on it. Cook on both sides until cooked to your liking, approximately 35–45 minutes. Use any extra marinade to baste the meat during cooking. Serve with salad and roast potatoes or with the Couscous and Lemon Salad (see page 225) and some lemon wedges for squeezing.

Carne
MASTERCLASS

Boning and butterflying a leg of lamb

Trim away large areas of solid fat, then cut away the bone from the leg by working the knife around it.

Cut back the flesh on either side of the bone, keeping the knife as close to the bone as possible.

Pass the knife under the bone to remove it completely.

Open out the meat and cut away any excess fat and gristle—but don't remove all the fat, as most of the soft fat will break down during the cooking, making the meat tastier and more juicy.

To butterfly the lamb, slice the thick sides in half and open out.

Then do the same again so the meat is twice its original size.

The lamb is then ready to grill or barbecue.

Rotolo di agnello con pecorino, menta e carciofi
Rolled Lamb with Pecorino, Mint, and Artichoke Stuffing

I ate this at Sora Lella in Rome. It's a cheap cut with the ingredients of the area added to it. I was impressed with the flavors and amused by the fact that—like the Brits—the Italians served mint with lamb. Use lightly cooked fresh artichoke hearts if you wish (see page 378), but I prefer the flavor of marinated ones for this dish. I usually have a jar in my cupboard.

Serves 6

4–5 lb leg of lamb, boned (you can ask your
  butcher to do this for you, or see page 288)
salt and freshly ground black pepper
30 mint leaves
2 oz semi-matured (*semi-stagionato*) pecorino,
  roughly cut into slivers
10 oz jar of marinated artichoke hearts in oil
  (6 oz drained weight), halved
2 garlic cloves, sliced
3 tablespoons olive oil
2 cups dry white wine
1¼ cups water

Preheat the oven to 475°F. Trim away any excess fat from the lamb and lay it out flat. Season well with salt and pepper. Place the mint, pecorino, artichokes, and garlic on the lamb and roll up. Secure with cotton string. Heat the oil in a large frying pan and sear the rolled lamb on all sides then pour away the excess oil. Transfer the lamb to an ovenproof casserole, deglaze the pan with the wine and then pour this into the casserole along with the lamb and the water. Cover, place in the very hot oven for 15 minutes, then reduce to 325°F and cook for 30 minutes. Remove the lid to allow the sauce to reduce, and cook for another 30 minutes or until cooked through.

Serve with new potatoes, wilted spinach, and plenty of crusty bread to mop up the juices.

Tip: A boned shoulder also works but increase the cooking time by 30 minutes to 1 hour.

Stuffing a leg of lamb

Open out the butterflied leg of lamb and lay the slices of ham on top, followed by the cheese and mint.

Top with the artichokes and season well with salt and pepper.

Roll up the lamb, enclosing the stuffing inside.

Tie up the roll with string so that the stuffing doesn't escape. Don't worry too much about butchers' knots—just keep the string as tight as you can.

Once cooked, untie the string and slice the meat to serve.

MASTERCLASS

Stracotto
Beef and Tomato Stew

This very easy beef stew is similar in flavor to a ragù and popular with everyone. Like all simple dishes, it can be used in other recipes too: for example, as a filling for *cappelletti* pasta (see page 187). Don't tell the Italians but I stir in half a jar of my friend Cyrus Todiwalla's curry pickle and it is transformed into a gorgeous beef curry. Leftovers are also great reheated with a little added chili powder then served in a baked potato with sour cream and grated cheese. Stracotto is so easy to prepare and useful, I now make double the quantity and have some permanently in the freezer.

Serves 6 as a main

¼ cup olive oil
4 tablespoons butter
1 large white onion, finely chopped
1 garlic clove
3 bay leaves
1 teaspoon freshly grated nutmeg
salt and freshly ground black pepper
2½ lb stewing steak
1 x 28 oz can Italian plum tomatoes

Put a large saucepan or flameproof casserole over medium heat and add the olive oil and butter. When these are hot, add the onion, garlic, bay leaves, nutmeg, salt and pepper and cook for 5 minutes, taking care not to let the onion burn. Then add the meat and brown on all sides for about 10 minutes.

Meanwhile, put the tomatoes into a bowl and reserve the can with the juice inside. Crush the tomatoes with your hands until pulpy. Add this to the browned meat. Now rinse out the can with 1 quart water and add this to the casserole. Cook uncovered for 3 hours, adding a little extra water if the sauce is looking dry and the meat is not yet tender. After this time the meat should be really tender and break into soft shards and the sauce should be reduced to a rich, sticky marvel.

Ragù alla Napoletana con braciole
Neapolitan Ragù with Beef Rolls

The tomato sauce is eaten with pasta, and the *braciole* are eaten afterwards with vegetables.

Serves 8

1½ lb boneless beef, round steak, rump steak, or chuck "shoulder clod"
3 large garlic cloves, finely sliced
salt and freshly ground black pepper
3 oz Parmesan shavings
3 tablespoons flat-leaf parsley, leaves coarsely torn
2 carrots, roughly chopped
2 celery ribs, roughly chopped
1 medium onion, roughly chopped
4 tablespoons extra virgin olive oil
2 x 14oz cans whole plum tomatoes
1 heaping tablespoon tomato purée
1¼ cups meat or vegetable stock or hot water

Slice the beef into sixteen pieces and use a meat mallet to bat out each slice thinly to about 6 x 3 inches wide and 1 inch thick. Lay the pieces out on a clean work surface and put two or three slices of garlic, spaced apart, on each one. Season the meat with salt and pepper. Divide the Parmesan shavings between the slices and top with the parsley, sharing it equally between the pieces.

Roll up each piece of meat to enclose the contents and secure each roll with a toothpick.

Heat the oil in a large saucepan and when hot, fry the vegetables and rolls for 10 minutes. Add the red wine and allow to reduce for a few minutes. Add the tomatoes and purée, stir and bring to the boil. Reduce the heat and leave the stew to simmer, partially covered, for 2 hours or until the beef is tender.

Remove the meat and set aside. Whizz the vegetables and juices in a blender to make a smooth sauce and season to taste. Remove the toothpicks from the rolls and put them back into the sauce to reheat before serving.

Rocco and Vincenzo

Rare

Medium

Well done

Carne

MASTERCLASS

How to tell when a steak is done

To tell when a steak is done to your liking, press the top of it while it is still in the pan or under the broiler. The resistance to touch will demonstrate how it is cooked. You can compare the feeling to various parts of your hand, using this simple guide.

Put your thumb and first finger together and prod the soft fleshy area at the base of your thumb with the index finger of your other hand. It will be soft to the touch like a "rare" steak feels. Next, move your middle finger to touch your thumb and feel the point again—it will feel like a "medium rare" steak. The third finger will feel like "medium" and the little finger like "well done."

TIPS ON BUYING AND COOKING STEAK

There are many types of steak available, such as ribeye, rump, Fiorentina or T-bone, porterhouse, sirloin, and filet, each with their own good points. When choosing ribeye or sirloin steak, look for one with marbling or thin veins of fat running through the meat. This fat will break down during cooking and offer moisture and flavor to the finished steak. A filet will not have as much flavor but the meat will be tender and should melt in your mouth.

Ageing You can buy steak aged for up to 35 days from good butchers. In Italy steak is eaten sooner than in the UK; it is a question of taste.

Trimming steak Some chefs cut the rind of fat off the steak while others leave it on to offer moisture and flavor. To avoid the steak curling up as the fat shrinks, however, it can be snipped with scissors at intervals along the length.

Seasoning steak In our cooking courses, many people ask why a steak in a restaurant tastes better than the ones they cook at home. Although this may be due to using a chargrill, it is usually more to do with the fact that a chef uses more salt and pepper than cooks do at home—it's as simple as that! There is also a debate between chefs as to whether steak should be seasoned before or after cooking. Both in the restaurants and in the school we always season our steaks well on both sides before cooking. If cooking the steaks in a pan, the oil should be very hot before adding the steaks.

For extra flavor, marinate steaks in a mixture of olive oil, salt, pepper, a couple of sprigs of rosemary or thyme, and two crushed garlic cloves. Leave it to marinate for at least 1 hour, or cover and refrigerate overnight.

For serving, try making a tagliata by slicing a steak into strips after cooking and drizzling with aged balsamic vinegar topped with Parmesan shavings and arugula.

Brasato al Barolo
Braised Beef with Barolo

In this classic Piedmontese dish, beef is braised slowly in Barolo, the local full-bodied red wine. The meat is studded with carrots and celery and, after two hours of cooking, becomes so tender it melts in your mouth. Strictly speaking, this should be started the day before because marinating the beef in wine further infuses it with flavor and tenderizes the meat. If time is short, however, this is still a great dish and will make a memorable feast.

Serves 8

2 carrots
2 celery stalks
3½–4 lb boneless beef bottom
  round
salt and freshly ground
  black pepper
⅓ cup olive oil
1 medium red onion, coarsely
  chopped
4 bay leaves
12 black peppercorns
3 sprigs of thyme
1 bottle Barolo or other
  full-bodied red wine
1 heaping tablespoon
  tomato paste
1¼ cups meat stock

Chop 1 carrot and 1 celery rib into eight sticks each. Decide which way the meat will be cut according to the grain—imagine that when it is carved, every slice should reveal circles of carrot and celery. Use a long sharp knife to make small but deep incisions (about 2 inches) in each end of the meat and push in the carrot and celery sticks. Season the meat all over.

Choose a pot large enough to accommodate the meat and heat the oil in it. Coarsely chop the remaining carrot and celery rib and cook with the onion for a few minutes. Add the bay leaves, peppercorns, and thyme.

Put the meat in the pan and brown on all sides; it should take around 10 minutes. Add the red wine and the tomato paste, stir to mix with the vegetables and bring to a boil. Reduce the heat and leave the stew to simmer for 2 hours or until the beef is tender.

Remove the meat and set aside. Puree the vegetables and juices in a blender to make a smooth sauce, or leave them as they are and season to taste. Slice the meat and serve with soft polenta or creamy mashed potatoes, topped with the sauce.

Tip: To reheat the brasato, cut the meat into slices and reheat in a frying pan with the sauce.

Filetto di manzo su crostone con Asiago e funghi

Beef Fillet on Crostone with Asagio Cheese and Wild Mushrooms

The combination of melting cheese, wild mushrooms, and tender steak is irresistible. If you cannot find Asiago, Fontina or gorgonzola also work well, either grated or thinly sliced. To plan ahead, grill the bread in advance, prepare the mushrooms and cheese, then fry the steaks and assemble the dish at the last minute.

4 thick slices of stale white crusty stale bread, cut to fit under the steaks

3 tablespoons olive oil

4 beef tenderloin steaks, 6–8 oz each

5 oz Asiago or Fontina cheese, coarsely grated or thinly sliced

salt and freshly ground black pepper

FOR THE MUSHROOMS

3 tablespoons extra virgin olive oil

2 garlic cloves, crushed

3 large sprigs of thyme

3–4 sprigs of rosemary

salt and freshly ground black pepper

1 lb mixed mushrooms (e.g. white cup, oyster, portabello, crimini, porcini), washed or brushed as necessary, thickly sliced

⅓ cup dry red wine

First, prepare the mushrooms. Heat the oil in a large frying pan over a high heat and, when hot, add the garlic, thyme, rosemary, salt and pepper. Cook for just a few seconds to flavor the oil, then add the mushrooms and cook over high heat, tossing or stirring frequently. When the water from the mushrooms has evaporated, add the wine and continue to cook over medium heat for about 5 minutes, until they are cooked through. Season to taste, then set aside in a warmed dish.

Heat the broiler to high. Toast the bread under the broiler (or in a toaster) until golden brown on both sides. Set aside on a grill pan or ovenproof serving dish.

Heat the olive oil in another frying pan and cork the steaks, two at a time, to your liking. (For instructions on how to tell when your steak is done see page 294.) Place a steak on each piece of toasted bread in the ovenproof dish. Pile a large spoonful of mushrooms on to each steak and top with a mound of grated cheese. Put the steaks under the broiler for 2–5 minutes or until the cheese is melted. Serve right away with any remaining mushrooms on the side. Serve with wilted spinach or green beans.

Spiedini di carne e salsicce alla Toscana
Tuscan Steak and Sausage Skewers

This recipe has become a family favorite: I can enlist the help of the children in making it and everyone loves eating it. It is based on an old Tuscan recipe for skewered sausages and pig's liver wrapped in caul and sandwiched between crunchy bread and herbs. For non-Tuscans it is an acquired taste but this version hits the spot and still utilizes the clever idea of having bread on the skewers to soak up the juices. As a child, one of my favourite dishes in an Italian restaurant was mixed grill so that I could have a bit of everything. This "recipe on a stick" is like that and the herbs give it so much flavor. Italian sausages are best as they contain no bread. Toulouse sausages also work if you like garlic. If you cannot find either, look for lean or gluten-free sausages that will hold their shape when cut in half. Chicken would also work here in place of one of the other meats.

Serves 6

12 oz sirloin or beef tenderloin steak
8 oz pork loin or tenderloin
1 lb Italian sausages (about 8)
4 oz pancetta or unsmoked bacon slices
6 oz country-style white bread
18 sage leaves or bay leaves, or some of each
6 sprigs of rosemary, cut into 12 pieces
⅓ cup extra virgin olive oil
salt and freshly ground black pepper
6 wooden or metal skewers

If you are using wooden skewers, soak them in water in a shallow dish for at least 20 minutes before use, to prevent them from burning later. Preheat the oven to 350°F.

Meanwhile, cut the steak and pork into 1½-inch squares, trimming off any gristle and excess fat. Cut each sausage in half, or into thirds if they are very big. Using a pair of scissors, cut the pancetta into 1½ inch squares or, if using bacon, cut each slice into three pieces. Cut the bread into 1 inch cubes. Divide all the ingredients into six equal piles.

Thread the prepared meats and sausages onto the skewers, alternating them with bread and interspersing the bay or sage leaves and rosemary between the cubes. Season them on all sides and place in a roasting pan. Drizzle the oil over the skewered ingredients, turning them as you do. Cook in the oven for 20–25 minutes, turning the skewers halfway through and basting them with the juices, until golden brown and cooked through. Serve on hot plates with any juices from the pan poured over the top. Peperonata or Caponata (see pages 106 and 370) and Lemon Couscous Salad (see page 225) are good with this.

Stefano's Tip: Cook the skewers on a rack over some partially-cooked potatoes in a roasting pan. The juices from the meat—and especially the sausages—will drain onto the potatoes, making them so irresistible you'll be at the gym tomorrow!

Choose the best sausages you can find and grill them over glowing embers for unbelievable flavor

Ragù alla Napoletana con carne
Neapolitan Ragù with Beef

Serves 6

This classic ragù is served all around Naples. Traditionally, a piece or pieces of meat are slow-cooked in tomatoes. The sauce is served with pasta and the meat eaten after. Some less-than-honest restaurants economize and omit the meat but still call it ragù. We challenged one waiter who told us that the meat was so tender it had "disappeared altogether."

3 tablespoons olive oil
1 large white onion, coarsely chopped
1 carrot, coarsely chopped
1 large celery rib, coarsely chopped
2¼ lb boneless chuck or stewing beef, cut into large bite-size pieces
⅓ cup red wine
¾ cup vegetable, chicken or beef stock
3 x 14 oz cans Italian plum tomatoes
2 sprigs of basil
salt and freshly ground black pepper

Heat the oil in a large flameproof casserole and cook the vegetables for a few minutes. Add the meat and cook until browned all over. Add the wine and reduce, then add the stock, tomatoes, basil, salt and pepper. Bring to a boil, then reduce to a simmer and leave, covered, for 3½–4 hours. Check it every 20 minutes or so and give it a good stir. If necessary, add a little water once or twice during the cooking time if you feel it is becoming too dry. Serve the sauce with pasta followed by the pieces of steak with vegetables.

Variation:
Ragù di carne alla Siciliana
Sicilian Ragù

Serves 10

I enjoyed my favorite version of this meat ragù in Sicily where our friends Ninfa and Teresa cooked pieces of stewing steak in the ragù in the same way as the Neapolitan version. However, about 30 minutes before the end of the cooking time, they added some meatballs (use a third of the recipe for Meatballs on page 300) after browning them first in a frying pan. They had also added 6 sausages, partially-cooked and halved, so that when you dipped into the big pot of sauce you could help yourself to meat, sausage, or meatballs—or in my case all three, all in the name of research, of course. Ninfa and Teresa scooped out ladlefuls of the sauce to eat with penne pasta, which was really delicious: like a tomato sauce but with all the flavor of the meat, too. Then they enjoyed the meat with bread and afterwards with salad, but heaps of mashed potatoes work well too.

Carpaccio di Manzo
Thinly Sliced Beef with Arugula, Parmesan, and Lemon

Carpaccio of beef originated in Harry's bar in Venice, taking its name from a painter who used a particular red that resembled the color of the meat. The term "carpaccio" is now widely used for anything that is thinly sliced—such as cod, tuna, or artichokes.

Serves 4

8 oz beef tenderloin steak
½ level teaspoon salt
juice of 1 lemon
5 tablespoons olive oil
1 tablespoon chopped
    flat-leaf parsley
a handful of arugula leaves
1 oz Parmesan shavings

Trim off and discard the fat and silverskin. Slice the meat very thinly and lay on 4 plates. (Freezing the meat for 30 minutes before slicing will make it easier to cut very thin slices.) Sprinkle with salt, lemon juice, oil and parsley, and top with the arugula and Parmesan.

Coda alla vaccinara
Oxtail alla Vaccinara

Oxtails used to be popular in the UK but we have tended to ignore it in recent years. Not so in Rome, from where this dish hails. *Vaccinara* refers to a butcher who specializes in beef. This dish comes from Testaccio, an area of Rome that housed the original abattoir for the whole city. We once had a taxi driver who drove us on a hell-raising journey through Rome to the airport while telling us in emotional terms that for generations his family had been butchers there. He regretted that he was the first member of his family to break the tradition of butchery. This is one of the dishes the butchers made at home, having been given the oxtails by the cattle-owners in exchange for their skills. Cook this in a lidded flameproof casserole, if you have one, or start the dish in a large frying pan and transfer to an ovenproof dish with a lid. It is a good idea to cook this dish the day before you want to eat it because, when left overnight, the fat comes to the surface and can be removed easily. Any leftover sauce can be eaten with pasta.

3 lb oxtails, cut into 2 in pieces
salt and freshly ground black pepper
flour, for dredging
3 tablespoons sunflower oil
3 tablespoons olive oil
4 oz pancetta or bacon, coarsely chopped
2 onions, coarsely chopped
1 large carrot, or 2 small ones, coarsely chopped
2 celery ribs, coarsely chopped
4 garlic cloves, crushed
1¾ cups red wine
1 x 28 oz can Italian plum tomatoes
1¼ cups water
5 cloves
3 bay leaves
2 cinnamon sticks (optional)
a large handful of flat-leaf parsley, including stems

Trim off as much fat as possible from the oxtails and leave them to soak in cold water for at least 4 hours or overnight. Drain, rinse, and pat them dry with kitchen paper. Season and flour the pieces and shake off any excess. Preheat the oven to 300°F.

Heat the sunflower oil in a heavy-bottomed flameproof casserole or in a large frying pan and cook the oxtails until golden brown all over. If you are using a frying pan, transfer the meat to a casserole. Discard any excess oil and wipe out the pan with paper towels.

Add the olive oil to the pan and cook the bacon, onion, carrot, celery, and garlic for about 10–15 minutes. When softened, add the *soffrito* to the casserole and place it over the heat. Add the wine, bring to a boil and reduce down for a couple of minutes, then add the tomatoes and water. Bring this to a boil, season with salt and pepper; add the cloves, bay leaves, cinnamon sticks, and parsley. Cover the casserole and reduce to a simmer for about 5 hours over low heat on the stovetop or transfer to the oven. During the cooking, stir the stew from time to time to make sure the oxtails do not stick.

Remove the casserole from the heat and skim off the fat or leave to cool and refrigerate until the next day, removing any fat as necessary before reheating. Serve with mashed potatoes or polenta with sautéed zucchini.

Polpettine di carne in sugo di Pomodoro
Meatballs in Tomato Sauce

Meatballs are popular all over Italy and take many shapes and sizes. *Polpettone* would refer to one big one such as a meatloaf; "ine" on the end of the word signifies "little ones," hence *polpettine*. These meatballs are good served on their own, with roasted red pepper sauce or cooked in the oven with tomato sauce. For this recipe, it's best to prepare the tomato passata first, so that it is simmering while you make the meatballs.

Makes 18 meatballs / Serves 6

1 quart Franca's Tomato Passata (see page 166)
12 oz ground beef
12 oz ground pork
5 oz soft white bread from a crusty loaf, coarsely torn
2 garlic cloves
½ cup chopped flat-leaf parsley
1 tablespoon basil
1 tablespoon thyme leaves
½ cup finely grated Parmesan
2 or 3 eggs, depending on size
salt and freshly ground black pepper
1 generous tablespoon extra virgin olive oil

Prepare the passata, unless you have some made. Put the white bread, garlic, parsley, basil and thyme into a food processor and process until crumbs are formed.

Use your hands to mix together the beef, breadcrumb mixture, Parmesan, eggs, salt and pepper in a large mixing bowl. Divide the mixture into 18 equal portions then roll them into balls (with wet hands is easiest). Set aside in a dish. The meatballs can be stacked if divided by a sheet of parchment paper. Chill in the fridge until needed.

Variation: Make a hole in the center of each meatball with your finger. Push in a cube of mozzarella, press the mixture together to close up the hole, and cook as above. The melting mozzarella is a delicious surprise.

Polpettone di Salvatore
Salvatore's Meatloaf

The key ingredient to this is the giant fat sausage called mortadella sold in all Italian delis. Salvatore, our Head Chef for many years, used to eat slices of it for breakfast every morning in warm, freshly cooked focaccia. Traditionally, meatloaf is made with parsley leaves but as necessity is the mother of invention and I was out of parsley at home one day, I used celery leaves instead and the result was delicious. I encourage you to try it both ways, but don't tell Salvatore! If you can't find mortadella use pancetta, salami, or bacon instead.

Serves 4

1 lb ground beef
3 oz mortadella, pancetta, or unsmoked bacon or a mixture of the two, finely chopped
¼ cup parsley or celery leaves, finely chopped
¼ cup finely grated Parmesan cheese
4 oz white rustic bread after crusts have been removed (see the masterclass on page 30)
1 garlic clove, finely chopped
2 eggs
olive oil, for greasing the roasting dish

Preheat the oven to 350°F. Tear the bread into pieces and soak the bread in milk for a few minutes. Squeeze it out and crumble into a bowl with the rest of the ingredients apart from the oil. Roll into a large oval shape and wrap it loosely in baking parchment either like a parcel or a candy with twisted ends. Put this onto a roasting pan and bake for around 45 minutes to 1 hour, until cooked through and the juices run clear. Serve on its own, with tomato sauce, mashed potatoes or a green salad in summer.

Variation: Whole boiled eggs can be enclosed inside the meatloaf, or it can be cooked in tomato sauce in the oven or on the stovetop after browning.

Polpettine Mondeghili
Beef and Lemon Patties

I was introduced to these *polpette* in Milan by Giusy, a lovely chef who took me under her wing. She originates from Sicily but had spent her working life in Milan and now runs a restaurant, Il Giardinetto, in via Tortona, specializing in Milanese traditions. These meatballs also remind me of my mum's rissoles which she made every Monday with leftovers from the Sunday roast. What I love about Giusy's version is that they are amusingly like her name: tender, juicy, and soft! She said the secret is to cook the meat first. Now these are a regular appearance in our house—I make a beef stock for a risotto or soup and use the meat to make these.

Makes 6

FOR THE POLPETTINE

8 oz boiled beef, minced or finely chopped in a food processor
4 oz bread from a fresh unsliced white loaf
1 tablespoon flat-leaf parsley leaves
zest of 1 small lemon
salt and freshly ground black pepper
1 level teaspoon salt
2 eggs, beaten
¼ cup finely grated Parmesan
¼ whole nutmeg, finely grated
2–3 tablespoons milk, as necessary
½ cup dry breadcrumbs, for coating (see page 30)
5 tablespoons olive oil

Put the minced beef into a large mixing bowl. Make breadcrumbs by pulsing hunks of bread with the parsley in a food processor. Add the crumbs to the meat along with the rest of the ingredients except the milk, dry breadcrumbs, and oil. Use your hands to squeeze and blend the mixture, adding the milk a spoonful at a time until a soft, malleable mixture is obtained. Form the *polpettine* by rolling egg-sized balls of the mixture between your hands, then flatten them slightly.

Put the dry breadcrumbs in a shallow bowl and dip the *polpettine* into the crumbs to coat. Heat the oil in a large frying pan and cook them in batches for 3–4 minutes on each side until golden brown. Remove from the pan and drain on paper towels before serving.

Cotoletta alla Milanese
Veal Milanese

I was shown this classic Milanese dish by a chef called Dino. He cooked it up for me in his tiny kitchen while simultaneously serving hundreds of other customers who packed out his restaurant, La Colonna—a great hot spot, favored by Milanese professionals. He didn't use salt or serve it with wedges of lemon as he felt that it was a shame to ruin the crispiness of the fried breadcrumbs; personally I feel that a good squeeze of lemon and a pinch of salt gives this dish a great edge and lightens it a bit. If you do not like to use veal, turkey is a good substitute—but don't tell Dino!

Serves 2

2 veal chops (preferably boneless),
½ cup dry breadcrumbs, for coating (see page 30)
2 eggs, lightly beaten
salt and freshly ground black pepper
2 tablespoons clarified butter
lemon wedges, to serve

Remove the bone from the chop, if necessary, and place both chops between two large sheets of parchment paper. Pound the meat with a meat mallet (or rolling pin) until it is very thin, by which time it will be about three times its original size. Traditionally the markings from the veins of a leaf are represented by scoring the veal, as its wavy edges resemble the shape of an oak leaf.

Spread the breadcrumbs on a big tray and put the beaten eggs, seasoned with salt and pepper, on a large plate. Pass each veal chop through the breadcrumbs, then dip into the egg and pass it through the breadcrumbs again.

Heat the butter in a large frying pan. When hot, cook the chops on both sides for 5–10 minutes until cooked through. Serve with a wedge of lemon.

Scaloppine al limone
Veal Escalope with Lemon

With all veal escalope recipes it is really important to assemble the ingredients beforehand and place them next to the hob: you want to be able to work quickly, as the veal takes literally minutes to cook. Have the plates heating in the oven beforehand, too, as the veal will cool immediately if put on to cold plates. Batting out the veal first will not only make your cut go further but will also tenderise the meat.

Serves 2

5–7 oz veal scallop, in one piece
salt and freshly ground black pepper
flour, for dredging
2 tablespoons olive oil
2 tablespoons butter
2 tablespoons white wine
juice of ½ lemon
finely grated zest of ½ lemon
2 tablespoons water

Ask the butcher to trim off any excess fat or sinew from the veal—or do it yourself.

Place the trimmed scallop on a chopping board and cover with plastic wrap. Use a meat mallet to pound the meat until it is as thin as possible. Once the scallop has been fully pounded, cut in half to feed two.

Season the veal with salt and pepper, then dip both sides of the scallops into flour. Shake off any excess so that only the thinnest coating of flour remains.

Put the olive oil and 2 teaspoons of the butter into a large frying pan over high heat. Once it is really hot, cook the scallops for about 1 minute on each side.

Pour off the fat from the frying pan, holding the veal in place with a fork, and deglaze the pan with the wine, lemon juice and zest for 1 minute. Add the water and the rest of the butter. Cook for about 1 minute. Serve the veal with the sauce poured over the top.

Saltimbocca alla Romana
Veal Saltimbocca

Saltimbocca means veal that is so delicious, 'it jumps into your mouth'—or so the translation goes. Italians will insist this should be made only with veal but try it with turkey or chicken too—and don't tell them! If you don't have a meat mallet, use a small saucepan instead.

Serves 6

6 veal scallops
12 sage leaves
12 slices of Parma ham or prosciutto
salt and freshly ground black pepper
flour, for dredging
3 tablespoons extra virgin olive oil, for frying
about ½ cup dry white wine
2 tablespoons butter

Cover each scallop with plastic wrap or parchment paper and use a meat mallet to pound the scallops to a thickness of approximately ¼ inch.

Remove the plastic wrap and place two sage leaves on each scallop. Carefully lay two slices of Parma ham over each scallop, keeping the sage leaves positioned underneath. If it doesn't stick well, wet your finger with cold water and wipe the meat surrounding the sage leaf. Then lay more plastic wrap over the scallop and flatten them a little more to ensure the meats together. Cover and place in the fridge for about 10 minutes, to seal.

Take the prepared scallops from the fridge and remove the plastic wrap. Put the flour ino a shallow bowl and lightly coat both sides of each scallop in flour, shaking off the excess. Heat the oil in a frying pan and fry the scallops until golden on both sides; this will take only a few minutes. Transfer the scallops to warmed serving plates.

Drain the oil from the pan, add the wine, reduce for a couple of minutes and stir in the butter. Serve this sauce with the scallops and some seasonal green vegetables.

Osso Buco
Milan-style Braised Veal

Osso buco means literally "bone with a hole." The dish is traditionally from Milan but is now, of course, cooked all over the world. This recipe is from Gino Borella who originates from Parma. He achieves the depth of flavor by using lots of herbs and long, slow cooking. His *gremolata* simply crowns this glorious wealth of flavors. Usually Osso buco is served with risotto Milanese, which contains the marrow fat from the bone.

Serves 6

Preheat the oven to 350°F. First prepare the vegetables for the *soffrito* by either chopping them extremely finely by hand or by pulsing in a food processor.

Next prepare the *gremolata* by mixing the finely chopped herbs with the lemon zest and pepper. Set aside.

Using a pair of scissors, snip around the fatty edges of the osso buco: this will help them stay in shape rather than split their sides. Season each one with salt and pepper, then lightly coat them with flour. Tap off the excess.

Put the *soffrito* mix, olive oil, bay leaves, lemon zest, garlic, and rosemary in a large ovenproof frying pan or flameproof casserole and cook for 5–10 minutes, until the vegetables are translucent.

Heat the sunflower oil in a second frying pan and, when hot, cook the osso buco until golden on both sides. Remove them from the pan and discard any excess fat; then add to the *soffrito* to the pan. Add the wine and allow to reduce for a couple of minutes before adding the tomato purée and stock. Transfer the pan to the oven and cook, uncovered, for about 1–1½ hours, until the osso buco is beautifully tender. Sprinkle with the *gremolata* and serve with risotto Milanese (see page 207).

6 veal shanks (osso buco), cut
  crosswise into 3-in pieces
salt and freshly ground
  black pepper
½ cup flour, for coating
3 bay leaves
2 strips of lemon zest,
  each about 4 in long
2 garlic cloves
2 sprigs of rosemary
⅓ cup sunflower oil
2½ cups dry white wine
1 tablespoon tomato purée
⅔ cup meat or vegetable stock

FOR THE SOFFRITO
1 large carrot
4–6 celery ribs
1 large onion
⅓ cup olive oil

FOR THE GREMOLATA
1 sprig of flat-leaf parsley,
  finely chopped
1 sprig of rosemary, leaves
  stripped and finely chopped
zest of 1 lemon
freshly ground black pepper

Involtini di vitello ripieni agli asparagi

Veal Stuffed with Asparagus and Ham in White Wine Sauce

When I learnt this recipe, the portly chef Edilio at Osteria di Maesta, in the region of Parma, was cutting shavings from an equally wide and round wheel of Parmesan. I thought that, just as the man and his dog begin to look alike, so does the chef and his ingredients! He said this recipe "properly" comes from this area, meaning that it uses the local Parma ham and Parmesan cheese.

Serves 4

1¼ lb asparagus spears, woody
  ends removed
4 veal scallops, 1 lb total
  weight
8 thin slices of cooked ham
4 oz Parmesan shavings
salt and freshly ground
  black pepper
8 slices of Parma ham
3 tablespoons extra virgin
  olive oil
4 tablespoons butter
15 sage leaves
⅔ cup dry white wine

Put the asparagus into a saucepan with enough salted boiling water to cover, and cook for 8–10 minutes, until soft. Drain, reserving the cooking water.

Place the scallops between two layers of plastic wrap and bat out with a meat mallet or the base of a small saucepan, until they are about 3mm thick. Cut each one in half to give you eight pieces long enough to roll around the asparagus. Lay the veal slices on the work surface and divide the cooked ham between them. Place two or three asparagus spears in the center of each one, trimmed to a size that will allow them to be rolled inside the meat without sticking out. Reserve any leftover asparagus. Put the Parmesan shavings on top and season with a little salt and pepper. Now roll up each *involtino*, securing them by wrapping each one in a slice of Parma ham.

When hot, cook the *involtini* with the sage leaves until browned on all sides. Pour in the white wine and reduce for a couple of minutes. Remove the rolls and set aside. Add the reserved cooking water and allow to reduce for 15–20 minutes over medium heat. Finally, add rolls back to the pan with the leftover asparagus, chopped into small pieces, and cook for a further couple of minutes. Season to taste.

To serve, remove the *involtini* and slice each one in half on the diagonal. Arrange four halves on each plate. Pour the white wine sauce over the top and serve with Parmesan and Nutmeg Mash (see page 387).

Scaloppine alla pizzaiola
Veal Escalope with Tomato and Oregano

The word *pizzaiola* in this title refers to the use of leftover ingredients from pizza toppings cooked together with meat. There are many variations to this classic recipe: you can top the veal with a slice of mozzarella and flash it under the grill, or you could add a heaping tablespoon of capers, for example.

Serves 2

5–7 oz veal scallop, in one piece
flour, for dredging
2 tablespoons olive oil
2 teaspoons butter

FOR THE SAUCE
1 tablespoon olive oil
1 garlic clove, smashed
1 x 14 oz can Italian plum tomatoes, crushed
a good pinch of oregano
salt and freshly ground black pepper
3 tablespoons dry white wine
1 tablespoon stock or water

Ask the butcher to trim off any excess fat or sinew from the scallop—or do it yourself.

To make the sauce, heat the olive oil and cook the garlic for a minute or two. Add the tomatoes and oregano, season with salt and pepper and continue to cook over a medium heat while you prepare the veal. If the sauce dries out too much, add a spoonful or two of water.

Place the veal on a chopping board and cover with plastic wrap. Use a meat mallet to pound the meat until it is as thin as possible. Once it has been fully beaten to twice the size: cut in half. Season the scallops with salt and pepper, then dip them into flour on both sides. Shake off any excess so that only the thinnest coating of flour remains.

Put the olive oil and butter in a large frying pan over high heat. Once it is really hot, cook the scallops for about 1 minute on each side. Pour off the fat, holding the scallops in place with a fork, then add the hot tomato sauce, white wine, and stock. Cook for about 1 minute, then remove the garlic clove. Serve the veal with the sauce poured over the top.

Tip: Chicken or turkey breast would work equally well in both these recipes.

Vitello ai funghi con timo e vino bianco
Veal with Wild Mushrooms, Thyme, and White Wine

This autumnal dish was inspired by a semi-successful foraging trip. Having found only four small porcini, we added shiitake and button mushrooms from the supermarket. You can use a mixture of wild and cultivated mushrooms, provided that some of them have a good strong flavor. If not, rehydrate some dried porcini and use the soaking water instead of the stock.

Serves 4

4 veal scallops, pounded as thin as possible
flour, for dredging
4 tablespoons extra virgin olive oil
salt and freshly ground black pepper

FOR THE MUSHROOMS
3 tablespoons extra virgin olive oil
2 garlic cloves, lightly crushed
2 sprigs of rosemary, leaves stripped
1 sprig of thyme, leaves stripped
8 oz wild mushrooms, washed and dried
3 tablespoons dry white wine
¾ cup chicken or meat stock
2 teaspoons butter

Prepare the mushrooms. Heat the oil in a frying pan until hot. Add the garlic, rosemary and thyme and cook for a couple of minutes. While the oil is still very hot, add the mushrooms and cook for a few minutes, until cooked through. Remove from the heat.

Season the scallops on both sides with salt and pepper. Put the flour in a shallow bowl and coat each scallop with the flour, shaking off the excess.

Heat the oil in another frying pan. When hot, cook the veal scallops for about 1 minute on each side, until browned. Add the wine and allow to reduce for a couple of minutes. Add the mushroom mixture, stir in the stock and reduce again for a couple of minutes. Stir in the butter; the sauce will thicken slightly and take on a shine.

Place the scallops on warmed plates, top with mushrooms, and pour the juices from the pan over the top.

Scaloppine al Marsala
Veal Scallops with Marsala

I remember this being cooked for me by one of our Sicilian chefs, Vincenzo, many years ago. He had a typically fiery temper but was incredibly talented and I have always remembered his veal dish. I hope this does justice to his memorable version.

Serves 2

5–7 oz veal scallop, in one piece
2 tablespoons pine nuts
salt and freshly ground black pepper
flour, for dredging
1–2 tablespoons olive oil
⅓ cup dry Marsala
2 tablespoons butter

Ask the butcher to trim off any excess fat or sinew from the scallop—or do it yourself.

Toast the pine nuts in a dry frying pan or under the broiler. Be vigilant: they burn easily. As soon as they are browned, remove from the pan and set aside on a plate to cool.

Place the trimmed scallop on a cutting board and cover with plastic wrap. Use a meat mallet to pound the veal until it is as thin as possible. Once the scallop is twice the size, cut in half.

Season the veal with salt and pepper, then dip the scallops into flour on both sides. Shake off any excess flour so that only the thinnest coating of flour remains.

Heat the oil in a pan and, when really hot, fry the veal for about 1 minute on each side, until cooked through.

Pour off the oil and put the pine nuts in the pan. Cook for about 10 seconds, stirring, until browned, then stir in the Marsala and the butter until melted and smooth. Transfer the veal to a hot plate. Let the sauce reduce for another 10–20 seconds, then pour it over the veal. Serve right away.

SALT

Salt is used quite generously in Italian cooking, in order to bring out the natural flavors of fresh fish, meat and vegetables. So much is written about the dangers of too much salt in our diet that some people have become paranoid about using it—but we all need some salt for our bodies to function properly. The problem of overload usually stems from the quantity we unwittingly eat in processed foods, not the salt we add when we cook with raw ingredients. From the earliest times, civilizations have understood the value of salt, not least for preserving food. Wars have been fought over it and taxes raised on it. In Italy, cities such as Venice built their wealth on the salt trade. The type of salt you use is important. Both sea salt and rock salt have a clean, distinctive flavor that means you don't have to use much to have an impact. We always use sea salt—an unrefined natural salt produced by evaporating sea water. Depending on the harvesting process, the resulting crystals can vary: some are harder and crunchier than others; some white and some gray. Rock salt, mined from salt beds, is usually more coarse than sea salt and more suited to grinding in a mill than crumbling with your fingers. Powdery table salt, on the other hand, processed and refined from rock salt, is stripped of most of its minerals, with substances added to allow it to flow.

Fegato alla Veneziana
Calf's Liver with Onions

This is what we know as "liver and onions;" although it has long been a popular English dish, its origins lie in Venice. The important part of the recipe is that you should have the same amounts of liver and onions. The onions are cooked long and slow, which makes them become sweet. They are then removed from the pan and the liver strips are cooked very quickly in the same pan.

Serves 4

4 tablespoons butter
3 tablespoons extra virgin olive oil
1 lb white onions, halved and thinly sliced
salt
14–16 oz calf's liver
flour, for dredging
3 tablespoons dry white wine
⅓ cup vegetable stock or hot water
freshly ground black pepper

Heat half the butter with the oil in a large frying pan and cook the onions over a low heat with a little salt until really soft—this will take about 45 minutes. Remove the onions using tongs, reserving the remaining oil and butter in the pan. Set the onions aside on a warmed dish.

Cut the liver into strips, 1–1½ inches wide, discarding any membrane. Season it generously with salt and pepper, then dredge in flour, shaking off the excess. Add the liver to the hot pan and fry quickly for a couple of minutes, stirring, until cooked and crisp on the outside but soft on the inside. Remove from the heat and add to the onions. Pour the wine into the pan and let it come to the boil. Put the onions and liver back into the pan and toss with the wine. Transfer the liver and onions from the pan on to warm serving plates. Put the pan back on the heat and pour in the stock, scraping up any brown bits from the bottom of the pan with a wooden spoon. Allow this sauce to bubble, then add the remaining butter. Pour the sauce through a fine sieve over the liver and onions. Serve with soft polenta or mashed potatoes.

Fegato con burro e salvia
Calf's Liver with Butter and Sage

This is another classic Italian liver dish that favors calf's liver as it is more tender than other types from older animals. Our chefs cook it daily for customers at our restaurants and over the years we have perfected the recipe, creating a brilliant dish in less than seven minutes, which makes this a great choice for a quick supper.

Serves 2

Season and flour the slices of liver and shake off the excess. Set aside. Heat the oil and garlic in a frying pan over a high heat and cook for 1–2 minutes. Add the liver to the pan and cook for 40 seconds on each side. Add the butter and sage and, as soon as the butter is melted, remove the pan from the heat.

Transfer the liver to warm plates and pour the butter, sage, and garlic over the top. Serve with mashed potatoes and Swiss chard or peas.

Tip: The 40-second cooking time comes after much experimentation, half a minute is often not enough and a minute a side too much. Try it for yourself but aim to have the liver slightly pink inside.

11–12 oz calf's liver, cut into
  2 or 4 slices, ¼ in thick
flour, for dredging
3 tablespoons oil
2 garlic cloves, left whole
4 tablespoons butter
10 sage leaves
salt and freshly ground
  black pepper

Porchetta alla Toscana
Roast Pork Belly with Tuscan Herbs

In porchetta is a way of cooking meat where it is boned and rolled with herbs then baked for several hours. In any Tuscan market you will find a *porchetta* van. The cooked pork is served in a *panino* with no accompaniment other than salt. We love this dish so much, we asked our local butcher to bring his *porchetta* van to our wedding. At midnight on a hot June evening we drank chilled Lambrusco and ate *porchetta* in *panini*— delicious! A number of Italy's regions claim *porchetta* as their own and each has its own version: wild fennel and garlic in Umbria, sage and garlic in Tuscany, assorted herbs in Le Marche, and rosemary and garlic in Rome.

Serves 8–10

3 lb boneless pork belly
salt
about 10 sage leaves, coarsely chopped
5 sprigs of rosemary, leaves stripped and
  finely chopped
4 garlic cloves, coarsely chopped
2 tablespoons extra virgin olive oil
freshly ground black pepper

Preheat the oven to 350°F. Lay the pork skin-side down on a work surface and make some shallow cuts in the flesh. Scatter 2 teaspoons of salt, the chopped herbs, and garlic over the surface and press them in with your hand. Roll up the belly and secure with string; it should be tied in about eight places along its length and once at each end.

Using a sharp knife, make some cuts in the skin of the rolled pork, drizzle with the olive oil, and season with salt and pepper, rubbing it in. Put the pork into a small roasting pan and place this inside a larger one. Put the pans in the oven and, using a pitcher or measuring cup, fill the larger one with cold water. Top it up as needed during the cooking period; the water evaporates and keeps the meat moist.

Cook for about 2 hours or until the juices run clear when pierced with a skewer. After cooking, allow to rest for 30 minutes in a warm place, covered with foil. Serve with bread or Lentil, Tomato, and Spinach Stew (see page 128).

Cotoletta di maiale al cavolo nero e cannellini
Pork Loin Steaks with Cavolo Nero and Cannellini Beans

Tuscany is the region where pork is said to be king of the table—and it frequently takes center-stage in meals. The steaks can be quickly cooked in the time it takes to prepare the dark green leaves of *cavolo nero* and warm the beans. This combination of cabbage and beans is often found in Tuscany where the locals are called the *mangiafagioli*, meaning bean-eaters. *Cavolo nero*, or black kale, is a winter cabbage full of vitamins to ward off winter ailments. It is now grown in the UK and elsewhere, is particularly good after the first frost.

Serves 4

5 tablespoons olive oil
1 medium white onion, finely chopped
2½ oz pancetta, chopped
2 garlic cloves, lightly crushed
2 sprigs of fresh thyme, leaves stripped
salt and freshly ground black pepper
10 oz cavolo nero, finely chopped
1 x 14 oz can cannellini beans, rinsed and
  drained
4 boneless pork loin chops
flour, for dredging
⅓ cup dry white wine
2 tablespoons butter

Heat 4 tablespoons of the oil in a large frying pan and sauté the onion, pancetta, garlic, and thyme; season with salt and pepper. Add the *cavolo nero* and sauté until it is wilted, stirring frequently. Add the cannellini beans to the pan and stir to heat through. Set aside on a warmed serving dish.

Season the pork on both sides and dip into the flour, shaking off the excess. Heat the remaining oil in a separate pan and cook the pork for 5 minutes, turning once, or until it is cooked through and the juices run clear when pierced with a skewer.

Set the pork aside on the beans and cavolo nero and pour off the fat from the pan. Deglaze the pan with the white wine and reduce for a couple of minutes. Add the butter and stir until melted and smooth. Pour the sauce over the pork and serve right away.

Carne
MASTERCLASS

Arista in Latte

Arista in Latte
Roast Pork in Milk

Cooking meat in milk is common throughout north Italy because it results in moist meat and a wonderfully rich and flavorful sauce. The milk transforms during the cooking from liquid to yogurt-like clusters which form a rich brown sauce. Valentina Harris advises me that if you give it a good whisk over the heat just before you are ready to serve, it helps to break up the sauce slightly, giving a smoother texture.

Serves 8–10

3½ lb pork loin, bone loosened and re-tied (see "Chining" below)
salt
4 tablespoons butter
3 tablespoons olive oil
3 cups whole milk

Season the outside of the pork with salt—but go easy with it, because pork is a naturally salty meat.

Heat the butter and oil over medium heat in a large, heavy-bottomed saucepan or flameproof casserole. Lower the pork into the pan and crisp the skin to a rich golden color, turning it every few minutes. It will take about 15 minutes to ensure all the edges are golden.

Reduce the heat slightly and add the milk very slowly so that it doesn't bubble up too much. Gradually bring it up to a simmer and partially cover the pan. Cook for 2 hours or until the juices run clear when pierced with a skewer.

Once cooked, transfer the meat to a cutting board and let it rest for 5 minutes, loosely covered with foil. Meanwhile, skim off some of the fat from the juices, then whisk over the heat to break up the milk a little. Carve the meat, place the slices on a hot plate, pour over the sauce and serve.

Tip: If you find you have undercooked the pork, lay the slices in an ovenproof dish, pour over the sauce and bake for 5–10 minutes at 350°F, until cooked through.

Chining

Remove the rind from the loin of pork for a leaner roast or leave it on and score with a sharp knife for a crusty-topped roast with crackling fat.

To chine a roast, cut as close to the ribs as possible to partially separate the flesh from the bones. Leave a "hinge" of meat in place to keep it together and, after cooking, this can simply be cut through. Leaving the bones with the meat means you gain flavor and prevent the meat from drying out.

Maiale con prugne e mele
Pot-roasted Loin of Pork with Prune, Apple, and Rosemary Stuffing

The sweet softness of the fruit here ensures this dish is neither dry nor lacking in flavor. Buy good-quality moist prunes. I find pot-roasting is one of the best ways of cooking pork as it keeps the moisture in the meat.

1 lb pitted prunes
1 cup dry Marsala or brandy
4½ lb loin of pork
3 large sprigs of rosemary
3 sprigs of thyme
salt and freshly ground black pepper
1 medium apple, peeled, cored and cut into
 ¼ in slices
4 oz *lardo di colonnata* (belly fat) or lard
2 cups white wine
¾ cup chicken or vegetable stock

Soak the prunes in the Marsala for at least 1–2 hours, preferably overnight, to soften. (If you want to speed up the softening process, heat the brandy and prunes in a pan over medium heat or in the microwave for a couple of minutes, then leave for 20 minutes.)

Chine the pork (see page 318) or ask your butcher to do it for you.

Place the rosemary and thyme, with a couple of pinches of salt and pepper, in the pocket. Put the apple slices on top and then the soaked prunes. Discard (or drink) any remaining Marsala or brandy. Now roll up the pork and secure firmly by tying pieces of cooking twine around the loin at 2 inch intervals so that it is really tight and all the stuffing is contained. Wrap the twine around once lengthwise and secure. Season the outside of the pork with salt and pepper.

Melt the lard in a large, deep flameproof casserole over medium heat. Brown the pork on all sides for about 10 minutes. Add the wine and allow to reduce for a few minutes. Add the stock, bring to the boil then reduce the heat and cover with a lid. Cook for 2½–3 hours. To test whether it is cooked through, insert a skewer into the center of the meat. The juices should run clear. Serve with soft polenta or mashed celery root and cavalo nero with chile.

Porchetta con semi di finocchio
Slow-Roasted Pork Belly with Fennel Seeds

This is a very simple yet effective recipe. It takes no time to prepare and, while it roasts away in the oven, you can relax, knowing the end result will be scrumptious. The idea is taken from the Umbrian version of *porchetta*, which is usually rolled, but I like the simplicity of this version where the belly is left flat. It is so delicious, it needs nothing more than crusty bread and a simple salad. In our family, we cut the pork into strips on a wooden board set in the middle of the table, and eat it with our fingers. In Sardinia, they eat pork such as this over thinly sliced bread to catch the juices.

Serves 8–10

4 teaspoons rock salt
4 teaspoons fennel seeds
3 lb pork belly, in one piece

Preheat the oven to 400°F.

Lightly crush the salt and fennel using a pestle and mortar. Put the pork belly in a small roasting pan and place this inside a larger pan. Transfer the two pans to the oven and, using a pitcher or measuring cup, fill the larger one with cold water. Keep topping it up as needed during the cooking period; the water evaporates and keeps the meat moist. Cook for 30 minutes, then reduce the temperature to 350°F and cook for another 2 hours or until the juices run clear when pierced with a skewer. After cooking, allow the *porchetta* to rest for 30 minutes in a warm place, covered loosely with foil.

Salsicce con fagioli
Sausage Casserole with Beans

This is one of Giancarlo's winter dishes, a warming family favorite that we serve on bonfire night and other chilly evenings. It can be made in advance and reheated without spoiling. In Italy we eat it with hunks of Tuscan bread to mop up the sauce but when we're in England we often serve it with mashed potatoes.

Serves 6

1 quantity of Soffritto (including rosemary and garlic),
  see page 125

FOR THE TOMATO SAUCE
6 tablespoons olive oil
1 red onion, chopped
2 garlic cloves, peeled and lightly crushed
1 red chile, seeded and chopped
1 x 28 oz can Italian plum tomatoes

olive oil, for frying
12 sausages
4 oz pancetta, finely chopped
⅓ cup red wine
2 x 14 oz cans cannellini beans, drained
1 cup hot vegetable stock

First, make the tomato sauce. Heat the olive oil in a frying pan. Add the onion and cook over medium heat for 8–10 minutes, then add the garlic and chile and cook for another 2 minutes. Be careful not to burn the garlic. Add the tomatoes, reduce the heat and simmer, stirring regularly, for about 30 minutes until the sauce is thick.

Make the *soffrito* (see page 125). When cooked, add the cannellini beans and heat through. Set aside.

Meanwhile heat a little olive oil in a second frying pan. Put the sausages and pancetta into the pan and cook for about 7–10 minutes, making sure the sausages are brown on all sides. When cooked, pour off the fat and add the wine. Allow to evaporate for a couple of minutes and pour the contents of the frying pan into the tomato sauce. Add the cannellini bean mixture and hot vegetable stock and leave to simmer for 15–20 minutes. Season to taste and serve.

Carne
MASTERCLASS

Salsicce fatte in casa del Sig. Belli
Mr. Belli's Homemade Sausages

The appropriately named Mr. Belli the Butcher is a very proud man—and rightly so. He owns a sparkling clean, well-stocked butcher's shop in Torrita di Siena in Tuscany. You can just tell both he and his staff care for the quality, cleanliness and display of their meats, fowl, and *salumi*. In his sausages, Mr Belli uses the finest Chianina beef from Tuscany and little else. It was a pleasure to watch him at his art as he deftly wound string between the sausages using the width of his hand to measure them into even lengths.

Makes 24–36 sausages

11 lb pork belly
8 garlic cloves
3 tablespoons salt
1 tablespoon ground black peppercorns
2 lengths of natural casings
cotton kitchen twine

Cut the pork belly into strips about 2 inches wide, or a size that will fit in your meat grinder.

Cut away and discard the tough skin from the strips, then put them into the meat grinder. Pass the meat a second time through the grinder. Pound the garlic, using a pestle and mortar. Spread the ground meat out on to a wooden board and distribute the garlic evenly. Then sprinkle with the salt and pepper and mix everything with your hands pulling the mixture backwards and forwards for about 10 minutes, to blend thoroughly

Stuff the mixture into the natural sausage casings. Do not overstuff them or the skins will split. Should this happen, push the stuffing to either side of the hole and start again. When the entire lengths are filled, wet your hands with water and run them down the length of the sausage to even out any bumps and overstuffing

Use the width of your hand as a measure to tie off sausages with twine, trying to get them evenly sized.

Keep a length of string on one end and, with this, hang up the sausages in a well-ventilated room for a day. This will strengthen the flavor of the sausages and allow them to dry out a little before cooking.

Stufato di salsicce, fave e patate
Sausage, Fava Bean, and Potato Casserole

The origins of this dish are actually in a combination of recipes for *contorni* (side dishes) that we were shown in Cilento, in south Campania. The result was so delicious that I had to be physically removed from the dish lest I do myself harm. We used Neapolitan sausages and pancetta, fresh fava beans shelled by our children, dried chiles, and these strange little edible bulbs known as *lampascione*. However, testing this dish back home, I found it to be equally delicious made with products available in the UK. Do buy the best-quality sausages you can find, with little or no added bread. If you cannot find Italian sausages, Toulouse sausages work well. Nearly all Italian sausages are simply ground meat, garlic, and pepper with herbs or spices added for regional variation.

Serves 6

1 quantity of Potatoes and
  Onions (or *lampascione*),
  (see page 389)
3 tablespoons extra virgin
  olive oil
6–8 best-quality sausages
4 garlic cloves, crushed
1 red chile, coarsely chopped
14 oz can Italian cherry or
  plum tomatoes
¾ cup water
2 tablespoons tomato purée
8 oz shelled fava beans, cooked

Heat the oil in a large flameproof casserole or saucepan and cook the sausages until nicely browned all over. Remove from the pan and slice into 1 inch pieces. Pour off most of the oil, add the garlic and chile and cook for a couple of minutes, then add the tomatoes, water and tomato purée. Bring to a boil and return the sausages to the pan with the potato recipe and the fava beans. Stir the ingredients together gently to combine, taking care not to break up the potatoes. Cover and cook over low heat for 30 minutes or until the sausages are cooked through. Serve in the casserole dish.

Luganica al vino rosso
Sausage Wheel in Red Wine

Luganica, *lucanica*, or *luganiga* sausages originate from Basilicata, but are now made in many regions. Made from pork shoulder, breadcrumbs, and spices, they are long and thin, sometimes sold as one long length, much like a thinner version of Cumberland sausage. The best way to cook them is to break off a length and curl it into a spiral, held in position by two or three wooden skewers. It can then be cooked very efficiently, turning it once with a pair of tongs rather than having to turn stubborn individual sausages. Italians generally cook these *alla brace*, on the barbecue, but in Sicily our friend Chiara cooked hers in a frying pan with a delicious red wine sauce.

1 lb *luganica* sausage
2 tablespoons olive oil
1 small onion, finely sliced
2 garlic cloves, chopped
1¼ cups red wine
1 sprig of rosemary
2 wooden skewers or 4 cocktail picks

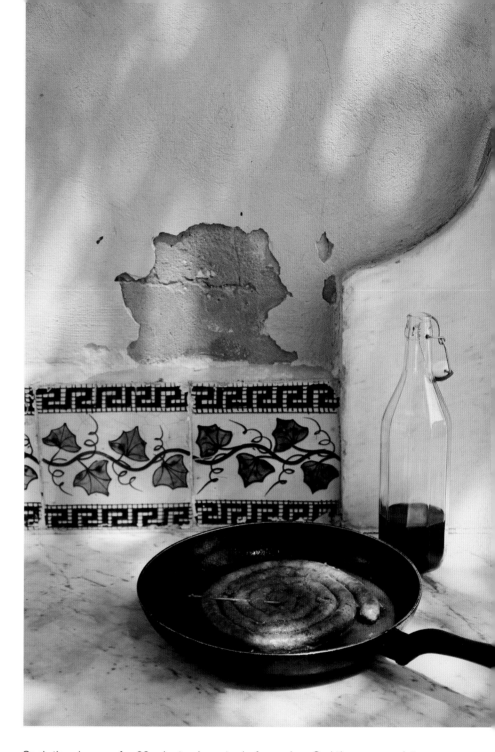

Soak the skewers for 30 minutes in water before using. Curl the sausage into 1 spiral or into 4 individual spirals and secure with the sticks. Heat the oil in a large, non-stick frying pan and cook the onion and garlic for 5 minutes. Put the sausage on top and cook on both sides until lightly browned. Add ¾ cup of the wine and continue to cook. Cover the pan and continue to cook for 15–20 minutes, until the sausage is cooked through. Remove the sausage, discard the skewers, and keep warm. Pour the remaining wine into the pan and let the sauce reduce for 5 minutes. Pour it over the sausages and serve with polenta or mashed potato.

Stufato di Capretto con Carciofi e Verza
Kid Goat with Artichokes and Cabbage

Goat is more common in the south of Italy. Its flavor is not as strong as people imagine and I was pleasantly surprised by this wonderful peasant-style dish. While testing it in our Caffé, the staff came running to try it, all saying how it reminded them of their grandparents. It was more popular in the past but is still served at Easter in some places. After just an hour of cooking the meat starts to become soft and tender and after two hours it is melting. We used ribs; if you use leg meat, cook it for longer.

Serves 6

¼ cup olive oil
salt and freshly ground black pepper
3 lb kid goat meat on the bone (ribs or leg meat), cut into bite-size pieces
2½ oz *lardo di colonnata*, coarsely chopped, or lardons
4 garlic cloves, peeled and lightly crushed
¼ cup white wine vinegar
a handful of parsley and 1 garlic clove, chopped
2½ quarts meat or vegetable stock
4 young artichokes, cleaned and quartered
8 oz Savoy cabbage, coarsely chopped
6 chunky slices of white bread

Heat the oil in a heavy-bottomed pan with a generous amount of salt and pepper. Fry the pieces of goat in the hot oil with the *lardo* and garlic for about 10–15 minutes, or until golden brown. Add the vinegar and the chopped parsley and garlic mixture. Let the mixture evaporate a little, then add the stock and the artichokes. Cover the pan and leave to cook slowly, until the goat is cooked through, stirring occasionally. This should take 1½–2 hours. Fifteen minutes before the end of cooking time, add the cabbage and stir through.

To serve, lay the bread in warmed soup bowls and ladle the stew on top of the bread. If you like a thicker sauce, some of the juices, cabbage, and artichokes can be pureed then stirred back into the pan.

Variation: The kid goat meat can be replaced with lamb, if you prefer.

Ragù di capretto
Kid Goat Ragù

Our chef, Monserrato, who cooked this for me loves *lardo*—pork belly fat cured with rosemary and salt. It adds a wonderful flavor to recipes and here it is finely chopped or blended with sage and rosemary. As it cooks, the smell of the herbs with the *lardo* comes up and hits you. *Lardo* is absorbed easily into other meats so is an ideal fat for ragù. The addition of the goat offal, if you can get it, means that you have different textures of meat in the ragù and a richness of flavor.

Serves 6–8

3 oz *lardo,* or lardons
2 large sprigs of sage (about 20 leaves)
2 sprigs of rosemary, leaves stripped
⅓ cup olive oil
salt and freshly ground black pepper
2 bay leaves
2 celery ribs, finely chopped
1 white onion, finely chopped
2 carrots, finely chopped
1 lb lean goat meat, chopped into bite-size pieces (add the leg bones to the pot for extra flavor)
goat spleen, heart and liver, if available
4 heaping tablespoons tomato paste
⅓ cup white wine
2 cups meat or vegetable stock

Chop the *lardo* with the sage and rosemary until it is well chopped and blended together. (Chopping them together means the herbs don't fly off in different directions.) Heat the oil with plenty of salt and pepper and fry the *lardo* mixture in hot oil with 2 bay leaves for a few minutes, then add the celery, onion, carrots, and goat meat with the bones. Chop the spleen, heart, and half the liver and add to the *soffrito*. After 15 minutes, add the tomato paste and stir well. Then pour in the wine and let it reduce for a few minutes. Add the stock, cover the pan, and allow the ragù to cook for 1–1½ hours. Check and stir every now and again and be prepared to add a little more stock as necessary so that the ragù doesn't burn. If you are not planning to eat it right away, allow it to cool, then reheat, adding a little stock if necessary.

Pollame e selvaggina

CHAPTER 8: POULTRY AND GAME

Pollame e selvaggina

INTRODUCTION

Giancarlo and I enjoyed very different childhoods in terms of the food we ate. Although his family had little available money, they kept guinea fowl, chickens, ducks, and rabbits, which enabled them to have a varied and quite adventurous diet. In our house, because my mother went out to work, we had convenience food during the week and home cooking only on weekends.

ven then, although I was brought up on roasts and casseroles, duck or pheasant were a special treat and I was in my twenties before I ever tasted goose or guinea fowl. The idea of pot-roasting a chicken or rabbit simply, so that the meat crisps and becomes really tasty, was something I only learned about during my travels in Italy, writing this book. The recipes for *Arrosto Misto* (page 360) and Pot-roast Chicken with Balsamic (page 334), served with a simple salad, are now some of my very favorite meals.

In Italy, many people still breed poultry and rabbits for the pot, either on their own land or on allotments, feeding them on household scraps—in the Veneto, however, you will find rabbit only in a ragù. Free-range birds are called *ruspante*.

Then, of course, there is hunting. Maybe not so many people go out hunting these days but there are still parts of Italy where they say the woods don't sing anymore because so many small birds, including songbirds, are considered fair game for hunters. Small birds such us blackbirds or quail are often threaded on to skewers and cooked *alla brace*, over the grill. In Tuscany, pot-roast or roast pigeon is popular, though many Italians take the same view as Venetians when it comes to rabbit, and will eat pigeon only if it is cooked in a ragù (see page 349).

In Italy, as in other countries, hunting has become a controversial subject over the last 10–15 years. Every so often the hunters lobby parliament to extend the hunting season, on one hand, while on the other, animal rights activists try to convince the public that some species are risking extinction. For example, the native Italian boar no longer exists: the boar you see in Italy nowadays is a bigger animal that originates from Eastern Europe.

During the last few years in Italy, *agriturismo venatorio* or "hunting hotels" have appeared, which stock game such as hare and pheasant that is released within a private area, so the hunter is sure to find some game. At the end of the hunt he must declare what he has killed and pay a different price for each species. Game birds such as quail and partridge are eaten right away and, because of the warmer climate, even pheasants are likely to be hung only for about two days. All are sold with their offal intact.

Something that I love, which is wonderful for a winter party, is *Scottiglia*, an old hunter's dish (see page 362), which is traditionally made with whatever small birds have been caught, and masses of basil and parsley. I refuse to use songbirds, however, so I make mine with guinea fowl, chicken, rabbit, and pheasant. It has the most amazing flavor—lovely with a big bowl of polenta.

Stronger game, such as venison, wild boar, or hare, is often marinated overnight in wine and cooked *agrodolce*, which means sweet and sour. Typical dishes involve vinegar or wine balancing the sweetness of onions, fruit, raisins, or even chocolate, in the case of wild boar. See the recipe for Roast Saddle of Venison with Woodland Fruits on page 357. Or you might find wild boar and venison hams, cured and air-dried in the same way as prosciutto. Duck and goose breasts are also sometimes smoked and served in thin slices as *antipasti*.

Chicken is popular in Italy, though much less so than in the US, and often it is cooked very simply. In Tuscany, *Pollo al Mattone* (see page 334), involves a small chicken being flattened under a terracotta brick, then grilled, with the addition only of olive oil, salt, and rosemary. Italian chickens are usually corn-fed, have a thick layer of fat on them and an intense flavor. They are sold complete with head, feet, and innards, all of which should be put to use.

To tell when poultry is done, insert a thermometer into the thickest area— it should read 170–180°F in order for it to be safe to eat. Alternatively, pierce the same area with a skewer and check to see that the juices run clear.

Cotoletta della domenica
Summer Sunday Chicken

This makes ideal picnic food, as the cooked chicken breasts travel well in a cooler. In spring and summer, when Italians head for the countryside, they frequently take this breaded chicken with them. Chicken panini can be assembled on site with lettuce and mayonnaise. The breadcrumb coating can be kept plain but this recipe comes from our friend Gregorio's aunt, Zia Rosa, from Sicily, who adds parsley and Parmesan to the crust. Apparently she fries off about 20 every Sunday morning to feed the numerous children in her family for their weekly picnic.

Serves 4

2 chicken breasts
2 eggs
¼ cup fine dry breadcrumbs, for coating
⅓ cup Parmesan, finely grated
2 teaspoons coarsely chopped flat-leaf parsley
salt and freshly ground black pepper
2–3 tablespoons flour, for dredging
sunflower oil, for frying

Pound the chicken breasts with a meat mallet or the bottom of a small pan until they are about ¼ inch thick. Cut into 4 or 8 pieces.

Break the egg into a shallow bowl and beat lightly. Mix the breadcrumbs, Parmesan, and parsley together in a second shallow bowl and put the flour in a third. If you are using a blender, break up the bread and add the parsley and Parmesan to the mixture.

Season the chicken well all over with salt and pepper. Dip into the flour, then the egg, then into the breadcrumb mixture. Heat about ½ inch of sunflower oil in a large frying pan and, when very hot, cook the chicken for about 3 minutes on either side until golden brown. Drain on paper towels. Serve with salad and fresh panini.

Tip: To test if your oil is hot enough for frying, drop a crumb of bread into it. If it browns quickly and makes the oil bubble around it, it is ready.

Variation: For a vegetarian option you can replace the chicken with thin slices of eggplant.

Pollo in umido al limone
Chicken and Lemon Casserole

Chicken and lemon always make a wonderful combination. This very easy casserole is a great supper dish and will sit happily on the stove until you are ready—so no need to worry about precise timings.

Serves 4–6

1 large chicken, cleaned and cut into pieces
salt and freshly ground black pepper
1 cup flour, for dredging
⅓ cup sunflower oil, for frying
2 ripe lemons
⅓ cup dry white wine

FOR THE SOFFRITTO
⅓ cup extra virgin olive oil
1 large white onion, finely chopped
3 celery ribs, finely chopped
3 medium carrots, finely chopped
1 long strip of lemon zest
3 garlic cloves, crushed
5 sprigs of rosemary
5 medium bay leaves
salt and freshly ground black pepper

Heat the oil for the *soffritto* in a flameproof casserole or lidded frying pan and cook all the ingredients together. Meanwhile, season the chicken pieces with salt and pepper, coat with flour and tap off the excess.

Heat the sunflower oil in a separate pan and cook the chicken pieces until golden brown. When the *soffritto* ingredients are soft and the chicken pieces golden brown on all sides, transfer the chicken to the casserole. Discard the remaining sunflower oil.

Squeeze the lemon juice over the chicken and add the lemon halves to the casserole. Stir well to combine, then add the wine and let it reduce for a couple of minutes until the strong smell of wine has dissipated. Add 2 cups water and cook over low heat, covered, for about 1 hour or until the chicken is cooked through and very tender, stirring occasionally to ensure the chicken doesn't stick to the pan. If there is still too much oil for your liking, spoon it out of the pan before serving. Serve with Parmesan mashed potatoes and *cavolo nero* or spinach.

Pollo all'aceto balsamico
Pot-roast Chicken with Balsamic

This is another recipe from my friend Gino who taught me, above all, to be brave. I kept taking his pan off the heat, fearful he was about to burn something, but he would slide it back and say "*lascia, lascia*," meaning "leave it." So I have learnt not to keep flipping the chicken over but to let it cook on one side to a rich golden brown, then to turn it over to do the same on the other side; this takes up to 15 minutes. And don't scrimp on the salt, either.

Serves 6–8

1 chicken, disjointed into 8 pieces
salt and freshly ground black pepper
8 slices of unsmoked pancetta or bacon, chopped into ¾ in pieces, or *lardo*
5 large garlic cloves, unpeeled, lightly crushed
1 long sprig of rosemary
⅔ cup dry white wine
⅔ cup stock or water
2 teaspoons balsamic vinegar

Season the chicken joints generously on both sides.

Heat the oil in a large, high-sided frying pan or big casserole dish and, when it is hot, add the chicken, pancetta, garlic and rosemary. Cook over high heat, partially covered. Let the meat brown well on both sides, turning the pieces once—allow about 10–15 minutes.

When they are brown, add the wine, let it reduce for a few minutes and then add the stock. Bring it to a boil then reduce the heat and let it cook for about 1 hour or until the chicken falls away from the bones easily. You can add a little more stock, if necessary.

Toward the end of the cooking time, if a lot of liquid remains, remove the lid for 10 minutes to reduce it. There should be enough to give each person about a tablespoon of sauce. Now dress the hot chicken with a good drizzle of balsamic vinegar and serve it right away, with salad and plenty of bread to mop up the juices.

Variation: Rabbit can be done in the same way—but disjoint the rabbit into four pieces and tie some pancetta around each piece, as it is a drier meat.

Pollo al mattone
Chicken Under a Brick

This rather strange-sounding Tuscan dish is thought to have Etruscan roots because tomb paintings from that era depict chickens being flattened by a stone over a grill. The chicken is marinated first, which means it has enough moisture not to need basting as it cooks. The marinade also gives it a wonderful flavor that will have you licking your fingers and coming back for more. So if you have a few old bricks in your garden, give them a good scrub and put them to good use. In restaurants a wire cage is made around the brick so that it can be grabbed easily with an oven mitt.

Serves 4

4 poussins (baby chickens)
2 red chiles, cut in half
1 garlic clove, smashed
4 sprigs of rosemary
⅓ cup olive oil
salt and freshly ground black pepper

Place the birds on a board. Insert a sharp chef's knife inside the first one and feel for the backbone along the bottom of the cavity. Twist the knife slightly outwards along one side of the spine and press down firmly on the knife on one side, then feel for the other side and cut along that in the same manner. Discard the spine and open out the chicken, snapping the wishbone as you do. Repeat with the other birds then place them in a non-metallic dish and layer the chile, garlic, rosemary, oil, salt and pepper between the poussins. Marinate for at least 1 hour or overnight.

Preheat the broiler, grill, or barbecue to its hottest setting. Put the poussins on the grill and place a brick on top of each one. Cook for 20–30 minutes or until they are cooked through. Check by inserting a probe or instant-read thermometer, if you have one—the internal temperature should read 190°F—or push a skewer into the densest area of each poussin and check that the juices run clear. Serve with Giorgio's Salad (see page 403).

Tip: The same can be done with a whole chicken, allowing a longer cooking time—approximately 45 minutes to 1 hour.

Gallina Padovana alla canevera
Padovan Chicken in a Bag

Padua is in the Veneto, the region around Venice, and this is one of its signature dishes. It is a sort of poached chicken recipe where the chicken was originally cooked in a pig's bladder and the air ventilated out with the use of a hollow cane or *canevera* in the local dialect. Fortunately, we now have plastic bags that will do the trick and roasting bags from most good supermarkets are ideal for just this. For safety's sake and so you don't lose the precious juices, I double-bag the chicken. The resulting flavors are intense and delicious, especially when the soft, moist chicken is served with the stuffing of apples and vegetables.

The quality of the chicken really shows in this dish, as the flavor is concentrated in the bag as it cooks. It's a really easy dish to put together: despite the need for a piece of cane and a plastic bag. I haven't specified the weight of the chicken as, for two people, you could use a poussin and adjust the stuffing ingredients to suit. You could also put extra breast meat in the bag, stuffed with extra finely chopped vegetables, to bump up the quantity. Equally, to feed a large family, you could use a massive chicken and put more stuffing ingredients inside. You should use as much stuffing as you can fit into the bird, as the resulting flavors of these are delicious. A poussin will take about 1 hour to cook and a large chicken about 2½ hours.

Serves 2–8, depending on the size of your chicken

Season the chicken inside and out, then fill the cavity with the mixed stuffing ingredients, through the larger hole, to maximum capacity. Fold over the flap of skin and secure with twine by tying the legs together tightly to close the cavity. Put the chicken in the bag with the closed cavity-end facing downward. Insert the length of cane into the bag but leave the end poking out of the top of the bag. Now tie the bag, around the cane, with string, winding it around the closure several times and leaving two 4-inch lengths of twine dangling from the knot.

Put the bag into a large saucepan or stock pot. Rest a long wooden spoon (or another length of cane) across the top of the pan, to one side, and tie the lengths of string on to it. (This is so that the bag doesn't fall completely into the water, the closure remains above the surface of the water and the cane sticks out of the pan, to one side.) Now fill the pan with enough water to cover the chicken in the bag. At this stage, the bird will bob up to the surface but, as it cooks and the steam comes out of the bag via the cane, it will fall. Bring the water to a boil then let it simmer gently for the required time, until the chicken is cooked through.

When cooked, take the chicken out of the bag and carve it as you wish. Serve the vegetables, too, and pour the juices from the bag over the chicken. I have served it hot with potatoes or allowed it to cool to room temperature and enjoyed it as a salad on a big wooden board, dressed with the juices from the bag.

1 chicken
salt and freshly ground
  black pepper

FOR THE STUFFING
1–2 apples, cored and chopped
  into 10 pieces
1 medium onion, coarsely
  chopped into 10 pieces
1 celery rib, coarsely
  chopped into 10 pieces
1 medium carrot, coarsely
  chopped into 10 pieces
1 cinnamon stick
1 large garlic clove, lightly
  crushed
10 cloves
2 bay leaves

2 roasting bags
1 length of cane, about 12 in
kitchen twine

Preheat the oven to 400°F.

Make a slit in the thicker end of each chicken breast with a long sharp knife. Push the knife inside towards the pointed end of the fillet and slide it back and forth with small movements to cut a long pocket inside the meat, without breaking through the flesh.

Push 1 tablespoon of pesto and a stick of mozzarella into each pocket and secure with a toothpick at the fat end. Put the flour, egg, and breadcrumbs on separate plates.

Heat enough oil in a frying pan to shallow-fry the chicken. Season the chicken well, then dip the breasts first in flour, then in egg and finally in the breadcrumbs. When the oil is hot, deep-fry the breasts just until golden brown on both sides.

Transfer to an ovenproof dish and bake for 10 minutes, or until the chicken is cooked through and the juices run clear when a skewer is inserted into the thickest part of the flesh. Serve with Giorgio's Salad (see page 403) and Lemon Roast Potatoes (see page 390).

Variation: These can also be shallow-fried over medium heat in a large, non-stick pan for 3 minutes on each side. Turn the chicken regularly to prevent it from sticking and finish cooking in the oven at 350°F for 15 minutes.

Petto di pollo farcito con pesto e mozzarella
Chicken Breasts Stuffed with Pesto and Mozzarella

These are like an Italian equivalent of chicken Kiev and make a great dish for children or a light lunch with salad. They are deep-fried and, when you cut them open, a wonderful aroma of basil and garlic steams out of the center, followed by the melting mozzarella. The best way to tell if the chicken breasts are cooked is with an instant-read thermometer to show the internal temperature has reached 190°F. If you don't have a probe, an alternative is to shallow fry them and complete the cooking in the oven. Because homemade pesto is so easy to make in a food processor, do make the effort, as it will really show in this dish.

Serves 4

4 skinless boneless chicken
  breast halves
4 tablespoons homemade pesto
  (or buy a good-quality brand)
1 x 4 oz ball of fresh mozzarella,
  cut into 4 long sticks
½ cup flour, for dredging
2 eggs, beaten
½ cup breadcrumbs
salt and freshly ground
  black pepper
sunflower oil, for deep-frying

4 toothpicks

Polletto ripieno di uva
Poussin Stuffed with Grapes

This is another recipe from Franco and Ann Taruschio. The cooking time will differ greatly between really small and large poussins. Those weighing 1 lb take an hour to cook but smaller ones can be done in 40 minutes. An instant-read thermometer is the best way of checking they are cooked. This also works really well with four quail or a whole chicken, with the same amount of stuffing. Try to find the sweetest Muscat grapes, which have a rich and musty taste like a good dessert wine.

Serves 4

4 poussins
salt and freshly ground
  black pepper
extra virgin olive oil, for
  drizzling
1 glass dry white wine
2 oz seedless green grapes
  (Muscat grapes are best)

FOR THE STUFFING
1 tablespoon finely chopped
  flat-leaf parsley
2 tablespoons finely chopped
  sage
1 thick slice of day-old bread,
  made into breadcrumbs
6 tablespoons melted butter
1 small onion, finely chopped
4 garlic cloves, finely chopped
8 oz seedless green grapes
⅓ cup dry white wine
salt and freshly ground
  black pepper

Preheat the oven to 350°F.

Firstly, prepare the stuffing. Pulse the herbs and fresh breadcrumbs in a blender or processor. Heat a little of the butter in a pan and cook the onion and garlic until golden. Remove from the heat and add the rest of the stuffing ingredients. Mix well together.

Season the insides of the poussins with salt and stuff each bird with the prepared stuffing, remembering to leave some grapes for the end. Drizzle with oil and season with salt and pepper. Roast the poussins for between 40 minutes and 1 hour, depending on the size of the birds, basting them from time to time with a little of the wine. Skim off the fat from the cooking juices as it collects.

Add the grapes to the cooking juices 5 minutes before serving. Serve the poussins with a little of the cooking juices poured over and a few grapes around them.

Pollame e selvaggina
MASTERCLASS

I learned to bone poultry many years ago but, like all skills, mine became rusty through lack of use. So, when writing this book, I took lessons from an Italian butcher. I actually really enjoy butchery now as I feel in control of a knife and the end result—my lunch. I urge you to try the recipe on the next page!

How to Bone a Chicken

Cut the chicken along the breastbone on either side. Keep the knife close to the bone all the time, separating the flesh from the bones.

Open out the breasts.

Cut off the neck, if needed.

Pull away the top half of the carcass and set it aside.

Cut the carcass in half, to release it.

Now loosen the remaining half of the carcass, pulling it away, and set aside.

Cut away the wings and reserve to cook with the bird.

Pull the legs up from the inside and cut around them to release the flesh. Scrape the meat downwards from around the bones. Set the legs aside.

Remove the wishbone and slice through the breast to open it out. Keep the bone to make a gravy (see page 355).

How to Roll a Boned Chicken

Turn the leg meat inwards and put one side over the other to close the gap in the center. Arrange the flesh into a rectangle.

Lay garlic cloves and sprigs of rosemary on the chicken and season well.

Roll up the chicken, tucking the flesh inside, ensuring that it is all covered with skin and no flesh is visible. Lay a sprig of rosemary on top.

Tie the chicken with kitchen twine to secure it, wrapping the twine lengthwise twice around the bird.

Then tie twine around the bird at intervals of 1½ inches. Tie the end of the twine securely to the original length-wise string and cut off the excess.

Recipe continued on the next page.

Pollame e selvaggina
MASTERCLASS

Pollo disossato al forno con rosmarino e aglio
Roast Boned Chicken with Rosemary and Garlic

With this recipe, as with the Rolled Lamb with Pecorino, Mint, and Artichoke Stuffing (see page 290), you end up tying up the meat around a simple stuffing, so any mistakes are easily disguised.

Preheat the oven to 350°F.

Bone and stuff the chicken as for the masterclass on page 339. Put the rolled chicken in a roasting pan and drizzle with about 1 tablespoon of olive oil. Put into the preheated oven for 1–1½ hours, depending on the size of the chicken. Test with an instant-read thermometer to see when the inside temperature reaches 190°F.

When carving, after the first slice, slide the rosemary sticks out if they are woody. Serve as it is or, to serve with gravy, follow the method on page 355 using your chicken bones.

Variation: Add some potatoes, carrots, onion, and garlic to the dish with the chicken. Turn the vegetables half way through and baste with the cooking juices.

1 boned chicken
4 sprigs of rosemary
10 garlic cloves
salt and freshly ground
  black pepper
1 tablespoon olive oil

3 cups chicken stock (see
page 140)

FOR THE MEATBALLS
4 oz fresh or slightly stale bread
1 large garlic clove, unpeeled
½ bunch flat-leaf parsley, larger
stems removed
a pinch of salt
1 lb cooked chicken
2 large eggs
½ cup Parmesan, finely grated
¼ whole nutmeg, finely grated
flour, for dredging
2–3 tablespoons olive oil, for
frying

FOR THE SAUCE
4 tablespoons dry white wine
4–5 sage leaves, coarsely chopped
1 tablespoon butter
1 teaspoon salt
freshly ground black pepper

Polpettine di Pollo
Chicken Meatballs

We often have leftover roast chicken in our fridge and this is a great way to use it up. I love recipes where nothing is wasted. This uses the bones for stock and the meat for meatballs. If I don't have any bones, I make up a simple vegetable stock instead or use a prepared broth. We usually end up eating this with fried roast potatoes but polenta or mashed potatoes would be good too, for absorbing the sauce. Be prepared to adjust the recipe slightly: if you don't have enough chicken you will need to reduce the quantity of breadcrumbs or add more egg to obtain a mixture the consistency of a stuffing that can be easily rolled into balls.

Serves 6/Makes 24–30 meatballs

Make your stock (see page 140), unless you already have some prepared. While the stock is simmering, put the bread, garlic, parsley, and a good pinch of salt into a food processor and pulse until you have breadcrumbs. Alternatively, finely chop the parsley and garlic with a large knife and grate the bread into crumbs (see page 30). Transfer the breadcrumb mixture to a large mixing bowl. Now mince the chicken in a food processor (or chop it finely with a knife) and add it to the bowl, along with the eggs, cheese, nutmeg, salt and pepper.

Mix everything with your hands until well blended, then using wet hands form into balls roughly the size of ping-pong balls. Roll the balls tightly, pressing the mixture to hold them together. Toss into flour, tap off the excess, then transfer to a tray.

Strain the stock into a large measuring cup or bowl, discarding the bones and onion.

Heat the oil in a large frying pan and, when hot, cook the meatballs (in batches, if necessary) until golden brown all over. Remove the meatballs and set aside on paper towels to drain. Pour off any excess oil and wipe the pan.

To make the sauce, pour the wine and sage leaves into the frying pan and allow the wine to reduce. Add the stock and boil rapidly until reduced by roughly one third. Return the meatballs to the pan and stir in the butter to thicken the sauce. Serve with heaps of Crunchy Parmesan and Celery Mash (see page 384) and Runner Beans with Parma Ham and Chile (see page 387).

Fagiano in umido all'arancia con castagne e uva secca

Pot-roast Pheasant with Orange, Chestnuts and Golden Raisins

The Borella family gave me this recipe for one of their favorite roasts served at Christmas time when they all ate together in Le Borelle, a tiny hamlet way up in the hills near Parma. I wish I had met the grandmother; she sounds like a formidable woman who kept her seven sons and two daughters in order, feeding them home-cooked food as well as walking several miles every day to take milk to the local Parmesan factory. I am sure she was a gold mine of recipes but sadly she never wrote any of them down. Her son Gino and grandson Stefano turned out to be fantastic chefs so I am sure she would be proud of her family tradition.

Serves 2–4, depending on the size of your pheasants

1 brace of pheasants (2)
2 large bay leaves
2 strips of *lardo di colonnata*, pancetta, or bacon
salt and freshly ground black pepper
⅓ cup olive oil
3 tablespoons white wine vinegar
⅔ cup white wine
1 cup golden raisins
zest of 1 orange, finely shredded
⅓ cup chicken or game stock
8 oz chestnuts, vacuum-packed or freshly roasted and peeled

Truss the pheasants, adding a bay leaf and a piece of *lardo* on the breast of each bird (see the quail masterclass on page 346). Season the birds with salt and pepper. Heat the olive oil in a large flameproof casserole and brown the pheasants over high heat, one at a time, if needed, turning frequently, until golden on all sides. Add the vinegar and allow it to reduce. Then add the wine and allow it to reduce again. Add the raisins and orange zest, stir well and pour in the stock.

Bring to a boil, then reduce the heat and simmer, covered, for about 1½ hours or until cooked through. Chop the chestnuts coarsely and add halfway through the cooking time.

Remove the pheasants from the casserole and set aside on a warm plate, loosely covered with a piece of foil and a kitchen towel. Boil the sauce rapidly to reduce it. Meanwhile, cut the pheasants into portions and return them to the sauce. If the sauce is very liquid, stir in a dusting of flour. Serve with mashed potatoes and cabbage or spinach.

Fagiano arrosto ripieno di castagne
Roast Pheasant Stuffed with Chestnuts

Observant readers may have spotted that there are two recipes containing pheasant and chestnuts in this book. When testing and sampling ways to cook pheasant, I found both recipes to be so delicious I couldn't bear to dispense with either. In the pot-roasted pheasant recipe on page 343, the chestnuts are used to thicken the sauce which, in my opinion, works extremely well because their mild flavor does not detract from the orange but merely softens it and enriches an otherwise thin sauce. In this recipe, the pheasant is roasted, which can often lead to a dry bird—but the chestnuts provide moisture, their flavor marries well with the pheasant and they bump up the quantity, so the scrawniest bird will feed up to ten people.

Serves 8–10

1 brace of pheasants (2)
salt and freshly ground black pepper
4 bay leaves
4 tablespoons butter, at room temperature
6 slices of pancetta or unsmoked bacon
3 celery ribs, cut into 1 in lengths
1 large red onion, peeled and cut into 8 wedges
2 carrots, cut into 1 in lengths
2 garlic cloves, unpeeled, lightly crushed
6 tablespoons olive oil
¾ cup dry red wine
⅓ cup chicken stock or water
1 tablespoon plum jam

FOR THE STUFFING

4 oz soft bread, for breadcrumbs
1 tablespoon chopped flat-leaf parsley
1 tablespoon thyme leaves
4–5 sage leaves, chopped
8 oz chestnuts, vacuum-packed or freshly roasted and peeled, roughly chopped
2 eggs

Preheat the oven to 375°F. Wash and dry the pheasants and season them inside and out with salt and pepper.

Place two bay leaves on top of each pheasant and smear butter over the breasts then lay the pancetta slices on top. Truss them, following the instructions for tying quail (see page 346).

To make the stuffing, pulse the bread in a food processor with the parsley, thyme, and sage until you have medium-fine breadcrumbs. Mix these with the rest of the stuffing ingredients and stuff the mixture inside the cavities of the birds. Roll any leftover stuffing into walnut-sized balls and set aside.

Place the pheasants side by side in a roasting pan surrounded by the vegetables. Drizzle olive oil over the birds and the vegetables and garlic. Season with a generous amount of salt and pepper. Cover each bird loosely with a square of foil and put into the oven. Cook for 45 minutes then remove the foil from the birds and reduce the temperature to 325°F. Pour in half the wine. Toss the vegetables and move them around in the pan so that they are well covered in wine and oil. Put the reserved stuffing balls on top of the vegetables. Continue to cook for another 30–45 minutes, depending on the size of your birds, or until cooked through. Use an instant-read thermometer to make sure the inner temperature reaches 75°C/165°F or stick a skewer into the deepest part of the bird and stuffing and check that the juices run clear. The tip of the skewer should feel very hot when removed: this is another indication that the stuffing is cooked thoroughly inside.

When cooked, remove the vegetables and stuffing balls from the pan with a slotted spoon and place on a warmed serving platter. Carve each bird into six or eight pieces. Put these on top of the vegetables and keep warm. Pour off two-thirds of the oil from the roasting pan and place over a medium heat. When hot, add the rest of the wine and allow it to reduce for 5 minutes. Stir in the stock and plum jam, let it bubble for a couple of minutes, then season to taste. Once you are happy with the consistency, pour the sauce into a warmed gravy boat. Serve the pheasant, vegetables, and sauce with polenta or roast potatoes.

Tip: Add a tablespoon of butter to the sauce at the end to thicken it and give a little shine.

Anatra all'arancia

Duck with Orange Sauce

This is said to have been one of the dishes that Caterina de Medici took with her to France when she married Henry II in 1533. Many people—mainly the French—disbelieve this story, as duck with orange sauce has become one of France's signature dishes. Italians, however, will tell you that it is Florentine in origin and that it is still served all over Tuscany today. I am with the Italians, of course! This is Giancarlo's version and one of my all-time favorites.

Serves 4

1 large duck, liver and giblets removed
salt
8 large oranges
1 cup granulated sugar
1¼ cups chicken stock (see page 140)

Preheat the oven to 350°F. Season the duck on the outside with salt, cut two of the oranges in half and place them inside the cavity. Roast the bird in the oven for about 1½–2 hours, until the skin appears golden and crispy (you will need to allow at least 45 minutes per 2 lb plus 20 minutes, but a longer cooking time will result in a less fatty meat).

To make the sauce, carefully cut away the zest (discarding any white pith) from 2 oranges and cut it into thin strips. Set it aside in a bowl. Peel away any remaining pith from the oranges, then remove the segments by sliding a knife on either side of each one so that the membrane stays in place and just the flesh comes away. Squeeze any remaining juice over the zest. Then juice the remaining 4 oranges. You should now have some shredded orange zest, some segments, and plenty of juice.

Put the sugar in a heavy-bottomed saucepan over medium heat. Cook without stirring until the sugar bubbles and takes on a coffee color. (Be careful: the hot caramel can spit at you, so it is a good idea to wear oven mitts.) Add the orange zest to the sugar and cook for 2 minutes, then add the segments and cook for another couple of minutes. Don't worry if lumps appear as they will melt away as the sauce simmers. Stir in the orange juice and simmer for 10 minutes. Add the stock and simmer gently for another 20 minutes. Set aside.

When the duck is cooked, remove it from the oven and allow to cool slightly. (Reserve the fat: it makes wonderful roast potatoes—see page 390.) To portion the duck, make a large cut along the backbone, then carefully remove each breast and cut it into three portions. Cut off the thigh/leg portions and divide each one in two, then finally cut off the wings.

Reheat the sauce. Place the duck portions in a large, deep pan and pour the sauce over the top. Simmer for 10 minutes, to allow the sauce to infuse the meat. Serve three portions of duck per person, with mashed or roast potatoes and carrot sformato (see page 382).

Anatra al Chianti con ciliegie
Duck with Cherries in Chianti

The combination of gamey meat and sweet, slightly sticky cherries is heavenly. This is a dish we developed for a banquet to be served at the beautiful *Castello di Gabbiano*, south of Florence. Italian cherries were just in season so we doused them in the Castello's Chianti and served this as a sauce with locally caught duck.

Serves 4

4 duck breast halves, skin on
salt and freshly ground
black pepper

FOR THE SAUCE
1 lb cherries, halved and pitted
⅔ cup orange juice
½ cup granulated sugar
2 cups red wine, such as
Gabbiano Chianti

Preheat the oven to 350°F.

To make the sauce, put the cherries in an ovenproof dish, pour in the orange juice, then sprinkle with half the sugar. Transfer the dish to the oven and bake for about 25 minutes or until the cherries have softened and browned a little. Remove from the oven and set aside.

Meanwhile, pour the wine into a saucepan with the remaining sugar and bring to a boil. Reduce the heat and leave to simmer for about 30 minutes to allow it to reduce to about one third of its volume (you want about ⅔ cup).

Season the duck breasts with salt and pepper. Heat a non-stick frying pan and, when hot, cook the breasts, skin-side down, for about 6 minutes, then turn them over and cook for another 4 minutes. This will give you medium-rare meat. If you prefer it well done, transfer the duck breasts to a baking sheet and roast in the oven for about 10–15 minutes.

Meanwhile, pour the cherries and the wine into a large frying pan and bring to a boil over high heat. Reduce the heat to a simmer and leave for around 5 minutes or until the sauce has reduced and thickened.

Slice the duck breasts and arrange them on warmed serving dishes. Pour the sauce over the top and serve with plenty of creamy polenta or mashed potatoes.

Ragù di Piccione
Pigeon Ragù

This is a great way to use up birds that have been killed as pests or on a shoot. Our chef, Monserrato, says the secret to this rich ragù is the stock he prepares from the carcasses, using only the breast meat for the ragù. As common with many good chefs, he tries to do this for whatever meat dish he is cooking, to extract the flavor from the bones. This is a trick that home cooks should copy: instead of discarding bones, make good use of them.

To make the stock, put all the ingredients in a large saucepan and bring to a boil. Leave to simmer for 30–40 minutes, uncovered, to intensify the flavor.

Finely chop the pancetta or pulse in a food processor with the herbs: it will form a thick paste which will break down during cooking. Heat the oil in a large frying pan or saucepan and add the celery, carrot, onion, garlic, and bay leaves, together with the minced pancetta. Cook these for 10–15 minutes, then add the pigeon meat. Stir thoroughly then leave to brown for 5 minutes. Add the tomato paste and wine, allow to reduce for a few minutes, then add 2 cups of the pigeon stock. Leave to cook for 20 minutes, stirring occasionally, then add another 2 cups of stock and leave to cook for about 1–1½ hours.

Serves 8

FOR THE STOCK

6 pigeon carcasses
1 onion, cut in half
2 celery ribs, coarsely chopped
1 carrot, coarsely chopped
1 large garlic clove, lightly crushed
2 quarts cold water
salt and freshly ground black pepper
2 tablespoons tomato purée

FOR THE RAGÙ

4 oz pancetta or unsmoked bacon
8 large sage leaves
2 sprigs of thyme
⅓ cup olive oil
1 celery rib, finely chopped by hand
  or in a food processor
1 carrot, finely chopped by hand
  or in a food processor
1 onion, finely chopped by hand
  or in a food processor
1 large garlic clove, finely chopped
2 bay leaves
breast meat from 6 pigeons, chopped into
  ¾ in cubes
2 heaping tablespoons tomato paste
⅔ cup red wine

Tip: To chop an onion, first make a series of vertical cuts, leaving the root intact, then a few horizontal cuts, then slice across the width, to obtain small pieces.

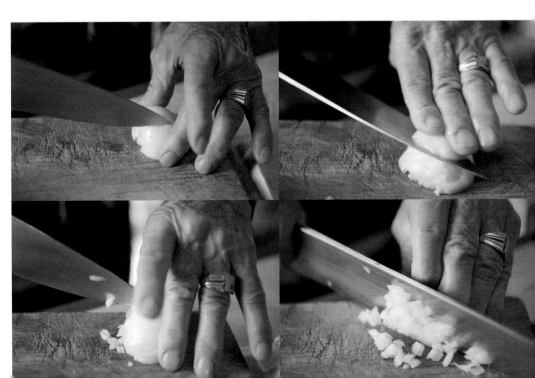

Pollame e selvaggina
MASTERCLASS

How to Prepare and Truss Quails and Other Small Birds

Use a towel to get a good grip and pluck off any remaining feathers. Alternatively, these can be burnt off using a blow torch or by holding above a gas flame on the stove. Lay a bay leaf over the breast of each bird.

Lay two pieces of *lardo* over each breast to hold the bay leaves in place. Then tie the *lardo* in place with kitchen twine, taking it over the breast and crossing it underneath.

Bring the two ends of twine up from underneath and cross them over the legs, tying the ends in a knot. Then hook the twine under the end of each leg and tie in a knot.

Wrap the twine around the middle of the bird, tying it underneath. Then tie each end of twine around the sides of bird. Pull the twine tight and finish tying underneath in a knot, then trim off the ends.

The finished tied birds have the *lardo* secured in place and the twine should be taut so that the breasts are plumped up.

Try the quail recipe on the next page

Arrosto Morto
Roast quails

Of all the methods for cooking poultry, pot-roasting seems to be the best way to cook small birds. With an adjustment to the cooking times, this recipe also works for guinea fowl, pigeon, partridge, or woodcock. The birds cook for longer than in the oven but the meat becomes so tender that the flesh falls from the bones and it is very easy to eat. Gino Borella showed me how to cook this dish and teamed it with Saffron and Mushroom Risotto (see page 208). When people ask what is my favorite recipe, despite the many dishes I love, it is this one that comes out on top every time. I have never known anyone not be impressed with the wealth of flavors it contains. It takes courage to make, however, and any stinting will spoil it, so be brave with the cooking time, oil, and salt.

Serves 6

6 quail
6 large bay leaves
6 strips of *lardo di colonnata*, pancetta
  or bacon
⅓ cup olive oil
⅔ cup dry white wine
1¾–2 cups stock, as necessary
salt and freshly ground black pepper
kitchen twine, for trussing

Choose a large lidded saucepan or flameproof casserole that will accommodate all six quail together. It doesn't matter if they are tightly packed together or even if they stand on end, as long as you can turn them occasionally.

Put the ball of twine into a box or saucepan and keep on hand on the work surface. That way you are not chasing it around the room like a new kitten.

Remove the wing tips, necks, and any remaining feathers from the quail. Lay the birds on a board with their legs on their chests and the wings crossed over the breasts. Truss the birds, placing a bay leaf and a piece of *lardo* over each breast (see page 350).

Heat the olive oil in the saucepan and, when hot, brown the birds very well all over. Keep the lid on but check every 5 minutes. This is where you have to be brave and trust Gino: keep cooking them until they are dark brown all over, turning them every so often, using tongs, to ensure even browning.

Now take the lid off and hold it as a shield while you pour in the wine: it will fizz and splatter in the heat, so beware! Let it reduce until it has almost dried out, then add 1¾ cups of the stock, put the lid back on and continue to cook over medium heat for about 1 hour, until the birds are cooked through and the meat falls easily from the bones. Add the remaining stock after about 30 minutes, if there is not enough liquid. Serve the quail on Mushroom Risotto or mashed potatoes with the sauce poured over them.

How to Bone a Rabbit

Set aside the liver and kidneys to use in the stuffing. Remove the legs from the back and front of the rabbit by feeling for the joints with your fingers and then cutting down with a sharp boning knife.

Use the tip of the knife to pull away the meat from the rib cage.

Then remove the spine in the same way, leaving as little meat as possible on the bones.

Don't worry too much if the meat doesn't come away in one piece from the ridged area of the spine: these holes with be patched over later with pancetta.

Scrape away the meat from the leg bones.

The finished filleted meat.

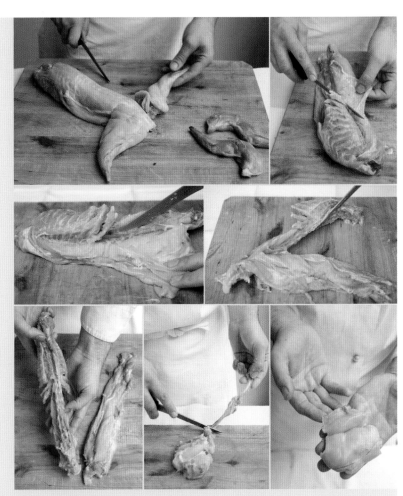

Pollame e selvaggina
MASTERCLASS

How to Stuff a Rabbit

Lay out strips of pancetta on a rectangle of plastic wrap.

Lay the pieces of filleted rabbit on top, forming a rectangle to fit over the pancetta. Try to achieve the same depth of flesh all over.

Lay another rectangle of plastic wrap on top and use the bottom of a small pan to pound the rabbit to a single thickness, to allow even cooking.

Remove the top layer of plastic wrap, then put the stuffing in a sausage shape on one long side of the rabbit. Use the bottom layer of plastic wrap to roll up the length tightly.

Remove the plastic wrap: the stuffed rabbit is ready to be cooked.

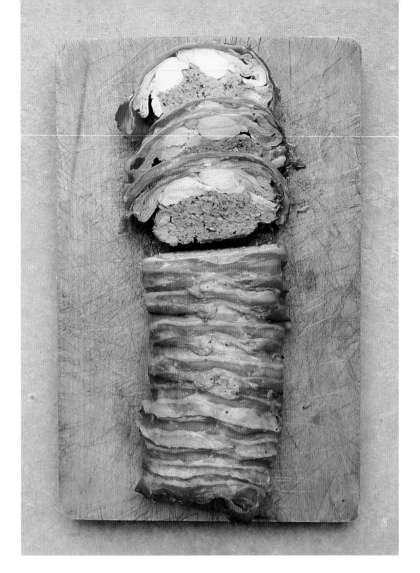

Coniglio ripieno al forno
Sabia's Stuffed Rabbit

This recipe can be prepared either with a boned rabbit or a whole one. Ask your butcher to do this or tackle it yourself following the instructions on page 353: it is tedious but boning the meat makes serving much easier. This recipe comes from Sabia, who lives in Abruzzo, in the center of Italy. The stuffing adds substance to the dish because rabbit—especially a wild one—can be very lean. Any leftovers are good sliced and eaten cold with a dressed salad.

Serves 6

1 rabbit, boned, bones and liver reserved for gravy or 1 whole rabbit, cleaned and innards removed
salt and freshly ground black pepper
olive oil, for greasing

FOR THE STUFFING
8 oz ground beef, pork or veal, or a mixture
1 cup finely grated Parmesan
1 garlic clove, finely chopped
2 tablespoons finely chopped flat-leaf parsley
2 eggs
¼ teaspoon grated nutmeg
12 slices of pancetta
⅓ cup dry white wine
salt and freshly ground black pepper

Preheat the oven to 350°F. Season the rabbit with salt and pepper inside and out. If you are using a boned rabbit, make sure the flesh is of an even thickness, filling in any gaps along the back with leg meat, and arrange it in a rectangle on a board.

Mix the stuffing ingredients in a bowl. If your rabbit is boned, spoon the filling along the center of the rectangle of rabbit, then roll it up and over the stuffing tightly. Lay the slices of pancetta vertically on a sheet of plastic wrap. Put the rolled rabbit on top (see page 349) and use the plastic wrap to roll up the parcel of rabbit tightly in the pancetta. Remove the plastic wrap and put the wrapped meat into a roasting pan lightly greased with olive oil. If the rabbit is whole, simply push the stuffing into the cavity and wrap the center of the body with the pancetta strips before placing it in the roasting pan.

Transfer the roasting pan to the oven and cook for 30 minutes. Pour the wine over the rabbit and reduce the temperature to 300°F. Cook for another 15–20 minutes or until the meat is cooked through and the pancetta is crisp. Serve with the pan juices or with gravy made from the bones, and roast potatoes, with a crisp salad to follow.

Fondo di Cottura
Gravy

Makes 1¼ cups—serves 6

The leftover bones from a roast give great flavor to a sauce so don't throw them away, or ask your butcher if you don't have any. Failing that, use the cooking fat and juices in the roasting pan.

a few bones, up to 2¼ lb in weight
1 carrot, cut into four pieces
1 celery rib, cut into four pieces
1 onion, peeled and cut into four pieces
1 sprig of rosemary
⅓ cup olive oil
⅓ cup white or red wine
2 bay leaves
3 cups of vegetable, chicken, meat stock or cooking water
2 teaspoons all-purpose flour
2 teaspoons butter
up to 2 tablespoons honey or jam

Place the bones, carrot, onion, celery, and rosemary in a shallow roasting pan, drizzle with the oil and roast in a preheated oven at 425°F until well browned (40–60 minutes). Remove from the oven and pour away most of the oil. Place the pan on the stove over high heat. If you are using the cooking juices from a roast, remove the roast and set aside to rest, covered loosely with foil and a kitchen towel. Heat the roasting pan on the stove. When the bones are sticking to the pan, add the wine and bay leaves. Let it reduce, scraping any residue from the bottom of the pan, then add the stock and bring to a boil, simmering for 5–10 minutes. Mix the flour and butter together into a paste and gradually whisk this into the sauce until it has thickened. Strain through a fine sieve, reheat, season, adding honey or jam to taste, and serve in a warmed gravy boat.

Pollame e selvaggina
MASTERCLASS

How to Joint a Rabbit

Remove the front legs, using a sharp cook's knife. Feel for the joint at the front leg with your fingers and put the knife down at the point between the bones. Use the other hand to bang down on the knife, to cut through.

Do the same on the back legs.

Remove the flaps of skin on either side of the belly.

Put the heel of the knife at the end of the rib cage and use the other hand to bang it down, to cut through.

Split the body into three pieces.

The beautiful butcher, Stefano!

Coniglio alla cacciatora
Tuscan Rabbit with Olives

This recipe belongs to our restaurant manager's mother, Nicoletta Salvato. During one of our "Italian Mamas" weeks, she came over from Tuscany to teach us some of her son Marco's favorite recipes—and this was one of them. It is typically Tuscan: a rich and full-flavored dish made out of something inexpensive. Note that larger wild rabbits will take longer to cook than small farmed ones, so adjust cooking times accordingly.

Serves 6

2½ lb rabbit, jointed into 8
salt and freshly ground
  black pepper
flour, for coating
¾ cup olive oil
4 tablespoons butter or *lardo*,
  cut into 1 in pieces
2 red onions, finely chopped
5 garlic cloves, lightly crushed
3 sprigs of thyme, leaves
  stripped
2 sprigs of rosemary, leaves
  stripped
⅔ cup red wine
1 x 28 oz can Italian plum
  tomatoes, crushed with
  your hands
2 cups vegetable or chicken
  stock or water
½ cup black olives

Season the rabbit pieces generously all over with salt and pepper, then coat them with flour, shaking off the excess. (The easiest way to do this is to put the rabbit and flour in a plastic bag and shake it.) Heat the oil and butter in the biggest frying pan you have (or use two). Cook the rabbit on all sides for about 10 minutes until well browned and crispy. Be patient—don't turn them more than once. Add the onion, garlic, and thyme or rosemary to the pan and cook until soft.

Pour in the wine, reduce for a few minutes until it separates from the oil, then add the tomatoes and stock or water. Bring to a boil, then let it simmer for 30 minutes. Add the black olives and cook for another 40 minutes or until the meat falls easily from the bones. Adjust the seasoning as necessary and serve on soft polenta.

Sella di capriolo con erbe e salsa ai frutti di bosco
Roast Saddle of Venison with Woodland Fruits and Red Wine Sauce

This is really good entertaining food—not food to make you laugh but food that tastes rich and amazing and impresses your guests. To me, this is restaurant food that you can cook at home. Our ancestors would have preserved berries in alcohol or made jam for winter; now we can pop into the supermarket and pick up a bag of frozen fruits but the thought of preserving summer fruit for winter is still there. We have friends with an allotment who freeze their glut of raspberries and, later in the season, we forage for blackberries and keep them frozen for just such an occasion.

Serves 10

10 lb saddle of venison, off the bone (if you get your
  butcher to do this, ask for the rib bones)
1 tablespoon olive oil
coarse salt

FOR THE SAUCE
venison ribs, for roasting
2 carrots, coarsely chopped
2 onions, coarsely chopped
3 celery ribs, coarsely chopped
1 bottle of good red wine
salt and freshly ground black pepper
1 lb bag of frozen forest fruits
4 oz plum jam
1 quart water
⅓ cup balsamic vinegar

FOR THE STUFFING
6 garlic cloves, unpeeled, lightly crushed
1 tablespoon fresh thyme leaves
salt and freshly ground black pepper

Preheat the oven to 350°F.

First, prepare the sauce. Put the venison bones in a roasting pan and roast them for 1 hour. Remove from the oven and transfer to a large saucepan with the juices from the dish. Add the carrots, onions, celery, and red wine, and season with salt and pepper. Bring to a boil and simmer for 45 minutes, then strain the liquid, discarding the bones and vegetables. Return to the saucepan and add the frozen fruits, jam, water, and balsamic vinegar. Reduce the liquid for 1 hour or until it has halved in volume. Taste and adjust the seasoning as necessary.

Meanwhile, prepare the boned venison for stuffing and roasting. Trim off any fat and lay any pieces of fillet previously attached to the bone in the center groove. These will fill out the meat so that you have a nice juicy lean bit in the center. Scatter in the garlic, thyme, salt and pepper to your liking. Having worked with chefs and Italians, I would tend to be generous with the seasoning. Don't think like an English person, think like an Italian mamma and use plenty of salt; the difference will be astonishing! Roll up the meat and truss with kitchen twine all the way down the length of the saddle.

Put the rolled saddle in a roasting pan, drizzle with olive oil and season with coarse salt. Roast in the oven for 40–45 minutes or until cooked (if you have an instant-read thermometer, the internal temperature should reach 130–150°F. Remove from the oven and leave to rest for 20 minutes. Serve in slices with the red wine sauce spooned over each portion. Any extra sauce can be served at the table.

Bistecca di cervo al Vin Santo e cipolline
Venison Steaks with Vin Santo and Pearl Onions

Vin Santo is a Tuscan fortified wine that we use a lot because Giancarlo is from Tuscany. I remember my father-in-law had barrels of *Vin Santo* with the dates it was made set in plaster on the outside. He never drank but always enjoyed giving me a glass of it when I arrived at his house. If you cannot get hold of *Vin Santo*, use Marsala or a dessert wine instead.

Serves 2

2 venison steaks, about 4 oz each
2 tablespoons sesame seeds
1 tablespoon olive oil
salt and freshly ground black pepper

FOR THE SAUCE
¾ cup **Vin Santo**
4 juniper berries, lightly crushed
4 black peppercorns
2 bay leaves
1 teaspoon honey
1 teaspoon sugar

FOR THE CARAMELIZED ONIONS
12 pearl or small boiling onions, peeled
2 cups water
2 tablespoons butter
2 tablespoons brown sugar

Make the sauce by reducing the *Vin Santo* with the juniper berries, peppercorns and bay leaves in a small saucepan over medium heat for 40 minutes, until the wine becomes a runny syrup.

Boil the onions in water for about 10 minutes, or until tender. Drain and set aside. Preheat the oven to 425°F.

Put the onions, butter, and sugar together in a frying pan and stir for 3–4 minutes until browned on all sides. Set aside in a small ovenproof dish.

Coat the venison pieces in sesame seeds. Pan-fry the venison in the olive oil on all sides. Hold a saucepan lid over the meat as it cooks, as the seeds pop and jump.

Transfer the venison to the dish with the onions, season and bake for 5 minutes or until cooked to your liking. Serve with the *Vin Santo* sauce, cabbage with pancetta, and roast potatoes.

Stufato di cervo con cannella e ginepro
Venison Stew with Cinnamon, Red Wine, and Juniper Berries

The combination of cinnamon and juniper is typical of the cooking of the mountainous northern regions of Italy. This dark—almost black—velvety stew is often served to hungry skiers in the Dolomites. It's rich and delicious but the flavors develop over time, so begin the day before you want to eat it, as this cut of venison improves when marinated overnight.

Serves 6

3 lb shoulder of venison, cubed for stewing

FOR THE MARINADE
2 carrots, coarsely chopped
1 large red onion, coarsely chopped
2 celery ribs, coarsely chopped
10 juniper berries, lightly crushed
10 peppercorns
1 sprig of sage
1 sprig of rosemary
1 bottle of red wine
5 bay leaves

FOR THE STEW
⅓ cup olive oil
4 garlic cloves, lightly crushed
salt and freshly ground black pepper
⅓ cup finely chopped rosemary
4 bay leaves
1¼ cups full-bodied red wine
¾ cup meat stock or water
1 teaspoon ground cinnamon or 1 long cinnamon stick, broken into 3 pieces

Trim any fat and sinew from the venison, as necessary. The meat should be lean.

Mix all the marinade ingredients together with the venison in a large, non-metallic bowl, cover and marinate overnight in the fridge. The next day, strain out the meat and vegetables and discard the liquid, sage, rosemary and bay leaves. Chop the vegetables, juniper, and peppercorns finely by hand, or pulse in a food processor, to obtain a *soffritto*.

Heat the oil in a frying pan, cook the garlic with salt and pepper for a couple of minutes, then add the *soffritto*. Cook for 5 minutes, then add the rosemary and bay leaves. Continue to cook for another 10 minutes, then add the meat. Brown all over and cook for about 15–20 minutes or until all the water has evaporated from the meat. Add the wine, let it reduce for 5 minutes, then add the stock and cinnamon. Bring to a boil, then reduce the heat and simmer for 50–60 minutes or until the meat is very tender. Serve with soft polenta and cabbage or *cavalo nero*.

Arrosto misto
Pot-Roast Hunter's Catch

This is one of those old recipes that would have been cooked in a cauldron. We still possess Giancarlo's grandmother's pot that would be suspended on a tripod over a fire. Most lean cuts of meat will work in this recipe and you don't have to use a mixture: chicken alone, would be fine. Brown the meat thoroughly: a dark appearance ensures a good flavor. Traditionally this dish uses pieces of *lardo di colonnata* (pork fat), which melt down during cooking.

Serves 6

6 tablespoons extra virgin olive oil
6 tablespoons butter or 3 oz *lardo*
3 lb meat (e.g. 1 rabbit or chicken disjointed into 8 pieces, or 2 duck legs and thighs and 1 lb pork loin, quartered)
1 celery rib, cut into ½ in lengths
1 large carrot, cut into 1 in lengths
1 medium red or white onion, cut into 8 pieces
4 garlic cloves, lightly crushed
2 sprigs of rosemary, broken into small pieces
5 bay leaves
⅓ cup white wine
¾–1¼ cups chicken stock
2 large potatoes, peeled and quartered

Heat the oil, butter, and *lardo* (if using) together in a large saucepan over a medium heat. When hot, add all the different meats together and fry for about 30 minutes or until well browned, turning the joints only once during the cooking time.

Next add the celery, carrots, onion, garlic, rosemary, and bay leaves and fry until golden. Pour in the wine and enough stock to almost cover the meat. Put the lid on askew to allow some steam to escape, and simmer for about 1½ hours, until the liquid has almost disappeared. Halfway through the cooking time, add the potatoes.

The liquid should reduce down to a sticky consistency and the meat and potatoes should be well cooked and browned all over. If the liquid disappears before the meat is cooked, add extra stock; conversely if there is too much liquid when the meat is cooked, remove the lid and boil hard to reduce the amount.

Scottiglia
Tuscan Hunter's Stew

The contents of *scottiglia* are entirely dependent on the season and the hunter's luck. Woodier herbs such as rosemary and thyme are usually used in Tuscan cooking but in this stew, soft green herbs are added by the handful. The choice of herbs and the mixture of meats gives the *scottiglia* an unusual depth of flavor and the long, slow cooking means the meat falls easily from the bone as you eat it.

Serves 8

⅓ cup olive oil
2 garlic cloves, coarsely
  chopped
1¼ lb red onions, finely
  chopped
a very large handful of flat-leaf
  parsley (about 2 oz), leaves
  stripped and coarsely chopped
a very large handful of basil
  (about 2 oz), coarsely chopped
a large sprig of rosemary,
  leave stripped and finely
  chopped
2½ lb mixed meats (pigeon,
  rabbit, guinea fowl, chicken,
  pheasant, partridge, or quail),
  large birds cut into 4 pieces
  and smaller ones left whole
salt and freshly ground
  black pepper
1¼ cups red wine
8 oz tomato paste
1 x 36 oz can Italian plum
  tomatoes, broken up with
  your fingers
4 large bay leaves
2½ cups chicken stock
1 loaf of crusty bread,
  thickly sliced

First make a *soffritto*. Heat the olive oil in a large flameproof casserole over medium heat. Add the garlic and onions and cook for 5 minutes, then add the herbs and cook for another 5–10 minutes, until the onions are soft.

Meanwhile, season the meats all over, add them to the pan and brown on all sides. Pour in the wine and leave to cook until it evaporates, stirring frequently. Add the tomato paste and stir again for a few minutes. Then add the canned tomatoes and bay leaves. Leave to cook until the tomato sauce thickens and the meat is cooked through. The cooking time will depend on the meats chosen and the size of the pieces but you should allow up to 3 hours' cooking time. Add the stock at intervals, little by little, until it is absorbed and the sauce darkens in color. Adjust the seasoning.

Toast the bread and arrange the slices in a warmed serving dish or in individual bowls. Pour the meat and its sauce over the bread and serve.

Bollito misto
Boiled meats

This dish is typical of northern Italy. This recipe—which makes a lot—is from Gino Borella. He uses onion skins to add colour to the stock then serves it as a broth with *cappelletti* or tortellini. The whole family loves to eat it with the sauces served in little terracotta dishes. In restaurants, *bollito misto* is sometimes served from a trolley, allowing you to choose your meat and sauce from a selection.

Makes enough for a party of 20!

1 *cottechino* (Italian sausage) or *zampone* (stuffed trotter)
2¼ lb ox tongue
5 lb beef brisket
2 chicken legs (about 1½ lb)
8 oz carrots, very coarsely chopped
1 lb celery, very coarsely chopped
1 large onion, unpeeled, cut in half
20 cloves, pushed into the onion
2 oz parsley stems
3 tablespoons coarse salt
7 quarts cold water
2 tomatoes (cut a cross through the stem in the top of each one)

Place the *cottechino* in a large saucepan of cold water and bring to a boil. Cook for 3½ hours (it is cooked separately from the rest of the ingredients, otherwise it spoils the flavor of the broth). If using *zampone*, cook it following the manufacturers' instructions—usually for about 30 minutes.

Put the remaining ingredients, except the tomatoes, into two large saucepans and cover with cold water. Bring to a boil and skim off the foam that collects, using a large spoon. Keep simmering, uncovered, for about 2 hours or until the meats are done. After 1 hour add the tomatoes. These will help to clarify the stock and give it a good color. If the water level drops, exposing the meat, add more hot water. You may have to add up to another quart—just ensure the meat is always covered. When all the meats are cooked through and very tender, remove them from the stock.

Peel and slice the tongue and carve the brisket. The chicken legs can be served as they are. Serve hot with *Salsa Verde* (see page 232) and a jar of *mostarda di frutta*, available from most Italian delicatessens.

Cinghiale con olive
Wild Boar with Olives

In Tuscany, wild boar hunting remains a very popular sport that men take very seriously. The meat, which is like pork but tougher, is very lean and healthy. We usually use leg of boar for this and stoned *Taggiasche* olives for a good flavor.

Serves 8

3½ lb wild boar, trimmed and cut into chunks

FOR THE MARINADE
1 bottle of red wine
1 carrot, cut into 3 pieces
1 celery rib, cut into 4 pieces
1 onion, cut into 8 pieces
zest of 1 orange, cut into strips
2 sprigs of rosemary
10 black peppercorns
10 juniper berries
10 cloves
6 bay leaves

FOR THE CASSEROLE
⅓ cup olive oil
2–3 sprigs of rosemary, leaves stripped and finely chopped
2 garlic cloves
5 bay leaves
2 tablespoons tomato paste
1 x 14 oz can Italian plum tomatoes
2 cups–1 quart meat or game stock
4 oz black olives, pitted

Put the wild boar pieces into a large, non-metallic container with the marinade ingredients and leave overnight, covered, in the fridge.

The following day, put the boar and vegetables into a colander, discarding the wine. Remove the vegetables and finely chop them by hand or in a food processor to make a *soffrito* (see page 125).

Heat the oil in a large frying pan and fry the *soffritto* for 15–20 minutes, stirring frequently, until soft and golden. Add the boar, rosemary, and garlic and fry for about 45–60 minutes, until the water has evaporated. Add the wine, allow it to reduce for a few minutes, then add the bay leaves, tomato paste, tomatoes, olives, and stock.

Cook for about 3 hours, or until tender, adding more stock if necessary. Serve with Crunchy Parmesan and Celery Mash (see page 384) or polenta.

e insalate

CHAPTER 9: VEGETABLES AND SALAD

Verdure e insalate

INTRODUCTION

In Italian, a greengrocer is called a *fruttivendolo*. I love that word. There is something so colorful and passionate about it, that really sums up the fruit and vegetable sellers I have met, especially in Sicily and Sardinia, who truly believe that their produce is better than anyone else could offer.

Sicilian greengrocer once told me why his produce was so full of flavor—and, indeed, why we were paying him so much! He told me that he drove twice a week to the place, near Etna, where his tomatoes were grown, and that the reason they were so good was that, as the rain fell, it poured down the mountain, collecting minerals on its journey and feeding them to the crops beneath. This, he said, combined with the strong sun, resulted in a concentrated flavor.

The Italians have been dedicated growers of crops since the days of the *Terramare*, early inhabitants who grew beans, vines, and wheat from the 15th to 8th century BC, taking full advantage of the sunshine and fertile land. The Etruscans and Romans were keen farmers too, and their legacy can be seen all over Italy today. As you travel around, you can scarcely see a patch of uncultivated land, from Liguria in the north—where growers have carved into the steep hillsides to form flat ground for vegetables, herbs, and flowers—all the way down to the slopes of Sicily.

Many Italians have a private or community garden, called an *orto,* where they will grow enough staple vegetables to supply their family throughout the summer—and often they will use traditional preserving techniques to keep them for the winter too. Even in towns and cities, people will grow chiles and basil on their balconies.

This devotion to eating vegetables straight from the garden, and the incredible surge of flavor you get from freshly harvested vegetables, is something I had always known about but never fully understood or appreciated until I grew carrots with my children for the first time. We have friends with a garden who often bring us their muddy vegetables and had always told us how quickly root vegetables lose their sugar once they are picked, but I had never put it to the test, so the children and I pulled up the baby carrots we had grown and literally ran to the house, washed them under the tap and ate them right away. They were so, so sweet; it was amazing to see the two children gorging themselves on carrots.

Many restaurants in Italy will serve a basket of local vegetables such as raw carrots, fennel, or celery with a *pinzimonio* made from oil, pepper, and salt—something that works only if the vegetables are packed with fresh flavor.

The difference between the Italian attitude to vegetables and our own was highlighted as far back as the late 16th and early 17th centuries by an Italian chef named Castelvetro, who lived in England. In a bid to encourage a greater use of vegetables and salads in the English diet, with its heavy use of meat and the popular sweets of the time (doesn't that sound familiar?), he wrote, "A brief account of all the roots, herbs and vegetables and fruits which, raw or cooked, are eaten in Italy." Although it was never published, a few copies were circulated and it was translated in recent times by Gillian Riley, a writer who truly understands the Italian idea of "cooking with love." She says of this short manuscript that it "remains as relevant today as it did in 1614; seasonal produce cooked and served with simplicity and affection is what we still seek and enjoy today in Italy."

In the markets, every trader knows that fresh produce needs to be of high quality, since the Italian customer is generally a knowledgeable one and Italian women are not shy of challenging on the issue of freshness—or price. They will want to taste, wherever possible, and pick over fennel bulbs, peppers, peaches, or cherries to select the best.

While markets in the north will usually supplement their local produce with fruits and vegetables grown in the warmer climate of the south, this is as far as imports go, in general. Apart from pineapples and bananas, which will be brought in, you will usually find only Italian fruits and vegetables when they are ripe and in season. A Tuscan chef, a good friend of ours, came to stay with us one winter and was amazed by the range of produce available in even the tiniest London supermarket. Though buying produce out of season went against the grain, she wasted no time in stocking up on fresh red chiles to take home for her friends.

For all the Italian love of fresh vegetables, this chapter was one of the hardest sections of the book to put together as, perhaps precisely because their vegetables are so full of flavor, Italians prefer to keep each one separate from the others and to serve them simply. Vegetables are served as side dishes to go with meat, and served on a small plate rather than with the main dish. Typical *antipasti* vegetables are served either grilled, preserved under oil or in vinegar, or boiled, for rather longer than most of us would consider cooking vegetables these days, then dressed with olive oil and salt. I must admit that I now love cooked green beans dressed with olive oil, red wine vinegar, and sliced garlic, the way Giancarlo's family have been eating them for years. Vegetable dishes such as this are generally served *tiepido*—at room temperature—rather than fridge cold, which really brings out the flavors.

In our restaurants, it has long been one of my jobs to work with the chefs, using Italian produce and dressings in ways they haven't considered, such as *salsa verde* over hot new potatoes and roasted red pepper sauce over roast potatoes—even poured over and then re-roasted—while the famous Piemontese dip *bagna-cauda* works brilliantly over roasted red peppers.

SALADS

When it comes to salads, in my view, Italians just don't make them as we have come to know them. While the British, Australians and Americans lead the world in new and interesting salad ideas, the Italian outlook, except in the most contemporary of restaurants, is much more conservative. Whereas we might combine some marinated artichokes with salad leaves and, say, some crunchy bacon, that just wouldn't be done in most Italian households. Instead you would serve your artichokes in one dish, and a *misticanza* or selection of lettuces and *cicoria* and endives in another, ready to dress at the table at the last minute with olive oil, salt, and wine vinegar.

In restaurants you might find mixed salads but they will rarely contain more than lettuce, tomato, cucumber, and sometimes grated carrot or corn (see my variation on this in Giorgio's salad, page 403).

So again, while some of the recipes in this section are traditional, there are others that we have developed in the restaurants, which combine Italian produce and ideas in a way that you might not always find in Italy.

With the fashion for healthy eating and light cooking (*La Cucina Leggera*) making headway in Italy, there are countless magazines devoted to this subject but they tend to focus on ideas from other countries and even the chains of salad restaurants that have opened up, offering a departure from pasta every lunchtime, don't offer anything like the range you might find in a high-end sandwich shop in Britain.

SPICES

Well-off Romans made great use of exotic, imported spices, possibly to disguise the flavor of decaying meat, or perhaps because a display of these expensive ingredients would show off the wealth of the host. It seems to me that the latter is most likely, since the rich could surely have afforded fresh meat.

During the dark ages spices disappeared from everyday diets and it was not until the middle ages that they once again arrived in Italy, in the north, through the trade routes into Venice; in the south, the influence of the Arab world spread via Sicily. In Medieval and Renaissance times, spices were once again seen as a symbol of prosperity.

Spices such as cinnamon, vanilla, chile, nutmeg, saffron, cloves, aniseed, colored peppercorns, ginger, coriander, and mustard were often used in large quantities and combinations more reminiscent of Indian cooking and, like herbs, they were valued for their medicinal properties and sometimes even considered to be mood-altering. Spices were often combined with sugar, even in savory dishes containing meat.

When French cooking became fashionable in the 1700s, the use of spices was almost abandoned and, for centuries, spicing in Italian cooking has been very conservative. Now younger, fashionable chefs are bringing spicesfl the likes of coriander, cumin, ginger, and star anisefl back into vogue.

Mustard, senape
Though most spices are used with discretion in traditional Italian cooking, the exception is mustard essence, which is the key ingredient in *mostarda di frutta* (mustard fruits), a syrupy concoction of mustard, sugar, and fruits traditionally served with *bollito misto*. There are different versions all over Italy but the most famous is *Mostarda di Cremona*, which hails from the city of Cremona in Lombardy.

HERBS

Aromatic herbs, known as *erbe aromatiche*, especially wild herbs (*erbe selvatiche*), play a big part in Italian cooking and figure strongly in some of the most famous recipes such as pesto and *salmoriglio*, the Sicilian dressing for fish made with oregano, lemon and parsley. In Liguria and Tuscany, where herbs grow in abundance, you will see people out and about with baskets, gathering wild herbs.

From the earliest times, herbs have also been valued for their restorative and medicinal powers. Cooks and apothecaries were not so far apart and the earliest recipes were often written down as if they were prescriptions (the Italian word for recipe, *ricetta*, is also the word for prescription). Giancarlo remembers his mother treating his ailments with a poultice (a paste made from herbs) when he was small. *Digestivi*, bitter after-dinner drinks containing herbs such as mugwort, rue, and wormwood, or the liqueur Fernet-Branca with its 27 herbs and spices, are still popular, as they are said to be good for the digestion.

The Roman writers Apicius and Pliny wrote about the place of herbs in cooking: Apicius described a single dish containing 60 herbs. Later the Italian Giacomo Castelvetro talked of *insalata di mischianza*, a salad full of herbs. His book was dedicated to Lucy, Countess of Bedford, a keen gardener, and it was a message to her in the England of 1614 to eat more fruit and vegetables.

His *insalata* contained "the first leaves of apple mint, nasturtium, spearmint, tarragon, leaves and flowers of borage, flowers of new fennel, the leaves of gentle rocket and lemony sorrel, the sweet flowers of rosemary and violet petals, washed and dressed with olive oil." Though some of the herbs such as *asofetida*, are more associated with Indian cooking these days, there are still many herbs used in Italy that we don't find everyday—in Puglia, for example, I ate boiled, chopped poppy leaves, which were peppery and delicious. I feel we should begin to grow herbs like myrtle and juniper in pots or window boxes, as the Italians do.

Preserving Herbs

Oregano, thyme, and sometimes marjoram are the only herbs that are used dried in Italian food; otherwise herbs are always fresh and, if they are not in season, they are simply not used. However, there are other ways of preserving herbs: I have seen people mixing finely chopped rosemary into salt, which not only preserves the rosemary but imparts a lovely flavor to the salt. Pesto, of course, is a prime example of preserving the summer flavors of basil in a jar, since it keeps well under a layer of oil in the fridge. Bags of herbs such as chopped parsley can be kept in the freezer, and oils can be flavored with rosemary, chile, or chopped bay leaves.

Key Herbs

The Ligurians are considered the gardeners of Italy, so many of these herbs feature heavily in dishes from that region.

Parsley, *prezzemolo*—has been used since classical times, when it was thought to cure kidney problems. Pliny claimed that parsley even cured sick fish in a pond. During Renaissance times, the humanist and Vatican librarian Bartolomeo Sacchi, known as Platina, author of a cookbook called "De honesta voluptate et valetudine" (On Right Pleasure and Good Health), said it cured dog and scorpion bites. Flat-leaf parsley is the most typical and it is used in so many dishes (*salsa verde* is basically a parsley sauce) that the Italian word for parsley, *prezzemolo* is also used to describe someone who seems to be everywhere and always crops up at parties.

Myrtle, *mirto*—is used all over Sardinia, where a typical dish is suckling pig cooked in a pit in the ground with myrtle leaves. It is thought that this cooking method was originally a way of hiding the existence of extra piglets from the *padrone* during feudal times.

Basil, *basilico*—the herb is such a symbol of Italian cooking that our chef Monserrato says he only has to chop basil and garlic together on a board to be transported back home to his family's kitchen in Italy, where everyone cooked together. Strongest in flavor when it is in flower, the herb differs slightly from region to region. Ligurian basil, for example, is milder and has a smaller leaf than its southern counterpart, which has a slightly minty taste. Traditionally thought to be good for stomach pains and sickness, and the key ingredient in pesto, in summer you will rarely see a tomato dish served without basil. Bruschetta, Pizza Margherita, *Insalata Caprese* (all of which feature the colors of the national flag)—all showcase basil.

Borage, *boraggine*—grows wild in Liguria and its little blue flowers can be eaten in salads. The leaves must be cooked before eating and have a mild flavor, reminiscent of cucumber. It is a key ingredient in *pansoti* (herb and cheese-filled ravioli), traditionally made with *preboggion*, a bundle of wild Ligurian herbs including parsley, borage, chervil, arugula, nettles, dandelions, and wild beets, which is also used to flavor *frittata* and stews. Borage was thought to be good for the soul and for relieving strained muscles.

Elderflower, *sambuco*—grows abundantly in Italy. The flowers can be mixed with batter and made into fritters, and are also used for making the liqueur Sambuca.

Fennel, *finocchio*—wild fennel is a long, thin plant that grows in the countryside or on roadsides. The thin stalks are chopped and used with fish and other dishes and the seeds are gathered and dried for use through the winter or for flavoring sausages, salami and, in Tuscany, *ragù*. In Sardinia, wild fennel is boiled and used to soothe toothaches, headaches, and inflammations. Plump bulbs of cultivated fennel are used raw or cooked and its distinctive anise flavor goes well with fish.

Juniper, *ginepro*—the berries are still collected from hillsides and used to flavor venison and game dishes. Juniper is also the flavoring in gin—see Monkfish with Gin and Juniper Berries (see page 255).

Mint, *menta*—is used with lamb, in fava bean pastes, in Sicilian sauces, and sometimes in salads. A particular variety is *nepetella* (*Calamintha nepeta*), or catmint or catnip, which has a small leaf and looks and smells like a cross between mint and thyme.

Marjoram, *maggiorana*—Ligurian cooking makes good use of this sweet herb, adding it to *pansoti*, vegetable tarts, and stuffed vegetables.

Nettles, *ortica*—appear in soups and *risotti* and at one time were boiled and cooled and used to treat stomachaches.

Rosemary, *rosmarino*—grown all over Italy, it is used with meats, especially lamb, beef, chicken, and rabbit—but rarely with fish, as it is considered too strong.

Sage, *salvia*—is essential in *porchetta*, chopped with garlic and salt. In the north it is cooked with butter and used as a sauce for filled pasta, sometimes combined with pine nuts. It is thought to have antiseptic qualities and to be good for sore throats.

Thyme, *timo*—good with fish and meat, it grows wild everywhere and is allegedly good for relieving hangovers!

Tarragon, *dragoncello*—I love the Italian name! Sometimes it is also known as *serpentaria*. It is mainly found in Tuscan dishes, usually in sauces, and is most typical in Siena.

Pomodori essiccati al forno
Oven-dried Tomatoes

In Tuscany I make these by leaving the cut tomatoes outside to dry in the hot sun, covered with a fly net which lets the light through but not the insects. Within about a day they're done and their concentrated taste is wonderful. We serve them with drinks or press them into focaccia before baking it. They would also be good thrown into a salad. You can, however, make very acceptable dried tomatoes in an ordinary oven. The best time to make them is toward the end of summer when tomatoes are ripe, sweet, and full of flavor. Use the best quality you can find.

Serves 4–6

12 oz cherry tomatoes, cut in
   half around the middle
1 teaspoon sugar
1 teaspoon salt
1 teaspoon finely chopped
   rosemary or thyme

Preheat the oven to 225°F. Lay the tomatoes cut-side up on a baking sheet. Sprinkle with the sugar, salt, and rosemary and bake for 1–1½ hours, depending on the size of the tomatoes.

Peperoni ripieni di soufflé al formaggio
Baked Red Peppers filled with Four-Cheese Soufflé

These peppers are light and easy to greens. Use any cheeses you have, but make sure one of them is blue for flavor.

Serves 4

4 red Romano or sweet bell
  peppers
⅔ cup whole milk
half a small onion, peeled
1 bay leaf
a good pinch of nutmeg
salt and freshly ground pepper
2 tablespoons butter
3 tablespoons all-purpose flour
¾ cup finely grated Parmesan
2 oz ricotta
2 oz Taleggio, cut into chunks
3 oz gorgonzola, cut into chunks
2 eggs, separated

Preheat the oven to 350°F. Cut the peppers in half lengthwise through the stem. Discard the seeds and membrane. Put on a baking sheet and bake for 7 minutes (not necessary for Romano peppers).

Put the milk, onion, bay leaf, nutmeg, pepper, and salt in a medium saucepan and bring to a boil. Melt the butter in a small pan and stir in the flour. Remove the bay leaf and onion. Cook for a few minutes, then add the mix to the milk and whisk. The mix will be very thick. When the mixtures are combined replace the whisk with a wooden spoon, add the cheeses and stir until melted.

Pour into a bowl and leave to cool for a few minutes, covered with plastic wrap. Whisk the egg whites in a bowl. Beat the yolks, add to the béchamel, then fold the egg whites into the rest of the ingredients in the saucepan. Spoon the soufflé mixture into the peppers and bake for 25 minutes until puffed and lightly browned.

Caponata
Sweet-and-Sour Eggplant

In Sicily, there are at least 40 variations to this recipe. It is usually served as part of *antipasti* with cured meats. It requires quite a lot of chopping and stirring, so you may want to double the recipe; it will keep in the fridge for a few days. Salting the eggplant in this recipe ensures they absorb less oil when fried.

Serves 4–6

1 large eggplant, diced
salt and freshly ground black pepper
2/3 cup olive oil
6 celery ribs, chopped
1 onion, chopped
1 tablespoon tomato paste
1 x 14 oz can Italian plum tomatoes
3 tablespoons sugar
3 tablespoons red wine vinegar
1 heaping teaspoon capers
12 green or black olives, pitted and chopped
2 tablespoons freshly chopped flat-leaf parsley
vegetable stock or water, as necessary

Spread out the diced eggplant in a colander, sprinkle with salt and set aside on a plate for about 30 minutes to 1 hour. Press gently to extract as much water as possible. Rinse the eggplant and dry well on paper towels or a clean tea towel.

Heat 4 tablespoons of the olive oil in a heavy-bottomed frying pan. Add the celery and sauté until lightly browned. Scoop out, using a slotted spoon, and set aside. Add another 2 tablespoons of the oil to the pan and cook the eggplant until browned and tender; you may need a little extra oil because the eggplant will really soak it up. Once again, scoop out and set aside to cool.

Pour the remaining oil into the pan and sauté the onion until golden. Add the tomato paste and tomatoes and simmer for 15 minutes or until reduced and thickened. Add the sugar and vinegar and cook for another 10 minutes, to make a rich sweet-and-sour sauce. Season with a little salt and plenty of pepper. Stir in the capers, olives, parsley, eggplant, and celery. If the mixture looks too dry, add a ladleful of stock or water to make a little more sauce. Taste and adjust the seasoning and be aware that the flavors will mellow as the caponata cools. Serve at room temperature.

Tip: Try a little shredded mint on top or add toasted pine nuts.

Melanzane alla Parmigiana con riso allo zafferano
Oven-baked Eggplant Layered with Mozzarella and Saffron Rice

Eggplants used to need salting to get rid of their bitterness until a botanist named Charles B. Heiser experimented with cultivating plants from selected seeds from eggplants that didn't taste bitter and produced larger fruits. Thanks to Charles, the modern cultivars don't need salting. It is said that a famous Sicilian chef some centuries ago came from the south to work for a grand old family in Parma and that it was he who introduced the common use of eggplant to the north and created this dish using the local cheese, *Parmigiano Reggiano*. This is a classic Italian vegetarian first or main course originally from the south of Italy but now made everywhere. In the west of Sicily where one of our chefs, Gregorio is from, they put a layer of saffron rice in the middle—but with or without, it's delicious.

Serves 6 as a main, 8 as a starter

FOR THE SAFFRON RICE
3 tablespoons olive oil
1/4 cup white onion, finely chopped
1 cup Arborio rice
4 x 4 oz packets of saffron
2/3 cup dry white wine
5 cups vegetable or chicken stock
salt and freshly ground black pepper

FOR THE EGGPLANT BAKE
2 tablespoons butter
sunflower oil, for frying
3 large eggplants
flour, for coating
1 quart of Franca's Tomato Passata
  (see page 166)
2 x 4 oz buffalo mozzarella, each sliced into
  8 pieces
1 cup Parmesan, grated

Butter an ovenproof dish measuring about 12 x 8 inches.

To make the saffron rice, heat the olive oil in a large saucepan and cook the onions until soft. Stir in the rice and allow it to "toast" for 3 minutes, then add the saffron. Stir through briefly for a minute, then add the wine. Allow it to bubble and reduce for a couple of minutes until the strong smell of wine dissipates. Next add the stock and seasoning and bring to a boil. Allow to cook for about 20 minutes or until the rice is tender. Remove from the heat and allow to cool; any remaining stock in the pan will soak into the rice.

Preheat the oven to 350°F. Heat a deep-fat fryer or a large frying pan with about 1¼ inches of sunflower oil until the oil reaches 325°F, or until a little piece of bread turns golden quickly and the oil bubbles around it. Cut the eggplants into ¼ inch thick slices and coat in the flour. Tap off the excess and fry the slices in batches in the oil until golden brown on both sides. Remove with

a slotted spoon and drain on paper towels to absorb the excess oil.

Coat the bottom of the prepared baking dish with a quarter of the tomato sauce. Scatter a quarter of the pieces of mozzarella and a quarter of the Parmesan on top. Cover with a layer of eggplant slices. Follow this with all of the rice then top with another quarter of mozzarella. Repeat with another layer of eggplant slices and another quarter of the tomato sauce. Scatter over another quarter of mozzarella and Parmesan, then the last layer of eggplant, tomato, mozzarella, and Parmesan on top. Transfer the dish to the oven and bake for about 30 minutes or until golden brown on top and bubbling all the way through.

Tip: If you are using a frying pan to cook the eggplants, don't be tempted to skimp on the oil or you will be forever having to get rid of the burnt bits of flour on the bottom of the pan. Should this happen, discard the oil, clean the pan and start again. Burnt flour will taint the flavor of the eggplant.

Zucchini fritti
Sautéed Zucchinis with Garlic and Chile

This simple vegetable dish is one we often quickly knock up at home to serve with chicken or meat main courses. Don't be put off by the amount of oil needed—any less and you will burn the zucchini. Most of it stays in the pan after frying anyway—and the flavor is wonderful.

Serves 4

⅓ cup extra virgin olive oil
½ red chile, thinly sliced
2 garlic cloves, crushed
2 medium zucchini, cut into
  ¼ in slices
salt and freshly ground
  black pepper

Heat the oil in a frying pan, add the chile and garlic and cook together for a minute. Add the zucchini slices, season with salt and pepper, and sauté in the pan for about 10 minutes until golden.

Don't be tempted to keep turning them: let the slices become golden underneath before turning them over.

Zucchine alla Poverella
Zucchini alla Poverella

This is originally a Pugliese dish. It is served as antipasto, or as a vegetable with meat or fish. Traditionally the zucchini are dried in the hot sun over the course of a day. In the British climate that is often difficult, so I have experimented with drying them in the oven, which seems to work just as well—and you don't have the problem of attracting bugs!

Serves 6

4 zucchini
1 generous tablespoon olive oil
1 tablespoon balsamic vinegar
8 mint leaves
salt and freshly ground black pepper

Preheat the oven to 225°F. Slice the zucchini into discs ½ inch thick. Lay them out on a baking sheet and dry in the oven for about 2 hours, turning them over halfway through. They should wrinkle and become dry on both sides. When done, remove from the oven and allow to cool.

Heat the oil in a large frying pan and, when hot, cook the zucchini on both sides until golden brown. Using a slotted spoon, lay them on a plate and drizzle with the balsamic vinegar. Scatter with salt, pepper, and mint leaves.

Carciofi alla Giudia
Jewish-style Deep-fried Artichokes

In the Jewish quarter of Rome there was a restaurant called Sora Margherita. It has now changed itself into a club, owing to an officious health and safety inspector telling them they had too many tables. There is no sign on the door and you have to fill in a membership card upon arrival. The tables are still close together and you have to wait to be seated but what awaits you amply makes up for that. The more-than-friendly staff greets you and advises you what is best to eat from their menu. My first treat was a deep-fried artichoke that looked like a large golden flower; the outer leaves had been transformed into salty crisps and the center into a tender heart.

Serves 4

4 artichokes
1 lemon
sunflower oil, for frying
salt

First, prepare the artichokes. Using your fingers, pull off the tough outer leaves. Trim the stem to within about 2 inches of the bottom. Peel the stem by scraping away the tough exterior with a sharp knife. Trim off the tips of the leaves with a sharp knife, cutting about ½ inch off the top of each leaf, and remove any prickly bits that you find on the inner leaves.

Holding the artichoke with one hand, gently open the leaves with the other as if opening a flower, petal by petal. Immediately place the artichoke in a bowl with enough cold water to cover it. Squeeze the juice of 1 lemon into the water—this prevents the artichokes from blackening. Prepare all four artichokes in the same way.

When ready to cook, remove the artichokes from the water and turn them upside down to drain. Pat them as dry as much as possible with paper towels and press them flat, flower end down, on a chopping board. This makes them open up as much as possible.

Heat enough sunflower oil in a deep-fat fryer or saucepan until very hot (test with a small piece of bread: if it sizzles and goes brown in 30 seconds the oil is ready). Carefully lower the artichoke (it may be easier to cook them one at a time) into the oil and turn it around gently, using a wooden spoon. The leaves should open up and become crisp. Fry for about 10 minutes until very brown. Once cooked, place each artichoke upside down on paper towels to absorb the oil. Scatter with salt and serve hot.

Verdure e insalate
MASTERCLASS

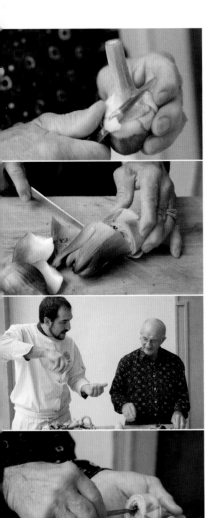

How to Clean an Artichoke

Firstly, remove a large number of the outer leaves; they can be tough to eat. Stop when the leaves become flexible and soft. Often this is when the color turns from deep purple to pale green.

Cut away the ends of the stems and scrape away the tough outer layer on the remaining part. Also trim away the tough area at the base of the bulb. Rub the cut surface with lemon juice.

Trim the remaining leaves to roughly half their length. You should finish up with something a little fatter than an artichoke heart and with a longer stem.

Scrape away any fuzzy choke from the center of the artichoke, as this is unpleasant to eat. Rub lemon juice inside and outside to prevent it from becoming brown, and leave it to soak in cold water with lemon juice added, while you prepare the rest of the ingredients.

Carciofi alla Romana
Roman Artichokes

I first ate these in Ristorante Alfredo in Rome. In Italy, the season for artichokes begins in December or January when artichokes arrive from the sunnier regions such as Sicily, Sardinia, Lazio, and Liguria. In markets, you often see the hearts of these tender young artichokes already peeled, bobbing around in buckets of water and lemon.

Serves 6

12 small or "baby" artichokes
1 small garlic clove, finely chopped
3 sprigs flat-leaf parsley,
 finely chopped
10 mint leaves, finely chopped
3 tablespoons olive oil
⅓ cup water
salt and freshly ground black pepper

Remove a large number of the outer leaves from the artichokes. The center is the most tender part and for this recipe you need the artichokes to be as tender as possible; you don't want to be eating chewy leaves. Trim the ends of the stems and scrape away the tough outer leaves with a sharp knife. Cut off at least ½ inch from the tips of the leaves. (Follow the step-by-step instructions on the left of this page.)

Mix together the finely chopped garlic and herbs and stuff the mixture into the artichoke centers.

Choose a saucepan or flameproof casserole that will accommodate all the artichokes tightly together and pour in the olive oil. Carefully pack the artichokes into the pan, heads down and stems up. Add the water and, if you have any of the herb mixture left over, add this too.

Place the pan over low to medium heat, cover, bring to a boil, then simmer for 45 minutes. Shake the pan frequently to make sure they don't stick. Add a little hot water if they become dry. Serve warm or at room temperature.

Traditionally, this dish is
made with mentuccia or wild
mint which grows only in
central Italy. Its small, light
green leaves have a strong
aroma and taste. If you don't
live in Italy or grow your own
mentuccia, normal mint makes
a good substitute!

Insalata di verdure grigliate
Grilled Vegetable Salad

This is so simple, you might ask why I am including it at all. I ate this dish in the Peck bar in Milan after a long journey: I wanted something light and fresh but I must admit to feeling slight disappointment when some dry-looking circles of eggplant arrived alongside similar peppers and zucchini. When the salad was dressed with balsamic and olive oil, however, the flavor was extraordinary. I now grill, broil, or oven-roast all my vegetables in this way, reducing the amount of oil. These vegetables are either served as antipasti or *contorni* (side dishes).

Serves 4–6

1 eggplant
2 red bell peppers
3 zucchini
2 tablespoons olive oil
a small handful of thyme sprigs
4 garlic cloves, unpeeled, lightly crushed
salt

FOR THE DRESSING
¼ cup olive oil
1½ tablespoons balsamic vinegar
salt and freshly ground black pepper

Preheat the oven to 400°F. Slice the eggplant into discs about ½ inch thick and lay them on a baking sheet lined with parchment paper. Set aside while you prepare the other vegetables.

Trim the peppers then cut them lengthwise into 1 inch thick slices: you should get around 8 slices from each pepper, depending on size. Halve the zucchini length-wise, then cut each half into four long wedges. Lay the zucchini and peppers on another baking sheet and brush with 2 tablespoons of oil. Sprinkle with salt and tuck the thyme sprigs under the peppers. Tuck the garlic between the vegetables.

Bake for 20 minutes. When they are cooked and lightly browned on the edges, remove the vegetables from the oven. Arrange them on a platter and drizzle with the oil and balsamic, and salt and pepper to taste. Serve warm or at room temperature but never cold from the fridge. You can add basil or mint leaves before serving or, for a more filling meal, mozzarella or goat cheese.

Cavolo rosso al forno con mele e cumino
Baked Red Cabbage, Apples, and Caraway Seeds

This is straight from the Italian/Austrian borders, up in the ski resorts of Trentino Alto Adige, where this dish is served with roast pork, sausages, or other drier meats such as chops. The buttery apples and raisins sweeten the cabbage, while the caraway seeds, which are typically used in rye bread from this region, give it a wonderful spice.

Serves 4–6

3 tablespoons butter
2 tablespoons extra virgin olive oil
12 oz red cabbage, shredded or thinly sliced
salt and freshly ground black pepper
1 heaping teaspoon caraway seeds
2 apples, peeled and sliced
¼ cup raisins (optional)
5 tablespoons red wine

Preheat the oven to 350°F.

Melt the butter with the oil in a large frying pan. When they are hot, add the red cabbage, salt and pepper and cook for about 5 minutes, stirring constantly. Add the caraway seeds, apple slices, and raisins and continue to cook over medium heat, stirring frequently, until the apple slices begin to soften and become pink with the cabbage juices.

Add the wine and reduce for a couple of minutes, then turn the cabbage into a lidded casserole (or use a lasagne dish and cover with foil). Bake, covered, for between 45 minutes and 1 hour, or until the cabbage has softened and started to brown.

Cavolo nero leaves

Cavolo nero stems

Cavolo nero con peperoncino e aglio
Cavolo Nero with Chile and Garlic

This member of the *Brassica* or cabbage family comes from Tuscany. It is a very good source of vitamins and iron and is at its best after the first frost. Any frugal Tuscan housewife would chop and boil the hard white stems in salted water for about 20–30 minutes, then toss in the leaves and serve it with a little butter. This recipe for preparing *cavolo nero* is also great served on toasted bread with a drizzle of good olive oil.

Pull the green parts away from the hard stems of the *cavolo nero* and wash them under cold water. Finely shred the leaves and put them in a steamer or in salted boiling water for 5–7 minutes, until just cooked. Drain, reserving a few tablespoons of the cooking water.

Heat the oil in a large frying pan and, when hot, add the garlic, chile, salt and pepper. Cook for a couple of minutes until they soften—but watch that they don't burn. Add the steamed leaves and cook for about 5 minutes, stirring constantly. If necessary, add a little of the reserved cooking water to stop them from sticking. The leaves should be wilted and coated in the chile and garlic oil.

Variation: This works equally well with spinach. Baby spinach can be "wilted" or cooked only and doesn't need pre-boiling.

1 head of *cavolo nero*
3 tablespoons olive oil
2 garlic cloves, lightly crushed
⅛–1 red chile, coarsely sliced
salt and freshly ground
  black pepper

Sformato di spinaci
Spinach Sformato

Sformato roughly translates as "formed" or "molded;" other than that, it is almost impossible to translate as this is neither soufflé nor mousse nor simple purée but something inbetween. Vegetables are cooked, then puréed and mixed with béchamel, cheese and egg to form a light, soufflé-textured molds that can be left in a big serving dish or turned out. They are often served as a starter: for example, Spinach Sformato with Pecorino Cheese Sauce or Potato Sformato with Cheese Sauce on Wilted Radicchio with Chickpeas. The molds, if you are using them, can be lined with cheese or breadcrumbs to give extra texture when they are turned out.

Makes 6 dariole molds measuring 2½ x 2½ inches, or 6 ramekins measuring 3½ x 1½ inches, or one small ovenproof dish measuring about 6½ x 8½ x 2½ inches

Preheat the oven to 350°F. Prepare the molds by buttering the insides, using your finger. Cut out a little circle of parchment paper to fit the bottom of each mold and press it down snugly. Then coat the inside with fine breadcrumbs or finely grated cheese, or leave it simply buttered.

To make the béchamel, heat the milk in a medium saucepan with the bay leaf, nutmeg, and salt and pepper. Melt the butter in a second, smaller pan and add the flour, stirring constantly. Cook for a couple of minutes to reduce the taste of the flour. When the milk is just about to boil, add the flour and butter mixture, whisking constantly. Keep over the heat until the sauce has thickened, then remove from the heat and set aside, with a sheet of plastic wrap touching the surface of the sauce to prevent a skin from forming.

Now squeeze the cooked spinach (or chop or prepare the vegetables you are going to add to the sauce—see variations); whatever you use, your vegetables should always contain as little water as possible. Add the spinach (or other vegetables) and the Parmesan to the béchamel and stir well to combine. Fold in the beaten egg whites. Pour the mixture into the prepared molds or into one baking dish and bake for 20 minutes for individual molds, or 25–30 minutes for a single dish.

To turn out the molds, run a knife around the edge of the sformato and then invert onto a serving plate. Serve with pecorino cheese sauce as a starter or vegetarian main course, or as a vegetable side dish.

You could also experiment with fennel, mushroom, and celery—but weaker flavors such as zucchini do not work as well as they are too watery.

1½ tablespoons butter, for greasing the molds
¼ cup fine dry breadcrumbs or finely grated Parmesan, for coating (optional)
1 cup milk
1 bay leaf
¼ nutmeg, freshly grated
2 tablespoons butter
3 tablespoons flour
1 lb spinach, cooked and squeezed (fresh spinach shrinks to half its original volume when cooked)
3 tablespoons finely grated Parmesan
2 egg whites, beaten
salt and freshly ground black pepper

Variations:

Sformato di carote
Carrot Sformato

Use 1 lb cooked and puréed carrots instead of spinach. Fills six dariole molds, as above, or an ovenproof dish approximately 8 x 11 x 2 inches.

Sformato di pastinaca
Parsnip Sformato

Use 1 lb cooked and puréed parsnips instead of spinach. Fills six dariole molds, as above, or an ovenproof dish approximately 8 x 11 x 2 inches.

Crema di Pecorino
Pecorino sauce

To make a cheese sauce, mix ½ quantity cheese to the quantity of cream and heat to the desired consistency.

Purè di fave e radicchio
Fava Bean Purée with Radicchio

The Pugliese are very good at growing beans and love to eat them with everything. After a short season, the beans are dried and used throughout the year even when fresh beans are available. Traditionally, fava bean mash is eaten with the local chicory: a long green leaf that grows wild. It can be very difficult to find but the mash also teams well with other bitter leaves such as radicchio or, as Caroline, a friend of mine who lives in Puglia, discovered, roasted red peppers. It is important to dress the purée with the best olive oil you have, preferably Pugliese. This duo is always eaten as a *primo,* not as a *contorno* (side dish), which I think is a shame: it would be wonderful with a roasted pork chop or some roasted fish. Dried fava beans can be found in some Chinese markets and in Middle Eastern food stores, as they are the staple behind the wonderfully named *foul medames*, a staple dish in Sudan and Egypt.

Serves 4

FOR THE FAVA BEAN MASH
8 oz dried shelled fava beans, with or without skins
1 large russet potato, scrubbed but not peeled
1 quart water (plus more, as necessary)
5 tablespoons extra virgin olive oil
salt

FOR THE RADICCHIO
3 tablespoons oil
½ white onion, sliced into rings
1 medium radicchio, long or round, thinly sliced
¼ cup vegetable stock or water
salt and freshly ground black pepper

Soak the beans overnight, then drain and discard the water. At this point the beans should be peeled if they were not already; the skins should slip off easily after being soaked. Put the beans and the potato in a saucepan, pour in the quart of fresh water, add salt and bring to a boil, then reduce the heat and simmer, uncovered, for an hour or until soft. Skim off the resulting scum with a spoon. Add a little more water, as necessary, but not too much because you need the cooking water to create a smooth purée: too much and you will end up with soup. When cooked, peel the potato. Then pass the beans, potato, and water through a *passatutto* or food mill, or mash until smooth. Season to taste, then stir in 3 tablespoons of the olive oil and drizzle the remainder on top. Set aside in a warmed serving dish.

To make the radicchio, heat the oil in a large frying pan and cook the onions for about 5–10 minutes, until softened. Add the radicchio and cook for a few minutes, stirring frequently, until it has wilted. Season to taste. Add the stock and allow to reduce for a few minutes, then serve with the mash.

Purè di patate con sedano e croccante di Parmigiano
Crunchy Parmesan and Celery Mash

This is a gorgeous mixture, full of flavor and texture, and great with stews or roast chicken.

Serves 8–10

1 quantity of Parmesan Crunch (see below)

2¼ lb russet potatoes, scrubbed but not peeled
salt
8 tablespoons butter
1 lb celery, finely chopped
¼ teaspoon finely grated nutmeg
up to 1 cup whole milk
freshly ground black pepper

Boil the potatoes in their skins, in salted water, until tender. Chop the celery finely by hand or in a food processor. Melt the butter in a pan and cook the celery for about 10 minutes, until softened. Remove from the heat and set aside. Once the potatoes are done, peel them then rub them through a *passatutto* or food mill into a saucepan. Add the milk a little at a time until you get a smooth purée over medium heat, season with salt, pepper, and nutmeg to taste. Mix in half of the Parmesan crunch, then put the mash into a warm serving bowl and garnish with the remaining crunch. For Parmesan mash, replace the celery and crunch with 1 cup of finely grated Parmesan.

Parmesan crunch
Spread out 1¼ cups finely grated Parmesan to ¼ inch depth onto a piece of parchment paper on a baking sheet, using a palette knife. Bake at 400°F for 5–8 minutes until pale golden brown. Allow to cool and break into pieces. Serve as it is with drinks or mix it into mashed potatoes.

Fave, cipolle e pancetta
Fava Beans and Pancetta

To peel or not to peel a fava bean? I am referring to the pale, gray-green wrinkly skin that covers the brighter green bean inside. I think life is just too short to peel them and, if they are young and tender or frozen, it really doesn't seem necessary. Any purists out there might want to peel them; nevertheless, Italians are mad about fava beans, eating them raw in spring with salt or cheese, boiling them in a variety of ways or drying them and eating the purée during winter months.

Serves 6

1 lb fava beans, fresh or frozen
salt
¼ cup extra virgin olive oil
4 oz pancetta, diced
freshly ground black pepper
¾ cup vegetable stock or water

Add a little chopped onion with the pancetta for added sweetness.

Bring a saucepan of salted water to a boil and cook the broad beans for 15 minutes, or until tender.

Meanwhile, heat the oil in a frying pan and cook the pancetta with some pepper. Once the beans are done, drain them and remove the skins if you wish (once they are cooked the skins slip off easily). Add the beans to the pancetta and cook for a few minutes, stirring frequently. Pour in the stock or water, bring to a boil and leave to simmer for 10–15 minutes or until cooked through.

Taccole con prosciutto di parma e peperoncino
Runner Beans with Parma Ham and Chile

This is another Gino Borella recipe. Runner beans are not as common in Italy—but they do exist. This dish was served to me as a starter but I like it best as an accompaniment to grilled or roast meat, chicken or sausages. Gino uses the tail of the Parma ham but you could also use pancetta, *guanciale*, *lardo,* or bacon.

Serves 6 as a side dish, 4 as a starter

1 lb runner beans or green beans, trimmed and cut into 3 on the diagonal
2 tablespoons extra virgin olive oil
2 garlic cloves, roughly sliced
½ green chile, thinly sliced
4 oz Parma ham or similar, cut into julienne
⅓ cup dry white wine
2 sprigs of fresh thyme
⅓ cup tomato passata (see page 166)

Cook the beans in salted boiling water until tender, then drain. Meanwhile, heat the oil in a large frying pan and cook the garlic, chile, and ham together for about 5 minutes, until the ham becomes crisp. Add the wine and reduce for a couple of minutes, scraping up any brown bits from the bottom of the pan with a wooden spoon—these will add flavor to the sauce. Next, add the thyme, tomato passata, and finally the beans, and stir well. Cook for a further 10 minutes to let the flavors blend.

Purè di patate con Parmigiano
Parmesan and nutmeg mash

Serves 6–8

2¼ lb russet potatoes, boiled in their skins
1 cup finely grated Parmesan
8 tablespoons salted butter
1 cup milk
¼–½ teaspoon freshly grated nutmeg (optional)
salt and freshly ground black pepper

As soon as the potatoes are cool enough to touch, peel them and put them through a *passatutto*, ricer, or mash them in a saucepan. Put the saucepan over medium heat and stir in the Parmesan, butter, milk, and nutmeg to blend well. Season to taste.

Insalata di zucca e cipolle rosse
Roast Pumpkin and Red Onion Salad

I love this autumnal, sweet salad with a little bit of crunch provided by the pine nuts. Serve it as a meal in itself or with roasted meats or as part of antipasti. In Italy they have enormous, long pumpkins with bright orange flesh, which are perfect for roasting or stuffing ravioli. The nearest equivalent is the butternut squash, which has an equally sweet and delicious flavor.

Serves 6

1¾ lb peeled and seeded pumpkin or butternut squash, cut into 8 even-sized slices
8 garlic cloves, unpeeled, lightly crushed
5 tablespoons olive oil
salt and freshly ground black pepper
2 tablespooons pine nuts (optional)
2 red onions, each cut into eight wedges
6 sprigs of thyme
1 lb lettuce, washed
2 tablespoons balsamic vinegar
1 oz Parmesan, shaved

Preheat the oven to 400°F. Put the pumpkin pieces and garlic cloves on a baking sheet and drizzle with two tablespoons of olive oil. Sprinkle with salt and pepper and roast in the oven for 20 minutes. Meanwhile, toast the pine nuts in a dry frying pan, if using.

Add the onion wedges to the baking sheet with another 1½ tablespoons of olive oil and extra salt and pepper. Tuck the thyme under the onions and pumpkin and cook for another 20 minutes, or until the pumpkin is tender and the onions lightly caramelized. Leave to cool to room temperature.

Separate the leaves of the lettuces and dress with 1½ tablespoons of olive oil and a little salt and pepper. Arrange the pumpkin and onions on top of the leaves, discarding the garlic and thyme. Drizzle with balsamic vinegar and a little extra olive oil. Scatter with the Parmesan shavings and pine nuts, if using.

Topinambour gratinate
Jerusalem Artichoke Gratin

Jerusalem artichokes are becoming more popular in Italy. Their unusual flavor certainly makes them stand out on the plate, but paired with simple roasted meat they are a real treat. This dish also makes a delicious vegetarian main course.

Serves 4–6 as a side dish

1½ lb Jerusalem artichokes, unpeeled
salt
2 cups milk
1 small onion
1 bay leaf
a generous pinch of nutmeg
freshly ground black pepper
5 tablespoons butter
½ cup flour
⅓ cup finely grated Parmesan

Preheat the oven to 350°F.

Cook the artichokes in their skins in salted boiling water, for about 5 minutes if they are very small, or for 15–20 minutes for larger ones, until they are soft, like potatoes. Drain, then slip off the skins. (Once cooked, skins will slip off more easily.) Slice the artichokes into ¼ inch slices.

Put the milk in a saucepan with the onion, bay leaf, nutmeg, and salt and pepper and allow to infuse by slowly bringing it to a boil.

Make a roux: melt the butter in a small saucepan and, when it has melted, add the flour and stir continuously over the heat for 3–4 minutes, to cook the flour through. Once the milk has boiled, remove and discard the onion and bay leaf, then whisk the roux into the milk. Continue to whisk until the sauce becomes thick and smooth. Adjust the seasoning to taste.

Put a layer of sauce in the bottom of a medium (about 11 inches) lasagne dish, then top with a layer of sliced artichokes. Scatter with some Parmesan, then repeat the layers until the ingredients are used up, finishing with a layer of Parmesan. Bake for between 45 minutes and 1 hour, or until the surface is bubbling and golden brown.

Verdure ripiene di Livia
Livia's Stuffed Zucchini Boats

Our friend Livia, who lives on a smallholding in Tuscany, uses her own vegetables, bread, and herbs in this recipe, while the meat—Chianina beef from the huge white cattle of Tuscany—comes from her local butcher. I buy the best meat I can find—not too lean, as a little fat gives a lot of flavor. Leftover stuffing can be made into meatballs. My children won't knowingly eat zucchini but will happily munch the meatballs, unaware that they are eating zucchini hidden within!

Serves 10–12

3 eggplants
5 zucchini
5 tablespoons extra virgin olive oil

FOR THE STUFFING
1 lb ground beef
3 garlic cloves, finely chopped
3 medium eggs, beaten
2 teaspoons salt
freshly ground black pepper
½ teaspoon grated nutmeg, optional
6 tablespoons fresh breadcrumbs
1 heaping tablespoon herbs such as parsley, marjoram, oregano, or fresh thyme
1 cup finely grated Parmesan

Preheat the oven to 350°F.

Cut the eggplants into quarters, then cut out the centres and reserve. Cut the zucchini in half, first lengthwise and then horizontally. Use a teaspoon to scoop out the flesh and reserve. Take care to leave a hollow in the center and leave an edge around the center to hold the stuffing: the zucchini will resemble little canoes.

Chop the zucchini flesh finely and mix together with the rest of the stuffing ingredients in a large bowl, using your hands.

Stuff the mixture into the cavities of the eggplants and zucchini, allowing the stuffing to mound above the cavities. Transfer the filled vegetables to a baking sheet, drizzle with olive oil and bake in the oven for about 15–20 minutes, or until they are browned and the meat is cooked through.

Patate e cipolle al forno
Oven-baked Potatoes and Onions

I was shown this dish in Cilento at the time when *lampascioni* (*Muscari comosum*), a type of grape hyacinth, were in season. Their bulbs have a subtle, slightly bitter flavor, highly prized by the southern Italians. One way in which they are cooked is by frying them with potatoes. I was informed that onions could be used in the same way.

Serves 4

1 lb potatoes, skins left on and cut into ½ in cubes
2 red onions, peeled and cut into ½ in cubes
5 garlic cloves, unpeeled and lightly crushed
⅓ cup olive oil
salt and freshly ground black pepper
2 sprigs of rosemary or thyme
3½ oz pancetta, roughly chopped (optional)

Preheat the oven to 400°F. Toss the ingredients together on a roasting dish and bake in a single layer for 20–30 minutes until cooked through. Shake and stir halfway through.

Patate arrosto con grasso di anatra e salvia
Sage and Dripping Roast Potatoes

We ate these at a restaurant in Tuscany, up in the hills, and were so impressed that we asked the owner his secret. He told us the key to his much-praised potatoes was the drained fat from all his roasted meats. He collected it each time, mixed it together, then tossed in some chopped sage at the end. When I thought about it, my mother always employed this method. She had a little brown pot in the fridge and each time we had a roast she would fill it with the leftover fat. (It always made the best fried bread too, before we all became health-conscious!) Marco, one of our Neapolitan chefs, told me that in Naples they always parboil the potatoes in white wine vinegar. He said it means they don't fall apart so easily and gives the potatoes a great flavor. Italians parboil potatoes for longer than we do but it works well and cuts down on the roasting time.

Serves 8–10

2¼ lb potatoes, peeled and cut into chunks about 1¼–1½ in across
2 bay leaves
10 black peppercorns
5 tablespoons white wine vinegar
⅓ cup fat from roast meats, or olive oil
4 garlic cloves, unpeeled, lightly crushed
2 sprigs of rosemary
coarse sea salt and freshly ground black pepper
a large handful of sage leaves, coarsely chopped

Preheat the oven to 350°F.

Boil the potatoes in salted water with the bay leaves, black peppercorns, and white wine vinegar for about 20 minutes or until a skewer passes easily through to the center. Heat the fat or oil with the rosemary and garlic in a shallow baking pan for 3–4 minutes, then add the drained potatoes. Discard the bay leaves and peppercorns. Season with plenty of sea salt and freshly ground black pepper. Separate the potatoes from one another so that they can crisp up on all sides. Bake for 20–30 minutes, until golden brown. Toss in the pan, using a metal spatula, halfway through the cooking time. About 5 minutes before they are ready, add the sage leaves to the potatoes and toss them around well. Serve in a warmed serving dish.

Patate arrosto al limone
Lemon-roasted Potatoes

This is an adaptation of a Valentina Harris recipe. She swears her roast potatoes are the best but I think they are even better with the skins left on. Less work, more nutrients is my motto!

Serves 8–10

2¼ russet potatoes, unpeeled, washed, and cut into 1 in cubes
8 garlic cloves, unpeeled, crushed lightly with the flat side of a knife
4 sprigs of fresh thyme or rosemary, left whole but crushed lightly
3 lemons, cut in half, strips of zest removed
6 tablespoons extra virgin olive oil
2 teaspoons salt
freshly ground black pepper

Put the cubed potatoes in a large bowl of water and leave for 30 minutes to remove some of the starch. Drain and dry on a clean kitchen towel. Preheat the oven to 350°F.

Put the potatoes in a large roasting dish and add the garlic cloves and herbs. Remove four strips of zest per lemon. Squeeze the juice from the lemons over the potatoes, then cut the lemons into quarters and add to the dish with the zest. Drizzle with olive oil and sprinkle with salt and pepper. Toss well to mix.

Transfer the dish to the oven and bake for 20–30 minutes, until the potatoes are browned all over. Halfway through the cooking time, baste the potatoes but be careful not to crush them too much. Remove the herbs and lemons before serving.

Insalata agrodolce
Bitter-sweet Salad

This salad is a union of the vegetables of the north with the fruits of the south. It was made up by our chef friend Gregorio Sicilian-fashion, by adding a little fresh orange to some salad leaves, making a delicious, bittersweet combination. In true chef-style, Gregorio julienned (thinly sliced the vegetables into sticks), which is worth the effort with this combination of colors—the end result is very pretty.

Makes 4 large portions or 6 small portions

Peel the oranges with a sharp knife to remove the white pith. Cut out the segments from their membranes and trim off any remaining pith. Put the segments into a large mixing bowl and squeeze the rest of the orange juice over them. Add the rest of the ingredients to the orange and use your fingers to combine them. Season to taste as necessary and transfer to a clean bowl to serve.

2 oranges
2 oz arugula leaves
½ white or red endive, cut into julienne strips
10 black olives, pitted
½ small red onion, cut into julienne (optional)
½ celery rib, cut into julienne strips
8 radishes, thinly sliced
3 tablespoons extra virgin olive oil
1 tablespoon red wine vinegar
salt and freshly ground black pepper

MUSHROOMS

All over Italy, on weekends you see families from all backgrounds parking everything from the latest four-wheel drives to battered Cinquecentos in little lanes and piling out with their baskets to go mushroom hunting in their favorite locations. I love the whole idea of the mushroom hunt and, as a woman who likes a bargain, the sense of getting something precious for nothing is especially appealing!

Italians love wild mushrooms, simply grilled and served with olive oil, parsley, garlic, salt and pepper, or sliced and cooked in olive oil and butter as in Giancarlo's Mushrooms (see page 395). So important are mushrooms in Italian cooking that, when other vegetables are cooked in this way, they are called "*al funghetto*" meaning "cooked in the same way as mushrooms." In season, wild mushrooms are a favorite in *risotto* and in sauces for pasta or meat, and are often preserved for use throughout the rest of the year, either dried, kept under oil (*sott'olio*), or pickled in vinegar (*sottaceto*).

Going on an Italian mushroom hunt is terribly exciting and secretive; I was told that in order to be a good mushroom hunter you have to be a good liar! The rule is that if you find a great spot for mushrooms, you never shout about it: you simply put your treasure in your basket and cover it up quickly in case you meet other hunters —and when you return from a successful hunt, you keep quiet about your lucky location or someone else might beat you to it next time. This secrecy serves another useful purpose: by preventing the invasion of the masses, it helps to preserve the woods and the conditions necessary for re-growth. Serious mushroom hunters help matters further by using a knife to cut the mushrooms, rather than pulling up too much from the ground.

The main species:

Porcini—without a doubt, the Italians consider these to be the kings of mushrooms. The French know them as *ceps* and in England they used to be called "penny bun," but the Italian *porcino*, meaning little pigs, really sums up their distinctive fat, round stems underneath meaty, brown caps. Although they are wonderful in risotto, sauces, stews, and salads, most Italians like to slice and cook them simply in butter or oil, parsley and garlic. They are also dried, for adding to dishes like risotto all year round.

Cantarelli—or *chanterelles*, as we and the French know them, are also popular, so much so that the pretty yellow trumpet-shaped mushroom, which smells like an apricot, is called different names from region to region, such as *finferlo*, *gallinaccio*, *galletta*, and even *margherita*. In France, the spring/summer chanterelle is also known as *girolle*. Often you will see chanterelles preserved in vinegar and served as part of an *antipasti*.

Cardarello—the best known of the oyster family is this King Oyster, also known as *cardoncello*. As the name suggests, the pale, brown-gray mushrooms have caps shaped rather like oysters. As well as growing wild on tree stumps in southern Italy, the mushrooms can be cultivated in sacks. In Puglia they are often baked with breadcrumbs and parsley.

Chiodini—the name means "little nails," which is what these little mushrooms look like. Sometimes they are known as honey mushrooms, or *famiglioli* (little families) because of the way they grow together on trees and old damp logs. They must always be cooked and are often blanched and then preserved in oil or vinegar.

Spugnoli—prized by the French as *morels*, and a favorite in Emilia-Romagna, the heads of the mushrooms, which look like sponges or honeycombs, are hollow, so they are good for stuffing, though they are also used in pasta and risotto and can be dried.

Ovoli—the orangey-red caps of these delicate-flavored mushrooms grow out of white sacs, which gives them an egg-like appearance. Their Latin name, *Amanita caesarea*, refers to the fact that they were a favorite with the Roman emperor but these days they are quite rare (and therefore expensive) and difficult to find outside Italy. Since they are in season at the same time as that other expensive ingredient, white truffles, they are sometimes served together.

Crimini—these are brown-capped cultivated button mushrooms, the biggest, most mature of which are these days known as the Portobello, which have become so popular and easily accessible.

Prataioli—these are white-capped field mushrooms.

Funghi alla diavola
Chillied Mushrooms in Red Wine

Giancarlo is forever cooking these at home. His mother used to make something similar as part of antipasti but we eat them on toast for breakfast or as a vegetable accompaniment to steak.

Serves 4–6, or more as antipasti

4 tablespoons olive oil
2 garlic cloves, crushed
  with the back of a knife
½–1 red chile
salt and freshly ground
  black pepper
1¼ lb button mushrooms,
  rinsed or wiped clean and
  left whole
⅔ cup red wine

Heat the oil in a large saucepan over medium heat and add the garlic, chile, salt and pepper. Cook for 1 minute to infuse the oil, then increase the heat, add the onion and cook for 3 minutes, stirring frequently to prevent burning.

Add the mushrooms, stirring frequently until they start to lose their water and begin to color. Then add the red wine and cook over medium heat for about 20 minutes, stirring occasionally, until the red wine has reduced, leaving a thick, rich onion sauce.

Insalata di rucola, pinoli e melagrana
Arugula, Pine Nut, and Pomegranate Salad

This is very pretty and jewel-like, good with roasted meats or cheese dishes such as *Sformato* (see page 382) or Baked Ricotta (see page 108).

Serves 4–6

1 handful of arugula per person, long stems stripped
½ cup pine nuts, lightly toasted
½ pomegranate, seeds only
2 tablespoons flat-leaf parsley leaves, coarsely torn

DRESSING
2 teaspoons honey
2 tablespoons extra virgin olive oil
1–2 tablespoons honey vinegar or lemon juice
salt and freshly ground black pepper

Mix the ingredients for the dressing together in a large bowl, seasoning to taste with salt and pepper. Add the arugula, pine nuts, and pomegranate seeds and toss to combine. Transfer to a clean dish and serve right away, sprinkled with parsley.

Funghi trifolati alla Giancarlo
Giancarlo's Mushrooms

Trifolati or *al funghetto* means "sliced like mushrooms" and when it is written on a menu it will mean that your vegetables—not necessarily mushrooms—have been sliced and fried, usually with some garlic and herbs. Mushrooms are often in need of a little flavor and, as Giancarlo says "you need to put the woods back into them." By that, he means the scent of dark, dank woods where mushrooms grow, created by adding some thyme and rosemary to infuse the woodsy, herby flavor back into typical supermarket mushrooms. All I know is that his tip of adding herbs and cooking them over high heat works. This mushroom recipe can used for *frittata*, *risotto*, as a topping on *crostini* (use 2 oz per slice), or *gnocchi* (stir in 4 tablespoons of cream for a wonderful mushroom sauce), and in the *Filetto di Manzo* recipe (see page 297).

Makes 10½ oz cooked weight, serves 4 as a side dish

4 tablespoons extra virgin olive oil
2 garlic cloves, crushed
3 large sprigs of thyme
3 sprigs of rosemary
½–1 red chile (depending on strength) finely sliced
1 lb mixed mushrooms (e.g. white cup, oyster, Portobello, crimini, porcini), rinsed or wiped clean as necessary, thickly sliced
a generous pinch of salt and freshly ground black pepper

Heat the oil in a large frying pan over high heat and, when hot, add the garlic, thyme, rosemary, chile, and salt and pepper. Cook for 1 minute, then add the mushrooms and cook them, still over high heat, tossing and stirring frequently. When the water from the mushrooms has evaporated and they have become browned and slightly crisp they are ready.

Insalata di pasta, mozzarella e pesto
Pasta and Pesto Salad

This simple yet delicious dish, which combines the best of Italy, has been a triumphant success when it is featured on our Caffè Caldesi menu and when I teach it at our cooking school. Our son Flavio loves to make and eat it. He has been known to discreetly pull the whole serving dish towards himself at the table and consume the lot before the rest of us have a chance!

Serves 4

8 oz shaped pasta, cooked, drained, and cooled
  under cold tap water
2 oz pesto (see page 164)
2 x 4 oz balls of fresh mozzarella, torn into pieces
8 oz cherry tomatoes, cut in half
4 large basil leaves, torn into pieces, to garnish

Put all the ingredients into a bowl, mix well, and serve sprinkled with basil leaves.

Carpaccio di carciofi
Raw Artichoke, Parmesan and Lemon Salad

The first tender young artichokes are best for this dish. They have small heads, long stems and are usually purple-green in color. Buy quite a few as most of the leaves are discarded or trimmed in this recipe so that what you are left with can be thinly sliced and eaten raw. Artichokes are related to cardoons whose long stems make a delicious vegetable. They are both part of the thistle family.

Serves 4

4 artichokes, trimmed
juice of ½ lemon
2 tablespoons olive oil
a good pinch of salt
1 oz Parmesan shavings
2 oz arugula

Clean the artichokes, following the instructions on page 378. Thinly slice the edible parts and, as you cut them, toss them in a non-metallic bowl with the lemon, oil, and salt to prevent them from discoloring. Leave them to marinate for at least 15 minutes or up to 2 hours.

Transfer the artichokes to a serving dish, scatter the arugula and Parmesan shavings on top, and serve.

Verdure arrosto di Franca
Franca's Roast Vegetables

I watched these being made in Franca's restaurant, Ristorante Sabatino, in Rome. I loved the way she casually splattered the tomato sauce onto the vegetables with a few flicks of her fingers like Jackson Pollock, and I loved the taste of the vegetables even more.

Serves 4

2 tablespoons olive oil
a small handful of flat-leaf parsley
¼ cup fresh breadcrumbs
2 tablespoons finely grated
  Parmesan
2 tablespoons *Pecorino Romano*
a large pinch of salt
1 eggplant, sliced lengthwise
  into ½-in thick slices
1 zucchini, sliced lengthwise
  into ½-in thick slices
2 red or yellow bell peppers,
  sliced into 6 pieces each,
  seeds removed
4 oz Franca's Tomato Passata
  (see page 166)

Preheat the oven to 400°F and grease a baking sheet with a little of the olive oil.

Pulse the parsley, breadcrumbs, cheeses, and salt together in a food processor.

Place the sliced vegetables on the baking sheet and sprinkle with the breadcrumb mixture.

Dip the fingers of one hand into the passata, then flick them to splatter the sauce over the vegetable slices. Drizzle with olive oil. Sprinkle an extra pinch of salt over the vegetables (if you wish) and transfer the baking sheet to the oven. Bake for 30 minutes, until cooked through and golden brown on top.

Cheese-stuffed Potato Cakes

In Puglia, I was served *tortino di patate* with pieces of cheese and Parma ham inside. Here I have provided the basic recipe, with the option of different cheeses.

Makes 8 small (½ cup) dariole molds or ramekins or 24 tiny molds

1¼ lb russet potatoes
4 tablespoons butter for the mash, plus
  extra for greasing and dotting on top
3 tablespoons Parmesan, finely grated, for
  coating the molds, plus ½ cup for the mash
  (optional)
2 eggs, beaten
4 oz Taleggio, mozzarella, stracchino, or young
  Parmesan (optional), cut into small cubes
1 tablespoon finely chopped rosemary
3–5 tablespoons milk

Scrub the potatoes and put them in a pan of salted water to boil. Meanwhile preheat the oven to 350°F. Prepare the molds by buttering the insides using your finger. Cut out a little circle of parchment paper for the bottom of each mold and press it down. Then dust the insides with Parmesan.

When the potatoes are cooked, drain them and, when cool enough to handle, remove the skins. Press them through a ricer back into a pan. Add the eggs, cheese and rosemary and place over medium heat. Mix in the butter and add the milk a little at a time, beating with a wooden spoon. Less or more milk may be necessary, depending on whether the potatoes are dryish or dampish. Season with salt and pepper.

Pour half the potato mixture into the prepared molds, then distribute the small cubes of cheese, if using, and cover with the remaining mixture. Tap the molds down firmly to get rid of any air pockets. Dot a little butter on top of each one. Bake in the oven for 20–25 minutes (15 minutes if they are tiny) or until golden brown and puffed up. Remove from the oven and work around the edge of the molds with a knife, to loosen them. Turn them out and peel off the paper. Serve right away or keep warm until you are ready to serve; but turn them out (right side-up) at the last minute, or they will dry out.

Endive Salad with Gorgonzola, Pine Nuts and Honey

Endives are part of the chicory family and have a gentle bitterness which, in this recipe, is balanced by honey. Endive leaves are the perfect shape to hold salads and we often eat this salad with our fingers using the leaves as large spoons. I'm a bit of a black pepper nut so I like this with a twist of pepper to finish but I have found, on my recent travels through Italy, that many people prefer to omit pepper from delicate salads like this. I leave it up to you to make the choice. The softer gorgonzola *dolce* works best here.

Serves 4

2 Belgian endives
4 oz gorgonzola (*dolce*)
2 tablespoons good-quality honey
1½ tablespoons olive oil
¼ cup pine nuts
black pepper (optional)

Cut off the root end from both endives and gently break off all the leaves, one by one, arranging them on a serving dish so that they resemble little boats to carry the ingredients.

Crumble the cheese over, ensuring that each leaf gets an equal helping. Drizzle the honey, raising the spoon high over the dish in concentric circles to create a lovely cobweb effect over the salad. Drizzle the olive oil in similar circular fashion.

Finally, toast the pine nuts lightly in a dry frying pan (be careful because they burn easily). Scatter them over the salad and serve with an optional twist of black pepper.

Bietole con pomodori, pinoli e olive
Swiss or Rainbow Chard with Tomatoes, Pine Nuts, and Olives

Chard has soft green leaves and very hard stems. Both parts of the plant can be eaten but they need to be cooked separately. This recipe uses tomatoes, but chard is equally tasty with lemon juice instead, both lending a pleasing acidity to the finished dish. Try to find *Taggiasca* or *Gaeta* olives and pit them yourself; they will taste far better.

Serves 4

1 head of Swiss or rainbow chard, green leaves
  stripped from the stems
3 tablespoons extra virgin olive oil
1 medium white onion, finely chopped
2 garlic cloves, coarsely chopped
2 oz olives, pitted and coarsely chopped
6 tablespoons pine nuts, toasted
vegetable stock, as needed
3 heaping tablespoons canned Italian plum
  tomatoes, or juice of 1 lemon
salt and freshly ground black pepper

Using a sharp knife, chop the chard stems into small cubes and cook in plenty of boiling salted water for 15 minutes, then drain. Meanwhile, wash the leaves well and chop coarsely.

Heat the olive oil in a large frying pan and cook the onion, garlic, salt and pepper until the onion is soft. Add the chopped and pitted olives and toasted pine nuts. Stir in the chard leaves, cover the pan and allow them to wilt for 5 minutes. Stir again, uncovered, for another 5 minutes. Add the boiled stems and stir to combine. Finally, stir in the tomatoes and heat through for 5 minutes, or add lemon juice to taste before serving. Taste and adjust the seasoning, if necessary.

Melanzane e pomodorini di Maria
Maria's Eggplant and Tomato Stew (sauce or side dish)

I wish I had a word for dishes that have several uses, as there are many of them in Italian cuisine. Maria is a Neapolitan shopkeeper and a good friend of ours. She leads a busy life, looking after her shops and family, so prefers quick and easy recipes that she knows her family will enjoy. This is one of them.

Serves 4

2–3 eggplants, depending on size
2/3 cup grapeseed oil or olive oil, for frying
salt, to taste
3 garlic cloves, lightly crushed
10 ripe medium tomatoes, chopped coarsely
  (or 1 x 14 oz can Italian tomatoes,
  preferably cherry)
1 sprig of basil

Chop the eggplants into sticks about ½ inch wide, discarding the center part containing the seeds. Heat the oil in a large frying pan and, when hot, add the eggplant. Cook for about 5 minutes or until pale golden brown and crispy. Use a slotted spoon to remove the eggplant from the pan and drain on paper towels. Sprinkle with a little salt.

Discard two-thirds of the oil and briefly cook the garlic in the remaining oil, then add the tomatoes and basil. If you are using fresh tomatoes, cook them for a few minutes to reduce their water content. If you are using canned tomatoes, cook for around 20 minutes. Return the eggplants to the pan, stir and season to taste. Serve this dish either as a *contorno* (side dish), with pasta, or as a vegetarian main course.

Variation: Add some chopped provola and some grated Parmesan and keep stirring over the heat to melt the cheeses into the sauce.

Panzanella di Livia
Livia's Bread and Onion Salad

This is an old recipe, doubtless invented as a way of making a meal out of stale bread, a few herbs and not much else. However, as the wealth of the population increased over the years, more ingredients were added to this recipe, such as chopped cucumber, tomato, radishes, or celery. Our friend Livia still uses up her bread in this way. You may have to experiment with different loaves of bread because not all varieties work; some do not bounce back to life and instead remain doughy. Tropea onions are sweeter than the normal red onions but, if you cannot get them, use ordinary red onions or scallions instead. Try to use the best vinegar you can find.

Serves 4

½ loaf of day-old Tuscan bread, 1 lb dry weight
1 small red Tropea onion, finely chopped
a handful of basil leaves, coarsely torn, plus extra for garnish
2 beefsteak tomatoes, coarsely chopped
3–5 tablespoons red or white wine vinegar
5–7 tablespoons extra virgin olive oil
salt and freshly ground black pepper

Break the bread into chunks and soak in water for 10–15 minutes. Meanwhile, chop and tear the onion, basil, and tomatoes and mix them in a large bowl with your hands. Add the vinegar to the oil in a small bowl and add seasoning to taste. Start with 3 tablespoons of vinegar and 7 tablespoons of oil; the amount you need depends on the absorbency of the bread.

Squeeze the water from the bread so that the bread is moist and bouncy. Combine it with the other ingredients in the bowl, tossing gently to mix, using your hands. Be gentle, otherwise the bread will break up too much. Taste and add more vinegar and oil as necessary, especially if all the liquid has been absorbed by the bread. Serve in a big bowl with more basil leaves torn on top.

Insalata di Giorgio
Giorgio's Salad

This is one for the children that the adults will enjoy too. A mixed salad can mean many things in Italy, from an elaborate and colorful but slightly common bowl of various ingredients to a simple mix of tomatoes and lettuce, to a very bitter combination of radicchio and chicory leaves. My children love the grated carrot and sweet corn and I end up digging my fork in too. It always amuses us that sweetcorn is called *mais* in Italian which sounds like "mice"—I make my own version of "mice salad" at home to encourage the kids to eat salad. In fact, Giorgio can now make it himself.

Serves 4

1 baby gem lettuce
6 oz cherry tomatoes, cut into
   quarters
5 tablespoons sweet corn
a small handful of parsley,
   coarsely chopped
½ green chile or ¼ red,
   thinly sliced
2 tablespoons extra virgin
   olive oil
1–2 tablespoons red wine vinegar
salt and pepper

Cut the core from the lettuce and arrange the leaves curling upwards on a large serving platter. Put the rest of the ingredients in a bowl and add salt and pepper to taste. Spoon the mixture into the salad leaves and serve.

Variations: Add chopped avocado and a tablespoon of lemon juice to the dressing.

Add 2 teaspoons finely chopped red onion, 1 tablespoon of coarsely torn basil leaves, or 1 grated carrot.

Instead of the corn, add a small, fresh ball of mozzarella, cut into cubes.

Insalata di arance rosse
Blood Orange Salad

This was the second treat I enjoyed at the hidden Jewish restaurant in Rome (see Deep-fried Artichokes, page 377). When something is simple and delicious why complicate it with other flavors? Use the best-quality extra virgin olive oil and olives you can find. I have made this salad with ordinary oranges, too, and it still works, but blood oranges are prettier.

Serves 4

3 blood oranges, peeled and sliced into ½ in-thick slices
1½ tablespoons extra virgin olive oil
12 black olives, pitted if desired
freshly ground black pepper

Lay the oranges on a plate, drizzle with the olive oil and grind some black pepper on top. Scatter the olives on top and serve.

Fagiolini con aceto
Greens Beans in Red Wine Vinegar

Italians cook their vegetables for longer than we do. Although the trend may be changing in more modern restaurants, it is happening slowly, as Italians prefer their vegetables well cooked. I have gotten used to this and actually love the flavor and texture of soft beans. This recipe is for summer, when the beans are in season. They are marinated in vinegar then served at room temperature—good with roast meats or a barbecue.

Serves 4

8 oz long green beans or runner beans
2 tablespoons red wine vinegar, to taste
3 tablespoons extra virgin olive oil
1 garlic clove, finely sliced
salt and freshly ground black pepper

Boil the beans in plenty of salted water for 5–8 minutes, until cooked. Drain and, while still hot, toss with the red wine vinegar, olive oil, garlic, salt and pepper. Adjust the seasoning and vinegar to taste. Leave for up to 2 hours, for the flavors to develop. Serve at room temperature.

Verza con pancetta e porri
Cabbage with Pancetta and Leeks

A great way to use this healthy vegetable—it can turn fussy eaters into cabbage lovers!

6 tablespoons olive oil
1 medium red onion, finely chopped
6 slices of pancetta or 3 slices of Canadian bacon, finely chopped
1 Savoy cabbage, finely shredded
salt and freshly ground black pepper
2 tablespoons butter (optional)

Heat the oil in a large frying pan and cook the onion until it is soft and clear. Add the pancetta and cook until lightly browned. Then toss in the cabbage, and salt and pepper, and stir well. Keep stirring until the cabbage is cooked: about 5–10 minutes, depending on the size of your pan. Add butter, if desired, and serve.

Carciofi alla Gino
Gino's Artichoke and Fava Bean Salad

This was one of the first dishes Gino Borella made for me. This way of cooking globe artichokes makes them wonderfully soft and tender. Small young artichokes are best for this: Violetto, Catanese, or Romanesco are good choices.

Serves 6

12 small artichokes (about 4½ lb, untrimmed)
½ lemon
½ bunch flat-leaf parsley
2 anchovy fillets
2 garlic cloves
⅓ cup dry white wine
⅓ cup extra virgin olive oil
¾ cup water
12 oz new potatoes, peeled or unpeeled
12 oz shelled fava beans

Pull off the tough outer leaves from the artichokes and trim the tops from the artichokes so they are about half their original length. Prepare as in the masterclass on page 378.

Chop the parsley, anchovies and garlic together and put them into a bowl. Pour in the wine and oil and mix together.

Dip the artichokes into this mixture and put them face down and stems up into a large saucepan or flameproof casserole. Add the potatoes and fava beans. Pour the rest of the parsley mixture over the top and rinse out the bowl using the water, and pour this into the pan too. Cover the surface of the vegetables with a piece of parchment paper or aluminium foil, to trap the steam in.

Put the lid on the pan and steam over medium heat, shaking the pan regularly, for between 45 minutes and 1½ hours, depending on the toughness of the artichokes. If the water has steamed away before the artichokes are cooked, add a little extra.

Serve hot, or at room temperature as a salad.

tartufo

TRUFFLES

My first encounter with a truffle was in Alba, late one night, in a small guest house. The owner had waited up for us and asked if we were hungry. Though all I wanted was my bed, when I discovered he was offering fresh *tagliolini* with butter and white truffle, I thought better of it. Sitting at a wooden table, drinking the local Barolo and tasting this delicacy, was a sublime moment I will never forget.

The flavor and aroma of truffles is like nothing else on earth; something happens between smelling and tasting, evoking a sexiness and seductiveness that is almost impossible to explain. To suggest dank, musky woods does little to describe the overwhelming feeling that, once tasted, you want more! The cost makes them all the more alluring.

What are they? Truffles are tubers but are related to mushrooms. They are *hypogenous fungi*, which means they grow fully underground and never emerge on the surface. They grow only in certain soils, close to trees such as willow, poplar, oak, chestnut, and pine, on a *mycelium*, which is a cobweb of filaments between tree roots. The truffles grow in symbiosis with the roots, acting as a filter for the water and, in turn, benefiting from nutrients from the tree. The type of tree and soil determine the flavor and aroma of the truffle, and experts can even determine which kind of tree, by the markings on the outside of the truffle.

White and Black Truffle Pasta

Perigord

Tuber albidum (Borchii)

Tuber aestivum (Scorzone)

Where and when to find truffles

The main areas for truffle production are Umbria, Piemonte, and Molise but there is also an area in Le Marche and Tuscany where truffles are harvested; and odd ones grow all over the country. Truffles are harvested or "hunted" all year round but the most famous white truffle, *tartufo bianco* (*Tuber magnatum* Pico) can be harvested for only 16 weeks from September to December.

Our friend Bruno Giorgi (see portrait), has been supplying our restaurants for years and, like all hunters, never reveals the good hunting grounds. Truffle hunters, *trifolau*, look for truffles mainly with the aid of dogs; pigs were once used but they tended to eat the truffles! Dogs, on the other hand, can be trained more easily. A truffle hound can be worth a fortune and there have been cases of other hunters stealing and poisoning dogs.

I went truffle hunting in Alba and it was exciting to see the dog following the scent and then stopping to dig furiously. With one command from his owner, the dog left the area and the hunter scraped the earth carefully to reveal the first black truffle. He gave the smaller ones to me, keeping the large ones to sell, and I shaved them over my pasta that evening.

VARIETIES

There are two main groups of truffles—white and black—which comprise various species, of which there are 17 edible ones that can be found in Italy. The main competitor is France, which produces the famous black Perigord truffle.

The white truffle

Tuber magnatum Pico, the white truffle, is rarer than the black truffle and both its flavor and aroma are more pungent and refined, which is why it is called "the king of truffles." It is also a much more expensive truffle due to its small production. Very rarely, a white truffle can reach more than 2¼ lb in weight, though they are usually much smaller than this. Their flesh is pale cream or brown with white marbling. This truffle is never cooked —it is only served fresh, shaved over warm or cold dishes. There are two main species of white truffle: *Tuber magnatum* Pico, and *Tuber albidum* (Borchii), the spring white truffle, which is less expensive.

The Black truffle

The black truffle or *tartufo nero* is more common than the white truffle and less aromatic and flavorful. Their size varies from around ¾ oz to 4 oz and they can be found throughout a longer period of the year. There are two main varieties: the black summer truffle, *Tuber aestivum* (Vitt.) is harvested between June and September; and of the winter truffles, *Tuber uncinatum* (A. D. Chatin) is harvested from September to mid-late December and *Tuber melanosporum* (Vitt.) from early December through to early March. The latter is the variety known in France as the Périgord truffle. Summer truffles have a less strong aroma and taste than winter truffles. As black truffles are less delicate than white, they can be used in cooking, so you will find them not only shaved raw but also in sauces and other dishes. You'll also find them preserved in jars, though I would seldom recommend them in this form.

Dolci

CHAPTER 10: DESSERTS

Dolci

INTRODUCTION

La passeggiata is still an important part of life in Italy. I love this tradition of dressing up after dinner at home and going out for "the stroll," inevitably finishing up at the *gelateria* to eat ice cream, have a drink and socialize—it seems so much healthier and better for the digestive system to get up and move after dinner. Lucky Italians, with their warmer climate—perhaps if we could be more certain of warm summer evenings, we might do the same.

talians are very fussy about their ice cream and everyone is a connoisseur. They will always have a favorite *gelateria* and an opinion as to why the ice cream that is served there is the best. Even though very few places make their own from scratch these days, as there are really good and quite gorgeous pastes made from fruit and nuts, such as pistachio and hazelnut, which save you grinding your own—these are added to your own recipe based on cream and eggs, so there is still plenty of scope for variation.

Because *la passeggiata* is so ingrained in Italian culture, most families don't go in for making elaborate desserts. If you are staying at home, you are more likely to finish a meal with just fresh fruit, or perhaps a *crostata*, a jam tart. In Tuscany, the trimmings of pastry are rolled into strips to make a lattice on top. Or there might be bottled fruits, such as cherries picked in season and preserved in alcohol. If you want a special dessert on a Sunday or for a special meal, you are more likely to buy one from the local *pasticceria*. A slight exception is in Naples and Sicily, where there is a bigger tradition of desserts, often combining the local speciality of candied fruits and nuts (a legacy of Arab rule in the 9th century) with ricotta.

In Tuscany, however, as I discovered while I was researching desserts with Giancarlo's family, most of the recipes seem to be a variation on a layer cake—and are often the kind of desserts that were all the rage in the UK in the seventies. There was a very funny moment when Giancarlo and I were filming "Return to Tuscany" for the BBC a few years ago. His Aunt Gina described a special dessert she made with plums from the garden and it sounded very exciting; it was only halfway through filming that I realized what she was making was a plum version of that seventies classic, pineapple upside-down cake!

However, just because they don't have a massive repertoire of homemade desserts doesn't mean Italians don't have a sweet tooth—it is just that they prefer their sugar (and caffeine) hit first thing in the morning, whereas we tend towards a savory breakfast, which is abhorrent to most Italians. Instead they will have cappuccino and a jammy pastry or a custard-filled doughnut.

There are also thousands of traditional cakes and cookies, usually made with nuts, such as almonds and hazelnuts (as in the famous amaretti), to slightly different recipes all around Italy. In Tuscany, the local *Cantucci*, made with almonds, are meant to be dipped into the famous sweet wine of the region, *Vin Santo*. Honey, the sweetener used by the Romans and for many centuries afterwards until sugar arrived from the East, is another key ingredient in cookie-making.

Although I would hate to offend the Italians, I often find their biscotti quite dry and plain, but wherever you travel, the locals seem to have an emotional bond with whatever crumbly little bite is traditional in their village or town, and they will insist on you trying them. Often the local *pasticceria* will present them as a gift on a shiny gold tray for you to take to someone's house when you are invited for dinner. The problem with following this custom is that, after a mammoth meal of the most delicious food, you will invariably be expected to finish up with a glass of homemade liqueur and several of the cookies you kindly brought with you. "No" will not be accepted as an answer.

Often special cakes and biscuits are associated with Saints' days, festivals and special occasions, such as *carnevale* in Venice—though, as I mentioned, these are more likely to be bought than made at home and are rarely eaten after a meal but more likely with a coffee during the day. At Christmas, both panettone, the light, domed spiced cake and *panforte*, the spiced gooey cake from Siena, fill the shops—again, they are better made by professional bakeries, which is why I haven't included recipes for them. In the north, close to the Austrian border, you find more of a tradition of pastries, often served in the Viennese-style coffee shops that first became fashionable in this part of Italy in the 1700s. This was the time when the influence of Austrian pastry chefs, followed by the French, first began to knock their Italian counterparts off the pedestal they had enjoyed throughout the kitchens of Europe.

Sicily is also widely regarded by pastry chefs over the world as one of the best places to eat patisserie, on par with Austria and France. Particularly in the capital of Palermo, the shops are crammed with desserts such as *cassata*, ice creams, and cakes, gaudily decorated with the local speciality of candied fruits.

Pasta Genovese
Genoese Sponge

Pasta Genovese is a very light sponge used for cakes, roulades, *cassata*, as a base for mousse, or on its own. In this method of making a sponge, the eggs are whisked whole rather than separated. The cake can be cut into discs and layered with *crema pasticerra* (pastry cream) and fruit. This recipe contains butter to make it moist—this can be omitted for a chewier result. The butter-free version is sometimes used for a *rotolo* (roulade), as it is quite flexible.

Makes a 10-inch cake. Serves 6–8, depending on how greedy you are!

⅔ cup sugar
4 eggs plus 1 egg yolk
seeds from 1 vanilla bean, or a capful of vanilla extract
zest of 1 orange and/or 1 lemon
1¼ cups "00" flour or all-purpose flour
4 tablespoons butter

Preheat the oven to 350°F. Grease and flour a 10-inch deep-sided spring-form cake pan. When the oven is hot, place the sugar on a baking sheet lined with parchment paper and heat in the oven for 5 minutes.

Whisk the eggs and egg yolk in a large bowl with an electric mixer, for 1 minute. Pour in the warm sugar and continue to whisk, adding the vanilla seeds and orange zest, until it leaves a ribbon trail on the surface. To check you've whisked enough, turn off the mixer and lift the beaters from the mix, making a circle with the beaters over the bowl; you should be able to see a line of the mixture sitting on the surface before sinking in. If there is no trail, continue to whisk. When it is ready, gently fold in the sifted flour. Melt the butter in a small pan and, when it is just melted, mix in with the rest of the ingredients. Pour the mixture into the prepared pan and smooth the top with a spatula.

Transfer to the oven and cook for 25–30 minutes or until golden brown and a skewer inserted into the centre comes out clean. When cooked, allow the cake to cool for at least 10 minutes, then remove from the tin by loosening it around the edges with a sharp knife before undoing the spring-form mechanism. If it doesn't come away easily from the base, slide a sharp knife underneath the cake. Leave to cool on a wire rack.

Drizzle the sponge with a liqueur of your choice such as Grand Marnier—we used the bright red Alchermes. Spread *crema pasticerra* in the middle and around the edges. Press on some chopped pistachios and dust with confectioners' sugar.

Torta di yogurt con mele e rosmarino
Rosemary and Apple Yogurt Cake

This was something my friend Livia showed me on one of our courses in Tuscany. I think it is widely known, because she found it in a magazine. However, after years of making it on her little farm in Tuscany, she showed me her Italian twist on the original, using her home-grown apples and rosemary.

Makes a 9 inch cake

butter or oil, for greasing
8 oz natural plain yogurt
2 eggs
1¼ cups sugar
⅓ cup sunflower or seed oil
2½ cups "00" or plain (all-purpose) flour
1 level tablespoon baking powder
1 tablespoon chopped rosemary
2 large or 3 small apples, peeled and sliced

Preheat the oven to 350°F. Grease a loose-bottomed 9-inch cake pan with sides about 2½ inches deep.

Whisk together the yogurt, eggs, sugar, and oil in a medium mixing bowl. Add the flour, baking powder and chopped rosemary, folding it in with a large metal spoon. Fold in the apples, then spoon the mixture into the pan. Cook for 40–50 minutes or until the top is golden and a skewer inserted into the center of the cake comes out clean.

Torta di arance e polenta
Orange and Polenta Cake

Polenta is usually cooked and served with savoury dishes but it can also be used to give a wonderful crunch to sweet recipes such as cookies or—in this instance—a cake.

Serves 8–10

1 cup unsalted butter
1¼ cups sugar
3 large free-range eggs
1 cup finely ground polenta
1 cup ground almonds
2 teaspoons baking powder
zest of 2 oranges

FOR THE ORANGE GLAZE
juice of 2 oranges
superfine sugar as necessary

Preheat the oven to 350°F. Whip the butter and sugar together until light and fluffy. Add the eggs, one at a time, and mix thoroughly. Once the mixture is combined, add all the dry ingredients and the zest.

Line the bottom and sides of a 10½ inch cake pan with parchment paper. Spoon the mixture into the pan, spread evenly and cook for about 35 minutes or until a skewer inserted into the center of the cake comes out clean. Remove from the oven and turn out onto a wire rack to cool.

To make the glaze, measure the juice and pour into a saucepan. Add the same weight of sugar to the pan and bring to a boil. Let it simmer for 5 minutes, then remove from the heat and allow to cool. Drizzle the orange glaze over the top. Serve with vanilla ice cream, crème fraîche, or mascarpone.

Torta Caprese
Chocolate and Almond Cake

This cake originates from the small town of Salerno, south of Naples. It is dense and delicious, and not difficult to make. It can be served as a dessert with ice cream, crème fraîche, or whipped cream or, for an unusual combination, cut into squares and served with a shot glass of Red Wine Jelly (see page 461).

Serves 8

8 oz dark (bittersweet) chocolate, minimum
  70 percent cocoa solids, broken into squares
8 tablespoons butter
4 eggs, separated
1¼ cups confectioners' sugar
1 cup ground almonds

Preheat the oven to 350°F. Grease a loose-bottomed 9-inch cake pan.

Melt the chocolate and butter in a heatproof bowl over a pan of barely simmering water (or in a microwave), taking care not to burn the chocolate.

Whisk the egg yolks and sugar together until light and fluffy. In a separate bowl, whisk the egg whites until they form soft peaks.

Add the melted chocolate and butter to the egg yolks and combine thoroughly. Mix in the ground almonds. Fold in the egg whites using either a whisk or a spatula. Mix well, then pour into the prepared cake pan. Transfer to the oven and bake for 25–30 minutes. The cake is done when it forms a crust on the outside. Don't expect an inserted skewer to come out clean because the center always remains moist. Serve at room temperature.

Budino di panettone
Panettone Pudding

Every Christmas we are given countless panettone and it is usually midsummer before they are used up! This is a very easy way to turn them into a rich, spicy pudding.

Serves 8–12

1 large panettone (2 lb), cut into
  2-inch thick slices
2 cups heavy cream
2 cups whole milk
2 vanilla beans, slit lengthwise, seeds scraped out
6 egg yolks
4 whole eggs
1 cup sugar

Preheat the oven to 300°F.

Place the panettone slices in a large baking dish, slightly overlapping if necessary (or cut the slices into triangles and lay them one on top of another). Pour the cream, milk, and vanilla—seeds and pods—into a saucepan and heat gently.

Add the whole eggs to the 6 yolks; add the sugar and mix well. Once the milk and cream mixture has heated through (do not allow it to boil), whisk it into the eggs. Remove the vanilla pods and pour the hot custard evenly over the panettone slices. Leave to soak for about 10 minutes, then place in the oven for 30 minutes or until the top is golden brown and the custard has set. Remove from the oven and allow to cool to room temperature. The pudding can be served as it is, chilled, or reheated in a microwave or oven.

Torta di ciliegie della Francesca
Francesca's Cherry Cake

This is another easy cake recipe made by our chef Monserrato's mother, Francesca, throughout the year, using different fruits of the season. Monserrato's favorite is one with cherries in *grappa*. I have used my own cherries in brandy instead and it's lovely—and even more delicious when matched with the reduced syrup from Cherries in Brandy (see page 484) poured over the top and served with a dollop of mascarpone.

(see page 484)

Makes a 10-inch cake/Serves 8

1 cup unsalted butter at room temperature, plus
  extra for greasing
1 x 15 oz can or jar cherries in syrup or liqueur
1¾ cups flour
2 heaping teaspoons baking powder
seeds from 1 vanilla bean
4 eggs, separated
1 cup sugar, plus extra for the syrup
  (about 1 cup)
finely grated zest of 1 lemon

Preheat the oven to 350°F. Grease a 10-inch springform cake pan and and line the bottom with a circle of parchment paper. Drain the cherries from their syrup or liqueur and reserve the liquid for the sauce. Pit the cherries and set aside.

Mix the flour with the baking powder and the seeds from the vanilla beans. Mix the egg yolks with the sugar briefly, then add the butter and lemon zest and beat together well with a wooden spoon. Whisk the egg whites until they are really thick, then gently fold into the egg mixture.

Next fold in the flour a little at a time. When it has all been incorporated, pour the mixture into the pan, then push in half the cherries, distributing them evenly in concentric circles over the cake. Transfer to the oven and bake for 20–30 minutes or until a wooden skewer inserted into the center comes out clean.

Measure the reserved cherry liquid—you will probably have about ¾ cup. Put the liquid and sugar into a small saucepan and bring to a boil. Reduce the heat and let it simmer for 10 minutes or so, until it starts to thicken. To test the syrup for density, remove the pan from the heat, pour a teaspoon of syrup on to a cold saucer and place in the fridge. After a couple of minutes, it will set and indicate how thick the syrup will be when cool. If it is too thick, add a little hot water to the pan off the heat and then bring to a boil again; if it is too runny, simmer for a little longer and repeat the saucer test. When you are happy with the consistency, allow the syrup to cool completely and serve it poured over the slices of cake.

Spongata
Nut tart with Honey and Mustard Fruits

This weird nut tart, a speciality of Parma, was introduced to me by Stefano Borella, whose family originates from the city. The use of *mostarda di frutta* (fruits preserved in mustard syrup) gives this sweet tart a spicy edge. It can be made in advance and is best served warm, with mascarpone or ice cream.

Makes a 10 inch tart/ Serves 8

FOR THE PASTRY (*PASTA FROLLA*)
8 tablespoons unsalted butter,
  at room temperature
½ cup sugar
1¾ cups all-purpose flour,
  sifted
2 egg yolks
seeds from 1 vanilla bean
grated zest of ½ lemon

FOR THE FILLING
1 cup walnuts, chopped
¾ cup ground almonds
¾ cup golden raisins
4 oz *mostarda di frutta*,
  chopped
⅓ cup sugar
6 tablespoons honey
1½ tablespoons butter
⅓ cup apricot jam
grated zest of 1 orange

Preheat the oven to 350°F. Grease a 9–10 inch tart pan with a removable bottom.

To make the pastry, combine the butter, sugar, and flour in a bowl and mix until well combined. Fold in the egg yolks, vanilla seeds, and lemon zest, and combine to form a dough. Wrap in plastic wrap and chill for at least 20 minutes, or preferably overnight.

To make the filling, combine all the ingredients in a mixing bowl.

Remove the pastry from the fridge and roll out on a lightly floured surface to prevent the pastry from sticking. Use it to line the tart tin, trimming off the excess.

Pour the filling into the pastry case and use the trimmings to make a lattice pattern over the tart. Bake for 40 minutes or until golden brown. Remove from the oven and allow to cool to room temperature before you cut it.

Tip: It is always better not to use the fan (convection) setting in your oven for pastries and cakes, as it will sometimes dry them out.

Torta contadina
Franca's Pear Cake

Franca is a very good friend of ours and a great cook. This is a cake she makes regularly at home. It's quick, easy, and delicious. She changes the flavor frequently according to the seasons, using fruits such as apricots or apples, or replacing the fruit with chocolate chips and walnuts.

Serves 8

1¾ cups "00" pasta flour or all-purpose flour

4 tablespoons baking powder

1 cup sugar

3 whole eggs

1 vanilla bean, slit lengthwise and seeds scraped out

zest of 1 lemon

½ cup whole milk

¾ cup raisins (optional)

½ cup pine nuts (optional)

8 tablespoons butter, at room temperature

2 pears, peeled, cored, and cut into eighths

½ cup semi-sweet chocolate morsels (optional)

Prepare a 10 inch cake pan with parchment paper by making a cartouche. Preheat the oven to 350°F.

Use a whisk to mix the flour, baking powder, sugar, eggs, vanilla, and lemon zest. Stir in the milk and mix until smooth. Use a spoon to stir in the pine nuts and raisins, if using. Stir well to combine. Tear the butter into small pieces and whisk them in.

Pour the mixture into the prepared pan and scatter or arrange (depending on whether you are going for the rustic or neat look!) the pears over the cake. Push the fruit into the mixture a little. Transfer the tin to the oven and bake for 20–30 minutes.

Tip: This cake is much better mixed by hand rather than with an electric mixer. The small lumps of butter left in the mixture melt, leaving holes that keep the cake light yet moist and buttery.

Babá
Rum baba

In Italy, Naples is the home of *babá* (small yeast cakes). In this recipe, the *babá* are flavored with rum but sometimes they are made in a miniature form, soaked in *limoncello*, and sold from jars on bar counters. Apparently, *babá* were so called by the exiled King of Poland, Stanislas Leczinsky, after his favorite story, Ali Baba, in *The Arabian Nights*.

Serves 8

3 x ¼ oz envelopes yeast
2 tablespoons tepid water
2 cups bread flour
2 tablespoons sugar
4 eggs
8 tablespoons butter, melted

FOR THE SOAKING SYRUP
2 cups water
2 cups rum
2 cups sugar

Preheat the oven to 350ºF. Dissolve the yeast in the water. Mix the flour, a pinch of salt, and sugar together in a bowl and add the yeast and water to the dry ingredients. Add the eggs and mix with an electric mixer (or use a food processor). Add the melted butter and keep beating for about 5 minutes, until smooth. Grease and flour eight dariole molds and put a little circle of parchment paper in the bottom of each. Pour the dough into the dariole molds and leave to rise until they have doubled in size; they should also spring back when touched. This will take between 30 minutes and 1 hour.

Bake for 20–25 minutes, or until golden brown, well risen and cooked through. Loosen the *babá* with a knife and turn them onto a cooling rack. They can be frozen at this point and soaked at another time.

In a pan, bring the syrup ingredients to a boil, then remove from the heat. Pour the syrup into a suitable container to fit all the *babá*. Leave them soaking in the liquid until ready to serve. Serve them with *crema pasticcera* (see page 424) and some preserved fruits in alcohol, such as cherries or apricots (see page 484).

Tempering Chocolate

It does take years to learn to do this properly—but at least if you get some experience, your resulting chocolate work will look better. There are types of bakers' chocolate available with added lecithin that make this process easier, but the flavor is not as good. All good quality chocolate is tempered in order to make it into a bar or block. In order to work with chocolate, you need to melt it, which un-tempers it. Therefore it needs to be re-tempered, which is the crystallization of the fats.

Make sure the bowl you use is completely dry and scrupulously clean, as chocolate must not come into contact with water. Heat the chocolate to roughly 100–115°F in the microwave or over a bain marie, making sure you don't burn it. If you don't have a thermometer, take it out a little before it is completely melted and stir to dissolve the remaining lumps. Overheating it will result in grainy chocolate. If you are using a bain-marie, as soon as the water comes to a boil, take it off the heat, then put the bowl containing the chocolate on top. Ensure that no steam comes up around the edge of the bowl.

Cool it down, stirring frequently, and leave it to cool to 82–86°F. It will change consistency slightly and start to thicken.

To check whether it is tempered, brush a little chocolate on to a piece of parchment paper. It should set within 5 minutes at room temperature and be glossy and even. If you look carefully at the surface, there should be no oily streaks. When it has reached the tempering stage, use it right away or reheat it momentarily to 88–90°F, to make it easier to work with. (Experienced pastry chefs test to see if it is ready by dabbing a little on their lower lip to test the temperature.) You can reheat chocolate up to four or five times; after that, it will deteriorate, but can still be used for a sauce or ganache.

MASTERCLASS

How To Make Chocolate Leaves

Select some perfect bay leaves and polish them with a piece of flannel or cotton: they must be completely dry. Brush each leaf with a coating of chocolate until it is well covered: it should be about 1mm thick.

Leave them to set at room temperature: this should take up to 5 minutes. When the chocolate has set, put the leaves in the fridge for 5–10 minutes. Carefully peel the leaves away from the chocolate and use them right away or store them in a cool place or in the fridge for a couple of days.

How To Pipe Chocolate

The chocolate should be tempered and cooled to 82–86°F. Use a plastic pastry bag or make your own from parchment paper. Fill the bag and fold over the edges to keep the chocolate inside.

Cut off the very tip of the bag, using scissors, then pipe swirls of melted chocolate onto the parchment paper and leave to set.

Crostata al cioccolato
Chocolate Tart

This is our supreme chocolate experience that we serve at our restaurant, Caldesi in Campagna, in Bray. It has undergone many changes along the way and we are now more than happy with the result—and so are our customers!

Serves 10

FOR THE PASTRY

6 tablespoons butter
1 cup "00" flour or all-purpose flour
½ cup confectioners' sugar
¼ cup unsweetened cocoa powder
1 egg

FOR THE CHOCOLATE FILLING

14 oz good-quality bittersweet chocolate, at least 70 percent cocoa solids
8 tablespoons butter
2 eggs
2 egg yolks
½ cup sugar

Preheat the oven to 325°F. Grease and flour a 9½ inch loose-bottomed tart pan.

To make the pastry, soften the butter, sift together the dry ingredients and mix in the butter, followed by the egg yolk and combine to form a dough. Leave to rest for 20 minutes. Roll out the pastry, line the prepared tin, then cover with a sheet of parchment paper and fill with baking beans or rice. Bake blind for 10–12 minutes. Remove from the oven, take out the beans and paper and return to the oven for 2 minutes. Remove the pastry from the oven and allow to cool. Meanwhile, make the filling.

Melt the chocolate with the butter in the microwave or in a heatproof bowl set over a pan of barely simmering water on the stove. As soon as they have melted, remove from the heat and leave to cool. Beat the eggs with the sugar in a mixing bowl, then mix with the cooled mixture.

Pour the filling into the pastry shell and bake for another 10–12 minutes (preferably without the convection fan). Leave to cool. Serve at room temperature or slightly warm, with mascarpone.

Dolci
MASTERCLASS

How To Make Curls

Using an offset spatula knife, spread melted chocolate onto a cool, dry surface to about 1mm thick. It should be around 8 inches wide and 4 inches in length. Try to achieve a smooth surface with a few sweeps of the spatula, without going backwards and forwards too many times as this will untemper the chocolate.

As soon as the chocolate starts to set, use a metal scraper or large chef's knife to push away ½ inch widths of chocolate. They will curl up and can be used as they are, or broken into smaller pieces.

To make shavings, follow the instructions for curls but firstly, as soon as the chocolate starts to set, score small squares into it.

Use the blade of the knife to scrape up the chocolate from the surface.

Torta della nonna
Grandmother's Pine nut and Custard Tart

This is a classic Italian dessert that graces most patisserie shop windows over Italy and one that is also made a great deal at home. Mention *torta della nonna* to Italians abroad and they go misty-eyed, as it reminds them of home.

Makes a 10 inch tart / Serves 8

1 quantity of Pastry (see page 426)

FOR THE CREMA PASTICCERA
2 cups whole milk
1 vanilla bean, split in half
1 long strip of orange or lemon rind
3 medium egg yolks
½ cup sugar
½ cup cornstarch
¼ cup Cointreau, Marsala, Strega, or Grand Marnier (optional)

TO DECORATE
¾ cup pinenuts
1 level tablespoon confectioners' sugar

Preheat the oven to 350°F. Grease a 10 inch loose-based tart pan with butter and dust with flour, tapping out the excess.

Make the pastry in a food processor, or by hand, following the method on page 426. Ideally, chill the pastry for 20 minutes in the fridge but, if time is short, roll it out between two layers of parchment paper or plastic wrap.

While the pastry rests, make the *crema pasticcera*. Put the milk in a saucepan with the vanilla bean and lemon rind over low heat. Mix together the egg yolks, sugar, and cornstarch in a bowl, using a wooden spoon. When the milk reaches a boil, remove the pan from the heat and add half the milk, a ladleful at a time, to the cornstarch mixture, stirring constantly. Pour the mixture back into the rest of the milk in the saucepan. Return to the heat for a few minutes, to thicken, still stirring.

Remove from the heat, stir in the liqueur, if using, transfer the mixture to a cold bowl and cover the surface with plastic wrap or damp parchment paper, to prevent a skin from forming. Allow it to cool with the vanilla bean still inside.

Roll out the pastry to a thickness of ¼ inch and use it to line the tart pan. If it cracks, use some leftover pastry to patch it—the result will be fine. Prick the bottom all over with a fork.

Pour in the cooled custard, discarding the vanilla bean and orange rind. Top with the pine nuts, packing them in to completely cover the surface. Sift the confectioners' sugar through a sieve or tea strainer over the top of the filling and bake for 25–30 minutes or until the pine nuts are beginning to brown and the pastry is cooked.

Remove from the oven and allow to cool before serving.

Torta del nonno
Grandfather's Chocolate Tart with Toasted Almonds

On an autumnal morning in Tuscany, this chocolate tart cries out to be eaten with a frothy cappuccino. The difference between this and its partner, *torta della nonna* (see previous page), is the filling of chocolate cream and toasted almonds, rather than pine nuts. The chocolate *crema pasticcera* also makes a great filling for doughnuts, cakes, or *zuppa inglese*, the Italian equivalent of trifle.

1 quantity of Pastry (see page 426):

FOR THE CHOCOLATE CREMA PASTICCERA
2 cups whole milk
3 egg yolks
½ cup sugar
¼ cup cornstarch
9 oz good-quality bittersweet chocolate, minimum 70 percent cocoa solids, grated or in drops

TO DECORATE
¾ cup sliced almonds
1 level tablespoon confectioners' sugar

Preheat the oven to 350°F. Grease a 10 inch loose-bottomed tart pan with butter and dust with flour, tapping out the excess.

Make the pastry, following the method on page 426. Ideally, chill the pastry for 20 minutes in the fridge while you make the filling.

While the pastry rests, make the *crema*. Put the milk in a saucepan over low heat. Mix together the egg yolks, sugar, and cornstarch in a bowl, using a wooden spoon. When the milk reaches a boil, remove from the heat and add a ladleful at a time to the cornstarch mixture, stirring constantly, until half of it has been incorporated. Pour the mixture back into the rest of the milk in the saucepan and add the chocolate. Return to the heat for a few minutes, to thicken the custard and melt the chocolate, still stirring. Remove from the heat, transfer the custard to a cold bowl and cover the surface with plastic wrap or damp parchment paper, to prevent a skin from forming.

Roll out the pastry to a thickness of ¼ inch and use it to line the tart pan. If it cracks, use some leftover pastry to patch it. Prick the bottom all over with a fork. Pour in the cooled custard. Top with the almonds, packing them in to completely cover the surface. Sift the confectioners' sugar through a sieve or tea strainer over the top of the filling and bake for 25–30 minutes, or until the almonds are beginning to brown and the pastry is cooked. Remove from the oven and allow to cool.

Crostatine di crema pasticcera
Berry Custard Tarts

What is better than picking your own fruit to cook with? These little custard tarts can be topped with any seasonal fruit. Our favorites are raspberries and blackberries together. In our house, I make the pastry, Giancarlo makes the custard and the children decorate the tarts. This Italian pastry is more interesting than an English shortcrust because it has the flavors of citrus zest and vanilla.

Makes a 10 inch tart or 4 x 4 inch individual tarts

Preheat the oven to 350°F. Grease a 10 inch fluted tart pan with a removable bottom.

Put the butter, flour, zest, and vanilla into a large bowl and rub together until you achieve a consistency of fine breadcrumbs. Keep your hands above the bowl, letting the crumbs fall, to aerate the mixture.

Add the egg and sugar, using your hands to mix and form a firm dough—simply squeeze the ingredients through your fingers until well blended. If the dough is a little dry, add a tablespoon of milk and blend well. You will only need this if the egg is small or the flour very absorbent. Ideally, chill the pastry for 20 minutes in the fridge but, if time is short, you can roll it out between two layers of parchment paper or plastic wrap. If it cracks, you can patch it up using trimmings from the pastry; the result will be fine.

Roll out the pastry to a thickness of ¼ inch and use it to line the tart tin. Prick the base all over with a fork. Transfer to the oven and bake for 20 minutes, or until it is a light golden color. Remove from the oven and allow to cool.

Meanwhile, make the custard. Put the milk in a saucepan with the vanilla seeds and pod and bring it to a gentle boil. Using an electric mixer, mix together the egg yolks, sugar, and cornstarch in a bowl, until pale and fluffy. When the milk is boiling, remove the pan from the heat and add half the milk, a ladleful at a time, to the cornstarch mixture, until it has been well incorporated. Pour the mixture back into the rest of the milk in the saucepan. Return to the heat for just a few minutes to thicken, stirring constantly. Remove from the heat and transfer the custard to a cold bowl. Cover the surface of the custard with plastic wrap to prevent a skin from forming. Allow to cool without removing the vanilla pod.

When cool discard the vanilla pod and fold in the cream. Fill the pastry shell with the cooled custard. Top with fresh fruits to decorate. You can go for a random look and pile the fruits on top or, starting from the outside, push in the individual berries to form concentric circles in alternating colors. For a really professional finish, brush the fruits with apricot glaze or jam (after warming it gently, to make it runny).

FOR THE PASTRY (MAKES 2¼ CUPS)

8 tablespoons unsalted butter at room temperature, plus extra for greasing (or use ½ butter and ½ lard)

1¼ cups "00" all-purpose flour, plus extra for dredging

2 teaspoons grated zest from 1 orange and/or 1 lemon

4 drops of vanilla extract, or the seeds scraped from ½ vanilla bean

1 medium egg

¼ cup sugar

1 tablespoon whole milk, if needed

FOR THE CUSTARD

1 cup whole milk

1 vanilla bean, slit lengthwise and seeds scraped out

2 eggs, separated

3 tablespoons granulated sugar

3 tablespoons cornstarch

½ cup heavy cream

TO DECORATE

strawberries, raspberries, or other soft fruits

apricot glaze or jam (optional)

426

Amore di fragole
Strawberry Amore

I couldn't resist this corny name! Italian menus are so poetic and the British are so unromantic in menu writing, stripping everything back to a dull list of ingredients. I had to indulge in a bit of poetry with this one as it's such a joyous, summery celebration of pastisserie. Try it and see if you don't burst into song!

Serves 8

1 quantity of Pastry (see previous page)
1 Genoese Sponge (see page 413)

½ cup heavy cream
4 teaspoons *maraschino*, Cointreau, Grand Marnier, or brandy
8 oz strawberries, hulled and halved

FOR THE *CREMA PASTICCERA*
1 cup whole milk
½ vanilla bean, slit lengthwise and seeds scraped out
3 medium egg yolks
¼ cup cornstarch
¼ cup sugar
3 tablespoons sweet or dry Marsala

FOR THE MERINGUE
2 egg whites
⅓ cup sugar

Preheat the oven to 350°F. Grease and flour a 9½ inch loose-bottomed tart pan. Roll out the pastry to ¼ inch thick and use it to line the tin. Line with foil or parchment and fill with baking beans or rice and bake blind for 25 minutes. Remove from the oven, take out the beans and leave to cool.

Using a long sharp knife, trim off the top of the Genoese Sponge (and give it to passing children). Now cut a disc about ½ inch thick from the rest of the cake. (What's left can be frozen for another day or topped in a different way.)

Make the *crema* (custard) according to the recipe on page 424 and leave it to cool. When cold, mix in the Marsala and *cream*. Put half of the *crema* into the pastry case, then top it with the sponge disc. Brush with the *maraschino*, to soften the sponge. Use an offset spatula to spread the rest of the *crema* mix over the sponge, then arrange the strawberries on top.

Now make the meringue. Whisk the egg whites and slowly add the sugar over a bain-marie until it forms a thick meringue. Use a piping bag and your imagination to pipe mounds of meringue onto the cake, between the strawberries. Use a blow torch to scorch the tops of the meringues or flash under a very hot broiler for just a couple of minutes, taking care not to cook the strawberries. Serve chilled.

Pastiera Napoletana
Neapolitan Easter Tart

We were given about six of these in one week during our stay in Naples over Easter. Some were very strongly flavored with orange-flower water, which I have to say I am not keen on as it reminds me of patchouli oil and incense-filled hippy shops from the early 1970s. Anyway, you can add it if you want to be traditional, or leave it out. (The aunt of one of my Italian friends admitted she didn't like it either and had left it out so, that way, it became our favorite tart.) This recipe makes a lot but it does keep for two or three days if covered and stored in the fridge. *Grano cotto* means cooked grains: it is wheat grain that has been soaked and cooked until it explodes and becomes soft. Tins or jars of ready prepared *grano cotto* are available at good Italian delis and online.

Serves 12

FOR THE PASTRY
2 quantities of Pastry (see page 426)
butter, for greasing the pan

FOR THE FILLING
1 lb ricotta
¾ cup sugar
4 egg yolks
4 oz candied fruit, finely chopped
1¾ lb canned *grano cotto*
½ teaspoon orange-flower water (optional)
2 teaspoons ground cinnamon

Grease a deep tart pan (about 11 x 1½ inches) and line it with parchment paper. Preheat the oven to 350°F.

Make the pastry, following the method on page 426, cover and chill for 20 minutes.

Meanwhile, to make the filling, mix the ricotta and sugar together in a large bowl. Add the egg yolks, candied fruit, *grano cotto*, orange-flower water, if using, and the cinnamon.

Roll out the pastry on a well-floured work surface until it is about ¼ inch thick. Line the pan with the pastry and spoon in the filling. Re-roll the pastry trimmings and cut them into strips ¾ inch wide. Lay these in rows about ¾ inch apart over the top of the tart. Then turn the tart and lay more pastry strips at right angles to the first ones, to create a lattice. Bake the tart in the oven for between 50 minutes and 1 hour until the pastry is nicely browned and the filling is bubbling hot.

Serve at room temperature. If you store it in the fridge, allow it to come to room temperature before serving.

Crostata di marmellata
Jam Tart

My friend Stefano's aunt, Zia Maria, made this simple tart very quickly during our photo shoot for the book. We weren't looking for any more recipes but it was so good it begged to be included. She bought her flour straight from the mill but I have found that "00" flour works just as well.

FOR THE PASTRY
2¾ cups "00" flour
½ cup sugar
8 tablespoons butter
2 eggs
2 tablespoons liqueur, such as Strega or Grand Marnier
½ packet of *pane d'angeli* or
2 teaspoons of baking powder

1 lb plum or other jam

Preheat the oven to 350°F. Pour the flour into a mound on the table or into a bowl and add the rest of the ingredients. Use your hands to bring the whole pile together. If the eggs are very large, you may need a bit more flour, so be prepared to adjust the quantities as necessary.

Grease a 10½ inch tart pan and dust with flour, tapping out the excess. Press the pastry into it with your fingers and, ideally, let it rest for 20 minutes in the fridge. Fill with jam and roll out strips of pastry from the trimmings and place on top, to form a lattice. Bake for around 20–25 minutes, until the pastry is cooked through.

Variation: Use the Spiced Honey Fig and Orange Jam from page 486 as a filling and decorate with walnuts.

If you don't have homemade jam, do buy a good quality "soft set" one. If I ever go to a summer fair at a church hall, I always stock up on homemade jams and marmalades for crostate such as these.

Budino di riso
Rice Pudding

Rice pudding is the ultimate comfort food: warm, sweet, and sticky. You can keep it relatively plain and omit the raisins and cinnamon or spice it up with some cardamom to give it an Arabic/Sicilian twist.

Serves 8

½ cup raisins
⅔ cup **Vin Santo**
2 quarts whole milk
2 cups heavy cream
2 cups risotto rice (Arborio)
1 vanilla bean, split lengthwise
2 cinnamon sticks
piece of lemon zest, about
  2 in long
1 cup honey

Put the raisins in a bowl with the *Vin Santo*, to soak.

Combine the milk and cream in a large saucepan with the rice, vanilla pod, cinnamon sticks, and lemon zest and bring to a boil over a medium heat.

Stir frequently, to prevent the rice from sticking, then leave to simmer for 30–40 minutes, or until the rice is done.

Add the soaked raisins, the *Vin Santo,* and honey and adjust the sweetness with more honey or sugar to suit your taste.

Arance candite
Candied Oranges

These make great edible gifts and are easy to make over three days. I make them every Christmas and enlist the help of the children to dip them in chocolate. Those that make it into a box are given to Giancarlo on Christmas Day. You can also use these oranges on ice cream, in *pastiera* (see page 428), or in *cantuccini*.

Makes 4 x 12 oz jars of oranges

4 large oranges, seedless if possible
2 cups cooking liquid (see method)
3 lb sugar (1 lb added each day)

To prepare the rind, score the skin of the oranges into quarters from stem to base, then peel away the skin and pith in four segments, using a spoon to slide between the flesh and pith. To prepare the oranges, slice the peeled fruits crosswise into circles about ½ inch thick.

Put the orange rind and slices into a large saucepan and cover with cold water. Bring to a boil, then simmer gently for 30 minutes, covering the pan with a lid or a *cartouche* of parchment paper to trap the steam inside.

Remove the oranges and rind using a slotted spoon and put them into a large bowl. Measure out 2 cups of the cooking liquid and discard the rest. Return the measured liquid to the pan and add 2 cups sugar. Bring it to a boil and skim off any scum that appears on the surface. As soon as it boils, pour it over the oranges. Leave for one day at room temperature, covered with parchment paper. A small saucer on the top will keep the paper weighted down over the oranges.

The following day, drain the oranges, again using a slotted spoon, and reserve the liquid. Pour this into a saucepan, add another 2 cups sugar and bring to a boil. Pour over the oranges, as before, and leave covered. On the third day, repeat the process. The oranges can then be stored airtight in sterilized jars.

Variation: For chocolate oranges, remove some of the oranges and leave on a wire rack to harden overnight, then dip them in tempered chocolate (see page 420) and leave on a rack to set.

Pere cotte ripiene di crema di ricotta all' arancia con salsa di cioccolato
Pears Filled with Orange Ricotta Cream, with Hot Chocolate Sauce

I first enjoyed this recipe in the Pasha restaurant in Puglia. Any variety of pears can be used but unripe ones are best as they withstand the poaching which gives them such a lovely flavor. Store the pears in the syrup in sterilized jars. Any leftover syrup can be used to moisten a cake or in a fruit salad.

Serves 6

6 large unripe pears (make sure they are uniformly hard)
chocolate leaves, to decorate (see Chocolate Masterclass, page 420)

FOR THE SYRUP
1 quart water
3 cups sugar
2 cinnamon sticks
zest (peeled off in strips) and juice of 1 lemon
1 vanilla bean, split in half lengthwise

FOR THE ORANGE RICOTTA CREAM
½ cup ricotta
6 tablespoons confectioners' sugar
finely grated zest of 1 small orange

FOR THE HOT CHOCOLATE SAUCE
3½ oz chocolate
⅓ cup heavy cream

Peel the pears, leaving the stems intact, and cut a little off the bottom of each one, so that they stand up right. Put them into a saucepan with the water, sugar, cinnamon, lemon zest, and juice and vanilla bean. Bring to a boil and cook until just soft. (Hard pears can take up to 1¼ hours but ripe ones cook in 15 minutes.)

Meanwhile, make the *ricotta* cream by mixing the ingredients together in a bowl, then pushing it through a fine sieve with a spatula. Set aside in the fridge.

Remove the cooked pears from the pan with a slotted spoon. Place them on a cutting board to cool. When they are cool to the touch, cut the top 1¼ inches off each pear, including the stem, and reserve. Cut a sliver off the base so they stand up straight. Using an apple corer or thin sharp knife, cut out the centers. Put the ricotta filling into a piping bag and pipe the filling into the pears (or use a small spoon). Put the tops back on the pears.

For the hot chocolate sauce, melt the chocolate with the cream in a small saucepan over low heat. Pour a pool of sauce onto each serving plate, place a pear in the center and garnish with a chocolate leaf.

Pesche all' amaretto
Baked Peaches with Amaretti Biscuits

Amaretti means "little bitter things" in Italian. The town of Saronno in Lombardy is famous for these little almond biscuits, which are sold individually, wrapped in decorative paper. They are similar to macaroons, made from ground sweet and bitter almonds. If peaches are not available, try plums or apricots instead.

Serves 4

4 peaches (ripe but quite firm)
8 amaretti cookies, crushed
1 level tablespoon butter, plus extra for greasing
1 tablespoon honey
1½ glasses Vin Santo (or dessert wine)
8 tablespoons demerara (raw) sugar

Preheat the oven to 350°F. Cut each peach in half and remove the pit.

Put them in a greased ovenproof dish and bake for 15 minutes while you make the stuffing. Mix the amaretti biscuits with the butter, honey, and *Vin Santo*.

Remove the peaches from the oven and increase the temperature to 400°F. Fill each peach half with some of the amaretti mixture. Sprinkle the demerara sugar over the top of the peaches and bake in the oven for about 10 minutes. Watch carefully, to ensure the sugar does not burn.

Allow two peach halves per person and serve with the juices from the baking dish and scoops of homemade vanilla ice cream.

Fichi al forno con buccia di arancia e zucchero di canna
Figs Roasted with Orange Zest and Raw Sugar

Figs are everywhere in Italy in late summer and are eaten raw with ham, drizzled with honey and served with cheese—or, in this case, baked. This recipe suits figs that sometimes need a little help with flavor. The honey and orange certainly do that, and the flavors are concentrated by baking.

Serves 4

8 figs
zest and juice of 1 orange
3 tablespoons mild honey, such as acacia
2 tablespoons demerara (raw) sugar
mascarpone, to serve

Preheat the oven to 400°F.

Cut each fig in half lengthwise, then place them cut-side up in a shallow baking pan. Drizzle over the juice of the orange and the honey. Mix the sugar and orange zest together and scatter over the figs. Bake for 20 minutes or until lightly golden.

Serve with a spoonful of mascarpone.

Dolci
MASTERCLASS

Making Ice Cream

The Coating stage

Most ice creams start as a custard. Care has to be taken at this stage as the custard can become scrambled eggs or separate. You can make the custard in a saucepan if confident or use a bain-marie (see glossary), which takes a little longer. In order to pasteurize the eggs, it is important that the custard should reach 185°F: "the coating stage." When you can coat the back of a spoon with the custard and scrape a mark through it that remains visible, it is ready. This test, however, does not guarantee you have reached the required temperature to kill any bacteria present. Therefore, it is more reliable to use a thermometer.

Cooling down

It is important the custard is cooled quickly to ensure bacteria cannot start breeding in the warm mixture. When the custard has reached 185°F, remove it from the heat and pour into a bowl. Stand this bowl over another, larger bowl filled with ice and water. When cool, churn the custard in an ice-cream maker, or freeze using the method on page 439. As soon as the ice cream is thick, stop churning, as over-churned ice cream will be grainy.

To make ice cream without an ice-cream maker

Pour the cooled ice cream mixture into a shallow dish, such as one you might use for lasagne, and put this in the freezer. After an hour or so ice crystals will form around the sides of the dish. Whisk these in with a fork or balloon whisk. Repeat every hour until the whole mixture is frozen and whisked through. If there are large lumps put the mixture through a food processor and re-freeze right away.

Gelato alla crema
Custard-based Ice Cream

Dolci

This is a basic ice cream custard mixture that is so often associated with the wonderful soft ice creams that you buy in Italian ice cream parlors. It is said that a genius of a man —aptly named Buontalenti—living in Renaissance Florence invented this egg custard ice cream, which at the time used honey, not sugar, and wine as a flavoring.

Makes about 3 cups / Serves 4–6

1¾ cups whole milk
⅔ cup cream
3 egg yolks
¾ cup sugar
flavorings of your choice
  (see below)

Put the milk and cream in a medium saucepan over medium heat until it reaches just below the boiling point. Meanwhile, mix the egg yolks and sugar in a heat-proof bowl, until well blended.

Pour about half of the hot milk on to the eggs and sugar and stir well. Pour this back into the saucepan and heat to 185°F, stirring, until it reaches the coating stage (see note above). Do not let the custard boil. Remove the pan from the heat and pour the custard into a bowl. Stand this bowl in another, larger one containing ice and water. When the custard is cool, churn it in an ice-cream maker or follow the instructions for the freezing method on page 439.

Flavorings:

Vanilla—scrape the seeds from a vanilla bean and add these and the pod to the mixture when heating the milk. Remove the pod from the cooled custard.

Cinnamon—add 1 teaspoon ground cinnamon or 1 cinnamon stick when heating the milk. Remove the stick when the custard has cooled.

Chocolate—add 4 oz good quality bittersweet chocolate pieces (minimum 70 percent cocoa solids) to the hot custard, off the heat, and stir until melted and smooth.

Pine nut—add 1½ cups toasted and coarsely ground pine nuts to the custard base as soon as it is made.

Walnut and honey—add 1 cup toasted ground walnuts to the custard base. Replace the sugar with honey. Serve with ice cream in hollowed-out walnut shells like the photo opposite.

Orange—add the finely grated zest of two oranges to the milk and cream before it is heated.

Gelato di fragole
Strawberry Ice Cream

This has to be one of the easiest fruit ice cream recipes—and it works every time. Also try making it with raspberries, black-currants, figs, cherries, mangoes, apricots, or peaches instead of the strawberries.

Serves 10–12

2¼ lb strawberries, hulled and cut in half
1⅓ cups sugar
2 cups heavy cream
½ cup whole milk

Put the strawberries in a saucepan with the sugar and bring to a boil. Simmer for 10–15 minutes, until the fruit has softened. Pass the strawberries and the juice through a fine sieve into a saucepan: this should make 2 cups of purée, depending on how much water is released from the strawberries; any left over can be used as a sauce. Add the cream and milk to the strawberries and stir well. Allow to cool.

When cool, churn in an ice-cream maker or follow the instructions for the freezing method on page 439.

Variation: For pear ice cream use 2¼ lb pears, peeled and quartered or canned. Follow the recipe for strawberry ice cream cooking the fresh pears until soft. This could take anything from 15–45 minutes depending on how ripe the pears are. If using canned pears, drain them and then dissolve the sugar with them over medium heat. Continue as above.

Gelato al Fior di Latte
Milk Ice Cream

Fior di latte is the name given to a cow's milk cheese similar to mozzarella, which is traditionally made with buffalo milk. However, in this context it refers to this egg-free ice cream made with cow's milk, which gives a delicate flavor and lighter feel compared to the normal custard-based version. It is very easy to make too, which is a bonus!

Serves 10–12

2 cups whole milk
1 cup sugar
1 vanilla bean, split lengthwise
2 cups heavy cream

Heat ¾ cup of the milk in a pan with the sugar and vanilla bean until the sugar has dissolved. Remove from the heat and allow to cool naturally or, to speed things up, in a bowl set over another bowl of ice and water. When it is cool, scrape any remaining seeds from the vanilla bean into the milk and discard the pod. Stir in the remaining milk and the cream. Churn in an ice-cream maker or follow the instructions for the freezing method on page 439.

Variation: For Stracciatella ice cream use 1 quantity of milk ice cream and 10½ oz milk or dark chocolate. Melt the chocolate in a heatproof bowl set over a pan of barely simmering water (or in a microwave). Scoop one third of the prepared ice cream into a container. Drizzle with one third of the chocolate in thin lines, zigzagging it over the surface: it will freeze right away. Add another third of the ice cream, followed by another third of the melted chocolate, zigzagging it as before. Repeat this with the remaining ice cream and chocolate, then return the ice cream to the freezer until needed. This is great served with Orange Syrup (see page 447) and little pieces of Candied Orange Zest (see page 430).

Croccante di pinoli o nocciola
Pine nut or Hazelnut Crunch

Makes 12–20, depending on size

2 cups sugar
2 cups pine nuts or hazelnuts, toasted

Line a baking sheet with parchment paper. Put half the sugar in a small saucepan and place it over high heat. Brush down the sides of the pan with a wet pastry brush to prevent the sugar from crystallizing. When it starts to smoke, add the rest of the sugar, little by little. When it is brown, remove the pan from the heat and mix in the nuts.

Pour the caramel directly onto the parchment. When it is not quite set but still malleable, cut it into shapes: long triangles or sticks, for example.

Leave to set completely. Cover with parchment paper or aluminum foil until you are ready to use it. Serve with ice cream or as candy.

Dolci
MASTERCLASS

Sorbetto di lime
Lime Sorbet

Serves 4

1 cup sugar
1 cup water
6 limes

Dissolve the sugar in half the water in a saucepan over medium heat, then remove the pan from the heat and cool over ice. Add the rest of the water. Halve 4 of the limes lengthwise before squeezing and reserve the skins. Grate the zest of 2 of the limes into the syrup and squeeze the juice from all the limes and strain it into the syrup. Churn the mixture in an ice-cream maker or follow the instructions for the freezer method on page 439. Serve in hollowed out lime halves.

Sorbetto al Frutto della Passione
Passion Fruit Sorbet

Serves 4

⅔ cup sugar
½ cup water
12 passion fruits
juice of 1 lemon

Dissolve the sugar in the water in a saucepan over medium heat, then leave to cool. Cut each passion fruit in half and scrape the seeds into a food processor, reserving the skins for later. Process them for about 10 seconds, to separate the pulp from the seeds. Strain the juice from the passion fruits and the lemon juice into the cooled sugar syrup. Churn the mixture in an ice-cream maker or follow the instructions for the freezer method on page 439. Serve in hollowed-out passion fruits. These can be prepared in advance and re-frozen.

Granita al Caffè
Coffee Granita

When your spirits are flagging and sleepiness is setting in, wake yourself up with this shot of icy cold espresso and sugar. Store it in the freezer for those moments when nothing else but caffeine and sugar will do the trick!

Makes 10 espresso cups

5 tablespoons sugar
2 cups freshly made hot
  espresso
brandy (optional)

Put a container big enough for the granita (about 1 quart) in the freezer to chill while you make the coffee.

Stir the sugar into the espresso as soon as it is made, so that it dissolves. Remove the container from the freezer and pour in the coffee. Return it to the freezer, to chill. After an hour, or as soon as it starts to set, stir it with a fork or whisk to break up the ice crystals. Repeat this until the granita is frozen throughout but completely broken up into small crystals.

For a smoother texture, process the frozen granita in a food processor for a few seconds. Put it back into the dish, then back into the freezer. Cover and freeze for up to 3 months. Granita melts very quickly, so serve straight from the freezer in chilled shot glasses or espresso cups.

Tip: For an extra kick, pour a shot of brandy in the bottom of some frozen shot glasses, top with coffee granita, and serve right away. This is also lovely topped with vanilla ice cream.

Granita al limone
Lemon Granita

Granita is a semi-frozen dessert of sugar, water, and flavorings. It originates from Sicily but is now found all over Italy. Sicilians eat granita all day long, to combat the baking heat and replenish their need for sugar. There are kiosks selling it on city streets and *gelato* machines in most bars to keep up with demand. Granita from a machine will be soft and smooth like a Slush Puppy; granita made at home will be crystalline and coarser but every bit as delicious. I was once "treated" to a Sicilian breakfast, which I looked forward to with a mixture of curiosity and greed. I sat in the hot sun surrounded by really loud, arguing Italians and sort of enjoyed an enormous soft brioche stuffed with lemon granita! It is not an experience I would rush back for; instead I prefer the sweet, sharp taste of lemon granita mixed with cold Prosecco in a glass or between the courses of a large dinner as a wake-up call for the palate.

Serves 4 as a large portion, or 8 shot glasses

¾ **cup granulated sugar**
2 **cups water**
¾ **cup lemon juice**
finely grated zest of 1 lemon

Put a container big enough for the granita (about 1 quart) in the freezer to chill while you make the syrup.

Put the sugar with half the water in a saucepan and stir over medium heat until the sugar has completely dissolved and you cannot see or feel (with the spoon) any crystals left. Mix it with the rest of the water, the lemon juice and zest, then put it in the chilled container and place it in the freezer. After an hour, or as soon as it starts to set, stir with a fork or whisk to break up the ice crystals. Repeat this until the granita is frozen throughout but completely broken up into small crystals.

For a smoother texture, process the frozen granita in a food processor for a few seconds. Cover and freeze for up to 3 months. Granita melts very quickly so serve it straight from the freezer, in chilled glasses.

Granita al Campari e arancia
Campari and Orange Granita

In smart restaurants, this might be something you are given between courses to cleanse your palate. You could also serve it in little shot glasses at a cocktail party. Another use, which occurred to me whilst under the influence of a gin and tonic (when else does inspiration occur?) is to use a large spoon of this instead of ice in your G&T.

Makes at least 20 shot glasses or 10 martini glasses

1 **cup Campari**
2⅓ **cups water**
1 **cup orange juice**
¾ **cup sugar**

Put a container big enough for the granita (about 1½ quarts) in the freezer to chill while you make the syrup.

Mix the liquid ingredients together, then pour roughly one quarter of this into a saucepan with the sugar. Heat for a few minutes, stirring, until the sugar has completely dissolved and you cannot see or feel (with the spoon) any crystals left. Mix it with the rest of the liquids and then put it into the chilled container and place in the freezer. After an hour, or as soon as it starts to set, stir with a fork or whisk to break up the ice crystals. Repeat this until the granita is frozen throughout but completely broken up into small crystals.

For a smoother texture, process the frozen granita in a food processor for a few seconds. Cover and freeze for up to 3 months. Granita melts very quickly so serve it straight from the freezer, in chilled glasses.

Semifreddo ai frutti del bosco
Marbled Fruits of the Forest Parfait

Semifreddo means "half-cold" in Italian and is, typically, an ice cream that is whipped before freezing, unlike the traditional, more solid ice cream that is whipped as it is being frozen, if it's made in an ice-cream machine, or at hourly intervals when using the handmade method. If it has a high egg content, it may have the texture of a frozen mousse. *Semifreddo* is relatively simple to make and has the benefit of being frozen as soon as it is made (without the further input that is required when making ice cream).

Serves 4–6

5 egg yolks
1¼ cups sugar (¾ cup for the cream; ½ cup for the fruit purée)
seeds scraped from 1 vanilla bean
1 cup heavy cream
1 lb frozen fruits of the forest or mixed berries

Line a loaf tin approximately 10 x 4 x 2 inches with plastic wrap or two strips of parchment paper.

Heat the berries with ½ cup of the sugar in a saucepan over medium heat until the sugar has dissolved. Remove from the heat and purée using a hand blender or a food processor. Allow to cool.

Heat the egg yolks and the remaining sugar together in a heatproof bowl set over a saucepan of simmering water, but make sure the bottom of the bowl is not touching the water. Continue heating and stirring until it is thick and creamy or until it reaches 185°F on a sugar thermometer. Add the vanilla seeds to the eggs and keep whisking. Remove from the heat.

Whip the cream to soft peaks, then gently fold into the egg yolks. Divide the mixture in half and into one half mix the puréed berries. Pour a little of the berry mixture into the prepared loaf tin followed by a little of the plain mixture. Repeat until both are used up and then, using a knife, swirl the two together. Put into the freezer for at least 4 hours to set (or overnight). Serve with some fresh berries if available or Simple Biscuits (see page 456).

Salsa di cioccolato caldo
Hot chocolate sauce

Makes 1 cup / Serves 6–8

1 cup heavy cream
8 oz bittersweet chocolate (over 70 percent cocoa solids)

Mix together the cream and chocolate in a pan over medium heat until melted. Serve right away in a warmed pitcher.

Semifreddo alla Nutella
Nutella Parfait

"What is life without Nutella?" is the advertisement in Italy for one of the nation's favorite products. Nutella is so popular, there is even a cookbook devoted to this hazelnut-based spread. Made by the Ferrero chocolate company in the 1940s, it is now sold all over the world, and even claims its own World Nutella Day!

Serves 8

2 cups heavy cream
10 egg yolks
¾ cup sugar
10½ oz Nutella

Line a mold with baking parchment paper or plastic wrap.

Heat the egg yolks and sugar together in a heatproof bowl set over a saucepan of simmering water (ensuring that the bottom of the bowl is not touching the water). Continue heating and stirring until it is thick and creamy, or until it reaches 185°F on a sugar thermometer. Remove from the heat.

Stir in the Nutella until smooth and leave to cool slightly while you whip the cream. Then fold in the cream. Pour the mixture into the prepared mold and put it into the freezer. Allow at least 4 hours to set (or overnight). Serve with hot chocolate sauce.

Crema fritta
Fried Custard Squares

These melt-in-the-mouth squares are popular in the Veneto and Liguria. They can be prepared in advance and kept in the fridge for a few hours before being fried. Serve with a fruit coulis or a glass of sweet wine.

Makes about 16 squares

FOR THE CREMA PASTICCERA
2 cups milk
1 vanilla bean
1 strip of orange or lemon rind
3 egg yolks
½ cup sugar
½ cup cornstarch

FOR THE BREADCRUMB COATING
1 cup fine dry breadcrumbs
3 egg whites

sunflower oil, for frying

Put the milk in a saucepan with the vanilla bean and orange or lemon rind over low heat. Put the egg yolks, sugar and cornstarch in a bowl and mix with a wooden spoon. When the milk is just boiling, remove the pan from the heat and add the milk, a ladleful at a time, to the cornstarch mixture, stirring constantly, until half of it has been incorporated. Pour the mixture back into the rest of the milk in the saucepan. Return to the heat for a few minutes, to thicken, still stirring. Remove from the heat, remove the vanilla bean and rind and transfer the custard to an 7 or 8-inch square baking sheet lined with plastic wrap. Cover the surface with plastic wrap to prevent a skin from forming. Allow to cool.

When cool, turn out the custard on to a chopping board and peel away the plastic wrap. Cut into 1½ inch squares.

For the coating, put the egg whites in a bowl and beat well. Put the breadcrumbs in a shallow dish. Dip each square of custard first into the egg whites to cover on all sides, then into the breadcrumbs, ensuring they are well coated.

Heat the oil in a deep-fat fryer to 340°F. Drop the squares, a few at a time, into the hot oil and fry until golden on all sides (this should take about 2–3 minutes). Drain on kitchen paper and allow to cool for a few minutes while you cook the rest.

Crostata di ricotta, limone e cannella
Ricotta, Lemon, and Cinnamon Tart

This tart is popular all over Italy and I have been shown versions of it by cooks from Milan to Sicily. There are countless variations, such as including more or less chocolate, or the addition of lemon—but there is always a pinch of spice in the form of cinnamon.

Serves 8

FOR THE SWEET PASTRY (PASTA FROLLA DOLCE)
4 tablespoons butter, plus extra for greasing
1¾ cups all-purpose flour, plus extra for dusting
½ cup sugar
zest of ½ orange or lemon
seeds scraped from a vanilla bean, or 4 drops of
  vanilla extract
2 egg yolks
4 tablespoons lard

FOR THE FILLING
2 egg yolks
1 cup sugar
1 lb cow's milk ricotta
⅛ teaspoon ground cinnamon
grated zest of ½ lemon
¼ cup good-quality semi-sweet chocolate morsels
  (minimum 70 percent cocoa solids)

Grease a 10-inch loose-bottomed tart pan with butter and dust with flour, tapping out the excess. Preheat the oven to 350°F.

Mix all the ingredients for the pastry together, by hand or in a food processor. Cover the dough with plastic wrap and let it rest in the fridge for at least 20 minutes, then roll it out on a lightly floured work surface and use it to line the tart pan, reserving the trimmings.

Mix all the ingredients together for the filling and spread evenly in the pastry shell. Roll out the pastry trimmings in a long rectangle and cut strips about ½ inch wide. Twist them and lay them across the tart, to form a lattice.

Cook for 40–45 minutes, or until a wooden skewer inserted into the center comes out clean and the top is golden brown. Serve at room temperature.

Meringhe
Meringue

Meringues are international. The classic Italian method is to heat the sugar first and then pour it onto whisked egg whites—but for this you really need a sugar thermometer.

This simpler recipe is from Stefano Borella, our friend and pastry chef for years. It works well, is uncomplicated and has many uses. It is, however, very sweet, so for some uses you may want to cut down the amount of sugar to 1½ times the amount of egg white, rather than double.

Makes 15–20 big meringues

1 cup egg whites (from about 8 eggs)
2 cups sugar

Preheat the oven to 225°F.

Put the egg whites with one third of the sugar in a glass or metal bowl, set over a saucepan of boiling water, ensuring that the bottom of the bowl is not in contact with the water. Whisk for 2–3 minutes, until stiff peaks form. Remove from the heat, add the rest of the sugar all at once and keep whisking until you have a glossy, firm meringue, which usually takes another 1–2 minutes.

Line a baking sheet with parchment paper. I like to use a heaping tablespoon of meringue and push it onto the parchment with a second spoon but, if you prefer, you can pipe the meringue for a smaller, neater result. If you like your meringues crunchy on the outside and soft inside, cook in the preheated oven for 30 minutes. If you prefer them crunchy all the way through, cook for 1½ hours, then turn off the oven and leave the meringues inside to cool, for at least 1 hour or overnight.

Variations:
For delicious strawberry meringues, add 8 oz coarsely chopped strawberries to the mixture. Sandwich them together with strawberry or vanilla ice cream and drizzle with some Baked Strawberry Jams (see page 490).

For chocolate meringues, add 6 tablespoons of coarsely chopped chocolate and 3 tablespoons of sifted unsweetened cocoa powder, and serve with vanilla ice cream and hot chocolate sauce (see page 442).

Pannacotta alla vaniglia
Vanilla Panna Cotta

This wonderful wobbly dessert originates in Piedmont in the north of Italy, where the use of cream is more prevalent. It has now, however, wobbled its way around the world as it is the perfect foil for so many flavors. After much experimentation, I have whittled it down to a simple formula of 2 cups liquid to 1 envelope (2½ leaves) of gelatin and 6 tablespoons sugar. The liquid can be made from a single ingredient or a combination of ingredients such as half-and-half or heavy cream, natural or Greek-style yogurt, milk, coffee liqueur, or fruit juices.

Serves 4 if using 4 oz dariole molds (see glossary)

2½ gelatin leaves, or 1 envelope of unflavored powdered gelatin
¾ cup whole milk
1¼ cups heavy cream
6 tablespoons sugar
seeds from a vanilla bean, or 1 teaspoon of vanilla extract

Soak the leaves of gelatin in a little cold water, or follow the packet instructions for softening the powdered gelatin.

Combine the milk and cream in a bowl, then pour about one quarter of this liquid into a saucepan and place over low heat with the vanilla. Add the sugar and stir until it has dissolved, then remove the saucepan from the heat.

Squeeze out the gelatin sheet and add them to the pan, or add the powdered gelatin. Stir until the gelatine has dissolved, returning the pan to the heat if necessary.

Strain the warmed liquid through a sieve (to remove any undissolved gelatine) into the remaining milk and cream in the bowl. Stir to combine. For speed of setting and to disperse the vanilla seeds evenly, put this bowl over another, larger bowl filled with ice and cold water. Leave to cool, stirring occasionally.

When the panna cotta is just starting to set, ladle it into suitable containers and place these in the fridge. The containers could be dariole molds, shot glasses, martini glasses, or so on. Of course, panna cotta does not have to be turned out, so use your imagination as far as toppings go.

Pannacotta al frutto della Passione
Passion Fruit Panna Cotta

Serves 4

2½ gelatin leaves, or 1 envelope powdered gelatin
2 cups Greek yogurt
4 oz passion fruit seeds and pulp (from about
  6 or 7 passion fruits)
½ cup sugar

Soak the gelatin leaves in a little cold water, or follow the packet instructions for softening the powdered gelatin. Turn the yogurt into a bowl and set aside.

Gently heat the passion fruit and sugar together for 5 minutes, until the sugar has dissolved, then remove from the heat. Squeeze out the gelatin sheets and add to the pan, or add the powdered gelatin. Stir until the gelatin has dissolved, returning the pan to the heat if necessary.

Strain the warmed liquid through a sieve (to remove any undissolved gelatin and the passion fruit seeds) into the yogurt in the bowl. Stir to combine. Cool the panna cotta (see page 444), then divide it between molds or glasses.

Sciroppo al frutto della passione
Passion Fruit Syrup

8 oz passion fruit seeds and pulp (from about
  12 passion fruits)
⅔ cup sugar
6 tablespoons water

Place the ingredients together in a saucepan and boil until the liquid becomes a syrup. Allow 10–15 minutes for it to reduce adequately.

Leave to cool. It is ready to use when it has reached room temperature. If it should thicken, simply reheat until it softens again to a liquid. Serve as a topping for panna cotta.

Variation:
For an orange syrup use ¾ cup orange juice, ½ cup sugar, and zest of 1 orange. Boil the ingredients together in a saucepan until the liquid becomes a syrup. Allow 10–15 minutes for it to reduce adequately. Leave to cool. It is ready to use when it has reached room temperature. If it should thicken, simply reheat until it softens to a liquid again. Pour over ice cream.

Pannacotta al basilico
Basil Panna Cotta

Unusual as it sounds, this is delicious. It has a light, summer flavor that never fails to impress. Dress it up with a few fresh strawberries if you want a contrasting color. For best results, soak the basil overnight in the milk.

Serves 4 if using 4 oz dariole molds

1 oz basil leaves, rinsed and dried
1¼ cups whole milk
2½ gelatin leaves, or 1 envelope powdered gelatin
6 tablespoons sugar
¾ cup heavy cream

Put the basil leaves into the milk, cover, and place in the fridge overnight. Depending on your choice of container, you may need to put a small saucer or pot lid on top of the basil to keep it submerged.

The following day, soak the sheets of gelatin in cold water, or follow the packet instructions for softening the powdered gelatin.

Heat the milk with the basil in a small saucepan and bring slowly to a boil. Add the sugar and stir until it has dissolved, then remove the saucepan from the heat. Squeeze out the gelatin sheets and add to the pan, or add the powdered gelatin. Stir until the gelatin has dissolved, returning the saucepan to the heat if necessary.

Put the cream in a bowl and strain the milk through a sieve into the bowl, pressing the basil with a wooden spoon to extract as much of its wonderful, pungent flavor as possible. Whisk the heavy cream and milk together vigorously, ensuring that you remove any lumps.

Transfer the mixture and the basil to a blender and process. Pass everything through a sieve into a bowl, to remove all the small pieces of basil. The liquid will be a lovely pale green color.

Cool the panna cotta (see page 444), then divide it between the molds or glasses.

Camicia da notte
Nutella Calzone

A recent craze over the past few years is to make a Nutella pizza. It makes a delicious topping and can be left open, topped with some shredded coconut, or folded over into the *calzone* shape. This version is called *camicia da notte*, meaning "nightshirt," as it was served in a bar around midnight. It is a gorgeous indulgence—and even better when accompanied by some sliced banana.

Serves 4

1 quantity of basic pizza dough (see page 66)

14 oz Nutella
4 tablespoons sugar
1 banana, cut into ½ in slices

Heat the oven to 475°F—or as hot as it will go. After the pizza dough has risen, cut it into four pieces and roll out each one into a circle about ¼ inch thick. Spread a very large tablespoon of Nutella (about 3½ oz) over one half of the pizza, leaving a gap of 1¼ inches from the edge. Lay the banana slices on top.

Fold the pizza in half and crimp the edges to seal.

Sprinkle each with 1 tablespoon sugar and bake in the oven for 5–10 minutes, or until golden brown. Remove from the oven and allow to cool slightly before serving.

Pannacotta al caffè
Coffee Panna Cotta

Serves 4 if using 4 oz dariole molds

2½ gelatin leaves, or 1 envelope powdered gelatin
¾ cup espresso coffee
1¼ cups heavy cream
6 tablespoons sugar

Soak the sheets of gelatin in cold water, or follow the packet instructions for softening the powdered gelatin.

Combine the coffee and cream in a bowl, then pour about one quarter of this liquid into a saucepan and place over low heat. Stir in the sugar and, once it has dissolved, remove the saucepan from the heat.

Squeeze out the gelatin sheets and add them to the pan, or add the powdered gelatin. Stir until the gelatin has dissolved, returning the saucepan to the heat if necessary.

Strain this warmed liquid through a sieve (to remove any undissolved gelatin) into the remaining coffee and cream in the bowl. Stir to combine. Cool the panna cotta (see page 444), then divide it between molds, glasses, or espresso cups. When set, pour the coffee caramel (photo and recipe opposite) over the top.

Caramello al caffè
Coffee Caramel Sauce

This is ideal for pouring over ice cream or coffee panna cotta.

1 cup sugar
⅓ cup espresso

Put the sugar in a heavy-bottomed saucepan over medium heat. Cook without stirring until the sugar bubbles and takes on a rich golden color. (Be careful: the hot caramel can spit at you so it is a good idea to wear oven mitts.) Gradually stir in the espresso while the caramel is bubbling. Leave to cool.

Zuppa Inglese Chocolate and Custard Trifle

Serves 4–6

⅓ cup rum, or *Alchermes*
  liqueur if you can find it
⅓ cup water
24 lady fingers

FOR THE CREMA
2 cups whole milk
½ vanilla bean, split in half
  lengthwise and seeds
  scraped out
3 egg yolks
¼ cup sugar
¼ cup cornstarch

FOR THE CHOCOLATE CREMA
2 cups whole milk
⅓ cup sugar
1 cup unsweetened cocoa
  powder
3 egg yolks
2 tablespoons cornstarch

Literally translated, *zuppa Inglese* means "English soup." It is thought that the Italians took the idea of English trifle and made it their own by adding the bright pink liqueur *Alchermes*, which is quite hard to find in the UK, so I use rum instead. In Florence, *zuppa Inglese* has a runny consistency, more like a sweet soup, while in Venice I found a version made from a jelly roll and coated with a layer of toasted meringue. In this recipe, it is made with both chocolate and vanilla custards, to be served in individual parfait or wine glasses, so you can see the layers, or in one dish.

First make the *crema*. Bring the milk, vanilla seeds, and pod to a low boil. Meanwhile, mix together the egg yolks, sugar, and cornstarch in a bowl with an electric mixer, until pale and fluffy. When the milk is boiling, remove from the heat and add half the milk, a ladleful at a time, to the cornstarch mixture. Then pour the custard mixture back into the rest of the milk in the saucepan and return to the heat for a few minutes, until it has thickened. Remove from the heat, cover the surface with plastic wrap to stop a skin from forming, and leave to cool.

For the chocolate *crema*, put 1 cup of the milk in a medium saucepan with the sugar and bring to a boil. Meanwhile, in a bowl mix the rest of the cold milk with the cocoa powder, cornstarch, and egg yolks. Whisk well to get rid of any lumps and pour the hot milk over the mixture gradually. Return the mixture to the saucepan and cook over medium heat for a few minutes until it thickens. Remove from the heat, cover the surface with plastic wrap to stop a skin from forming and leave to cool.

Mix the rum with ⅓ cup water in a bowl. Break one lady finger in half and dip it into the diluted rum just long enough for the liquid to penetrate into the biscuit but not so long that it becomes soggy. Put it straight into a serving glass. Do this with five more biscuits, to make a layer. (Or use a large serving bowl, about 12 x 8 inches, and cover the bottom of the dish with a single layer of rum-soaked biscuits.)

Cover with a layer of the *crema*, then a layer of chocolate *crema*. Repeat the layers, ending with a final layer of *crema*. Chill until ready to serve.

Cioccolata in tazza
Hot Chocolate Cream in a Cup

This recipe is a chocoholic's idea of heaven, as my son Giorgio will vouch. We discovered it in a restaurant called *Il Mulino di Sopra*, meaning "the mill above," just outside Parma. It was a converted water mill and you could watch the rushing water through a window. The menu indicated that if you wanted this dessert, it had to be ordered 20 minutes in advance, so Giorgio ordered it before we had even chosen our starters! The friendly chef kindly gave him the recipe. We have since discovered that, if you pour out a couple of small cups for the children, you can then add a shot of brandy to the remainder for an impressive mid-morning hot chocolate or an indulgent dinner party special.

Makes 10 espresso cups

1 cup whole milk
1 cup heavy cream
½ cup sugar
5 egg yolks
5 oz good-quality bittersweet chocolate (minimum 70 percent cocoa solids), in pieces or drops
3 tablespoons brandy (optional)

Whisk the milk, cream, sugar, and egg yolks in a saucepan, stirring constantly. Then place over medium heat and bring almost to the boiling point. It needs to reach 190°F to sterilize the egg and thicken the custard. If you don't have a thermometer, check that the custard coats the back of a wooden spoon and, if you run your fingernail through it, the line remains visible. Remove from the heat, add the chocolate and whisk to melt. Add the brandy, if using. Serve hot in small coffee cups and drink it, or dip in strawberries, bananas, cake, etc. If left to cool the chocolate will set and can then be eaten the next day.

Crema di Amaretto
Amaretto Cream

This simple cream has the power to turn a humble tart or pudding into a dreamy dessert. Try it with poached fruits such as pears in red wine, or Figs Roasted with Orange Zest and Brown Sugar (see page 433). Amaretto liqueur comes from Saronno in Lombardy, northern Italy. Made from the kernels of apricots or almonds (or both), it has a sweet almond flavor.

⅓ cup mascarpone
⅓ cup heavy cream
2 tablespoons sugar
2–3 tablespoons Amaretto

Mix all the ingredients together in a medium bowl, using a hand whisk. Adjust the amount of liqueur and sugar to taste, and keep chilled. To serve, use 2 spoons to form *quenelles*.

Variation: Use Grand Marnier, Cointreau or brandy instead of Amaretto. Add a little orange or lemon zest for a citrus punch.

Baci di dama
Chocolate and Hazelnut Biscuits

Baci di dama translates literally as "ladies's kisses." Hazel trees are plentiful in the area of Piemonte in the north of Italy, where the nuts are frequently used in desserts and, indeed, to make the famous chocolate and hazelnut spread, Nutella. If you can, buy hazelnuts already skinned, but if you cannot find them, toast unskinned ones first to loosen the skins. With nuts, I have learned never to trust a package's sell-by date, but to taste them first. If they have gone rancid, there is no point in using them because the unpleasant taste will be carried through, so do buy the freshest nuts you can find.

Makes 30–40 biscuits

1 cup hazelnuts, shelled and skinned
1 cup ground almonds
5 tablespoons sugar
1½ cups all-purpose flour
12 tablespoons salted butter, softened
½ jar of Nutella, to sandwich the biscuits together

Preheat the oven to 350°F. If the hazelnuts are unskinned, spread them out on a baking sheet and toast them in the oven for about 5 minutes until the skins become crispy. Put them on a clean kitchen towel and fold one half over the top. Roll them in the cloth, pressing down with the palm of your hands. This will loosen and collect the skins.

Line one or two baking sheets with parchment paper. Grind the hazelnuts finely in a food processor. Put all the dry ingredients in a bowl and mix in the butter. Form into small balls the size of large marbles: about ¾ inch across. Flatten each one gently between your fingers to make them into more of a patty shape. Place on the parchment, spaced well apart, and bake for 20 minutes, or until golden. Remove from the oven and allow to cool.

Spread half of the biscuits with a little dot of Nutella, allowing for the fact that, when you press them together, the filling will spread; then press the other biscuits on top. Try to match sizes of each top and base accurately so that they are even. Serve with coffee. These will keep, stored in an airtight container, for a couple of days.

Zabaglione

Zabaglione is said to have originated in Venice and was made with sweet Cypriot wine and honey. Over the years, the wine has given way to Marsala, a dessert wine from Sicily, and the honey to white sugar; you could, if you wish, opt for honey if you prefer a more natural ingredient. Vin Santo also makes a good replacement for the Marsala. The Neapolitan word *zapillare* means foaming and that is the result of whisking the ingredients together over heat. Zabaglione became one of the classic desserts of Italian restaurants in the 1970s, served in long-stemmed glasses. Now, however, it is also served as a sauce over fresh or chilled fruits.

Serves 2–4

4 egg yolks, plus 1 whole egg
¼ cup sugar
3 tablespoons Marsala *secco*

Whisk the eggs, sugar and Marsala together in a bowl. Place the bowl over a large saucepan of boiling water and continue to whisk. When you lift the whisk, it should leave a trail in the bowl: this is called "the ribbon stage." Taste to see whether you need more liqueur or sugar. Pour into glasses and serve immediately.

Tip: Cool any leftovers and whip with fresh cream for a *semifreddo*. Spoon over fresh fruits, sprinkle with sugar and caramelize using a blow torch.

Cartellate
Spiced Fried Pastries

I was shown this recipe by an amazing lady, Rita, who shares her great-grandmother's *masseria* in Mola, Puglia with her five cats. *Cartellate* are spiral pastries, traditionally eaten at Christmas time in northern Puglia, where they are doused in *vincotto* (concentrated grape must)— though I prefer the alternative of honey and cinnamon. The origins supposedly go back to St. Nicholas of Bari (one of the original Fathers Christmas), born in Patara, which was under Greek control at the time. Considering the proximity of Puglia and Greece, perhaps the recipe is Greek. The pastry is made with white wine and olive oil, which makes it very strong and elastic, and it is also used for the Scallion and Leek Pie (see page 71).

Makes approximately 20 spirals

FOR THE WHITE WINE PASTRY
butter, for greasing
2¼ cups "00" or all-purpose flour, plus extra for dusting
3 tablespoons olive oil
⅓ cup dry white wine
½ teaspoon salt

sunflower oil, for deep frying
3 tablespoons honey
3 tablespoons dry white wine or water
confectioners' sugar, for dusting
ground cinnamon, for dusting

Mix together the ingredients for the pastry in a large bowl, adding the wine little by little until you have a soft, pliable dough. Roll out the pastry very thinly on a lightly floured work surface until it is transparent—you should be able to see the work surface through it. (Rita told me that when you can blow underneath it, the pastry is ready.) Cut it into strips measuring 1¼ inches wide, and roughly 14 inches long, using a pastry wheel, and pinch the strands together in half at 1¼ inch intervals along the length. Then curl the strips round, pressing the openings together until a spiral is formed.

Leave the *cartellate*, uncovered, for 5–8 hours, or until they have dried. They can be made the night before you want to serve them.

Preheat the oil in a deep-fat fryer to 340°F, drop in the spirals, hole-side down first, and cook for about 4 minutes, until golden. Turn them over and fry until the second side is also golden. (Alternatively, you can cook the cartellate in hot sunflower oil to a depth of about 2 inches in a large frying pan.) Remove with a slotted spoon and drain on paper towels.

Bring the honey and wine or water to a boil in a large frying pan. Drop the *cartellate* into the pan, hole-side down, turn them over until well coated, then transfer to a plate. Sprinkle with cinnamon and sugar. Serve hot or leave to cool at room temperature.

Tiramisu

Literally translated, this is a "pick me up," as the sugar and espresso lift the spirits. This is Giancarlo's recipe and, instead of the more usual Marsala or brandy, he uses *Vin Santo*, the Tuscan fortified wine. Tiramisu freezes well so it is worth making two at a time and freezing one. Remove from the freezer and leave it overnight in the fridge to thaw out before serving. I think tiramisu looks better in individual glasses than spooned out from a larger dish, but I leave that up to you. Since this uses raw eggs, buy the best quality and do not serve to the pregnant, or elderly.

Serves 8–12 people.
enough for a 10 × 10 inch serving dish
or 8–12 individual glasses

6 eggs, separated
¾ cup sugar
8 oz mascarpone
⅔ cup heavy cream
⅔ cup espresso coffee, hot
⅔ cup *Vin Santo* or Marsala
24 *savoiardi* (lady finger) biscuits
2 oz good-quality bittersweet chocolate (minimum
  70 percent cocoa solids), grated

Beat the egg yolks and sugar together until light and fluffy. Whisk in the mascarpone. Whip the cream to soft peaks in one bowl and whisk the egg whites to soft peaks in another. Gently fold the cream, egg yolk mixture and egg whites together, incorporating as much air as possible.

Pour the espresso and *Vin Santo* into a large bowl, ready for dipping the biscuits.

Cover the bottom of a large dish or individual glasses with a ¾ inch layer of the cream, then a layer of biscuits that have been dipped quickly into the espresso and wine mixture. You must dip and layer the biscuits individually as you go, otherwise they become too soggy.

Continue to build up the layers of cream and biscuits, ending with a layer of cream. Chill, covered, in the fridge for 24 hours. Dust with grated chocolate to serve.

Biscotti semplici semplici
Simple Biscotti

I was inspired to make a lemon version of these, having tasted circles of soft pastry topped with fine pieces of lemon zest on a vanilla biscuit and fine pieces of orange zest on chocolate biscuits served with espresso at the end of a meal at Parizzi, a glamorous modern restaurant in Parma. My version has the lemon zest inside. When I was making them I started to think of other classic Italian flavors and came up with the basil and rosemary versions. The whole world of herbs and citrus fruits is open for experimentation on these, so try different combinations like orange zest and chocolate or rosemary and thyme. Children like to help with these, too, and you can cut them into all sorts of shapes, such as long thin triangles to stick out of ice cream sundaes, or little squares to serve with coffee. Have fun!

Makes 20–30 biscuits, depending on the size of the cutter

8 tablespoons softened butter
¼ cup sugar
1½ cups "00" or all-purpose flour, plus extra for dusting
flavouring of your choice (see variations below)
1 tablespoon milk, if necessary

Preheat the oven to 350°F. Mix the butter, sugar, and flour, together with your chosen flavoring, in a bowl, with your hands, or in a food processor. If the dough is very crumbly, add a little milk. At this stage, the pastry can be stored, wrapped in plastic wrap, in the fridge. You will need to bring it back to room temperature before rolling it out.

Dust your work surface and rolling pin with flour and roll out the pastry to ¼ inch thick. Cut the pastry into shapes, using a cutter, or cut triangles with a sharp knife. Lay the biscuits on a tray lined with baking parchment and bake in the oven for 8–10 minutes or until lightly golden. Remove from the oven and allow to cool on a wire rack.

Variations:
Basil biscotti To the above quantity of dough, add 1 tablespoon chopped basil.
Lemon or orange biscotti To the above quantity of dough, add 1 level tablespoon finely grated lemon or orange zest.
Rosemary biscotti To the above quantity of dough, add 2 teaspoons finely chopped rosemary.
Vanilla biscotti To the above quantity of dough, add the seeds from one vanilla bean.
Chocolate biscotti Omit ¼ cup of flour and replace with ¼ cup unsweetened cocoa powder instead.

Zaleti
Vanilla and Orange Polenta Biscuits

This recipe comes from Franco Gatto, who used to work at one of our restaurants. Franco comes from the Veneto where polenta in all its forms abounds. I love the crunch of the *polenta* combined with the citrus fruits.

Makes 20–25 biscuits

½ cup golden raisins
⅓ cup warm milk
8 tablespoons butter
1 cup polenta or cornmeal
⅓ cup caster sugar
1 cup "00" or all-purpose flour
3 tablespoons pine nuts
2 egg yolks
zest of 1 lemon
zest of 1 orange
1 vanilla bean, split in half lengthwise, seeds scraped out, or 1–2 drops of vanilla extract

Preheat the oven to 350°F and line a baking sheet with baking parchment.

Soak the raisins in the warm milk and reserve. Melt the butter and allow to cool a little before using. Put all the remaining ingredients in a bowl, incorporate the butter and mix well. Drain the raisins, discarding the milk, and add to the mixture. When the ingredients are totally combined, shape the biscuits into *quenelles* (see page 451) and place on the baking sheet, leaving space for the biscuits to expand.

Bake for about 12 minutes or until golden brown. Remove from the oven and place on a wire rack to cool.

Cantuccini con arance e pistacchi
Orange and Pistachio Biscuits

Cantuccini—or *biscotti* as they are sometimes known—are now famous the world over in coffee shops and Italian restaurants. *Biscotti* means "twice cooked" and is the generic name for this type of biscuit. *Cantuccini* are smaller versions, the "*ini*" denoting "small." The biscuits can be made either as fat fingers or cut wafer thin, and flavored with various nuts, dried fruits, or chocolate drops.

½ cup whole blanched almonds
½ cup shelled pistachios
2¼ cups all-purpose flour, preferably "00"
¾ cup sugar
1 teaspoon baking powder
2 large eggs, lightly beaten
4 teaspoons mixed candied peel
1 teaspoon vanilla extract, or seeds scraped from
** a vanilla pod**
zest of 1 orange
confectioners' sugar, for dusting

Preheat the oven to 350°F. Spread out the almonds on a baking sheet and lightly toast in the oven for about 5 minutes, taking care not to burn them.

To give a brighter green look to the pistachios, blanch them in boiling water for a couple of minutes, then drain. Slip off the skins.

Mix together the flour, sugar, and baking powder in a large mixing bowl. Stir in the nuts, eggs, candied peel, vanilla extract or seeds, and orange zest. Stir to form a thick but soft dough. Divide the mixture into thirds. Form each third into a sausage shape by rolling it, with your hands, in icing sugar. Place the rolls on a baking tray lined with baking parchment and flatten slightly. Bake for 20 minutes, until golden brown.

Remove from the oven. Cut each roll diagonally into strips ¼ inch–½ inch wide. Spread the strips in a single layer on 1 or 2 baking trays and return to the oven for 2–3 minutes. Leave to cool before serving. Enjoy dunked into a glass of *Vin Santo* or other sweet wine.

Sfinci
Cinnamon
Doughnuts

I helped make these at our friend Fabrizio's mad house, where so many people dropped in to say "hello." We gave away so many *sfinci,* I was worried that I wouldn't get to try one. I smiled between clenched teeth at the guests, watching them enjoy these sweet delicacies as I slaved over a pan of hot oil. Finally it was my turn to sit down and savor these warm, sticky sweets with a glass of cold white wine. These are usually eaten on San Martino, which is November 11th, but I think they work at any time of year. If you don't eat them up in one day, cover loosely with a clean kitchen towel and enjoy them the next day.

Makes 50

¾ cup rice
salt
1 medium russet potato
2 cups "00" flour or
  all-purpose flour
2 cups fine semolina
1 oz fresh yeast
approximately 1¼ cups
  tepid water
finely grated zest of
  ½ large lemon
sunflower oil, for frying
½ cup sugar
1 teaspoon ground cinnamon

Boil the rice in 1 quart of water with a little salt. Boil the potato, whole in its skin, in a separate pan. When the rice is done, put it through a *passatutto* or ricer. When the potato is done, peel and pass it through a *passatutto* or mash finely with a fork. Add ½ teaspoon of salt to the flour and semolina and mix together. Add the potato and rice to the flour and semolina and crumble in the fresh yeast. Add the rest of the water, little by little, to form a very wet dough; it should be thick and sticky. Leave to rise, covered, in a warm place, for an hour or so, until the mixture has risen and bubbles have appeared.

Heat the oil in a medium saucepan or deep-fat fryer until really hot. Wet a teaspoon with a little water and pick up a heaping spoonful of dough. With a wet thumb, carefully push it into the hot oil. It will make a rumbling noise, like something erupting from the bottom of the pan. When it bobs up to the top, let it brown on one side, then flip over, using tongs, and let it brown on the other side.

When browned, let the *sfinci* drain on paper towels, then toss them in the cinnamon and sugar. Serve right away.

Beignets
Choux Buns

These are Giancarlo's favorites—whenever we are in Italy, the first thing we do is order a cappuccino and devour at least 2 or 3 *beignets* each. My favorite is hazelnut; Giancarlo likes chocolate.

Makes 25 beignets

½ cup water
4 tablespoons butter
½ teaspoon sugar
a pinch of salt
¾ cup bread flour
2 eggs

Preheat the oven to 400°F. Line a baking tray with parchment paper.

Put the water, butter, sugar, and salt in a medium saucepan over low heat. When the butter has melted, bring it to a boil and watch it. Have a wooden spoon ready in your hand and, as soon as it comes to the boil, pour in the flour, all at once. Vigorously beat the mixture with the spoon until the flour is well incorporated. Now use a hand or electric mixer to add the eggs, a little at a time, until you have a smooth glossy mixture. Pipe out little mounds measuring about 1¼ inches across and ¾ inch high, spaced about 3 inches apart—you should get around 25 buns. Bake for 15 minutes, then reduce the oven temperature to 325°F and bake for another 10–15 minutes, until golden brown and firm inside. Leave to cool before filling. To fill the beignets use half the quantity of *crema pasticcera* on page 424 or half the quantity of *chocolate crema pasticcera* on page 425. Alternatively, fill with ice cream.

Frittelle con zabaione
Crunchy Doughnuts with Zabaglione Cream

In a tiny street in Venice, near the Piazza San Marco, is the Rosa Salva pâtisserie. Venetians squeeze inside to enjoy an espresso and choose from the mouth-watering array of cakes—*fatte in casa*—made on the premises: *beignets* (golden nuggets of filled choux pastry), *frittelle con zabaione* (fried doughnuts filled with *zabaglione* cream) and delicate little biscuits sprinkled with powdered sugar.

Makes 12–14 doughnuts

1 quantity of choux pastry (see previous page)

FOR THE CREMA
1¼ cups whole milk
½ vanilla bean, split in half lengthwise,
  and seeds scraped out
3 egg yolks
¼ cup sugar
¼ cup cornstarch
3 tablespoons Marsala

½ cup sugar, for coating

First make the *crema*. Bring the milk to a gentle boil with the vanilla bean and seeds. Meanwhile, mix the egg yolks, sugar and cornstarch in a bowl, using an electric mixer, until well blended. When the milk is just boiling, remove from the heat and add half of it, a ladleful at a time, to the cornstarch mixture. Pour this mixture back into the rest of the milk in the saucepan and return to the heat for a few minutes, until thick. Remove from the heat and stir in the Marsala, cover the surface with plastic wrap to stop a skin from forming, and leave to cool. Meanwhile, make the choux pastry (see previous page).

Preheat the oil to 350°F, or until a small piece of bread quickly turns golden brown when dropped in. Drop teaspoons of dough into the hot oil and fry the doughnuts, in batches, for about 8–10 minutes, until they are golden brown and cooked through. Drain and cool on kitchen paper.

When they have reached room temperature, break the doughnuts open a little and spoon in the custard or fill a piping bag and use the tip of it to make a little hole in the doughnut and pipe in the custard. Toss in sugar to coat and serve warm, or allow to cool.

Gelatina di vino rosso
Red Wine Jelly

This idea came from the famous restaurant Aimo e Nadia in Milan. Aimo used Amarone wine, one of my favorites. He serves his jelly in slices between pieces of dark chocolate. I've always liked bitter chocolate and red wine, much to the horror of my winetasting friends, so I was pleased to see I wasn't alone in enjoying this combination. My suggestion, however, to complete this indulgence, is to serve the jelly in shot glasses with chocolate tart (see page 422).

Serves 4

5 gelatin leaves
1 bottle red wine, Chianti or your favorite
  Italian full-bodied red wine
⅔ cup sugar

Soak the gelatin leaves in cold water. Pour the red wine into a medium saucepan and add the sugar. Bring to a boil, stirring occasionally. When it boils, remove from the heat. Take the gelatin, squeeze out the water, and drop it into the hot wine, stirring to ensure that it is well mixed in.

Pour the jelly into a cold jug and leave to cool. When cold (but not setting), pour into glasses or jelly molds.

Tip: If you are in a hurry, pour the jelly into a bowl and stand it over another bowl a third full of ice and cold water.

Gelatina di bellini
Prosecco and Peach Jelly

Serves 10 in champagne flutes

5 gelatin leaves
1 bottle of Prosecco
½ cup golden caster sugar
1 peach, peeled and cut into ½ in cubes

Soak the gelatin leaves in cold water. Heat a little of the Prosecco with the sugar in a saucepan until it melts. Remove from the heat and add the soaked and squeezed out gelatine. Stir until dissolved. Mix with the rest of the Prosecco and cool in a bowl in the fridge or over ice until it just starts to set. Mix in the peach pieces and pour into a jug. Fill your glasses. Chill until set.

Frutta di marzapane
Marzipan Fruits

Marzipan was originally made in a pestle and mortar by pounding almonds with sugar. Traditionally it was flavored with orange water or vanilla. *Pasta di mandorle*, made with almonds, sugar, and egg, is similar to marzipan and used for modelling into fruits and other shapes. Both types of paste were introduced to Sicily during the Arab invasion and then moved into the rest of Europe, particularly during the Middle Ages, when highly skilled patisserie chefs would make them into ornate edible models of castles, animals, and other exotic creations. In England, such confectionery was known as *marchpane*. Instead of making marzipan, I use the ready-made version, sold in 7–8 oz packages or tins. They work very well and I now make these fruits every Christmas with my children.

Dolci
MASTERCLASS

Stecche di bomboloni
Doughnut Sticks

Richard Bertinet showed us this recipe and our patisserie expert, Stefano Borella, adapted it, dipping the sticks in *crema pasticcera* flavored with *strega* and serving the sticks with a blackberry and Sambuca coulis.

Makes about 40 doughnut strips

1 quantity of *crema* (see page 426)

½ oz fresh yeast
1 cup tepid milk
5 tablespoons butter
5 cups flour
¼ cup sugar
2 tablespoons salt
2 large eggs
oil, for deep frying
sugar or cinnamon sugar, for coating
3 tablespoons *strega* or other liqueur

Dissolve the yeast in the milk with your fingers or a small whisk. In a mixing bowl, rub the butter into the flour, using your fingertips, then add the sugar and salt. Pour in the milk and eggs and mix together with a spoon, then use your hands. Bring the dough out of the bowl onto a floured work surface and knead, with the help of a plastic dough scraper, until a smooth and elastic dough is formed. This should take about 10 minutes. Put the dough into an oiled bowl, cover with a cloth, and leave in a warm place to rise until doubled in volume.

When risen, turn out the dough on a floured work surface and roll it out to a thickness of ¼ inch. Cut the dough into sticks about 3½ inches long and 1¼ inch wide. Place on a floured tray, cover with a kitchen towel, and leave to rise to double the size. This second rising should take around 30 minutes. Meanwhile, heat the oil in a deep-fat fryer or large saucepan to 340°F.

When the sticks have risen, drop them, a few at a time, into the hot oil for about 5 minutes, turning them halfway through, until golden brown in color. Drain on paper towels, then dip into sugar or cinnamon sugar.

Mix the *crema* with *strega* and pour into a bowl for dipping and serve with blackberries in *grappa* or cherries in syrup. Any homemade jam is good too, or dilute blackberry or blueberry jam with *sambuca* or another liqueur and serve this for dipping the doughnut sticks.

Makes about 8–12 pieces of fruit, using an 8–inch block

If you intend to hang the fruit, model the shapes around a piece of green florist's wire, or use the stems from apples, or small twigs from the garden, to make realistic stems. Leave the fruits to dry overnight, then the next day they can be painted with food coloring and left to dry once more. If they have wires, hang them on the Christmas tree; or eat the unwired versions. Do let people know if they contain inedible parts!

Formaggi

CHAPTER 11: CHEESE

Formaggi
INTRODUCTION

I only realized how crucial cheese is to Italian cooking when I had to come up with some ideas for a student at our school who couldn't eat dairy products. I should have remembered that I once made a spectacular faux pas when friends came to dinner and I included Italian cheese in every course, completely forgetting that one of our friends hated cheese—but when you are cooking Italian food it is second nature to add Parmesan, pecorino, ricotta, mozzarella, or mascarpone to so many dishes. They add body and flavor—and Parmesan (or *Grana Padano*) and pecorino are used almost like flavor enhancers, to bring out the taste of fellow ingredients, rather than make a dish actually taste cheesy.

talians think of cheese, whether it is made from cow, sheep, goat, or buffalo milk, as a great source of easily-digested energy (even as an aphrodisiac, in the case of Parmesan), and it is eaten before the dessert course or fruit at a formal meal, often with quince jam, honey, caramelized walnuts, or semi-dried grapes; and in most homes it will be included as part of the *antipasti*, a light meal or as a snack. One of the first things I ate with Giancarlo's family was pecorino with ripe pears and a little honey drizzled over the two (a combination that dates back to Roman times). And I can still taste the fresh fava beans we peeled and ate in Puglia with shavings of the local pecorino.

When friends come around, I sometimes serve *crostini*, along with slices of *bresaola* rolled around some arugula leaves and Parmesan, and I put out finger-sized wedges of young pecorino or sweet (*dolce*) gorgonzola cheese with a pot of acacia honey, so people can put a tiny spoonful on top. Very gooey and sticky and gorgeous—there is something about the combination of Italian cheese and honey that works so well. I might also put out other cheeses such as *Vezzena di Malga* or a *Canestrato Pecorino* and buy a jar of good *mostarda di frutta* (mustard fruits) to serve with them.

Until recent times, very few Italian cheeses beyond the most famous, such as Parmesan, gorgonzola, and mozzarella, were known outside Italy, but these days more and more artisan, smaller production cheeses are finding their way into specialist cheese shops and delicatessens. And we aren't the only ones discovering previously unheard of Italian cheeses—so are the Italians. Fabio Antoniazzi of *La Credenza*, who brings us our cheeses, grew up in Conegliano, at the foot of the Dolomites, and when he was young, his family only ever had *Asiago* or *Montasio* cheese on the table at home, just as my husband Giancarlo only knew Tuscan cheese as a boy.

Nowadays, Fabio spends his time travelling the country, discovering more and more regional styles that he is excited about, from the north (particularly the Alps, where the greatest number of local examples seem to be made)

to Sicily. Even in regions such as Molise and Basilicata there are some wonderful cheeses, the likes of *Provolone* and artisan aged pecorinos.

And in Veneto there are cheeses that are put into wine to preserve them, as originally it was too expensive to coat them in oil, so they are called *ubriaco*—"drunken" cheeses.

With the help of the Slow Food movement, very old cheeses are being saved from extinction, such as *Montebore* from Piedmont, which dates from the 15th century and is made with cow's and sheep's milk in three layers, so that it looks like a little wedding cake. Local producers with small, free-ranging herds are being supported, and old traditions are being maintained, so that the cheeses "stay pure." For example, near Piedmont, they use a particular breed of cow to give the milk to make *Toma*.

Typical of the small cheese makers Fabio has discovered are the Madaio family, who have been making and maturing cheese using buffalo's, goat's, and sheep's milk, for four generations in the Cilento National Park area in Campania and have built special cellars on their farms (as they are not allowed to use the old caves, due to health and safety regulations). They have even been able to take the molds from the original caves and reproduce them in the cellars to create the same environment, and they continue to make the cheese in the same way as their ancestors did.

Fabio is fascinated by such local traditions and loves the seasonality of cheeses—something we rarely think about in this country, when cheese is on sale all year round.

According to Fabio, if you see a fresh goat cheese on sale on January 10th, you should be worried, as this is the wrong time of year for a goat to be making cheese! He feels the natural cycle should be maintained, which means that goat cheese should be non-existent for two months of the year (between January and beginning of March) when the goats are pregnant and don't have milk. Surely we can go without goat cheese for two months!

A BIT OF CHEESE HISTORY

Cheese has been made since pre-historic times in Italy. The Greek colonies in Sicily in the 5th century BC were famous for their cheese-making skills and they taught the Etruscans and Romans. The Roman scholar Pliny wrote about cheese stimulating love-making. The Latin for cheese was *caseus*, which in turn became *cacio* in Italian, a word that is still used today in parts of Italy. When cheeses were molded they were put into a "form"—or *forma* in Latin—which became the more familiar *formaggio* in Italian.

In the days of the Romans cheese was made from sheep's and goat's milk and Gillian Riley, in her *Oxford Companion to Italian Food*, talks about Archestratus (the Greek poet who lived in Syracuse in Sicily) using cheese grated over fish, which is interesting, as these days Italians have a well-known aversion to mixing fish and cheese together. Later, around the time of Jesus, the Romans made cheese out of cow's milk as well as goat's and sheep's milk, and their soldiers were fed a diet of bread, cheese and garlic to ward off diseases. The Romans used rennet (an enzyme that coagulates milk) from the stomach of sheep or kid goats, or a vegetable rennet found in fig sap or thistle flowers. I was told that, in Tuscany, cheese used to be made with rennet from artichoke flowers.

It is amazing how many Italian ideas for using cheese date back to Roman times. Again, according to Gillian Riley, the Romans were also the first to smoke cheese and to add flavor by rolling it in thyme or black pepper. Cheese is not only used in sauces (see Flaming Pecorino on page 477) but sometimes incorporated into the dough before baking (see the recipe for Easter Cheese Bread on page 56), or fried. The recipe for Ricotta, Lemon, and Cinnamon Tart on page 443 is derived from an old Roman recipe using ricotta and honey. During the dark ages, though, it was often monks who kept the art of cheese-making alive, and when you read the history of many local cheeses, there is often a reference to a monastery.

Formaggi italiani
ITALIAN CHEESES

These are some of the cheeses you are most likely to be able to find outside Italy, in Italian delicatessens and specialist cheese shops.

Asiago

A semi-fat cheese made from cow's milk and named after the area in Veneto near Vicenza where it is made. It is a cheese that has been made since the middle ages but, until recent years, wasn't well known outside the Veneto. There are two kinds of *Asiago*. The one we have at the restaurants is *Asiago pressato*, which is a young cheese with lots of holes, a springy rind and quite a delicate flavor. The second kind, *Asiago d'allevo*, is still delicate, but more tangy. It is called *mezzano* at three months old or *vecchio* at nine months old or more, when it becomes good for grating.

Burrata

I watched this beautiful, rich cheese being made in Cilento, the area south of Naples, where a small production is made from buffalo milk, though it is traditionally a speciality of Puglia, where it is made with cow's milk. It is similar to mozzarella, but the pouch of cheese is filled with buttery cream and tied closed. Often it comes traditionally wrapped in bright green *asphodel* (lily) leaves, and it should be eaten absolutely fresh. Often it will be served with extra virgin olive oil drizzled over it, and black pepper.

Caciocavallo

A very old and typically southern Italian cow's milk cheese whose name means "horseback," it belongs to the *pasta filata* family, which includes mozzarella, and is shaped like a pouch, tied with string—its name is said to come from the fact that the cheeses are matured by hanging in pairs over a beam, as if astride a horse. The young cheese is quite mild and smooth but it becomes more tangy and hard with age.

Castelmagno

From Piedmont, this is an ancient cheese, mentioned as far back as the 12th century, that is made with cow's milk, with some sheep or goat's milk usually added. It is white when it is young, and naturally blue-veined when it is more mature, and has a semi-hard, crumbly texture and salty flavor.

Fontina

This semi-soft cow's milk cheese, made in the Val d'Aosta in the north of Italy, was written about in 1477 but was possibly found on Roman tables. Traditional for *fonduta* (see page 472), it has a slightly sweet, nutty taste and, like Parmesan, acts as a flavor enhancer in cooking.

Gorgonzola

Italy's famous blue cheese comes in two styles: *dolce* (sweet), which is the young mild-tasting cheese; and *piccante*, which is more mature, and stronger and more salty-tasting, with marked blue-green veining.

Grana Padano

Grana simply means grainy and, since Parmesan is also a *grana* cheese, for many years, until *Parmigiano Reggiano* received DOP status in 1996 (which meant that true Parmesan could only be made in a limited area of Italy) it was sold around the world as parmesan. The wheels of cheese look very similar and both cheeses are made in a similar way. *Grana Padano* hails from Lombardy and has its own DOP, though it can be made in a much wider area. The cheese was first made by Cistercian monks 1000 years ago and, in the north of Italy in particular, it is used in cooking in any way that you might use Parmesan: for example, in risotto. As always, Italians will debate which is best—but most agree that *Grana Padano* is lighter, slightly more sweet and moist, whereas *Parmigiano Reggiano* has a more complex, salty flavor and crystalline texture.

Marzolino

This cheese is made to a very old tradition, brought to Tuscany by Sardinian shepherds, which became very popular amongst the nobles in Catherine de Medici's time. Apparently, when she went to France to marry Henry II, she took with her olive oil and *marzolino* cheese. When young, the cheese is white and relatively soft; in the more mature cheeses the skin becomes a reddish color and the flavor more tangy.

Mascarpone

This creamy, soft white, subtly-flavored cheese originally comes from Lodi in Lombardy but is now made across the region. As with ricotta, purists would say it isn't actually a cheese, as it is made from cream—and if you eat it fresh, you can appreciate the floral scents which are a result of the special grasses and herbs fed to the cows. Most of the mascarpone we see outside of Italy, however, is sold in tubs and has a longer shelf-life. It is a key ingredient in *tiramisu*, the now world-famous dessert from Treviso, and also in *crema al mascarpone*, made by whipping the cheese with sugar, eggs and rum and serving the mixture in glasses or cups, sometimes with a base of crumbled *amaretti*.

Mozzarella

Though mozzarella can be made from cow's milk (which should really be called *fior di latte*), the best is made fresh from the milk of the water buffalo that first arrived in Italy from China in the 6th century AD and which graze in and around Campania. Mozzarella, along with *burrata*, *provolone,* and *caciocavallo*, is one of the group called *pasta filata*, meaning "stretchy cheese." This refers to the process in which the curd is cut up and has boiling water poured over it to make it melt. It is then stirred with a stick and strings of melting cheese are formed that look like a thick cobweb. This mass is then gathered up and smaller lumps are pinched off by hand, which is what gives the cheese its distinctive shape and slightly frilly edge. Sold floating in watery whey, the pure white mozzarella is delicate, fresh and fragrant, with a slightly tangy flavor, and the very best is eaten just on its own, or with tomatoes and olives in *insalata caprese*.

Montasio

This cheese is attributed to a 14th century monk who was in charge of the mountain huts in the Montasio mountains in the Veneto/Friuli region, where the herds of cows were taken in the summer. It can be eaten young, semi-aged, or aged, when it is often used for grating.

Parmigiano Reggiano (see page 474)

Pecorino (see page 476)

Provolone

This curd cheese was originally made with buffalo and cow's milk, but nowadays it is more likely to be made solely with cow's milk. Calf's rennet is used for the sweet *provolone* and lamb's rennet for the spicier version. Mainly made in Campania and Puglia, but also in other regions, including the north, it is pale yellow with a smooth, shiny skin, and is molded into various shapes, often according to the tradition of the region in which it is made. They might be melon, cone, *salami*, or flask-shaped, or they can be small (*provolette*), or medium (*provole*).

Ricotta (see page 470)

Robiola

Sometimes round, sometimes square, these really soft, creamy cheeses from Piedmont might be made with any combination of cow's, sheep's, or goat's milk.

Stracchino

Creamy, melting, and sweet, this is one of my favorite cheeses and I have always wondered why it is not readily available outside Italy. From Lombardy in the north, *stracchino* is also the name for a group of cheeses that used to be made at the end of summer when the cows were tired (*stracca* in local dialect). Nowadays it is made all year round. Other cheeses in the *stracchino* family include *crescenza*, a light, elastic cheese that is often used in sauces and for melting.

Taleggio

Though the name *Taleggio* has only been used since the early 20th century, these cow's milk cheeses have a history going back to the 10th and 11th centuries when they were first made in the Val Taleggio region of Lombardy. As they mature they are "washed" with a salt-water brine, and some of the most famous are matured in the caves of Valsassina in Como. The young cheeses are quite mild but they can become tangier as they get older.

Formaggi

MASTERCLASS

Ricotta

Ricotta means "re-cooked" in Italian. Technically it isn't a cheese at all, as it is made from whey, while cheeses are made from curds. It is a by-product made by re-cooking some of the whey that is left over from making cheese—the rest is traditionally fed to animals, especially pigs. Creamy and white, and not dissimilar to cottage cheese in texture, ricotta can be used in salty and savory dishes. Ricotta is also sometimes smoked, for use in savory dishes, which helps to preserve it and also gives it a wonderful flavor.

Ricotta al limone
Ricotta with Lemon

This version of ricotta is easy to make at home, using whole milk instead of whey, and lemon juice, rather than the traditional rennet, to introduce acid. Use buffalo milk, if you can find it (see suppliers list): it has a higher buttermilk and fat content (though it is lower in cholesterol).

Makes approximately 8 oz

2 quarts whole milk, preferably buffalo milk
1 level teaspoon salt
4 tablespoons lemon juice

Place four layers of cheesecloth or muslin in a colander and set it inside a bowl. Have this ready near the stove. Heat the milk and salt to a simmer. When the milk is just about to boil, reduce the heat so the milk simmers, then stir in 3 tablespoons of lemon juice. Keep stirring and, after a couple of minutes, lumps will appear: these are the curds.

Use a slotted spoon to lift out the curds and put them into the muslin in the colander. Keep doing this until no more curds appear. To make sure you have taken all the curds out of the whey, stir in another tablespoon of lemon juice. Spoon the remaining curds into the muslin. Allow the cheese to drain for a couple of minutes, then put it into a mold to drain further. If you don't have one, poke some holes in the bottom of a yogurt container with a corkscrew, then stand this in another, slightly larger pot. Use the cheese right away—or, when it reaches room temperature, it can be stored in the fridge for a couple of days.

Note:
If the milk doesn't separate, simply add a few more drops of lemon juice until it does.

Mozzarella in carrozza
Deep-fried Mozzarella

In carrozza literally translates as "in a carriage," a fanciful description of the precious *mozzarella* being cushioned and carried by slices of soft white bread. *Carrozza* are great as part of a spread of *antipasti* or as a light lunch with salad dressed in walnut oil and some Oven-dried Tomatoes (see page 372).

Serves 4 as antipasti or 2 for a lunch

4 slices of good-quality white bread
2 anchovy fillets, each cut into 4
2 x 4 oz balls buffalo mozzarella (or cow's milk mozzarella)
sunflower oil, for frying
flour, for coating, in a flat dish
1 egg, beaten, in a flat dish
6 tablespoons fine dry breadcrumbs, in a flat dish

Put two slices of bread on the work surface. Lay four anchovy pieces on each slice. Cut the mozzarella balls into slices and lay them over the anchovies, leaving the crusts of the bread clear. Put the other slices of bread on top and press down with the palm of your hand, to seal the sandwich. Cut off the crusts (and give them to the birds in your garden).

Heat the sunflower oil in a frying pan or deep-fat fryer to about 340°F. Test the temperature by dropping in a small piece of bread: if it sizzles and becomes brown within a couple of minutes, the oil is ready.

Dip the sandwiches first in flour, then in egg, then in breadcrumbs to coat them all over. Carefully place in the hot oil and deep-fry for about 10 minutes or until golden brown, turning halfway through cooking time. Drain on paper towels and serve immediately.

Crostini con marmellata e formaggio
Cheese Crostini with Jam (see photo on page 476)

Jam is frequently served with cheese in Italy. I have had pecorino with strawberry jam, ricotta with marmalade, and smoked *scamorza* with fig jam. To do this, simply spread some toasted bread with fig jam and then grate some cheese such as smoked *scamorza* or pecorino over the top. Melt it under the broiler, grind some black pepper on top, scatter with some chopped parsley and serve.

Sformato di formaggio
Sformato of Cheese

These can be served with a Fresh Tomato Sauce (see page 102), Roasted Red Pepper Sauce (see page 104), or a dressed green salad. They are good either hot or at room temperature. If you want to make them a day ahead, they can be reheated for 10 minutes in the oven, in a bain-marie, at 350°F.

Serves 6

butter, for greasing
a handful of fine breadcrumbs or 2 tablespoons finely grated Parmesan, for lining the molds
8 oz ricotta (sheep's or cow's milk)
4 tablespoons heavy cream, mascarpone or Greek-style yogurt
½ cup finely grated Parmesan or pecorino
¼ nutmeg, finely grated
1 tablespoon finely chopped herbs (thyme, oregano or rosemary)
3 eggs
salt and freshly ground black pepper

Preheat the oven to 325°F. Select six molds, such as thin metal dariole molds, or ramekins. Butter them inside and line the bottom of each one with a circle of parchment paper. Dust the rest of the inside of the mold with either breadcrumbs or Parmesan. Shake out the excess.

In a mixing bowl, combine the ricotta, cream or yogurt, cheese, nutmeg, herbs, salt and pepper. In another bowl, whisk the eggs until frothy, then combine them with the rest of the ingredients. (Check the seasoning, if you don't mind eating raw eggs). Pour this mixture into the moulds until they are three-quarters full.

Stand the molds in an ovenproof dish, such as a lasagne dish, and put this into the oven. Pour a jug of water around the molds to come halfway up the sides.

Cook for around 40 minutes or until they are golden brown and slightly risen. Remove from the oven and leave to rest for a few minutes. When you are ready to serve them, work around the edge with a round-bladed knife and turn out. Serve on individual plates with sauce or salad.

Fonduta
Cheese Soup

As the province of Piedmont borders Switzerland, there is bound to be a crossover of recipes between the Italian and Swiss way of cooking local produce. However, this isn't as simple as using Italian cheeses to make a fondue; there is no ceramic bowl with cows painted on it set over a little candle and served with forks for dipping. In this recipe, Piedmont cheese (such as *Asiago* or *Fontina*)—is soaked in milk for hours before being transformed into a velvety, thick soup. It's rich, filling and utterly addictive.

1½ lb melting cheese (e.g. *fontalle*, *valdostana*, *Fontina*, *Asiago* or *Toma*)
2 cups milk
5 egg yolks

Crumble the cheese into small lumps about the size of your fingertip, into a medium bowl. Pour in the milk until the cheese is just covered and leave to rest for 2–3 hours in the fridge.

Drain the milk into a bowl, then pour off half of it. Put the remaining milk and cheese into a saucepan and add the egg yolks. Set the pan over a low heat and cook until the cheese has completely melted. Do not let it boil and keep stirring continuously with a wooden spoon. It will thicken; you want it to be the consistency of thick custard. Serve in warmed bowls with crusty bread and—if you are lucky enough to get hold of some—shavings of white or black truffle.

Gelato al Parmigiano
Parmesan Ice Cream

This recipe is based on one that my friend India told me about. She was dining high up in the mountains of northern Italy and was served truffle risotto with Parmesan ice cream that melted into the rice and ran down the sides like lava from a volcano. It sounded great so I have created a Parmesan ice cream. The truffle risotto recipe can be found on page 210.

Makes 2 cups, serves 8–10

1 cup milk
⅓ cup heavy cream
2 bay leaves
4 oz Parmesan, shaved
2 tablespoons Marsala dolce (sweet)
8 oz ricotta
salt (if necessary)

Put the milk, cream, and bay leaves in a medium saucepan and bring to the boil. Remove from the heat and add the shavings of Parmesan, stirring to melt them into the milk. Add the Marsala and then transfer to a freezerproof container to cool. Remove the bay leaves and add the ricotta, whisking it in to smooth out any lumps.

Put the container in the freezer (I usually leave the whisk in too). After 30 minutes, whisk again to make the consistency lighter and fluffier. Repeat the freezing and whisking a couple of times, then remove the whisk and leave in the fridge if you are going to use it that day. Otherwise freeze completely and remember to bring it out of the freezer and put into the fridge the day before you need it.

Serve in scoops over risotto, soups, hot toast, or over mashed potato. You can also make the semi-frozen iced cream into *quenelles* using two teaspoons. Put these on a tray covered with baking parchment and freeze them individually, ready to be dropped onto hot risotto straight from the freezer.

Tomino avvolto nel prosciutto di Parma
Tomino Wrapped with Parma Ham

Tomino are little circular cheeses made from full-cream milk from a cow, goat or sheep—or sometimes all three—from the alpine valleys of Piedmont. As indicated by the "*-ino*" at the end of the word, they are smaller versions of the large *Toma* cheese from the same area. They are often eaten on their own with herby oil poured over them. I saw *Tomino* wrapped in ham in Bologna and was determined to try it at home. I love the flavor of the cooked ham with the melting cheese and together they blend particularly well with the sweet balsamic and toasted pine nuts.

Serves 4

1 round or long radicchio
2 tablespoons olive oil
2 tablespoons honey
2 tablespoons pine nuts
4 *Tomino*
4 slices Parma ham
2 teaspoons aged balsamic vinegar
salt and freshly ground black pepper

Preheat the oven to 350°F. Split the radicchio lengthwise into four pieces. Lay them on to a baking sheet and drizzle with the olive oil and honey. Season with salt and pepper and scatter over the pine nuts. Bake for 10 minutes or until the radicchio are slightly softened and lightly browned. Remove from the oven and set aside.

Wrap each *Tomino* in a slice of Parma ham and set aside. Arrange the radicchio on serving plates with the pine nuts and any juices from the pan poured over the top.

Heat a non-stick frying pan and dry-fry the cheeses over a medium heat until the ham is lightly browned and begins to crisp, and the cheese starts to melt inside. Lay each wrapped cheese on the radicchio and serve with crusty bread. Drizzle with some syrupy balsamic vinegar.

Parmigiano Reggiano and Grana Padano

PARMESAN CHEESE

Parmesan is probably the most famous cheese in the world, though in fact it is outsold by *Grana Padano*, which looks and tastes very similar, and has been made in Lombardy for over a thousand years, pre-dating Parmesan by about 200 years. Both belong to the family of *grana* or "grainy" cheeses and for many years, outside Italy, *Grana Padano* was considered a type of parmesan. Then EC laws made it illegal to call a cheese Parmesan unless it was produced to traditional specifications within a designated area. *Parmigiano Reggiano*, as the authentic cheese from the region is known, can these days only be made in the original production areas of Reggio Emilia and Parma, as well as in Modena and part of Bologna, on the left bank of the river Reno, and Mantua, on the right bank of the river Po. Approximately 10,000 *caseifici* or dairies around the hills and valleys supply the milk for only 600 or so cheese houses.

When the new law came in, it had the effect of raising the price and image of *Parmigiano Reggiano* overnight. It also left producers of *Grana Padano* with an identity crisis outside Italy. Like Parmesan, the cheese has its own PDO (protected designation of origin); however, it can be made over a much bigger area: throughout most of the Po Valley from Piemonte and Lombardy to Veneto, and as far as Trento. Only slowly has it found a niche for itself again in the rest of the world and as it can be cheaper it is often used as an alternative to Parmesan.

I sometimes think you would need to be a real connoisseur to tell the difference—though many Italians will say they can tell the difference blindfolded, and there is a big debate over which cheese is best. If you come from Lombardy you may well prefer, and only ever use, *Grana Padano*; in other regions you might use it for cooking but serve *Parmigiano Reggiano* as a table cheese, as it is often considered a little saltier and more complex, and has a slightly more crystalline texture which many people like; whereas *Grana Padano* can be a little lighter, creamier, and sweeter—and,

some say, fruitier, even with a hint of pineapple. This may be to do with the fact that *Grana Padano* is often eaten slightly younger. In both cases, you can buy cheeses at different stages of maturity, though *Grana Padano* is usually aged for between 9 and 24 months, and often eaten at around 16–18 months. You can also buy *riserva* cheeses, which must meet stringent criteria and must be aged for at least 20–24 months. By contrast, most people consider a *Parmigiano Reggiano* aged for 24 months to be just right for eating. In some restaurants, a wheel of *Parmigiano Reggiano stravecchio* (over two years old) will be brought to your table at the end of a meal, and the inside scooped out with a special short-handled knife, which allows the cheese to break apart according to its natural structure.

The production methods are very similar for both cheeses but there are important differences. Although both cheeses are made from a combination of morning and evening milkings, in the case of *Parmigiano Reggiano*, the fattier milk from the evening milking is first separated and the skimmed milk mixed with the whole milk the following morning.

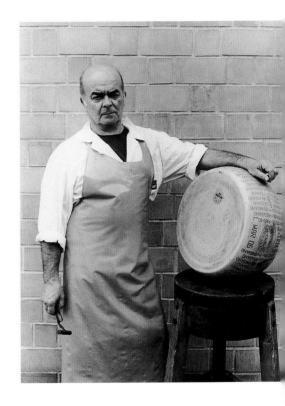

On the rind of a wheel of Parmesan you will see the code number of the dairy and the date of production, along with the branded mark of the consortium on it. The words *Parmigiano Reggiano* are also inscribed around the rind in pin-dot writing, so that part of the name appears on every wedge. On the rind of a wheel of *Grana Padano* you will see the name of the consortium within a diamond mark, with the number of the dairy that made it and the date of production within a four-leaf clover.

Many of the cheeses of both styles are made from the milk of large herds of cows kept in barns because, these days, it is considered that the lifestyle of cows who laze around indoors produces richer, creamier milk. However, it is possible to find *Parmigiano di Montagna* or *Parmigiano Reggiano Vacche Rosse,* which is made in the mountains from cows kept in fields. Such mountain Parmesan has a deeper, stronger flavor and is less sweet.

Crema di formaggio
Gino's Potted Cheese Spread

This is a recipe that Gino's mother used to make. Her family kept cows in the high pastures of the hills outside Parma. Every day the cows would be milked and every day she and the other women of the area would walk miles downhill following a bumpy path full of potholes (hence the expression "no use crying over spilt milk!"), carrying a yoke with open pails of milk. Unlike in the UK, where this way of life came to an end a hundred or so years ago, in Italy it was still taking place only 50 years ago. Eventually the women's walk was replaced by a van that came to collect the milk from the distant farms. What a welcome relief that van must have been. The women would be given cheese and butter in return for their milk and this amount would be deducted from the amount they were paid for the milk. Apparently the farmer collecting the milk would hide as the women arrived, in order to avoid paying them as frequently as they would have liked! Gino's mother would finely grate any leftover cheese and mix it, as in the following recipe details, in order to preserve it further.

Makes 8 oz, enough to spread on 10–12 crostini (2½ x 2¼ inches)

1½ cups *Pecorino Toscano* or Parmesan (or a mixture of the two), finely grated
3 tablespoons olive oil
4 tablespoons dry white wine
a good pinch of chili powder (optional)

Mix the ingredients together in a medium bowl and adjust the chili powder to taste, if using. Use right away or spoon into a standard sized jar and press it down. Cover with a layer of oil and store in the fridge for up to a month. Gino suggests serving this on *crostini* with honey drizzled over the top, or with caramelized figs, or arugula.

Pecorino

In various regions of Italy there are pecorino cheeses made from sheep's milk that share many similarities, particularly in the way they are rubbed with olive oil, and some also with tomato paste. The origins of this ancient cheese go back 2000 years. These days there are five distinct types (described below), which are defined and protected by Italian law. You might also come across Pecorino di Fossa, aged in cellars and traditional pits in Umbria; Pecorino Affinato in Vinaccia; and Pecorino Tartufo, made with black and white truffles.

Pecorino comes in varying degrees of ripeness, from young to mature, according to the style. Mature pecorino, which can be sweet, nutty, and piquant, is often used instead of Parmesan for grating, or served with fruit and honey after a meal.

Pecorino Romano is a sharp, zesty sheep's milk cheese made in Latium (Lazio), Tuscany, and Sardinia. Aged for at least five months for the table, it is also hardened for at least eight months to give a fairly strong-tasting cheese for grating.

Pecorino Fiore Sardo can be lightly smoked and ripened for a few months for the table, and for more than six months for grating, at which point it develops a sharper flavor.

Pecorino Sardo has a *dolce* (mild) version, aged for 40–60 days, and a *piccante*, a hard cheese, aged for at least two months. There is an old and curious delicacy called *casu marzu* ("rotten Pecorino" or "maggot cheese"), where the larvae of the cheese fly are introduced into the *Pecorino Sardo*. These days it is (technically) illegal to sell the cheese.

Pecorino Toscano is made with sheep's milk from herds in Tuscany and a few towns near Perugia and Viterbo. Though aged for at least four months, it is a relatively mild cheese, traditionally eaten simply with a slice of pear.

Pecorino Siciliano is aged for at least four months and is the strongest and most spicy of the pecorino cheeses.

Pecorino al flambé
Flaming Pecorino

I saw this dish in the famous restaurant, Andreini, in Alghero, Sardinia. Cristiano the chef/owner set fire to a Sardinian pecorino cheese that had been hollowed out inside. He scraped the cheese from around the hollow then added cooked *tagliolini* pasta with brandy and cream. The hot pasta blended with the melted cheese and it was served right away. You need to find the strongest alcohol possible (minimum 60 percent proof), such as the *alcol puro* that they have in Italy. UK laws prohibit us using alcohol like this, apparently because we would all become raving alcoholics, according to my local French off-licence, so I bring it back from Italy when I can, or use the strongest alcohol I can find.

Serves 2

6 oz *linguine* or *tagliolini*,
  fresh or dried
salt
1 whole pecorino
1 tablespoons butter
½ white onion, finely chopped
2 tablespoons sage leaves,
  coarsely chopped
freshly ground black pepper
4 tablespoons dry white wine
4 tablespoons stock or pasta
  cooking water
2 tablespoons heavy cream
2 tablespoons alcohol
  (minimum 60 percent)
2 tablespoons brandy

Cook the pasta in boiling salted water. If using fresh pasta, do this after you have made the sauce; if using dried pasta, start to cook it while you make the sauce.

Hollow out the pecorino, reserving about 3 oz of scrapings in the bottom of the cheese.

Melt the butter in a frying pan and fry the onion, chopped sage, pepper and salt. When softened, add the white wine over a high heat and allow it to reduce for a minute or two. Then add the stock to the pan and let it reduce, as before. Add the cream and stir through.

Using a ladle, pour the alcohol and brandy into the cheese and set fire to it, using a taper or long match. When the flame has died away, scrape enough pecorino from around the edges for two portions of pasta (approximately 3 oz) and leave this in the bottom of the cheese.

When the pasta is cooked, drain and add it to the sauce in the pan. Stir to combine, then put it into the pecorino and toss it around inside, using tongs, to mix it with the cheese scrapings. Serve in warmed bowls, sprinkled with black pepper.

Conserve e

Liquori

CHAPTER 12: PRESERVES & LIQUEURS

Conserve e Liquori
INTRODUCTION

There is something magical (I really mean that) about swapping homemade food with someone. When our friends Vicky and Stephen came round with their buffalo milk to teach me how to make ricotta, in exchange I gave them a loaf of spelt bread and a jar of quince jam.

think homemade preserves, in particular, appeal to our instincts for self-sufficiency and survival by taking seasonal produce and making it into something that will last. And the pride you have when you use a tomato or other fruit picked from your garden, or a berry collected from the wild, rather than one bought from a shop, is even greater.

When I first began making my own bread and preserves, I remember the moment when I took my first bite of wholewheat bread with plum jam: it was gloriously tasty and marvellously self-satisfying. Now my cupboards are brimming with jars.

The preserving of fruits from summer to eat during the winter months is one of the oldest forms of cooking. Although it is rarer these days, many families still gather together in Italy to bottle ripe tomatoes for winter, or to help with the family olive harvest; and many a *nonna* will still make jam or preserved vegetables for her family.

My fear is that when this knowledgeable generation of women is gone, their recipes will be lost with them, unless their daughters take over, so I have been busily working with grandmothers in kitchens, scribbling down tips and measurements in order to "preserve the preserves" for future generations! This is not easy, as they rarely weigh any ingredients but simply judge quantities by looking and tasting.

Whether the origins are in poverty or whether it is just that they enjoy the endless search for perfect seasonal produce, the Italians are foragers. Less and less so, perhaps, as they move into the cities, and supermarkets become more popular, but still you see families out gathering "things" from the hillsides and woods. It might be wild herbs, fennel, chicory, or arugula, mushrooms, truffles, fruits, berries or nuts—some for eating immediately, and the rest to be preserved and enjoyed for the rest of the year.

When we ran our cooking course in Tuscany, almost every day I saw an old man and woman busily collecting in the distant field, their backs bent double. I could never manage to see (even through binoculars!) what it was they were gathering, but it must have been worth it, since their bags were always crammed full.

Preserving means altering the natural breakdown of the ingredient you wish to preserve. There are various methods which create conditions that inhibit micro-organisms from reproducing and prevent the food from decaying: you might use a strong alcohol such as *grappa*, brandy, or strong rum, an acidic substance such as vinegar or lemon juice, a sugary solution, or oil.

Jams

In Italian, jam is frequently referred to as *marmellata*, which can be confusing, as we think of marmalade as being made with citrus fruits and jams with other fruits. Even more confusingly, *conserva* is usually used to describe preserved tomatoes, whereas we have become used to seeing "conserve" on jam labels. Something new that was introduced to me by our friends Livia and Nello in Tuscany is baking jam in the oven. They love to use their outside oven for jam making, and I have had success translating their recipe to the domestic oven (see page 490).

The Italians I have worked with on preserving do not seem preoccupied with pectin—in fact, some of them didn't really know what it is, despite the fact that they have been making jams for years. I suppose they simply use their instincts whereas, if you read English books on preserving, they will always emphasize that getting the pectin level right is a crucial aspect of the job. The natural pectin found in fruits is what, when mixed with sugar, will make your jam set. It is found under the skin (particularly in the case of apples, pears, and citrus fruits) and also in the pith and seeds and, to a lesser extent, in the juice.

Fruit that is ripe but not overripe will contain more pectin. If a fruit is low in pectin, it is necessary to use more sugar, to add another fruit with a higher pectin level, or to add lemon juice, in order to make it set more easily.

KATIE'S PRESERVING TIPS

"Every fruit has its season" or so the proverb goes. Always use fruit at the peak of its natural season. Whether the fruit comes from the tree in your back garden, the market, or from on sale at the local supermarket, pick out the best specimens to preserve. Bruised and half rotten fruit will spoil the color and flavor of the finished preserve. Wash the fruit well under cold running water to eliminate any insects or traces of pesticide.

If you can, use organic fruit to ensure your end result is as natural and harmless as possible. Many Italians grow their own fruit or collect it from the wild but, as the organic market grows in Italy, this is the preferred choice of many. It is especially important with citrus fruits known as *agrumi* as you will want to use the skin. Although any protective wax can be removed, some chemicals could have penetrated the skin, so seek out fruits that are unwaxed as well as organic. Wonderful lemons and oranges are available from the southern coasts of Italy and the island of Sicily—so for a true Italian flavor, see if you can find these.

I use a large, heavy-bottomed saucepan for my preserving that is wide enough for the water to evaporate from the cooking fruit. Preserving pans are ideal but I have never invested in one as I already have far too many saucepans in my kitchen! Avoid aluminium pans as the acidity of the fruit reacts with them.

Stir frequently using a wooden spoon with a long handle so that the jam doesn't stick to the bottom of the pan.

It can speed up the process if you put the sugar and fruit together and leave it overnight, so there is less stirring to do the next day.

Skim the surface of the jam frequently while cooking, to remove the impurities. Some fruits will need this more than others. Small fruits can be seeded in this way, as the seeds bubble up to the surface.

Delia Smith recommends stirring a tablespoon of butter into the jam at the end to disperse and eliminate the foam.

For flavored oil (see page 486) or Limoncello, bottles can be sterilized in boiling water for 10 minutes.

Use lids that are coated in plastic for preserves containing vinegar, or the metal will deteriorate. Either use a lid that you know came from a product containing vinegar, such as pickles, or buy them new.

Even if you are using perfectly ripe, sweet fruit, sugar is needed for preservation. If you end up with more than a 60 percent sugar content in a jam (from added sugar as well as the natural sugar in the fruit), it will be hard for micro-organisms to breed. The quantity of sugar needed will depend on the type of fruit and its ripeness, as will the cooking time, though it has to be sufficiently long to ensure a good conservation period. In Italy there is only one kind of sugar available which is halfway between superfine sugar and granulated sugar—either will do for these recipes.

When is the jam ready?

As a general guide, the setting point of jam is 220°F. Using a jam thermometer is a very useful way of telling when you are near setting point, but it is not essential. The Italians I have worked with prefer to judge by eye when the jam is thick enough and it is time to stop cooking. It is important to stop at the right time, as cooking jam for too long will crystallize the sugar and make it thick and solid, but cooking it for too short a time means it won't set, even to a soft stage, and it is also more likely to become moldy. Look out for the bubbles; when the jam is ready the bubbles will be smaller and, in the case of citrus fruit, the color will become darker.

Cold saucer test

To test for setting point without a thermometer, put about three saucers in the freezer before you start, so that they become very cold. When the jam is starting to thicken and you think you are near setting point, put a teaspoon of bubbling jam on to one of the cold saucers and put it back in the freezer. If it forms a skin on the surface after a few minutes and wrinkles to the touch, it is at setting point; if it remains runny, boil it for longer.

Sterilizing the jars

There are many ways to sterilise jars. In Italy, they simply wash them well and then, after filling, boil them in hot water (a bain-marie) to create a vacuum and sterilize the contents. Giancarlo's Aunt Gina washes out the jars with a little *grappa* just before using them, to kill any bacteria.

Generally speaking, the British way is to sterilize the jars before filling them. I usually re-use jars of various shapes and sizes over and over again but avoid large ones, as often the contents will not be eaten quickly enough before mold begins to form.

I use an Anglo-Italian way of sterilizing and bottling, which works for me. Always sterilize the jars just before you need them so that they are not hanging around gathering further bacteria. Wash the jars and lids, using very hot water and detergent, then rinse them well to eliminate any trace of the detergent. Boil the lids in water for 10 minutes, to sterilize them. Put the jars upside-down, to drain on an oven rack at 225°F for 15 minutes. Alternatively, wash the jars and their lids in a dishwasher on a hot cycle.

Filling the jars

While still hot, fill the jars with your hot jam, marmalade, or other liquid. Filling the jars while they are still hot will mean they are less likely to crack and that they haven't been hanging around too long, exposed to unwanted micro-organisms. Leave a ¾ inch gap at the top to form a vacuum. Always seal the jars

Unwanted guests in preserves

The rule of preserve-making is to get whatever you are making into the jar with the least number of micro-organisms present. There are three ways to help prevent this. Firstly, sterilize jars to kill any "unwanted guests," and make sure you use very clean equipment and work surfaces. Secondly, follow the quantities and methods given in recipes correctly: provided you produce the right alcohol, sugary, or acidic solutions, it is hard for micro-organisms to breed. (When you preserve vegetables under oil, micro-organisms will be denied oxygen so their reproduction is inhibited.) Thirdly, make sure you cook fruit or vegetables at high temperatures, so that any micro-organisms are killed.

On the safe side

If, when you open your preserves, you discover that the vacuum on the lid has failed and it is domed, not sunken, or if there is mold on the jam or an unpleasant aroma from your preserve, it is much better to err on the safe side and throw the contents away, however painful this may feel after all your efforts! Once a jar of your preserve is open, always store it in the fridge.

as soon as they are filled. Put the lids on tightly unless using screw-band lids, which should be left slightly loose, then tightened after boiling.

Creating a vacuum

Lay a cloth or wire rack on the bottom of a large saucepan. Put the jars on top and fill with warm water so they are completely covered. If there are not enough jars to fill the pan, wrap a cotton kitchen towel around them to support them and stop clattering against one another. Heat the pan until the water is boiling, then simmer for 15 minutes. If they are very large, boil them for 20–30 minutes.

Turn off the heat and let the jars cool to room temperature before removing them from the water. As they cool you should hear a clicking sound as the lids are sucked in when the vacuum has formed. Dry the jars, label them, and store your preserves in a dark cupboard.

In some recipes, it will state that the fruits or vegetables should not come into contact with heat, as with fruits preserved in alcohol (the alcohol is enough to kill any bacteria); and also with vegetables preserved under oil, as the oil will close off oxygen. In these cases, after sterilizing the jars, place them upside-down on a rack and leave them to cool to room temperature before filling.

Preserved tomatoes

San Marzano tomatoes are the best for preserving as they contain less water and they have more flesh than other varieties. Peeled, uncooked tomatoes, *pomodori pelati* are bottled, sometimes with the addition of basil, when there is a summer glut.

For *conserva* or passata, the tomatoes are cooked with a little salt and with or without aromatic herbs such as basil or garlic (see Gregorio's Cherry Tomato Passata, page 166, and Giovanna's Fresh Tomato Sauce, page 102). Passata is cooked for over an hour, the exact time depending on the wateriness of the tomatoes, then passed through a sieve, to eliminate the skins and pips and give a smooth sauce which can be added to other dishes or poured over a pan of fried onions and garlic to make a sauce for pasta, fish, or meat.

Frutta Sotto Spirito
FRUITS IN SPIRIT

More in grappa
Blackberries in Grappa

When blackberries abound in the hedgerows, pick as many as you can and preserve them in grappa. This not only makes a wonderful dessert with ice cream but can be strained into champagne flûtes and topped up with prosecco. This is also delicious when reduced to a runny jam consistency and served with venison or duck.

Makes about 2 lb (3 or 4 jars)

1½ lb blackberries
5 cloves
zest of 1 lemon, cut into long strips
3 cups grappa
½ cup caster sugar
4 star anise

Pick over the blackberries, discarding stems and leaves, and wash them if necessary. Stick the cloves into the lemon zest so that they can be retrieved later. Put all the ingredients in a medium saucepan and bring to the boil, then simmer for 30 minutes. Discard the lemon zest and cloves but leave in the star anise. Put into sterilized jars (see instructions on page 482).

Albicocche in Vecchia Romagna
Apricots in Vecchia Romagna Brandy

Make this in summer with just ripe apricots and Italian *Vecchia Romagna* brandy. It makes a wonderful Christmas present after six months maturing in the jars.

Makes about 2 x 24 oz jars

1 cup sugar
1¼ cups water
2¼ lb ripe apricots
1 long cinnamon stick, broken in half
2 star anise
1¼ cups *Vecchia Romagna* or other brandy

Sterilize two jars according to the method on page 482. Dissolve the sugar in the water in a medium saucepan. When just boiling, plunge the apricots into the syrup for a few seconds, then remove with a slotted spoon and put into the jars.

Add the cinnamon stick and star anise to the pan and leave to cook until the syrup thickens a little. Pour the brandy into the jars. Pour the syrup over the apricots and put star anise and a cinnamon stick in each.

Variation:
Ciliegie in brandy
Cherries in Brandy

Makes about 4 x 12 oz jars

2¼ lb cherries
2 cups sugar
1 quart brandy

Leaving the stalks intact, wash the cherries and dry them on kitchen paper. Put them into the jars with the sugar and top up with brandy. Seal and leave in a cool place for at least 2 weeks. Turn upside-down occasionally to help dissolve the sugar.

Frutta Sciroppata
FRUITS IN SYRUP

Ciliegie sciroppate
Cherries in Syrup

In Italy, summer fruits are frequently preserved in syrup for the winter months. It may be a dying trend in these more health-conscious times but I admit it is something I like to do with my children and they really enjoy them, while I prefer the ones in grappa or brandy! Perhaps we shouldn't turn our backs on canned fruit as an occasional treat; after all, a few years back every household bottled fruits to extend their use into winter, and this tradition has evolved into canned fruits available in all supermarkets. Canned pears are soft and easy to use in tarts and for a *coulis* and tinned cherries often have more flavor than fresh ones. Once you have your own bottled fruits, I am convinced you will use them up quickly.

Makes about 4 x 12 oz jars

3¼ lb cherries
1 cup sugar
1 quart water

Pick over the fruit, making sure they are unbruised and ripe. Leaving the stems intact, wash the cherries and dry them on kitchen paper. Sterilize the jars (see page 482), then distribute the fruit between them.

To make the syrup, put the sugar and water in a medium saucepan. As soon as it boils and the sugar is completely dissolved, remove the pan from the heat and set aside to cool. When the syrup is at room temperature, pour it evenly over the fruit in the jars. Seal with the lids and sterilise in a large pan of boiling water for 5 minutes (see page 482).

Tip: It is a good idea not to use large jars because, once they are opened, the fruit deteriorates in a few days. It is better to bottle smaller amounts and to use them up quickly. Store opened jars in the fridge.

Pears, apricots and peaches also work very well in syrup.

Marmellata speziata di fichi e arance
Spiced Honey Fig and Orange Jam

If you have a friendly greengrocer, they should be able to order a box of these figs for you when they are in season. Our *fruttivendolo,* or greengrocer, the wonderfully named Paolo Puddu, always tells me when fruits are at their best in terms of ripeness and cost, so that I can make jams at the right time of year. This is a great jam, made at the end of summer and ready for winter when the spicy flavors come into their own. This jam could also be used in the *Crostata di Marmellata* recipe on page 428.

Makes about 6 x 12 oz jars

juice of 2 oranges
10 cloves
6¾ lb honey figs
¾ cup sugar
2 cinnamon sticks
3 lengths of orange peel, about 8 in long
1 vanilla bean, split in half

Squeeze the oranges, then push the cloves into one of the leftover skins and set aside. This will help to flavor the jam with cloves but no one will accidentally eat one.

Remove the very tip of each fig, where the stem would have been attached, and halve or quarter them if they are very large. Place the figs with the rest of the ingredients, including the clove-spiked orange, in a large heavy-based saucepan over a medium heat. Bring to the boil, then cook, stirring frequently, until the figs have become soft and most of the liquid has evaporated. After about 2 hours, you should have a thickish jam. Test for setting point (see page 482). Remove the orange half and pour into sterilized jars and seal, placing the jars in boiling water, as described on page 482.

Carciofi sott' olio di Rina
Rina's Artichokes under Oil

Makes 2 x 12 oz jars

10 fresh artichokes
⅔ cup white wine vinegar
1 cup white wine
2 bay leaves
10 peppercorns
1 tablespoon rock salt
1 cup olive oil

Prepare the jars and lids according to the instructions on page 482. Meanwhile, trim the artichokes as described on on page 378 and cut them into quarters.

Bring the vinegar and wine to the boil, with the bay leaves, peppercorns, and salt. Add the artichokes, in two batches if necessary, and boil for 8–10 minutes, if they are young and tender, or longer if they are older and tougher. When cooked and just softened, drain them upside-down on a tea towel for 10–15 minutes. When dry, pack tightly into the prepared jars and then, pushing them to one side with a knife or spatula, pour in the oil. Put on the lids and keep in a cool, dark place for at least a month (and up to a year).

Variation:
For peppers and eggplant under oil follow the recipe instructions above, using 2 peppers and 1 aubergine— cut into ½ inch sticks the length of the peppers.

Paté di pomodori secchi, capperi e olive
Sun-dried Tomato, Caper, and Olive Paste

I first ate this paste on freshly cooked focaccia. It was made by a friend, Chiara, in Sicily, using her own sun-dried tomatoes. I make mine from store-cupboard ingredients bought from my local supermarket, which is less romantic but just as tasty! Store the paste in a jar in the fridge for up to one month, topped up with more olive oil to cover the surface.

4 oz sun-dried tomatoes
4 oz good-quality olives, pitted
⅓ cup extra virgin olive oil
1 tablespoon capers, rinsed
½ dried or fresh red chile, coarsely chopped
a good pinch of salt

Pulse all the ingredients together in a food processor and adjust the seasoning to taste.

Conserva di pomodori e peperoncino
Tomato and Chile Jam

San Marzano plum tomatoes are ideal for this recipe. They have little juice and are mainly all pulp, which is why these are the ones Italians can or use to make passata. You can use standard round ones, but make sure they are ripe for maximum flavor. Round tomatoes will have to be squeezed as they have a much higher water content and it would take a very long time to boil it off.

Cut the tomatoes in half and, if they are a very watery variety, squeeze them to remove most of the juice and seeds. Put them into a large saucepan with the other ingredients over a medium heat, stirring frequently. Boil for 1½–2½ hours, or until the volume has decreased by half and it has reached a thick but just runny consistency.

When cooked, season to taste, adding salt or sugar as necessary. Remove the basil and put through a *passatutto* or food mill to get rid of tomato seeds and skins. Cook for another 30 minutes. Put into sterilized jars (see page 482) and boil to create a vacuum. Serve with pecorino or smoked *scamorza*, or with Baked Ricotta (see page 108).

Fills 2 standard jars / Makes 2 lb

5½ lb plum tomatoes, preferably *San Marzano*, rinsed and destalked
3 cups sugar
1–2 red chiles, fresh or dried, coarsely chopped
2 sprigs of basil
a large pinch of salt

Marmellata di arance di Nonna Rosa
Nonna Rosa's Orange Marmalade

Nonna Rosa is a Sicilian grandmother who lives on a smallholding and cooks with her own produce. I talked to her about a marmalade that I had eaten in Cilento, south of Naples, that used lemons and oranges, and was served poured over fresh buffalo ricotta. She told me she had always put lemons in her marmalade to add a twist of bitterness to the sweet oranges (it doesn't work with Seville, as they are too bitter). I asked her about pectin and setting agents but she looked at me blankly, saying she always makes it this way and it always works!

Shred the orange zest according to your taste for fine or chunky marmalade. Next, remove the pith from the oranges and then segment them. If the segments are large, cut each one into two or three pieces. Put the flesh and zest into a large, heavy-bottomed saucepan suitable for jam-making.

Do the same with the lemons: removing and shredding the zest, discarding the pith, and then separating the segments. Again, cut them as necessary if the segments are too big. Add them with the sugar.

Bring the contents of the pan to the boil, then reduce the heat to a slow, bubbling simmer. Leave uncovered to bubble away for 1½–2½ hours; the juice in the fruit will determine how long it will take. Test for setting point (see page 482), then fill and sterilize the jars as described on page 482.

Enjoy with toasted bread, made into a *crostata* (see page 428) or, as I did, poured over fresh ricotta.

Makes about 5–6 x 12 oz jars

zest of 3 oranges
3 lb sweet oranges,
  peeled weight (about
  20 oranges)
3 cups sugar

Marmellata di susine e more
Plum and Blackberry Jam

Makes about 5 x 12 oz jars

2¼ lb Victoria plums
14 oz blackberries
2 cups caster sugar

Follow the instructions opposite for apricot jam.

Tip: You can either leave the jam with visible fruit pieces or purée with a hand blender or *passatutto* if you prefer a smooth consistency. Reheat to boiling point again before bottling.

Marmellata di albicocche
Apricot Jam

In my trials I have found that apricot jam has a more interesting flavor if you cook the fruit with the pits in. They can be removed later, by hand, with a spoon or by pushing the jam through a *passatutto*. Most Italians use the same weight of fruit to sugar but I have cut down the amount of the sugar in this recipe—though you may need to add more if your apricots are less than mature.

Makes about 5 × 12 oz jars

2¼ lb apricots
2–2½ cups granulated sugar

Halve the apricots and put them into a large saucepan, leaving the pits intact or removing them, as you wish. Add the sugar and slowly bring to the boil. Simmer the jam for about 1½ hours or until it has reduced to a thick, jammy consistency that you are happy with. You can do the test on a cold saucer to test this (see page 482).

The apricots should be soft and squash easily with a wooden spoon. If the flesh resists being squashed, cook the fruit for longer. Taste the jam carefully without scorching your tongue and add more sugar if necessary. When you are happy with the consistency and flavor, remove from the heat and bottle as described in the masterclass. If you are removing the stones after cooking reheat the jam to boiling point again to sterilize before bottling.

Marmellata di pesche
Peach Marmalade

Makes about 5 × 12 oz jars

2¼ lb peeled and pitted peaches, chopped into bite-size pieces
2–2½ cups sugar

Follow the instructions for apricot jam but peel the peaches and chop the flesh into bite-size pieces. Discard the pits.

Marmellata di fragole
Baked Strawberry Jam

This jam is made in the oven, which is safer than having it boiling on the stove. You need to be careful when transferring it to and from the oven but otherwise children can certainly be involved in the jam-making process. The jam is soft-set, with a consistency similar to a thick purée. It can be used for jam tarts, as a cake filling or, as my children like it, at the bottom of a homemade jelly.

Makes 4 x 1-cup jars

6¾ lb strawberries, hulled, washed, and drained
juice of 2 lemons
1½–2 cups sugar

Preheat the oven to 400°F.

Put the strawberries in a large preserving pan or oven-proof dish. Pour in the lemon juice and mix well. Bake for 20–30 minutes, or until the strawberries have softened, stirring every 10 minutes. Remove from the oven and leave to cool slightly.

Purée the fruit either in a food processor or by passing it through a *passatutto* (food mill), then return it to the pan or dish. Stir in enough sugar to sweeten the fruit to your taste. Return the jam to the oven for a further 30–40 minutes, or until it has thickened to a soft-set consistency, stirring every 10 minutes.

Meanwhile, sterilize four jars and lids by washing them in very hot soapy water or in a dishwasher. Place them in the oven for a couple of minutes to warm up—this will prevent them from cracking when the hot jam is poured into them.

Remove the jam from the oven and immediately pour it through a funnel into the jars. Allow a ¾ inch gap at the top of each jar and screw the lids on tightly. (The gap is crucial as it will form a vacuum when the jars are rheated.) Create a vacuum, following the instructions on page 482.

Frustringolo (Lonza di fichi)
Fig Salami

This popular Italian accompaniment to cheese is Franco Taruschio's recipe. He sources his ingredients from Arab shops, reasoning that the quality and prices are good because the Arabs are fans of nuts and dried fruits. We now make and serve it regularly on the cheese platter in our restaurant in Bray; I also love it mid-morning, with an espresso. This recipe does make a large quantity but the logs last for months if wrapped in foil. Fig salami also makes a great gift, done up in brown paper and ribbon, with a mystique and a touch of the spicy Middle Eastern world about it.

Makes 6 logs about 12 x 2½ inches

4½ lb dried honey figs (ideally without flour dusted on top), chopped finely or minced
1 lb almonds, roughly chopped
1 lb walnuts, roughly chopped
5 oz natural candied peel, finely chopped
4 cups chopped dates
4 oz whole pistachios
6 oz bitter chocolate, chopped
1 liqueur glass of brandy
1 liqueur glass of Strega
1 liqueur glass of anisette
1 liqueur glass of crème de menthe
2 teaspoons ground cinnamon
seeds scraped from a vanilla bean
confectioners' sugar, for dusting

Pour the dry ingredients onto a clean work surface (or into a large bowl) and make a well in the center. Pour in the liquids and use your hands to mix the whole lot together.

Divide the mixture into 6 equal portions. Dust a board and your hands with confectioners' sugar and roll out into *salami,* about 2½ inches wide and 12 inches long.

Wrap each one in rice paper and then parcel it up in parchment paper. Leave to mature in a dry, cool place for about a month before using. After a month, wrap each *salame* in foil and store in a dry place. This is great with pecorino.

Marmellata di mele cotogne
Quince Jam

My friend Livia from Tuscany gave me this recipe: she eats it with bread or in a *crostata* but, being English, I prefer it with cheese such as pecorino or Cheddar. Quinces are naturally high in pectin; choose unblemished fruits for a jam with a good pink color.

2¼ lb quinces
3 cups caster sugar
⅓ cup water, if necessary

Makes 1kg jam (2 × 18 oz jars, or 4 × 9 oz jars)

Blanch the quinces in boiling water for a couple of minutes. Drain and set aside to cool. Peel the skins and cut them into four. Remove the cores and cut the flesh into bite-size pieces. Put the flesh and sugar into a saucepan and place over a medium heat. Bring to the boil and allow to simmer for up to 3 hours, until the quinces have broken down and become soft. If necessary, add a little water to loosen the mixture and allow it cook for longer. The ripeness of the quinces will affect the cooking time but it will be between 2 and 3 hours. Purée the mixture through a processor or blender.

Pour into sterilized jars and bang the jar lightly to disperse air bubbles. If necessary, push the jam to the edges of the jar with a clean knife. Seal with the lids and refer to page 482 for sterilizing the jars and creating a vacuum.

GLOSSARY OF TERMS AND INGREDIENTS

Al cartoccio Cooked in a paper or foil parcel; usually refers to fish, but could be meat or pasta.

Al funghetto Literally "cut like mushrooms"; cut into thin slices.

Al vapore Steamed.

Alla Translates as "to the"; used in titles of food, e.g. *Patate alla Giancarlo*, meaning potatoes cooked in the style of Giancarlo.

Alla griglia, alla brace, ai ferri Cooked on a grill over embers.

Antipasti Collection of small dishes eaten at the beginning of a meal to stimulate the appetite.

Arrosto Roast.

Baccalà Dried and salted cod.

Bagnomaria (bain-marie) A method of cooking in which one container is placed over another containing simmering water, either on the hob (e.g. for zabaglione) or in the oven (e.g. for *sformato*).

Baking blind Initial cooking of pastry cases without filling. Beans or rice wrapped in plastic wrap or parchment paper are generally used as a filling, to maintain the shape of the case.

Bard To wrap strips of pancetta or *lardo* around meat to stop it drying out during cooking (e.g. for Pot Roast Quails).

Baste To spoon hot cooking fat and juices over food while it cooks to stop it drying out and keep the dish moist.

Battuto See *Soffritto*.

Bignè Small filled choux pastry buns.

Biscotti Generic term for cookies.

Bisque Concentrated shellfish stock used to give flavor to fish dishes.

Blanch To cook a vegetable quickly by dipping it into boiling hot water for a minute or so.

Bottarga Dried fish roe, also known as *muggine*.

Braise, brasare To cook meat slowly with vegetables (e.g. for *Brasato al barolo*).

Brodo Stock.

Burro manie (beurre manie) Equal amounts of butter and flour blended together. Small amounts are whisked into sauces to thicken them without forming lumps.

Butterfly To open out a joint of meat (e.g. a leg of lamb).

Caramel Sugar or sometimes sugar and water reduced to a thick consistency and brown in color.

Carpaccio Thinly sliced raw meat, fish or vegetables.

Cartouche Fold a square of parchment paper in half and then in half again. Then fold again making an elongated triangle. Put the sharpest end of this into the center of a round dish and measure outwards to the size you need. Tear or cut the paper and open out a near-perfect circle. Use this to cover food that is being poached or to line a cake tin.

Caul Cobweb of fatty membrane from the stomach of an animal.

Chining Almost removing the backbone from a joint of meat.

Chinnoise A fine sieve.

Choux See *Pasta choux*.

Condita Dressed with, such as oil and vinegar on salad.

Coulis Thick, usually sweetened purée of fruit.

Cream To beat together butter and sugar into a light, fluffy, thick cream.

Crema A cream such as *crema pasticcera* or custard.

Crespelle Pancakes; often served stuffed and rolled with a sauce and Parmesan.

Croccante Crunchy.

Crostata Tart.

Crostini Small toasted breads topped with a variety of ingredients and eaten as *Antipasti*.

Crostoni Larger toasted breads often rubbed with garlic and drizzled with olive oil. Sometimes served alongside soup or put at the base of a soup bowl and topped with soup.

Dariole moulds Thin metal forms to make pannacotta and *Sformato*.

De-glaze To add wine or stock to a pan containing lightly burnt cooking juices and fat to make a sauce.

Fiorentina T-bone steak, typical of Tuscany.

Florentine Foods from Florence; typically containing spinach (such as pancakes), or a biscuit made with chocolate or dried fruit.

Folding Gently and lightly mixing ingredients together with a big metal spoon without losing air.

Friggere To fry.

Fritte (-i) Fried, such as *Calamari fritti* (fried squid).

Fumetto Fish stock or thin soup, usually clear rather than colored.

Ganache A mixture of chocolate and cream to make either a sauce, chocolate filling, or coating for a cake.

Gelatina Gelatin, a setting agent derived from bones.

Impasto A mix, from the verb *impastare*, meaning "to mix."

In crosta In a crust; e.g. *crosta di sale*, a salt crust, or *crosta di erbe*, a herb crust.

In padella In a skillet.

In umido Food cooked in liquid so that it doesn't dry out (e.g. meat cooked in tomatoes).

Infuse To use a strong flavor such as a herb or garlic to lend character to a bland liquid (e.g. leaving basil in milk overnight for Basil pannacotta).

Insalata Salad.

Julienne Vegetables cut into matchstick-size pieces.

Lardo White fat from the back, sides, and belly of a pig preserved in marble containers with salt and rosemary; thinly sliced and eaten with bread or used to flavor potatoes or meat dishes. *Le lardellature* means moistening food by studding it with sticks of lardo.

Lesso, carne lessata Boiled foods, such as *bollito misto*, a selection of boiled meats.

Macerate Small pieces of food, such as fruit, left in syrup or liquor to soften and become flavored.

Marinata (marinade) Liquid used to marinate food.

Marinate To leave food in flavored liquid for tenderness and flavor (e.g. steak left in olive oil, rosemary, and garlic).

Milanese Bashed-out meat coated in breadcrumbs and fried.

Mugnaia (meurnière) Sauce made from butter, flour, and lemon, often containing chopped parsley.

Parboil To partially cook food in boiling water (e.g. potatoes before roasting).

Pass To push food through a sieve or *passatutto* to make it smoother.

Passata Soup or sauce passed through a *passatutto* or sieve to eliminate skin, seeds, or lumps.

Passatutto Food mill.

Pasta Pasta or pastry.

Pasta choux Choux pastry.

Pasta frolla Shortcrust pastry, used for making cakes and tarts.

Pasta Genovese Genovese sponge cake.

Pasta sfoglia Puff pastry.

Pastella Batter.

Poussin Baby chicken.

Prove To allow dough to rise, usually after shaping before baking.

Purè (purée) To blend food until smooth using a blender, liquidizer, or food processor.

Ragù Sauce with visible pieces, usually served with pasta, fish, or meat (e.g. *Ragù alla Bolognese*).

Reduce To allow liquids to concentrate over heat; boiling a sauce to concentrate flavors, slightly thicken it and reduce the quantity as the water evaporates.

Rest To allow food to settle; for dough or pastry this allows gluten to shrink back after being kneaded or rolled to prevent shrinkage during cooking. With meats, makes them more tender after roasting or frying.

Ribbon trail When a mix is beaten thickly enough for it to leave a trail if dropped from a spoon (e.g. for *Pasta Genovese*).

Ripieno Stuffing.

Roux Unequal mixture of butter and flour used to thicken sauces.

Saba, sapa, vin cotto Grape juice and skins allowed to reduce; used to dress foods and make sauces.

Salsa Sauce.

Saltato Sauté; literally translates as "jumped" as the food is continuously tossed or stirred while being fried.

Salumi Generic term for cured meats.

Sear, seal To fry or grill meat quickly to form a cooked coating.

Sformato Cross between a purée, a bake and a mousse.

Simmer Gentle boil.

Soffritto Base for a sauce, stew, or soup, usually made from finely chopped celery, carrot, and onion.

Soft peaks Egg white or cream lightly whipped so that soft peaks form; they bend over at the top.

Spezzatino Stew containing chunks of meat.

Spiedini Skewers.

Stiff peaks Egg white or cream whipped for so long that stiff peaks form; they stay rigid at the top.

Stoccafisso Dried cod.

Stufato Slowly cooked (e.g *Stufato di Agnello,* or lamb stew).

Sugo Smooth sauce usually served with pasta (e.g. *Sugo di Pomodoro*).

Timballo (timbale) Food cooked in a mold and turned out.

Torta Cake or tart.

Vellutata Creamed (e.g. for a smooth soup).

BIBLIOGRAPHY

Artusi, Pellegrino
L'Arte di Mangiare Bene
(Giunti Marzocco, Italy, 1960)

Bardi, Carla
Prosciutto, The Italian Pantry
(The Wine Appreciation Guild,
North America, 2004)

Bertinet, Richard
Crust, Bread to Get Your Teeth Into
(Kyle Cathie Limited, London, 2007)

Bertinet, Richard
Dough, Simple Contemporary Bread
(Kyle Cathie Limited, London, 2005)

Bugialli, Giuliano
Foods of Sicily and Sardinia and the
Smaller Islands
(Rizzoli International Publications, Inc, New
York, 1996)

Castelvetro, Giacomo
The Fruit, Herbs and Vegetables
of Italy
(Penguin Group, London, 1989)

Corbin, Pam
The River Cottage Preserves
Handbook
(Bloomsbury Publishing, London, 2008)

Da Mosto, Francesco
Francesco's Kitchen
(Ebury Press, London, 2007)

David, Elizabeth
Italian Food
(Penguin Books, London, 1963)

Del Conte, Anna
The Classic Food of Northern Italy
(Pavilion Books Limited, London, 1995)

Del Conte, Anna
Gastronomy of Italy
(Bantam Press, London, 1987)

Demetra
Pane, i Segretti per Farlo
(Demetra, Italy, 1999)

Demetra
Scuola di Cucina, Tutte le Tecniche
(Giunti Editore, Milan, 2003)

Editoriale Domus
Il Cucchiaio d'Argento, La Grande
Cucina Regionale
(Editoriale Domus, Italy, 2007)

Fearnley-Whittingstall, Hugh
The River Cottage Meat Book
(Hodder and Stoughton, Great Britain,
2004)

**Fearnley-Whittingstall, Hugh
and Fisher, Nick**
The River Cottage Fish Book
(Bloomsbury Publishing, London, 2007)

Ferrigno, Ursula
The New Family Bread Book
(Mitchell Beazley, London, 2007)

Field, Carol
The Italian Baker
(Harper Collins, New York, 1985)

Fisher, Marta
Marmellate, Confetture, Sciroppi
(Cybele & Co, Italy, 2002)

Francesconi, Jeanne Carola
La Vera Cucina di Napoli
(Newton Compton, Italy, 2006)

Gray, Patience
Honey from a Weed
(Prospect Books, Devon, 2002)

Hazan, Marcella
The Classic Italian Cookbook
(Alfred A. Knopf, United States, 1976)

Lidell, Caroline and Weir, Robin
Ices, the Definitive Guide
(Grub Street, London, 2003)

McGee, Harold
On Food and Cooking
(Hodder and Stoughton, Great Britain,
2004)

Ploner, Richard
Il Pane delle Dolomiti
(Athesia SpA, Italy, 2006)

Plotkin, Fred
Italy for the Gourmet Traveller
(Kyle Cathie Limited, London, 1997)

Pini, Stephen
The Fishmongers' Company
Cook Book
(The Fishmongers' Company, London,
2002)

Riley, Gillian
The Oxford Companion to
Italian Food
(Oxford University Press, New York, 2007)

Roggero, Savina
Meat, Cooking all'Italiana
(Thomas Y. Crowell Company, United
States, 1975)

Sheldon Johns, Pamela
Proscuitto, Pancetta, Salame
(Ten Speed Press, United States, 2004)

Stevens, Daniel
The River Cottage Bread Book
(Bloomsbury Publishing, London, 2009)

Taruschio, Ann and Franco
Leaves from the Walnut Tree
(Pavilion Books Limited, London, 1997)

Vignozzi, Sara
Carne! Meat Dishes the Italian Way
(McRae Books, Italy, 1998)

INDEX

504